ADMINISTERING INTERPRETATION

just ideas

transformative ideals of justice in ethical and political thought

series editors

Drucilla Cornell

Roger Berkowitz

ADMINISTERING INTERPRETATION

DERRIDA, AGAMBEN, AND
THE POLITICAL THEOLOGY OF LAW

Peter Goodrich and Michel Rosenfeld, Editors

FORDHAM UNIVERSITY PRESS

NEW YORK   2019

Fordham University Press gratefully acknowledges financial assistance and support provided for the publication of this book by The Benjamin Cardozo School of Law, Yeshiva University.

Copyright © 2019 Fordham University Press

All rights reserved. No part of this publication may be reproduced, stored in a retrieval system, or transmitted in any form or by any means—electronic, mechanical, photocopy, recording, or any other—except for brief quotations in printed reviews, without the prior permission of the publisher.

Fordham University Press has no responsibility for the persistence or accuracy of URLs for external or third-party Internet websites referred to in this publication and does not guarantee that any content on such websites is, or will remain, accurate or appropriate.

Fordham University Press also publishes its books in a variety of electronic formats. Some content that appears in print may not be available in electronic books.

Visit us online at www.fordhampress.com.

Library of Congress Cataloging-in-Publication Data

Names: Goodrich, Peter, 1954– editor. | Rosenfeld, Michel, 1948– editor.
Title: Administering interpretation : Derrida, Agamben, and the political theology of law / Peter Goodrich and Michel Rosenfeld, editors.
Description: First edition. | New York, NY : Fordham University Press, 2019. | Includes bibliographical references and index.
Identifiers: LCCN 2018060277| ISBN 9780823283798 (cloth : alk. paper) | ISBN
   9780823283781 (pbk. : alk. paper)
Subjects: LCSH: Law—Philosophy. | Derrida, Jacques—Influence. | Agamben, Giorgio, 1942– —Influence.
Classification: LCC K235 .A353 2019 | DDC 340/.1—dc23
LC record available at https://lccn.loc.gov/2018060277

Printed in the United States of America

21 20 19   5 4 3 2 1

First edition

Contents

Introduction
Peter Goodrich and Michel Rosenfeld ... 1

I Reconstructing Interpretative Communities

1. Interpretations as Hypotheses
   Bernhard Schlink ... 11
2. Antonin Scalia, Bernhard Schlink, and Lancelot Andrewes: Reading *Heller*
   Stanley Fish ... 22
3. The Interpreter, the Analyst, and the Scientist
   Jeanne L. Schroeder ... 38
4. Law against Justice and Solidarity: Rereading Derrida and Agamben at the Margins of the One and the Many
   Michel Rosenfeld ... 54

II Derrida and Dissimulation

5. Jacques Derrida Never Wrote about Law
   Pierre Legrand ... 105
6. Derrida's Legal Times: Decision, Declaration, Deferral, and Event
   Bernadette Meyler ... 147
7. Derrida's Shylock: The Letter and the Life of Law
   Katrin Trüstedt ... 168

III The Justice of Administration

8. A Postmodern *Hetoimasia*—Feigning Sovereignty during the State of Exception
Marinos Diamantides … 189

9. *Contra Iurem*: Giorgio Agamben's Two Ontologies
Laurent de Sutter … 234

IV CounterPlaces, CounterTimes

10. Cities of Refuge, Rebel Cities, and the City to Come
Giovanna Borradori … 253

11. A Ghost Story: Electoral Reform and Hong Kong Popular Theater
Marco Wan … 272

12. Appearing under Erasure: Of War, Disappearance, and the Contretemps
Allen Feldman … 290

List of Contributors … 323
Index … 329

ADMINISTERING INTERPRETATION

Introduction

Peter Goodrich and Michel Rosenfeld

Interpretation, according to Giambattista Vico, has its etymological roots in *interpatrari*, in mingling with or entering the discourse of the fathers. While the etymology is dubious, the concept is peculiarly applicable to legal interpretation, where the search for authority, for prior and precedent determinations, whether contained in a code or in judicial decisions, plays an inordinate role in the elaboration of meaning and the deciding of disputes. Whatever jurisdiction is in play, the assumption that underpins the task of interpreting legal texts is that there is an authority which will dictate and delimit the choice of the decision maker and ideally will stipulate a certain, which is to say indisputable, outcome. The conflict of legal interpretations is confined historically to disputes within an established corpus of authoritative texts within a monotheistic tradition of truth and in its corresponding juristic form of verdict, or statement of the truth.

While it may appear anachronistic to address legal interpretation via its religious roots and specifically its monotheistic genesis and environs, it is necessary to recognize the continuing sense in which hermeneutics is at base a scriptural discipline. It entails faith in the text and a core belief in the textual basis of legal decision. Even *in partibus infidelium,* among those who do not believe or have left the strictures of explicit religious faith in favor of Continental theory, culture wars, deconstruction, or *oikonomia,* the hermeneutic character of the disciplines remains and dictates a shared method, if not common outcomes. However much the essays in this volume may differ in approach and theme, in political orientation and affective scope, the focus on interpretation as a way to make discursive sense of an inherited textual corpus is a constant and shared parameter of debate among judges, lawyers, interdisciplinary scholars, novelists, and public intellectuals. The point to be stressed here is that the apparent chasm between U.S. and European legal theory or the radical diversity of approaches to legal interpretation derived from disciplines external to law can otherwise appear both disconcerting and syncretic. Our starting point is thus a counterintuitive commonality among those who apparently have nothing in common, civilian and common lawyers, U.S. pragmatists and Continental (French) theorists, analytic philosophy of language and deconstruction, and, finally, its successor theory of *oikonomia* and the empty space of sovereignty.

The starting point is close to Vico's stipulation of the task of interpretation as coming to terms with and making something of the textual tradition of law in its patristic and exegetical forms. The political theology of law remains a pivotal element in debate, initially and quite literally in the derivation and application of a biblically based hermeneutics to legal texts. There is a scripture, as indeed there is with all the Renaissance disciplines, and law differs only in its proximity to biblical exegesis and in its accessing of the regalia of power as wielded through interpretation. Thus Bernhard Schlink begins his defense of legal decision as consensus through a protocol of falsification by way of reference to early experiences and familial inculcation of the interpretation of the Bible as a distinctive and different approach to meaning that nonetheless shares with law the impulse to postulation of precepts. Judge Schlink is mindful of the requirement of decision in cases and distinguishes legal interpretation from other hermeneutic pursuits, specifically the literary and the spiritual, through a scientific model of falsification. There is no legal truth, but there are decisions, and these determinations of disputes gain consensus through being tested and not falsified. Interpretation is the hinge on which the case revolves. It is precisely against consensus and in propagation of correct decisions that the contrarian Stanley Fish pitches his critique of Schlink. Reviving, or better resurrecting, the dead figure of the author, Fish finds the metaphor of textual genesis in the intention of the writer that resolves the conflict of interpretations. Something is meant, and it is that intended meaning which can be uncovered or discovered by careful textual analysis. The text has a father, a progenitor, and a law in the semiotic sense of a figure that sent it.

If the starting point of debate is the search for textual authority, lodged in consensus or in authorship, or as Jeanne L. Schroeder puts it, in an imaginary stability, a putative symbolic truth, the figure provoking and at least covertly animating the dispute is that of Jacques Derrida, and specifically his neologism of deconstruction. The method of deconstruction arrests the linear progression of interpretation and dictates time and the recognition of the incalculable as the necessary though impossible criteria of just decision. Briefly fashionable in the 1990s, the specter of deconstruction haunts both the legal and the literary academies in the United States as the portentous and unstable figure of "French theory," or as François Cusset puts it, the campus drug derridium. It is deconstruction that, as much as and before any other "post" movement, swept through the culture and acted particularly in law as a species of threat. Indeterminacy, the absence of the consensus, the aporia of decidability, the impossibility of the certainty that lawyers crave, both challenged doctrine and raised the question of justice as being in conflict with law. For Derrida, theory is necessary to interpretation because all meaning is a philological and philosophical investigation, open to contestation, and contingent in the sense of openness to alternatives and as a perpetual work in process. There are, within the deconstructive frame, only positions, one might say specters of meaning, within a text without end. The lawyer's necessary yet artificial interruptions of the interpretation of the text generate moments of hiatus of meaning in which the possibility of justice has to step in and play the role of law.

As against the concepts of consensus and certainty, however advocated, the broader and lingering debate on legal interpretation seeks to convert the perceived threat of deconstruction into a productivity. The exquisitely detailed attention to language that Derrida offered promises significant gains and opportunities for legal interpretation that have yet to be fully explored. There is an ethics to interpretation, a temporality and materiality to texts that legal scholars and doctrine have yet to fully explore. There is also a significant divide in that it is predominantly the European, and most usually the Anglophone, legal academy that has pursued, taught, and worked through the implications of deconstruction, its potentiality for expanding the concept of legal interpretation, while the U.S. legal academy, traumatized by the brief success of critical legal studies, has turned away from any expansive reception of Derrida's work and has increasingly anathematized whatever phantasm is perceived to lurk behind that nomination. As Duncan Kennedy has formulated it, the hermeneutics of suspicion has denounced Derrida, or at least the uncertainty and immorality that his work is contended to stand for, as extraneous, divisive, suspect, and at root fraudulent. Its "critiquiness" stands not so much for something, as in the way of clarity, certainty, and proper promulgation of the norms of law. In an old trope, revived from the era of legal realism, deconstruction was deemed and denounced as nihilistic, and thus has been little taught and, as Pierre Legrand meticulously details, even less understood in the U.S. legal academy.

It is true, as Bernadette Meyler points out, that jurisprudence or philosophy of law has little pedagogical place or institutional role in the U.S. legal academy, and so the potential of grammatology or deconstruction in the theorization and practice of interpretation remains yet to come. Debates tend to be specific to substantive legal disciplines, and so it is interpretation in the law of contract, constitutional interpretation, statutory meanings, and the like that provides the principal access to methods and debates that generally neither aspire nor rise to the level of hermeneutics. It is thus a significant part of the purpose of this collection—this Collect, this prayer—to reintroduce the potential of theory and the possibilities of justice that interpretation at best portends. Janus-faced, the work aims to look back, to recollect, to resurrect and reinvigorate a debate that flared briefly and then vanished, as to the literary and philosophical parameters and resources of legal hermeneutics in a context still hostile to the impracticality of interdisciplinary endeavors and wary of the perceived pretentiousness of critique. The legal resistance to theory, borne on the back of U.S. exceptionalism, is indeed at a high point. Clinical training, skills, professional practice are the keywords, the buzz, in American law schools, and as such, the intricacies and impracticalities, the time necessary for theory as the source of the clinic and the protocol that generates practice, get undermined and overlooked in the rush to commerce. Deconstruction proffers the prospect and makes the argument that this is never decided, that interpretation will always come back, that clinical practice is precisely the pursuit, as Michel Rosenfeld postulates, of justice or at the very least of just interpretations. The neglect of theory demotes the office of the jurist and frays the ethical bonds of legal community, leaving both subject and interpretation to the vagaries of the unconscious and the infidelities of the imaginary. Crumbling and slippage, or in Fish's radical diction, evil, take the place of scholarship and extended deliberation alike. Easy answers replace hard cases.

Jurisprudence, broadly meaning legal theory, is still, by way of comparison and contrast, compulsory in a majority of law schools in common law jurisdictions outside the United States, and theory is much more likely to be integrated into the substantive curriculum in the teaching of public law, human rights, and international law. Hermeneutics, deconstruction, and theories of *oikonomia* and state apparatuses are incorporated into doctrinal elaborations in private and public law in a manner that is largely unknown in the U.S. legal academy, where, at most, it is economics and at a stretch identity politics that lay a claim to space in the increasingly clinically oriented curriculum. The resistance to theory means indeed that Derrida is largely an unknown name and unread theory in the new generation of legal scholars, and Giorgio Agamben is an even more distant figure, despite his training as a lawyer. Perhaps it is more accurate to say that legal theory is a minor concern in marginal spaces insofar as the contributions in this work are predominantly from law professors, albeit eccentric and halcyon representatives of the academy as currently oriented. *Ars iuris* for the sake of *ars iuris* is a failing memory, a distant cry.

The last point and theme relating to comparative trends in legal interpretation is that in the absence of theory it becomes internal to legal doctrine and narrowly confined to variations on commonsense themes of literalism and purposivism. If that is a necessarily general description of a discourse that is judicially generated and oriented, it also fits with the thesis propagated by Agamben and taken up in the latter portion of the present volume, namely, that administration has become the dominant mode of governance operating as a legally generated exception to the criteria of strict law. Economy as the disposition of social forces, as the alignment, capture, and reproduction of social spaces, of subjects as such, defines and determines administration according to a logic of self-reproduction, the autopoietic replication of any given apparatus or assemblage of blank continuance. For Agamben, law is displaced by a pure assemblage of apparatuses, which he defines through a theological genealogy of administration out of the hidden theology of *oikonomia*. The father administrates the household, which is to say, disposes and distributes its elements according to the desire for glory and continuance, and in a comparable manner the state administrates civil society, purporting to follow sovereign dictate and established law while simply acting according to the criteria of administrative self-reproduction, according to an economy of interpretation that propels the subject in a choral and acclamatory fashion toward a paternalistic conception of its own good. Administration, in this schema, exists simply to reproduce itself and operates accordingly through the pure desiderata of its own reinstallation. The apparatus is consecrated to the goals of administration, to "the exit of things from the sphere of human law" and subjective value: "Every apparatus implies a process of subjectification without which it cannot function as an apparatus of governance," to which is added the salutary proposition that in a disciplinary society, "apparatuses aim to create—through a series of practices, discourses, and bodies of knowledge—docile, yet free, bodies that assume their identity and their freedom as subjects in the very process of their desubjectification."[1]

The apparatus, or dispositor as Agamben prefers to translate the term, signals the end of the universal as an explanatory category. Singularities need explanation, cases, practices, subjects, the processes of variation, and modes of multiplicity are the objects of governance and disposition and as such are the materialities that focus interpretation. Adrift, because law historically favors norm and generality, *universalia* and other dogmas, a certain dualism emerges. Borrowing from the *Pure Theory of Law*, the work of the Austrian jurist Hans Kelsen, Agamben depicts a dual ontology of the social.[2] The dualism of the "is" and the "ought" becomes Hellenized as that of "estô" and "esti," of being and that which ought to be, the ontology of command, as the interpretative economy of administration. The apparatus of governance as will and disposition, as the circular command of what ought to be, generates a division between theory and practice, the empirical and the governmental. It is in this vein that Agamben recirculates the baroque maxim that the king rules but does not govern, arguing in essence that sovereignty is spectacular and necessary in choral and acclamatory terms, but the enthroned glory of rule is antinomically related to administration, which has its own hermetic logic of practice based around apparatuses of governance that are constituted by assemblages of subjective capture. The apparatus of the war machine, in Allen Feldman's analysis, thus operates by virtue of a scopic regime that generates a divergent temporality, a counter time, and the desubjectified subject of the enemy as the corpse, as the "ought to be" of nonbeing, the forensics of legitimated disappearance. For Marinos Diamantides as well, the spectacular appearances of sovereign and law, the scopic regime of the social, belies a practice that is quite antinomic to the stated politics or advertised programs of political parties. One thing is said and another is systematically done: atheists kiss the hands of bishops and bow to the church, socialists pay obeisance to hierophants, because these ritual modes of recognition of sovereignty have no practical role to play, indeed are necessary but separate from the functioning of the apparatuses of governmental reproduction.

Translated into the dialogue over legal interpretation, Agamben's theory and its reception in European jurisprudence provide something of a continuation of Derrida's grammatological concerns. In arguing, particularly in *The Kingdom and the Glory*, that the spectacular domain of sovereign power bears little to no relation to the practice of governance, the theory of *oikonomia*, of social disposition according to multiple apparatuses of administration operating to capture and reproduce subjects, the hermeneutics of suspicion is introduced into the apprehension and reconstruction of legal meaning.³ For Derrida, the text was an artifact, and its plenitude of meanings called for justice in the sense of time, patience, care in refusing precedent or prior determinations of sense, Hans-Georg Gadamer's "prejudice" as prejudgment, in favor of attending to the plurality of textual and intertextual connotations. As Legrand points out, Derrida was not a lawyer, and one consequence of that is a degree of distance and a certain freedom in his analysis of justice in relation to law. Deconstruction, as he famously formulated it, could play with social science; it could take its time, plead for justice, listen for the other in the shell of the self. For Agamben, as a lawyer, there is a greater emphasis on sources and the lineage of textual meaning as recuperated through far-flung philological and etymological excavations. In a fashion comparable in many respects to the work of the French jurist Pierre Legendre, Agamben's goal is to reconstruct the Christian theology and way of life that is harbored in and acted out through the social and legal texts of the Western tradition. In tracing the cenobitic roots of Western administrative offices and forms of life, the point is made again and again that the spaces and affects, places and roles, of the Western subject are dictated by the categories of faith and the modus vivendi of religious community. The legal text, in this analysis, is the paramount but indistinct avenue of instantiation of inherited categories of the symbolic. Law opens the door to the social, establishes its structure and sites, but then disappears into or is absorbed by the administrative assemblages of subjectification and reproduction. It is in this sense a paradox, a self-abrogating meaning in the form of the exception, that institutes a law without law in the form of administrative practice.

Where Derrida's philosophy of interpretation was sometimes perceived as threatening to the legal academy because in its survey of the plurality of the text it was perceived to stall meaning, Agamben proffers a rather more stringent sense of the predetermination of both affect and interpretation. Where Marco Wan traces the ghosts, the hauntology of a cultural past, in Hong Kong cinema, and postulates a political morphology to these specters, Agamben offers a more comprehensive angelology of social forms. Even the heresiarchs hide behind the Christian figures of truth because they are what is there, they constitute the symbolic, and because their significance lies paradoxically in their profound lack of meaning, in their absence from the administrative practices that they legitimate and unleash as self-perpetuating powers. What is left to analyze and interpret within this frame is the antinomy of meaning and practice, the scission of text and decision, norm and instance of deciding, the dictation of what ought to be and the event of what is. For Derrida and Agamben, the specters—the no more one, more than one of these subjects—reexamined in the multiple forays of this collection, the economy of interpretation is for both a practice of opening to meaning and in that very aperture opening meaning to itself. For both thinkers, it is the fissures in the text, the enigmas and other references to forgotten eruditions, hidden practices, excluded causes, thwarted freedoms, that excite the interpreter's attention. The shared cause is that of the diversification of interpretation and the opening of law to its own hermeneutic wealth, to the plurality of traditions and multiplicity and potential of the severality of jurisdictions that compose the discourse, the texts of the jurists. It is, then, in the end, a primary purpose of interpretation to address the open in the sense of the future, the nonexistent, inchoate, and unformed life to come. In this dimension, in the futureity of the hermeut's task, the adventure is and remains that of sculpting a window into the not yet, the community and democracy of meaning to come.

NOTES

1. Giorgio Agamben, *What Is an Apparatus?* (Stanford, Calif.: Stanford University Press, 2009), 19–20.

2. For this commentary on Kelsen's Kantian-inspired critique, see Giorgio Agamben, Opus Dei: *An Archaeology of Duty* (Stanford, Calif.: Stanford University Press, 2013), 123–25.

3. On the otiose character or impracticality of sovereignty, see Giorgio Agamben, *The Kingdom and the Glory: For a Theological Genealogy of Economy and Government*, translated by Lorenzo Chiesa, with Matteo Mandarini (Stanford, Calif.: Stanford University Press, 2011), 68.

Reconstructing Interpretative Communities

Interpretations as Hypotheses

Bernhard Schlink

I

I grew up with the Bible being read and interpreted every evening. After dinner my family remained seated around the table and read one chapter, my parents, my three siblings, and I taking turns verse by verse, and then my father, a professor of divinity, interpreted what we had read. Before I learned how to read, an American Bible with illustrations—it must have been a postwar gift by an American reeducation institution—was opened before me so that I had a picture to look at.

Did I learn anything for my life as a lawyer and legal interpreter? When my teachers in Gymnasium tried to familiarize me with literature, obviously, they presented a different kind of interpretation. I got a sense of the difference between interpreting something that is meant to govern our life and interpreting something meant to inspire us, to widen and deepen our understanding of the human condition. Not that the Bible is not meant to inspire us. It can even be entertaining; one winter, after my father had us read Paul's Epistles one after the other, we children rebelled and demanded something more exciting, and he gave in. All winter, we reveled in the sex and crime of the book of Kings. But again and again, the Bible is about norms, about what is right and what is wrong, what we may and what we must not do. Then the interpretation is not far from the interpretation of legal norms.

The interpretations of legal norms, which are abstract and general, are also abstract and general. The interpretations of literary texts or historical documents, which are specific and individual, are also specific and individual. The interpretation of the Bible is both.

The interpretation of a literary text or a historical document tries to find out what the specific author meant or how his or her specific contemporaries understood the text or document, or how it fits into a specific context, be it the context of other works by the same author, or of works by other authors, or of other cultural or political or social events or creations of the same period. Sometimes literary interpretation is not interested in the author, his or her contemporaries or contexts, and attempts only to satisfy our wish for something new and fun, surprising and stimulating. It can present a determined Hamlet instead of a hesitant Hamlet, Faust as a petit bourgeois rather than a character with deepest and highest aspirations, and Antigone as a comic instead of a tragic figure and still work, that is, make the audience of the performance enjoy, wonder, and think. But this too remains something specific and individual, an individual interpretation for an individual audience, on this specific stage at this specific moment.

Of course, literary theory enjoys abstract and general insights, and poems and stories, novels and plays, can trigger all kinds of abstract and general ideas about beauty, truth, justice, guilt, and so forth. But they are either discussed as the abstract or general ideas of the specific author or his or her times, or they are discussed in and of themselves, and the text and its interpretation are merely the occasion to do so. When one discusses the abstract and general ideas about justice, law, and tradition that Sophocles presented and that his contemporaries found in Antigone, one stays with Sophocles and in his times. When one discusses justice, law, and tradition as today's abstract and general issues, one may be inspired by Sophocles's Antigone but leave its interpretation behind.

The interpretation of a legal norm may also try to find out what the author meant or how the norm was and is understood by others and how it fits into its legal context. It may also be an interpretation for an individual audience, the parties on a specific stage, the courtroom where their specific case is argued and decided. Still, it is never just an interpretation for this specific case with these individual parties. Legal interpretation is always an interpretation for all cases like this case and for all parties like these parties. It offers a legal solution for a legal problem that can arise in different cases with different parties. If a norm is phrased or paraphrased as an *if-then* sentence—if this factual constellation occurs, then these are the legal consequences—the interpretation aims to cover all cases that are similar enough to fall under the *if*-clause and all variations that the legal consequences can take on.

Interpreting "Congress shall make no law abridging the freedom of speech" or "if someone speaks, his or her freedom must not be abridged" means elaborating on who this someone is—every citizen and also the public employee? People and also organizations? On what speech is—the verbal and also the nonverbal expression? The expression by symbols and also the expression through action? On what an abridgement of freedom is—previous censorship and also subsequent sanctions? A prohibition what to say and also a prohibition when and where and how to say it? And so forth. The interpretation may be driven by a specific conflict between individual parties and may research individual cases past and present and may argue hypotheticals looking like individual cases. The result is always an abstract and general insight; the speaker, the speech, and the abridgement of freedom all are interpreted as abstract and general categories.

2

There are two kinds of *if-then* sentences, those that predict factual consequences of factual constellations and those that demand legal consequences for factual constellations. In other words, there are *then*-clauses that predict what is expected to happen, and there are *then*-clauses that stipulate what must or must not happen. In the first case, if the expectation turns out wrong, if what the *then*-clause predicts does not happen, the *if-then* sentence is falsified. In the second case, if the norm is not fulfilled, if what must happen does not happen or what must not happen happens anyway, the norm is still a valid norm, at least as long as violations of the norm do not become rampant. If a meteorologist predicts that sudden, heavy temperature drops mean rain and the temperature drops and it does not rain, we learn that the prediction was wrong. If a norm stipulates that damages have to be compensated and someone who caused damages and should pay compensation avoids doing so, the norm remains unquestioned.[1]

But even though the normative and the factual *if-then* sentences differ in this important respect, they also have something important in common. Both are abstract and general, both express something that claims relevance for an infinite number of instances, whether these instances be legal constellations or natural or social events.

Having as their reference an infinite universe of discourse, they can never be verified, never be proved right. Never can one exclude the possibility that something that proves them wrong will not come up. They can only be falsified, proved wrong. Of course, they can show their worth by not being proved wrong over a long period of time. But this worth can always be shattered; there is no guarantee that a new case or the rethinking of the legal consequences that an established interpretation took for granted will not falsify the established interpretation or that a new natural or social event will not falsify an established theory.

This is what I mean by interpretations as hypotheses. Legal interpretations present a norm as demanding a certain category of legal consequences for a certain category of factual constellations. They are abstract and general *if-then* statements about factual constellations and their legal consequences. Like scientific hypotheses that cover an infinite universe, they cannot be verified but only falsified. They are hypotheses—their validity is inescapably as hypothetical as that of scientific hypotheses.

3

Since interpretations and scientific hypotheses cannot be proved right, there can also be no rules that have only to be followed to discover the right interpretation or hypothesis. There can only be rules for falsifying hypotheses and interpretations. To put it differently and maybe more positively: there can only be rules for justifying interpretations and scientific hypotheses, justifying them preliminarily by demonstrating that all ways to falsify them, currently available, have been tried and tested without resulting in a falsification.

That there can be no rules for discovering the right interpretation, as there can be no rules for discovering the right scientific hypothesis, gives the context of discovery its characteristic freedom. Anything can be used to come up with an interpretation or scientific hypothesis interesting enough to be considered and tested. Dmitry Mendeleyev dreamed the periodic system of elements as a game of solitaire[2]; August Kekulé dreamed the benzene ring as a snake biting its tail.[3] Most of us have experienced thinking long and hard about a problem, going to bed clueless, and waking up with the solution.

This is what legal realism and its German counterpart, the *Freie Rechtsschule*,[4] got right and also wrong. They got it right that lawyers, attorneys, judges don't necessarily find their idea for an interpretation by going from interpretative step one to step two to step three to step four. They find their ideas by thinking about what feels right, right in terms of justice, or politics, or efficiency, by talking about their cases in a more or less scholarly way to colleagues and friends, husbands and wives, by liking or hating the parties of a case, by feeling burdened from a meal too heavy or cheery after a glass of champagne in the afternoon. They may, like Mendeleyev and Kekulé, find the interpretation in dreams. But like Mendeleyev and Kekulé, once they get out of bed, they have to test the interpretation that came to them. They have to try to falsify it in all currently available ways. They have to justify it by demonstrating that they have tested it without the result being falsification.

This is what legal realism and *Freie Rechtsschule* got wrong. The context of discovery and the context of justification are governed by different principles.[5] In the context of discovery, anything goes, so long as it is imaginative and creative. What matters in the context of justification are the possibly falsifying instances; they have to be agreed on; the discovered interpretation has to be tested against them; the test must not result in falsification. Legal realism and *Freie Rechtsschule* got it right that lawyers find their interpretations in erratic ways. They missed that lawyers have to test and falsify or justify their finds—and that they do.

That they missed it is understandable. The standards for interpretation that legal scholarship and jurisprudence have developed over time were, and are even now, normally presented as standards for finding the right interpretation. That is precisely what they cannot be, what they cannot effect. So legal realism and *Freie Rechtsschule* had an easy triumph by showing that the finding of an interpretation can happen in strange and weird ways. But it is finally an empty triumph, because what matters is not the context of discovery but the context of justification.

Not to be misunderstood—the two contexts are not neatly separated. Lawyers don't first go through the context of discovery and then through the context of justification. They have an idea of an interpretation, test it against the possibly falsifying instances that come to mind, easily drop it or modify it, test it again, have another idea that they like better or that they find a way to combine with the first, and so forth.[6] They move in a circle—a variation of the hermeneutic circle.[7]

They don't keep moving in it forever. There is a final draft of an interpretation and a final test. And when the interpretation passes the final test, when it is finally not falsified, it is justified and accepted—at least, for the moment.

4

How do the tests work, the tests that accompany the move through the hermeneutic circle and also the final test? How are legal interpretations falsified?

Scientific hypotheses are falsified by reality or, to be precise, by a new understanding of reality or, to be even more precise, by a new consensus about how to understand reality.[8] Once the scientific community agrees that a situation X that under the *if-then* of a hypothesis should result in situation Y results in situation Z instead, the hypothesis is falsified.

How are legal interpretations falsified?

In various ways. New cases, new factual constellations can show that an interpretation is wrong. Let me give a German example. A tax norm that gave publishers certain benefits was interpreted as privileging all publishers (*Verleger*) regardless of what they published—books, magazines, newspapers, records. When videos came on the market, a medium less bought than rented, the question came up about whether their publishers should also enjoy the privilege. Yes, the lawyers for the video publishers argued that publishers are publishers, and all publishers have always been treated equally. It is not that easy, was the counterargument; what the argument of the lawyers for the video publishers overlooks is the fact that wholesale traders in beer and other beverages are traditionally called "beer publishers" (*Bierverleger*), but were never meant and also never claimed to be privileged by the tax norm; to privilege them would be plainly absurd. The counterargument didn't decide how the publishers of videos were to be treated. It falsified the interpretation that to enjoy the privilege it was enough to be called a publisher. The right treatment of publishers of videos had to be found through a different interpretation.

The rethinking of the legal consequences that an interpretation has accepted as part of a norm can also falsify the interpretation. Let me, slightly simplified, offer another German example.[9] Person A drives along a street open only to the vehicles of residents and others who are delivering to residents or visiting them without being a resident, but in a careful and orderly manner. Suddenly person B, a resident, drives out of his driveway, not looking left or right, and crashes into A's car. B argues causality and the illegality of A's behavior—if A had not driven down the residential street, the accident would not have happened; and to drive down the residential street was illegal for A—and claims damages. Indeed, the causation of an accident through illegal behavior had traditionally been accepted as sufficient ground for damages. But in the case of A and B, the court—followed by academic opinion—regarded this result as unjust, incompatible with normative principles inherent in the legal system. It decided to understand causation and illegality as necessary but not sufficient conditions for the full recovery of damages. It required as a further condition that the illegality of the behavior caused the damage, as was not the case here because the same accident would have happened if a resident had driven down the street. Again the struggle for the adequate interpretation does not end here. How the connection between the illegality of the behavior and the damage, of course not a simple causal connection, has to look, how the illegality of A's behavior has to be weighed in relation to B's behavior, how the damage may have to be split—these are all open questions. But the rethinking of the legal consequences had falsified the interpretation under which the causation of an accident through illegal behavior was sufficient ground for damages.

5

As these two examples demonstrate, the occurrence of a new factual constellation and the rethinking of the legal consequences are not two neatly separated falsifying instances. They are intertwined. And the new factual constellation is of importance and the legal consequences have to be rethought because, in the first example, the text of the norm is read more thoroughly and taken more seriously, and, in both examples, the intention of the legislature is presumed to want to avoid absurd or unjust legal consequences.

Scientific hypotheses are falsified by consensus about how to understand reality. Legal interpretations are also falsified by consensus: about what the text of the norm says, about what the legislature intended, and about the consequences of a legal interpretation being compatible or incompatible with the rest of the legal system and its normative principles. Again, these three instances of falsification are intertwined; the legislature knows that it can legislate only text, not intentions; the intentions to be considered can be those only of an idealized legislature, not of the actual several hundred members of the legislative body of whom some intend this and some intend that and some nothing because all they want is to get it over with and go home; the idealized intentions—the intent of the legislature—aim at consequences that are at least compatible with the rest of the legal system and its normative principles.[10]

That these three consensuses matter is not due to methodological principles of interpretation. It is due to the constitutional state within which the interpretation takes place. In the constitutional state the power of the word replaces the power of brute force as far as possible; therefore the words of the law—the text of legislation—have to be taken seriously. In the democratic constitutional state the law must be created by the will of the people through its representatives; therefore the intentions of the elected legislators matter. And in the constitutional state under the rule of law the citizens have the right to know what to expect as the legal consequences of their actions and must therefore be able to rely on the consistency of the legal system.[11]

The struggle to establish a consensus about text, intentions, and consequences is the lawyer's daily bread. Often enough the consensus is not easily established, and sometimes it is not established at all. The questions asked in the attempt to establish the consensus are the old, familiar questions: What does the text really say? What did the legislature intend? What are the consequences of this or that interpretation?

6

Since the old, familiar questions reappear in the falsification model of interpretation, what is its advantage? Is it just, as we say in German, old wine in new skins? What is gained by understanding presumed instances of verification as mere instances of falsification?

Understanding legal interpretations as the hypotheses that they are confirms that there is no one right interpretation and that the quest for it goes astray. There are many interpretations that have not been falsified, not only over time but also at any given time. The falsifying instances, consensus based as they are, are too weak to reduce the competing interpretations to one; there will always be several interpretations worth considering. But even though the falsifying instances may be weak, they are strong enough to finish interpretations. Again and again it happens that an interpretation is shown to be incompatible with the text or the intentions or the consequences as they are consensually understood.

Since there will always be competing interpretations, while there can only be one decision, judges have to choose. The responsibility of judging goes farther than interpreting; it includes choosing between interpretations, and the judge cannot hide behind interpretation and what it requires him or her to do. There is a variety of viewpoints under which judges choose. Stare decisis; whether a decision works; whether it keeps social forces, prone to conflict, in equilibrium; whether it pacifies; whether it is fair; whether it is proportional—these and more are all legitimate points of view. But applying them is not interpretation, unless they are made norms by a constitution or statute, as, for instance, the principle of proportionality is in the German and other legal systems. There are also illegitimate viewpoints, among them political or religious affiliations, gender bias, and laziness, this often-ignored factor that makes judges choose the interpretation that makes things easy for them. The role of the judge as servant of the law decides what is legitimate and what illegitimate—not a hard decision.

Judging is more than interpreting. It ends the debate over the interpretation to be chosen; it chooses between possible interpretations; it chooses between the relevant points of view; it finishes all consideration; it decides. But this decision embodies neither an aporia nor a paradox, is nothing mystical or mythical, not the conservation and at the same time the destruction of law, no incursion of the irrational into the rational or of violence into discourse, as we sometimes can read.[12] The step from considering to choosing, from calculating to deciding, is simply the point where theory becomes practice. And wherever theory becomes practice, be it a house that has been designed and is now being built, an operation that the surgeons wondered how to perform and now go to perform, something ends and something begins. Theory ends and practice begins.

But theory doesn't disappear. If a decision uses a falsified interpretation, it is wrong, even if it is the decision of a court of last instance, unappealable, unchangeable. That practice creates a new, unchangeable reality doesn't make the practice right. A dental treatment is a mistake, even though the healthy tooth that the dentist mistakenly pulled out instead of the bad one cannot be put in again.

7

Looking back to the Bible reading and interpreting in my family, I think I might also have caught a glimpse of the practical role of interpretation in religion—as opposed to the notional role of interpretation in literature.

Literary interpretation is the core of dealing with literature. Dealing with literature begins with reading and ends with interpreting, and since it is impossible to read without interpreting, we can say that dealing with literature begins and ends with interpretation. In religion, as in law, interpretation is just an element, a crucial element, but still just an element of something much bigger. It is an element of a world with institutions, traditions, the need for abstract and general instructions, different kinds of practice, the need to bridge the gap between theory and practice, the hope to bring people faith. This world determines what interpretation in religion and in law is.

I understand that lawyers have turned to the field of law and literature with delight. Lawyers are readers, many lawyers read literature, many lawyers love literature. And to get students interested and engaged with problems of legal philosophy and jurisprudence, justice and injustice, law and morality, guilt and punishment, literature sometimes works better than philosophical and jurisprudential texts proper.

But if lawyers look for methodological cousinhood and inspiration, literature may not be the first choice. Theology, psychiatry and psychology, engineering—any area where interpretation has to come up with abstract and general instructions, and where interpretation plays a role as a hinge between theory and practice—may be closer to law than literature.

NOTES

1. Cf. Niklas Luhmann, *Das Recht der Gesellschaft* (Frankfurt am Main: Suhrkamp, 1995), 133–35.

2. John Boghosian Arden, *Science, Theology, and Consciousness* (Westport, Conn.: Praeger, 1998), 59; Gerard Irwin Nierenberg, *The Art of Creative Thinking* (New York: Cornerstone Library, 1986), 201.

3. John Read, *From Alchemy to Chemistry* (London: Dover, 1957), 179–81.

4. The protagonists of the movement being Ernst Fuchs, Hermann Kantorowicz (Gnaeus Flavius), and Eugen Ehrlich.

5. Cf. Franz Wieacker, *Privatrechtsgeschichte der Neuzeit* (Göttingen: Vandenhoeck und Ruprecht, 1967), 580–82.

6. Cf. Karl Larenz, *Methodenlehre*, 6th ed. (Heidelberg: Springer, 1991), 206–14, 211.

7. Martin Heidegger, *Sein und Zeit*, 11th ed. (Tübingen: Max Niemeyer Verlag, 1967), § 32, pp. 152–54); Hans-Georg Gadamer, *Wahrheit und Methode*, 7th ed. (Tübingen: Mohr Siebeck, 2010), 1:270–81.

8. Karl R. Popper, *Logik der Forschung*, 3rd ed. (Tübingen: Mohr Siebeck, 1969), 71–76.

9. Bundesgerichtshof, *Neue Juristische Wochenschrift*, December 9, 1969; *Neue Juristische Wochenschrift*, 1970, 421–23, also *Juristenzeitung*, 1970, 186–88.

10. Bernhard Schlink, "Bemerkungen zum Stand der Methodendiskussion in der Verfassungsrechtswissenschaft," *Der Staat* 19 (1980): 73–107 (esp. 88–107).

11. Friedrich Müller and Ralph Christensen, *Juristische Methodik*, 9th ed. (Berlin: Duncker & Humblot, 2004), 1:517–27.

12. Jacques Derrida, "Deconstruction and the Possibility of Justice," *Cardozo Law Review* 11 (1990): 919–1047.

Antonin Scalia, Bernhard Schlink, and Lancelot Andrewes
Reading *Heller*

Stanley Fish

I

At both the beginning and the end of his essay "Interpretations as Hypotheses," Bernhard Schlink distinguishes between literary interpretation, on the one hand, and legal and biblical interpretation, on the other.[1] Literary interpretation, he says, is specific to an author and his or her time, and has as its aim the determination of the author's meaning. It is not impossible that literary interpretation will lead to other actions—to a conversion, to political activism, to the performance of patriotism—but such an additional stage of action is contingent, not necessary. Getting a literary interpretation right (a notion Schlink challenges, I think wrongly), or at least believing that you have done so, is its own reward; nothing more is required. In contrast, legal and biblical interpretation take place in a normative field; determining the meaning of a statute or a clause in the Constitution or a verse in the Bible is necessarily preliminary to rendering a verdict, or commanding an act or the cessation of an act, or renouncing one's practices or being born again. The

Bible speaks to all lives and demands their reformation; the law speaks to all cases analogous to the present one and announces a decision to which future legal actors are to some extent bound. It follows, then—and this is Schlink's conclusion—that if lawyers are looking for "methodological cousinhood," they should probably look not to literature but to "any area where interpretation has to come up with abstract and general instructions," instructions, that is, which extend far beyond the present instance.[2]

Another way to put this would be to say that biblical and legal interpretation are serious activities; much hangs on them; and while they may certainly involve ingenuity and wit, they steer clear of frivolity. Literary interpretation, on the other hand, can on occasion be played like a parlor game. "Sometimes," says Schlink, "literary interpretation is not interested in the author . . . and attempts only to satisfy our wish for something new and fun, surprising and stimulating. It can present a determined Hamlet instead of a hesitant Hamlet . . . and Antigone as a comic instead of a tragic figure and still work, that is, make the audience of the performance enjoy, wonder, and think."[3] Now, I don't think that such performances can count as interpretation, for in my view interpretation is limited to the effort to figure out what a purposive agent had in mind when he or she produced these words and images; an activity not tethered to an interest in the author may be "surprising and stimulating" and productive of "fun," as Schlink observes, but it isn't interpretation.[4] A reading of Hamlet in which the prince is determined and resolute is an interpretation only if the interpreter believes that Shakespeare intended it. If he does not so believe, he is not interpreting, although what he is doing may arrest our attention. That argument, to which I shall return, is fully compatible with Schlink's distinction between a normative activity whose performance involves lessons we must heed—be they legal or moral—and an activity whose performance we enjoy for its own sake and wonder at for the pyrotechnic skills it displays.

Schlink doesn't make the point, but I suspect that he would join me in saying that it is probably not a good idea to mix the two kinds up: that is, to announce that one is playing a serious game and then proceed merely to play; and he might think, as I do, that it would be a positively bad idea to draw, or claim to draw, normative conclusions from a procedure—if that is the word—that followed no mandated normative path. Schlink is certainly right to say that "there can be no rules for discovering the right interpretation," but there is a rule the flouting of which will result not in wrong interpretation but in something that is not an interpretation at all.[5] That rule (probably not the best word) is one I have already given: if you're not concerned with what the author or authors had in mind, you're not interpreting; you're just playing around. This is my version of Schlink's insistence that interpretations have to be capable of being tested and justified; a so-called interpretation that could not pass the test or one that could not fail—because its production followed no rules and therefore it could not be held to any—must be rejected. Such an interpretation could not, in Schlink's vocabulary—a vocabulary I challenge later on—even be "falsified" because it is not a candidate for being true or false.

A spectacular example of just that kind of faux interpretation, of an analysis that is not really in the hunt, can be found in Antonin Scalia's opinion in *District of Columbia v. Heller*.[6] The case turns on a Washington, D.C., law that by banning the registration of handguns effectively prevents citizens from keeping a handgun at home for self-defense.[7] The question debated by the majority and the four dissenters is whether the statute runs afoul of the Second Amendment: "A well-regulated Militia, being necessary to the security of a free State, the right of the people to keep and bear arms shall not be infringed."[8] Justice John Paul Stevens, writing in dissent, declares that the Second Amendment "was adopted to protect the right of the people of each of the several states to maintain a well-regulated militia."[9] Justice Scalia, writing for the majority, finds that the amendment gives citizens "an individual right to possess a firearm unconnected with service in a militia, and to use that firearm for traditionally lawful purposes, such as self-defense within the home."[10] Each side claims that its position rests on the "natural meaning" of the words of the text.[11] They differ, however, on how to determine exactly what that "natural meaning" is.

Scalia, as everyone knows, was a textualist, someone who believes that correct interpretations are to be arrived at by examining the language of the text independently either of its author's intention or of the history (biographical or legislative) that led up to its formation.[12] It turns out that the textualist method (or as I shall argue, nonmethod) is a perfect fit with Scalia's thesis that the right granted by the Second Amendment is "unconnected with service in a militia."[13] The obvious obstacle this thesis must overcome is the prefatory clause, "A well-regulated Militia, being necessary to the security of a free State."[14] How can this clause (technically an "absolute construction"[15]), with its emphasis on militia service and no mention at all of self-defense, be "unconnected" or disconnected from the assertion of a right in the operative clause?[16] The answer is at once brilliant and dazzlingly simple: unconnect or disconnect them syntactically and by so doing disconnect the meaning of the amendment from a linear reading of its words. Syntax, rather than being the vehicle of meaning, becomes a placeholder for meanings that emerge independently of it, a frozen visual field whose components can be read in any way and in any direction: right-left, left-right, up-down, down-up. Unmoored from the constraint of linearity, that is, from the pressure of what comes before and what comes after, words can be turned this way and that, can be played with until they display the meaning the interpreter desires. This sounds like the opposite of textualism, but in fact it is textualism followed to its logical, and massively irresponsible, conclusion.

Scalia's first move in this game is decisive, and it is a doozy: he reads the second, operative, clause first.[17] What this does is allow him to establish its meaning apart from any interpretive pressure exerted by the prefatory clause; and after having done that, he can turn around and say, with a straight face, that the first clause "does not limit the latter grammatically."[18] How could it, given that he has explained its grammar in isolation? Scalia disconnects the second clause from the first and then observes, in all innocence, that they are, well, disconnected; and if they are disconnected in syntactic fact, they can be said to be disconnected in semantic fact; their meanings have nothing to do with each other because the contiguity that binds them together in a temporal flow has been removed when the order of their consideration is reversed.

After acknowledging that he has begun "our textual analysis with the operative clause," Scalia promises to "return to the prefatory clause," but only, he says, "to ensure that our reading of the operative clause is consistent with the announced purpose."[19] He himself does not announce the prefatory clause's purpose until he has established (in isolation) the meaning of the operative clause. Only then does he tell us that the purpose of the clause (but not of the amendment as a whole) is "to prevent elimination of the militia."[20] He can safely assert this because he has already denied to the clause any limiting effect on what follows it. Its literal absence from his analysis for many pages allows him to assert that the purpose of the amendment is to affirm a right—the right of citizens to defend themselves by bearing arms—they had always had apart from any participation in military service. To be sure, participation in military service is made more effective by the affirmation of that right, but is not what the amendment safeguards; it is a secondary beneficiary of the amendment's primary purpose. That is, while the Second Amendment's central function is to "codify" (Scalia's word) the right of the people to keep arms for self-defense, it has the additional and happy consequence of preventing the elimination of militias.[21] That consequence, however, is just a fortunate by-product of the codified right, not the content of it. "The prefatory clause does not suggest that preserving the militia was the only reason Americans valued the right."[22] The main reason, he insists, is to preserve "self-defense and hunting."[23] Again, this conclusion is enabled by the reversal of temporal order: first establish the meaning of the operative clause as if it had no antecedent, and then go back and see if the orphaned prefatory clause can be made to fit with what you have established. I would say that the chances of success are 100 percent.

If Scalia's reasoning strikes you as strained, even tortured, it is nothing compared with what happens when he turns to the individual words of the operative clause. Having severed the clause from the one preceding it, and thereby made it into an independent entity that can be interrogated in a vacuum, he proceeds to do the same thing to each and every word. That is, rather than determine a word's meaning by attending to its place and function in a syntactic structure and to its relationships with the other words in that structure, he catalogs the meanings the words have had in *other* texts, texts that have no relation at all to the production and ratification of this one. Scalia spends nine pages on the phrase "to keep and bear arms,"[24] but he does not treat the phrase as a unit that has a well-known idiomatic meaning identified by Justice Stevens: "to possess arms . . . for military purposes."[25] Instead he addresses each word in turn, but not really in turn; rather, he takes them up in the order convenient to the interpretation he wants to reach: "Before addressing the verbs 'keep' and 'bear,' we interpret their object: 'Arms.'"[26] That is, he starts with the last word and thereby ensures that the words preceding it will play no part in its interpretation. The work of interpretation will be done by texts and authors with no connection to the text at hand. So he asks how did Samuel Johnson define *arms* and how did Timothy Cunningham (author of a 1771 legal dictionary) define *arms* and how did Trusler or Blackstone define *arms*?[27] After he has played around with *arms* for a while, he performs the same operation on *bear* and *keep* and finds that these words—considered single, stand-alone verbal units—often occurred in contexts "referring to possessing arms for militiamen and *everyone else.*"[28] That is, he finds usages of *arms*, *keep*, and *bear* that were unconnected with service in a militia. Who would have doubted it? One would have thought that the question is what these quite ordinary words mean as they are combined in *this* sentence, produced at *this* time, by *these* authors, not what range of meanings might have been assigned them by a series of dictionaries. By what logic does discovering that *arms*, *keep*, and *bear* often appeared in nonmilitary contexts lead to the conclusion that they do so here?

The answer is "by the logic of textualism," which forbids inquiries into actual authorship and actual intentions, and mandates, instead, an extensive investigation of word usage with a view to determining how the words of the text in question would have been defined by contemporary dictionaries and contemporary usage.[29] Textualism's self-description has it allowing the text to speak for itself without the interposition of an interpretive machine; but the method of textualism, at least as exemplified by Scalia's performance in *Heller*, reminds us that texts are inert—only black marks on a white background—until they have been placed in a context that gives them interpretive life. The key question is, what is the right context, the context that will at once constrain and guide the process? For an intentionalist like Stevens, the right context will be what the author or authors had in mind. For a living constitutionalist, as Justice Stephen Breyer is in his dissent, the right context will be the present-day urgencies that have given rise to the constitutional question. The living constitutionalist will want to know if the words of the Constitution can be squared with the rational purposes of a legislature, and he will try as hard as he can to bring the two into harmony. But a textualist has foresworn both these contexts—the intentional one and the one that foregrounds the goals of legislatures—and he is left only with the bare words and with nothing animating them. His only recourse, given what he has denied himself, is to animate them with their own histories, to maintain, in effect, that it is the words, in the fullness of their historical lexical profiles, that have authored the texts in which they appear.

The trouble with animating words by reference to their histories as found in dictionaries or in statistical compilations of usage is that the context is too open and too plural to do the work required of it. A dictionary lists too many possible meanings of a word and goes in too many directions to serve as an interpretive guide. Statistical evidence of usage likewise offers averages and distributional tables without any mechanism for specifying which statistic is interpretively relevant *in this particular case*. As Frank Easterbrook explains, a dictionary "is a museum of words, an historical catalog rather than a means to decode the work of legislatures."[30] For a textualist like Scalia, however, this inability of lexical history to narrow meaning down because the history is so rich and varied is an opportunity and an advantage.

Freed from the constraints of syntax, context, and intention, the so-called interpreter can roam around in the wonderful world of ever-proliferating meanings until he lights upon one that supports his antecedent preference. Advertising itself as a methodological constraint on subjective and willful interpreters, textualism in fact licenses interpreters to be as willful and creative as they like so long as they are able to point to friendly dictionary entries, a category that will never be empty. Textualism, in short, is a form of fiction making claiming for itself a grounding in objective verbal reality. The so-called Linguists' Brief, responding to the court of appeals ruling from which Scalia took some of his arguments, puts it very nicely: "The court defined the words 'bear' and 'arms' separately, then reconstituted them into a new, ahistorical expression meaning 'the carrying of arms for private purposes such as self-defense.'"[31] "Ahistorical" is too polite; entirely made up would be more accurate.

2

This, then, is my complaint against Scalia's so-called method: it is without a foundation and without any constraint because the constraints both of syntax and of intention have been removed. The result is what the dissent (in a footnote) characterizes as interpretive "atomism"—the detaching of verbal units from the structures that confer meaning on them so that, tethered to nothing and hanging in midair, they can be given the meaning the interpreter has selected in advance.[32] It works; in fact it cannot fail; root around in the vast empire of usage long enough and you will always find something that suits.

There is a tradition, however, in which this same methodological arbitrariness is blameless and interpretively sound. It is a religious tradition that finds its expression in seventeenth-century sermons. It is called "crumbling," and it involves "riffing" on the individual words of a biblical passage rather than attending to the place those words have in an unfolding syntax.[33] Meaning is regarded not as something that emerges at the end of a temporal unit but as something that can be accessed spatially, as it were, by allowing words to suggest associations (of sound or sense) that then suggest associations, which then suggest associations, and so on.[34] It is as if each word were looked up in a large dictionary like the *Oxford English Dictionary*, and the entire range of entries put in play, with the play being arrested only when the interpreter comes upon something that confirms the point he has had up his sleeve from the beginning. It sounds very much like what Scalia does in *Heller*, but in fact it is different, for in the sermons the inability of the interpreter to fail is a function not of his method but of the God-centered world he lives in.

Here is an example from a sermon preached in 1620 by Lancelot Andrewes.[35] The sermon takes its starting point from a passage in the twentieth chapter of the Gospel according to John.[36] In the passage, Mary Magdalene is looking for the body of Christ, peers into the sepulcher that no longer houses him, and weeps at her inability to find him: "and as she wept, she stooped down, and looked into the sepulcher."[37] Listen to what Andrewes does with this simple recitation of a simple action: "That is, she did so weepe as she did seeke . . . Weeping without seeking is but to small purpose. But her weeping hindered not her seeking. Her sorrow dulled not her diligence. And diligence is a character of love, comes from the same roote, *dilectio* and *diligentia* from *diligo*, both."[38] Andrewes meditates in the manner of free association on the individual words, or rather on the consonants and vowels they share. First the relationship between "weeping" and "seeking" is elaborated; and then (this is the amazing moment) "seeking" morphs into "sorrow" because both begin with an *s*, and the *d* in "hindered" is doubled into "dulled" and "diligence" ("Her sorrow dulled not her diligence"). And then diligence is declared to be a character of love in two senses: it is an essential ingredient of love, and the two share a character, an alphabetic letter in Latin, and by virtue of that phonetic likeness is like love at the root. In the course of this explicatory tour de force, syntax ceases to be the generator of meaning and is instead a scaffolding on which bundles of meaning are hung.

Those who objected to crumbling, reports Meredith Neuman in her book *Jeremiah's Scribes*, complained that "a too minute attendance upon the minutiae of the text detracted from the common sense of the words."[39] That, of course, was exactly the point. The "common sense of the words" is the sense they acquire at the end of the linear entity we know as a sentence. The meaning of an individual word is never present at the instance of its utterance; meaning is always elsewhere, always deferred, yet to be realized. And it gets worse. The meaning arrived at, at the end of the sentence, the meaning that forms what grammarians call a "complete thought," is itself incomplete, despite the rhetorical finality of the sentence's period, for there is always more that has not been said. Nor will the incompleteness of a single sentence be redeemed by the production of more sentences; for if no one sentence delivers the whole meaning, the serial addition of sentences won't do so either; you can't reach completeness by piling up incompletenesses. The big picture where everything can be seen and understood in all its significance is always one sentence ahead; no sentence or sequence of sentences, however long, can ever be meaning-*full*.

But in the world Andrewes inhabits, full and complete meaning is everywhere, all around you, not at the end of sentences but at every point in a structure that is not linear but spatial. Put the right pressure on any word, no matter where it is positioned in a syntax, and it will deliver all the meaning you could ever want; you don't have to seek it, and you can't miss it because human strivings, in life and in sentences, are not its source. It is a pregiven meaning and it has been given by the God whose benevolent omnipresence is the message declared by every item in the world—the *uni*-verse—he has created. To those whose hearts and minds are filled with a faith in this pregiven, never-failing, never less than complete meaning, to those who take seriously the commonplace that the world is God's book, everything they see, hear, and read bears the preknown meaning that sustains the world and is its content—the twofold love of God and of our neighbor for his sake. In his *On Christian Doctrine*, Augustine explains that you can't go wrong if you affirm that meaning, even if you make interpretative errors. Were the cleverest man alive to construct an interpretation that "does not tend to build up this two-fold love," he will have failed in understanding.[40] And, conversely, the slow-witted man who gets the philology and the etymology wrong will nevertheless have hit the mark "if his mistaken interpretation tends to build up love."[41] You can't make a mistake if you see and read in the right spirit.

In the passage Andrewes explicates, Mary Magdalene apparently makes a big mistake. Jesus stands right in front of her, but she doesn't recognize him and "supposes him to be the gardener."[42] Andrewes comments: "Though she might seem to err in some sense, yet in some other she was in the right. For in a sense, and in a good sense, Christ may well be said to be a gardener and indeed is one . . . The first, the fairest, garden (Paradise) He was the gardener, it was of his planting . . . So gardener in that sense. But not in that alone . . . He it is that gardens our souls, . . . sows and plants them with the true roots and seeds of righteousness, waters them with the dew of his grace."[43] And so Andrewes concludes, he appeared "in his own likeness" when he appeared, at least to Mary Magdalene, as a gardener. Indeed, any likeness, if it is one that illustrates his qualities, will be his own, for he is everything that is truly meaningful; he is what everything is "like" if it is seen correctly. You can be looking for him in all the wrong places, but still find him because there is no place where he is not. Andrewes makes this point in a remarkable sentence: "He is found of them that seeke Him not, but of them that seeke Him never but found."[44] The sentence's syntactic rhetoric, turning on the adversative *but*, seems to contrast two classes, those who find him and those who don't. But the second *but* ("never but found") undoes the first and makes the two classes one. Neither can fail to find him. Errors on the level of mundane perception and faulty interpretation will always be redeemed by the meaning that necessarily includes and baptizes them.

3

Nothing comparable redeems Scalia's textualism. Crumbling works for Andrewes and for other Anglican preachers because the sense to be discovered is pre-inscribed in all phenomena. Therefore it doesn't matter where you begin—the last word first, the first clause second—or whether you hop around all over the place; the one true meaning is always and already available and you can't possibly miss it. There is only one interpretive conclusion, and it is never more than a half step away no matter where a meandering imagination has taken you. In the world Scalia lives in, however—the secular world of rational deduction, the world of the law—sense is to be discovered rather than presupposed. Meaning must be put together and argued for, and therefore it really matters where you begin and in what order and on the basis of what reasons you proceed to a conclusion that is not simply waiting for you everywhere. The chain of reasoning must be a true chain, with its links soldered together in a way that can be followed, verified, or shown to be falsified (to return to Schlink's vocabulary). If meaning is not pregiven, as it is for Andrewes, if meaning must be fashioned by human agents, the path to its discovery must be clearly marked and the evidence must be closely tied to the object of interpretation. Scalia's evidence is not closely tied to the object of interpretation, because his first move, as I have shown, is to break that object up and then interpret, if that is the word, the disjointed pieces.

Schlink declares that "if a decision uses a falsified interpretation, it is wrong," and by a falsified interpretation, he means an interpretation that cannot account for the "factual constellations" that give rise to it. For example, the interpretation of a tax norm that would extend benefits to anyone calling himself a publisher will be falsified, he says, by the fact that wholesale beer traders also call themselves publishers.[45] But I would argue that the interpretation would not be so much falsified by the use of "publisher" to mean beer merchants as it would be rendered less persuasive, at least for a time; for the lawyer on the other side could still go back to the drawing board and come up with an interpretation that neutralized or outflanked the inconvenient usage. Falsification, with its suggestion of scientific procedure, is, I think, the wrong word to describe what happens when an interpretation fails. I agree with Schlink that "the struggle to establish a consensus about text, intentions, and consequences is the lawyer's daily bread,"[46] but I would argue that the finished loaf, the consensus, is baked/established not by logic but by rhetoric in the best sense of that freighted word—the art of building an argument that hangs together and displays premises and evidence in a manner that draws from the audience a rational assent. My analysis of Scalia's interpretation has not falsified it but shown it to be something that doesn't hang together. And it doesn't hang together because it is not really an interpretation at all but a demonstration of textualism's inability to come to grips with the object to which it pledges fidelity. At best (and also at worst) it belongs in Schlink's category of interpretive extravaganzas that are fun, although it may not be fun to live in its wake. The opinion can't be falsified because, as I remarked earlier, it doesn't rise to the level of being either true or false; it's just a bag of tricks, and it is a bag of tricks licensed by Scalia's "method," which, far from being the guarantor of constraint as he claims, is the very antithesis of constraint. Scalia objects to living constitutionalism because he believes that it abandons the text to the willful interpreter. Textualism, at least in this case, not only abandons the text; it disassembles the text while claiming all the while to be its protector, and it does so in order to reassemble the text in a form that will support the outcome the interpreter prefers. Nor could it be otherwise: textualism is *necessarily* result oriented because having detached the text from the intentional, historical context that gives it meaning, it has nowhere else to go but to enact the interpreter's desires. At least living constitutionalism is honest in its frank avowal of the political motives that textualism loudly disclaims and rhetorically pushes away.

4

Scalia's *Heller* opinion can be seen as a footnote—a very important one—to one of the most celebrated and influential debates in Anglo-American jurisprudence, the argument (in the pages of the *Harvard Law Review*) between

H. L. A. Hart and Lon L. Fuller over whether Nazi law was in fact law.[47] Hart famously declared that while Nazi law may have been bad law (he certainly thinks it was), it was nonetheless law because it exhibited the features that identify law—statutes, tribunals, trials, verdicts, rules of evidence, penalties, and so forth.[48] Fuller replied that a body of law that is not animated by some moral, aspirational vision will not hang together, will not constitute a system, will have no consistency or coherence, will have no genuine relationships between its parts, will not, in short, be law.[49]

Although it may seem puzzling at first, this debate about morality and law takes a turn into interpretive theory when Hart and Fuller offer opposing accounts of how to figure out what the hypothetical ordinance "no vehicles permitted in the park" means. Hart correctly locates the interpretive problem (if there is one) in the word *vehicle*. What exactly does it cover? An automobile surely, he says. But what about "bicycles, roller skates, toy automobiles"?[50]

Hart answers his question by calling for a study of the lexical history of the word, which, he says, has a core meaning and some not-so-core meanings, meanings that reside in what he calls "the penumbra."[51] Penumbral meanings cannot be read off the text, but must be guessed at or deduced from circumstances; the jurist who finds himself in the penumbra is on his own, exercising the kind of discretion appropriate to legislators: when the direction the text supplies has run out, "the intelligent decision of penumbral questions is one made not mechanically but in the light of aims, purposes and policies."[52]

To this analysis Fuller replies that none of this fancy reasoning and lexicography is necessary. All one has to do is ask a simple question: What did the framers of the ordinance have in mind? That is, what did they want either to encourage or to prevent? "We ask ourselves, What can this rule be for? What evil does it seek to avert? What good is it intended to promote?"[53] Once that question is answered—the purpose is to preserve quiet or protect pedestrians or minimize pollution—it is immediately obvious whether a particular object (like a toy automobile) is a vehicle of the kind the ordinance aims at. Hart, Fuller explains, thinks of words as existing in the abstract and so in need of the directing constraint that dictionaries and lexical histories can provide.[54] A word so conceived is an "inert datum of meaning," floating in air because it is "isolated from the effects of purpose and structure," the true sources of constraint.[55] So isolated a word can mean anything one likes.

It is in this characterization of textualism/positivism as an interpretive method that breaks free of the constraints of purpose and structure that we find the link between the "no vehicles in the park" example and the larger issue of whether Nazi law was really law. Fuller's criticism of the Nazi regime matches point for point his criticism of Hart's theory of interpretation. In the Third Reich, Fuller reminds us, laws were often secret, leaving the citizen ignorant of what actions could or could not be legally performed; if laws were not secret, they were inconsistently enforced or not enforced at all; and many of the laws that were enforced were retroactively declared.[56] The result was a legal landscape of stand-alone bits unrelated to one another because no "internal morality" or informing spirit united them into something that could be called a system.[57] Unconstrained by any overriding purpose (except the purpose to do the regime's will, whatever it might be at the moment), the German lawyer was "prepared to accept as 'law' anything that . . . was printed at government expense and seemed to come '*von oben herab.*'"[58] The homology is perfect: the textualist/positivist "method" of reducing texts to infinitely manipulable pieces of data and the Nazi regime's "method" of promulgating directives that were faithful to its arbitrary and changing will rather than to any overarching principle were mirror images of each other. A bad theory of interpretation and an evil regime emerged in tandem, and Fuller goes so far as to agree with Gustav Radbruch's contention that "a general acceptance of the positivistic philosophy . . . made smoother the route to dictatorship."[59] Because textualist positivism encourages piecemeal interpretation of disconnected entities and closes its eye to any constraining moral or intentional perspective, it is, Fuller more than implies, the perfect judicial/linguistic interpretive theory for the implementation of the Nazi program. The conclusion is not one he explicitly draws, but it is waiting to be announced: not only is textualism incoherent as an interpretive practice; it is evil.

NOTES

1. See Schlink, this volume.
2. Ibid., 20.
3. Ibid., 12.
4. Ibid., 12.
5. Ibid., 14.
6. District of Columbia v. Heller, 554 U.S. 570 (2008).
7. Ibid., 574.

8. U.S. Const., amend. II.
9. District of Columbia v. Heller, 637.
10. Ibid., 577.
11. Compare Scalia's majority, "From our review of founding-era sources, we conclude that this *natural meaning* was also the meaning that 'bear arms' had in the 18th century" (ibid., 584; emphasis added), with Stevens's dissent, "When, as in this case, there is no such qualifier, the most *natural meaning* is the military one" (ibid., 649; emphasis added).
12. See, e.g., Antonin Scalia and Bryan A. Garner, *Reading Law: The Interpretation of Legal Texts* (St. Paul, Minn.: Thomson/West, 2012), 16: "The exclusive reliance on text when interpreting text is known as *textualism*. We believe that this approach elicits both better drafting and better decision making."
13. District of Columbia v. Heller, 577.
14. U.S. Const., amend. II.
15. "In its grammatical usage, an absolute construction is so called because it is independent of its grammatical surroundings" (Julian Wolfreys, *Occasional Deconstructions* [Albany: State University of New York Press, 2004], 126).
16. For examples of Justice Scalia disconnecting the right in the operative clause from notions of military service, see District of Columbia v. Heller: finding that all written examples of the phrase "keep arms" from the founding period "favor viewing the right to 'keep Arms' as an individual right *unconnected* with militia service" (582; emphasis added); finding that three founding-era legal scholars "understood [the Second Amendment] to protect an individual right *unconnected* with militia service" (605; emphasis added); finding that "the 19th-century cases that interpreted the Second Amendment universally support an individual right *unconnected* to militia service" (610; emphasis added); finding that "every late-19th-century legal scholar that we have read interpreted the Second Amendment to secure an individual right *unconnected* with militia service" (616; emphasis added).
17. See District of Columbia v. Heller, 578.
18. Ibid., 577.
19. Ibid., 578.
20. Ibid., 599.
21. Ibid., 603.
22. Ibid., 599.
23. Ibid.
24. Ibid., 582–91.
25. Ibid., 646.
26. Ibid., 581.
27. Ibid., 581–84.
28. Ibid., 583.

29. See, e.g., Scalia and Garner, *Reading Law*, 12: "In their full context, words mean what they conveyed to reasonable people at the time they were written."

30. Frank H. Easterbrook, "Text, History, and Structure in Statutory Interpretation," *Harvard Journal of Law and Public Policy* 17, no. 1 (1994): 67.

31. Brief for Professors of Linguistics and English, District of Columbia v. Heller, 554 U.S. 570 (2008) (No. 07-290), 2008 WL 157194, 4–5.

32. District of Columbia v. Heller, 650n14: "The Court's atomistic, word-by-word approach to construing the Amendment calls to mind the parable of the six blind men and the elephant, [in which] each blind man approaches a single elephant; touching a different part of the elephant's body in isolation, each concludes that he has learned its true nature. . . . Each of them, of course, has fundamentally failed to grasp the nature of the creature."

33. See generally Meredith Marie Neuman, "Crumbling, Collating, and Enabling," in *Jeremiah's Scribes: Creating Sermon Literature in Puritan New England* (Philadelphia: University of Pennsylvania Press, 2013), 140–72.

34. Neuman, "Crumbling, Collating, and Enabling."

35. Lancelot Andrewes, "Sermons on the Resurrection Preached on Easter-Day" (1620), anglicanhistory.org/lact/andrewes/v3/easter1620.html.

36. John 20:11–17.

37. Ibid.

38. Andrewes, "Sermons" (emphasis added).

39. Neuman, "Crumbling, Collating, and Enabling," 149.

40. Augustine, *On Christian Doctrine*, trans. J. F. Shaw (Mineola, N.Y.: Dover Publications, 2009), 26.

41. Ibid.

42. John 20:15.

43. Andrewes, "Sermons."

44. Ibid.

45. Schlink, 16.

46. Ibid.

47. The seminal articles of the debate were H. L. A. Hart, "Positivism and the Separation of Law and Morals," *Harvard Law Review* 71 (1958): 593; and Lon L. Fuller, "Positivism and Fidelity to Law—a Reply to Professor Hart," *Harvard Law Review* 71 (1958): 630.

48. See Hart, "Positivism and the Separation of Law and Morals," 618–20.

49. See Fuller, "Positivism and Fidelity to Law," 645–47.

50. Hart, "Positivism and the Separation of Law and Morals," 607.

51. Ibid., 607–11.

52. Ibid., 614.

53. Fuller, "Positivism and Fidelity to Law," 663.

54. Ibid., 664–65.
55. Ibid., 669.
56. Ibid., 651.
57. Ibid., 645.
58. Ibid., 659.
59. Ibid., 657.

The Interpreter, the Scientist, and the Analyst

Jeanne L. Schroeder

Despite their differences, Stanley Fish and Bernhard Schlink agree that there are correct and incorrect interpretations of legal materials.[1] They also agree that, in legal interpretation, it is the text's meaning, not the interpreter's opinion, that is to be revealed.

Schlink and Fish agree that the method for finding a *correct* interpretation cannot be reduced to a finite series of rules. To put this another way, interpretation requires judgment, and, as Immanuel Kant argued, judgment cannot be taught.[2]

Each, however, offers a negative rule to recognize incorrect interpretations. Schlink asserts that incorrect legal interpretations can be eliminated through the scientific method of falsification. Fish claims that any proposed interpretation that is not concerned with the author's state of mind is not an interpretation at all and must be rejected.

Unfortunately, Fish's insistence that "interpretation is limited to the effort to figure out what a purposive agent had in mind when he or she produced these words and images" is problematic for reasons beyond the base issue that Schlink raises as to what it means for a collective body such as a legislature, bar committee promulgating a uniform statute or restatement, generations of judges developing a body of common law to have an intent. In this essay I am concerned that his references to authorial intent could be read to downplay the role of the interpreter as an active subject—which I don't believe is Fish's position. Although interpretation is objective in that it always involves the examination of an object (i.e., a text), interpretation is not *merely* objective. Communication is collaboration; interpretation needs an interpreter. As such, it is intersubjective.

But interpretation cannot be limited entirely to the intersubjective order of the "symbolic" in which language, as well as law, is located. The symbolic can never be disentangled from the orders of the imaginary and the real that are its logical boundaries.[3] Interpretation has a subjective aspect because it requires the creative act of the interpreter's imagination.

Schlink is correct that hypothesis formation is essential to interpretation. He distinguishes between the subjective moment in developing an initial working interpretation and the subsequent objective or intersubjective process of testing it.

INTERPRETATION AND IMAGINATION

In this essay, I comment on Fish's and Schlink's positions from the position of speculative theory, concentrating on Lacanian psychoanalytic theory. Interpretation falls within what Jacques Lacan calls the "analyst's discourse."[4]

According to Bruce Fink, in Lacan's most well-known essay on linguistics, "The Instance of the Letter in the Unconscious, or Reason Since Freud,"[5] he does not so much explain his theory of interpretation as demonstrate it. By intentionally making his texts infuriatingly opaque, Lacan forces us to confront the arduous process of interpretation that we often accomplish so quickly that we are not even aware of what we are doing. This process includes, as Schlink insists, the imaginative act he calls hypothesis formation.

Lacan asserts that the symbolic—the order of intersubjective relations including language and law—is logically open-ended and in a process of slippage. Let me start by concentrating on what Lacan does not mean. It is tempting to misread this as the proposition that signification is arbitrary and one interpretation is as good as any other. In fact, this type of sophistry is the farthest thing from Lacanianism. As Slavoj Žižek explains (invoking Donald Rumsfeld), psychoanalysis is the search for "unknown knowns."[6]

That is, psychoanalysis is grounded in the proposition that "truth" can be established through articulation that makes the unknown-known known. Similarly, interpretation is a process of revealing the meaning that is initially hidden in a text.

Lacan starts with the common linguistic proposition that language consists of signifiers referring to signifieds. Language does not, however, refer directly to the object world itself. Rather, each signified is itself another signifier.[7] Language is, then, an unending and open chain of signification. This is why it is in a constant state of flux and slippage. The question is, can we stop this slippage to establish the certainty of meaning?

Lacan offers several descriptions of how stable meaning is established or, in Fink's words, "precipitates out, or crystalizes,"[8] out of slippery signification. One way is the creation of a master signifier: a signifier that is also its own signified, that is, it stands only for itself. This can be thought of as a declarative assertion or hypothesis, such as "the statute means x."

Stability is, however, the hallmark of the *subjective* order of the imaginary, not the *intersubjective* order of the symbolic. It is the interpreter who uses her imagination to impose a master signifier.

It is easy to misread my insistence on the necessary role of imagination as implying that an interpreter "makes up" an interpretation. Famously, Lacan said that "every truth has the *structure* of a fiction" not that truth is fictional.[9]

The subjective Lacanian imaginary is a way to temporarily halt the slippage of the symbolic. Law, however, must be intersubjective (symbolic): it applies to all who are similarly situated. The certainty of interpretation is, therefore, always contingent. In Schlink's words, our interpretation is a hypothesis that must be tested, and refined or rejected based on the evidence. In Fish's words, it must be justified through argument and rhetoric.

Fink illustrates Lacan's point with the following example:

> If I say that "Dick and Jane were exposed, when they were young children and in a repeated manner, to . . ." the listener does not know how to understand "exposed" until I finish the sentence with "harmful radiation," "foreign languages," or even "their uncle the exhibitionist." . . .
> The end of the sentence determines how the listener understands or "rereads" the beginning of the sentence; the end of the sentence fixes the meaning(s), putting an end to the sliding (without necessary reducing multiple meanings to one single meaning).[10]

In other words, when one begins reading, one encounters ambiguity. The verb *exposed* when juxtaposed with the term *young children* could mean many things. Fink suggests that the reader starts generating alternative hypotheses and must choose among them. In this example, the choice might seem inevitable because only one interpretation would be consistent with words encountered at the end of the sentence. Indeed, in the ordinary course, one might not even experience oneself as interpreting at all. The point, however, is that the reader, using her imagination, *retroactively* draws meaning out of signification.

When one encounters a difficult text, such as Lacan's "The Instance of the Letter," or a complex statute or frustrating legal dispute, one becomes painfully aware how difficult interpretation can be. The crucial point is that although this process requires the reader to use her imagination and make choices, the choices are among potential meanings within the text itself. As Fink says, the problem is not that the text has no meaning so that the reader must supply it, but that it often is overflowing with *potential* meanings, not all of which can be correct.[11]

One can see here how Fink's reading of Lacan is consistent with Fish's damning account of Judge Antonin Scalia's textualism in his opinion in *Heller*.[12] In Scalia's reading of the Second Amendment of the U.S. Constitution, he takes each clause and word separately without "the constraints of syntax, context, and intention" and then scours dictionaries for convenient definitions unmoored from the text. As such, he preserves the plethora of *potential* meanings so that he can pick and choose the one that serves *his* pregiven, normative ends. Although Scalia claims to be bound to the text, in fact, his method frees him from it. "Far from being the guarantor of constraint as he claims, [it] is the very antithesis of constraint." Whatever this exercise might be, it is not interpretation.

ABDUCTION

Schlink distinguishes between hypothesis formation and proof. This former is what the American philosopher Charles Sanders Peirce called "abduction"—which he argued was as essential a part of the scientific process as deduction and induction.[13] Crucially, the scientist does not "find" hypotheses to test, she imagines them.

Peirce explains the abductive process as follows. First one observes a surprising fact. Then one tries to formulate an explanation that, if true, would change the fact from being surprising to a matter of course.[14] That is, abduction is guessing what might be the case. The apparent explanatory power of an abduction is a good reason to adopt it as a working hypothesis. As Thomas Sebeok and Jean Umiker-Sebeok have shown, that famous fictional paradigm of logical deduction, Sherlock Holmes, is, in fact, no such thing. He is a master of *abduction*: He claims he never guesses,[15] when in fact that is all he ever does.[16] Abduction, however, is the beginning, not the end, of interpretation—it is not proof.

Consequently, although Schlink agrees with the proposition of "legal realism and its German counterpart, the Freie Rechtsschule," that lawyers, attorneys, and judges "find their ideas by thinking about what feels right," he criticizes these movements for making the Sherlockian mistake of conflating abduction and deduction. As he says, "The context of discovery and the context of justification are governed by different principles."

Schlink is correct in agreeing with the realists that legal interpreters "don't necessarily find their idea for an interpretation by going from interpretative step one to step two to step three to step four." That is, abduction cannot be reduced to a specific set of rules. Lacan was deeply influenced by Kant, who, he thought, was the true founder of psychoanalysis[17] precisely because he insisted that judgment cannot be reduced to rules and we can never really know how we come to make decisions. In Kant's words, "The depths of the human heart are unfathomable."[18]

Nevertheless, I believe that Peirce would disagree with Schlink's assertion that "in the context of discovery, anything goes, so long as it is imaginative and creative." Peirce thought that philosophers should study the process of hypothesis formation precisely because there are better and worse methods. Abduction is not just guessing; it is *intelligent* guessing.

And here we rehabilitate Sherlock. He was a very good guesser because he did the hard work of careful study, observation, and critique. He was critically aware that his abductions had to account for all the evidence. Consequently, he was never satisfied with his initial abduction but would seek additional evidence for the purposes of modifying it. As I have said elsewhere:

> The process consists of the gathering of small facts, what Holmes called "trifles." The investigator then tries to formulate a plausible story that fits the facts (plausible in the sense of being both possible and probable . . .). Having developed initial stories, the investigator seeks additional trifles.

The development of alternate stories depends on the trifles gathered, the gathering of trifles, the act of observation, is itself determined by the story. One can see only what one is looking for. The stories are themselves questions. Abduction, then, is the art of asking good questions and making good guesses, which are themselves further questions.[19]

In other words, in practice (as Schlink admits), hypothesis formation and proof "cannot be neatly separated 'into two steps.'"

Schlink's proposition that we don't know whether or not we make an initial judgment on the basis of reasons and evidence is consistent with the teachings of Kant and Lacan, and perhaps neuroscience. We make tentative decisions and then retroactively critique them. We can never know, however, what caused our decision. The process of retroactive justification and interpretation is so natural to humans that, as Fink's example illustrates, in the ordinary case we are unaware that we are even doing so. This is precisely why it seems so alien when we confront the hard cases in which we become aware of the hermeneutic process.

It is standard in legal academics to assume that rationality consists of consciously "weighing" the evidence and arguments to make a decision (going from step one to step two, etc.). Schlink, however, suggests that some such process characterizes hypothesis proof. Consequently, Karl Popper insists (and Schlink implies) that although abduction (i.e., hypothesis creation) is irrational (i.e., anything goes), proof is rational.

The speculative and psychoanalytic traditions would argue otherwise. The fact that a thought process is partly unconscious does not necessarily mean that it is irrational. Indeed, computers are not (yet) conscious but "think" in a purely logical, algorithmic way—indeed, so rigidly that they can be stupid in the sense of lacking common sense. Similarly, psychoanalysis holds that the *unconscious* is structured like language.[20]

This brings us back to the analyst and interpretation. The point of interpretation is to reveal unknown knowns, the still-undiscovered content in the text itself. Good analysis takes the hard work of interrogation and examination. It also requires introspection of one's own motives.

Consequently, if "anything goes" in hypothesis formation, it is only in the weak sense that as an empirical matter in any specific case, law might be, to invoke the familiar cliché, what a judge had for breakfast, or the champagne she had with lunch (to give Schlink's example). However, the ethical interpreter will not stop with her original abduction.

This is one reason why, in Schlink's words,

> the standards for interpretation that legal scholarship and jurisprudence have developed over time were, and are even now, normally presented as standards for finding the right interpretation. That is precisely what they cannot be, what they cannot effect.

Similarly, while insisting on the crucial importance of abduction, Peirce argues that the truth value of an abduction must be established by some other means. These would include the more well-known logics of deduction and induction as well as the adoption of an additional "meta-abductive theory" as to why one's guesses are likely to be right.[21] A meta-abductive theory "relates the proposed hypothesis to truth by positing a link or innate parallelism between the mind and the external world of our experience."[22] The reason why Sherlock Holmes is almost always right is not just because he was very skilled at abduction. Rather, it was because his creator-deity, Arthur Conan Doyle, structured his fictional world to match Sherlock's mind and vice versa.[23] Sherlock is what Kant called a marionette of God.[24]

This is reflected in Fish's account of Lancelot Andrewes's seventeenth-century biblical interpretative technique of "crumbling," which he contrasts to Scalia's "textualist" Constitutional interpretation. Crumbling and textualism might seem similar at first blush because each isolates single words from a text and analyzes them individually out of context. The difference is that, in reaching his conclusions, Andrewes relies on a Peircean meta-abduction. We are God's creatures and the Bible, as God's book, has "a pregiven meaning and it has been given by the God whose benevolent omnipresence is the message declared by every item in the world—the *uni*-verse—he has created." No matter where you look, you will see God because God is everywhere. Consequently, "You can't make a mistake if you see and read in the right spirit." To put this another way, we can look at each word in a holy text separately, because God's Word is wholly present in each word. In contrast, "nothing comparable redeems Scalia's textualism," which is disingenuous.

Because the legal interpreter cannot rely on God to lead her to the truth, she must find some other way to justify her interpretations. Fish argues that this can only done by "building an argument that hangs together and displays premises and evidence in a manner that draws from the audience a rational assent."

FALSIFICATION

Here, I part company with Schlink. He is correct that we cannot reduce abduction to a set of rules. But, he suggests that we can so reduce *disproof*. I fear that by doing so he undermines the power of his argument by conflating hypothesis refinement with falsification.

The assertion that falsification is the hallmark of scientific method and, therefore, the gold standard for proof is most closely associated with Popper.[25] The assumption that this is widely accepted among scientists and philosophers is very common among lawyers. Indeed, the U.S. Supreme Court referenced it in the *Daubert* case establishing the standard for admissibility of scientific evidence.[26] It formed the basis of the long-running television series *MythBusters*.

Among those who think about science, however, things are not so neat. And it is hard to imagine how to move from scientific method of experimentation and controlled observation to legal analysis, other than by questionable analogy. Indeed, Popper described his project in *The Logic of Scientific Discovery* as the "demarcation theory."[27] That is, he was trying to how science *differs from* other disciplines.

The application of law as a practice can never be a purely deductive enterprise. While another famous Holmes—Oliver Wendell Jr.—perhaps goes too far in asserting that "the life of the law has not been logic: it has been experience,"[28] nevertheless, experience and common sense are important and crucial elements of legal reasoning. Each new case presents a new fact pattern so that one is always applying the law by analogy to previous interpretations of the law. In a common-law country like the United States we are particularly sensitive to the fact that law generally progresses by induction and analogic reasoning as well as deduction.

The black swan problem of induction or verification has been well known since at least David Hume.[29] The fact that every swan you have ever seen or heard about has been white gives you a very good reason to believe that all swans are white. It does, however, not rule out the *logical* possibility that black swans exist. And, indeed, it turns out that Australian swans are black.

Famously, Popper thought that he "solved" the problem of induction.[30] One cannot prove a hypothesis through induction. One may, however, be able to *disprove* it. Consequently, he argued that the scientific method consists of falsification: The rigorous search for data that would disprove the hypothesis. Indeed, Popper went so far as to assert that although he agrees that hypothesis formation is necessarily subjective, a matter of "psychology,"[31] nevertheless, falsification could purge scientific theory from individual subjectivity.[32] If so, the source of theories and the method of abduction would be irrelevant.[33] As Schlink suggests, anything goes. Unfortunately, this is not necessarily true. When one falsifies a hypothesis, one might be left with nothing, not the truth. Consequently, Peirce and other theorists of abduction insist on distinguishing between good and bad guessing.

Philosophy of science has not treated Popper kindly. His theory of falsification, albeit elegant, has been largely supplanted.[34] For example, W. V. O. Quine and J. S. Ullian reject Popperian falsification, defend induction, and adopt a coherence theory of knowledge.[35] Even Popper's student and ardent defender, Imre Lakatos, admits that scientists not only do not but, in fact, *cannot* reject hypotheses as "falsified" merely because experiments and observation produce empirical anomalies.[36] Lakatos argues that, by necessity, anomalies always exist between observed results and theories, which, after all, are simplified models of the world."[37] Consequently, when scientists encounter data inconsistent with their initial hypotheses, they rarely reject them. Rather, they refine them by adding auxiliary hypotheses.

Because of this, Paul Feyerabend suggests that as an empirical matter, scientists do not limit themselves to falsification or any one method, but recognize that different methods, including verification and common sense, may be more or less adequate for different tasks.[38] Consequently, he seems to suggest that all scientific method—not merely hypothesis formation—might be described as "anything goes."[39]

As Fish notes, Schlink's own description of hypothesis formation is not falsification. Schlink states:

> Lawyers don't first go through the context of discovery and then through the context of justification. They have an idea of an interpretation, test it against the possibly falsifying instances that come to mind, easily drop it or modify it, test it again, have another idea that they like better or that they find a way to combine with the first, and so forth. They move in a circle—a variation of the hermeneutic circle.

It should be clear by now that I am, in fact, in substantial agreement with Schlink's intuitions—his abductions about abduction. What I question is his professed faith in falsification, which threatens to make "anything goes" an acceptable approach toward hypothesis formation.

If falsification is problematic in science, it is more so in law. There is no *rule* that tells us when a newly discovered legal fact disproves our legal interpretations. As Fish insists, consensus "is baked/established not by logic but by rhetoric in the best sense of that freighted word—the art of building an argument that hangs together and displays premises and evidence in a manner that draws from the audience a rational assent."

Legal analysis, at least in the common-law tradition, proceeds largely through argument by analogy. Lawyers disagree as to whether a new case is like or dislike a previous case. This is true even though there are, no doubt, many cases where the interpreter has great confidence in her judgment (or that there is a general consensus among the relevant community) that the similarities of the new fact pattern to previous cases prevail over the differences, or vice versa. Nevertheless, at some level of generalization almost any two cases can look alike, and at some level of specification, no two are similar.

Indeed, Schlink's "defense" of falsification replicates Lakatos's critique. Schlink says:

> If a legal interpretation in a previous case would seem to lead to a unjust result in a subsequent case, the judge could decide to develop an *auxiliary* exception to the old interpretation, rather than overruling her previous interpretation. Indeed, if the earlier case was decided by a superior court, basic principles of precedent would require her to try to do so. (emphasis added)

It is precisely the possibility or necessity of abducing auxiliaries that makes falsification problematic, if not incoherent. Indeed, Schlink's examples of legal falsification illustrate precisely why theorists of science (and practicing scientists) find it an inadequate description of scientific method.

Fish and I are also largely in agreement that Schlink's example of judicial falsification is no such thing. According to Schlink, the creators of videos argued that a certain benefit under German tax law should apply to anyone who was called a "publisher" in German. The government countered by pointing out that German brewers of beer are also traditionally known as "publishers." No one seriously believes that the tax law applies to them. Schlink asserts that this "falsifies" the video producers' interpretation of the law.

I would say, in contrast, that this is an example of how the observation of a potentially anomalous result—a Sherlockian trifle—leads to the creation of an auxiliary to the original hypothesis. The auxiliary might be that the statute covers anyone falling within that subset of persons who are called "publishers" traditionally covered by the statute. This could be supported by an argument by analogy or, as Fish suggests, a purposive analysis that would try to derive legislative intent or another argument that hangs together.

Although I agree with Fish's conclusion that falsification is "the wrong word to describe what happens when an interpretation fails," I must distance myself from one of his reasons. He states that "interpretation could not . . . even be 'falsified' because it is not a candidate for being true or false." He is no doubt right that an interpretation is not a brute fact that is either true or false (indeed, philosophers of science disagree as to whether scientific hypotheses can be true in this sense). However, they can be "true" in Alain Badiou's perhaps idiosyncratic understanding of "truth" as the ethical act of *being* true to something: that is, fidelity. As such, it is opposed to knowledge.[40] That is, a true interpretation is one that is faithful to the text.

Fish suggests that Schlink's case invokes comparisons to H. L. A. Hart's infamous "vehicle in the park" interpretative hypothetical. I offer an example from American law. In *United Housing v. Forman* the U.S. Supreme Court needed to decide whether interests in Co-op City—a state-sponsored affordable housing complex in Queens, New York City—constituted securities for the purposes of the federal securities laws.[41] The statutory definitions of "security" in the two federal securities acts consist of laundry lists of enumerated investments, including "stock." According to the opinion, the legislation establishing Co-op City referred to its interests as "stock."[42] The plaintiffs, who wanted to invoke the protections of federal law, argued that anything called "stock" was a security for the purpose of federal law, much like the German lawyers argued that anyone who was called a "publisher" fell within the relevant tax law.

Although the Court did not expressly say so, this could not be the case because the English word *stock* can refer to a wide variety of disparate things such as cattle, broth, inventory, and theater companies, to name a few. It seems highly unlikely—indeed absurd—to suggest that Congress intended to subject cowpunchers to the jurisdiction of the Securities and Exchange Commission.

To put this in Schlink's vocabulary, the Court found that the plaintiff's initial hypothesis did not fit or explain all the circumstances. Specifically, it would mean that a legal right economically equivalent to a residential real estate lease—traditionally the bailiwick of state law—would be governed by federal law. Consequently, referring both to congressional intent and common sense, the Supreme Court modified the plaintiffs' hypothesis. It agreed that, indeed, all "stock" is a security,[43] but that the mere invocation of the word *stock* was not dispositive. Rather, the Court had to determine the substantive definition of the term *stock* in the context of the federal securities law that is intended to protect certain investors. In this context, it found that *stock* means "equity securities" that traditionally have certain characteristics (such as the right to vote, the right to dividends, free alienability). The interests in Co-op City were sui generis, lacking these characteristics of equity. Consequently, they were not *stock* as that term is used in securities law despite their name given by the state. In other words, the Court did not so much falsify and abandon the initial hypothesis as modify it.

THE LEAP OF FAITH

Schlink compares the practice of abduction followed by deduction leading to a new abduction, and so on, with the hermeneutic circle. But, as in the game of musical chairs, at some point the music stops and we must act. As he says,

> They don't keep moving in it forever. There is a final draft of an interpretation and a *final test. And when the interpretation passes the final test,* when it is finally not falsified, it is justified and accepted—at least, for the moment. (emphasis added)

The problem is that none of us, let alone a judge, has the luxury of time to wait until the final test is administered. She must act now and apply her interpretation to the matter before her. As Schlink, the former judge, understands, "Judging is more than interpreting . . . it chooses between possible interpretations."

However, there can be no rule—falsification or other—that determines which to choose from. The speculative tradition understands rationality and freedom to be retroactive, not prospective. We decide first—we use our imagination to temporarily reduce signification to meaning—and only afterward introspectively attempt to justify the act in light of logic, evidence, and legal and ethical values. We must repeatedly return to our interpretations and refine them as we gather more and more trifles—the process that Schlink identifies but inaccurately calls falsification. As the common law presupposes, we will only know the law retroactively in the future after the *next* case is decided.

Consequently, when we act on our interpretations, we are forced to make Peirce's meta-abductive leap. Tragically, the judge does not have Andrewes's God or Sherlock's Doyle to ensure that she makes the right choice. We are not Kantian marionettes.

Freedom consists of accepting and adopting our decisions and their ethical implications. This is why judging—*pace* Hart—is always a moral act.[44] This is one meaning of Sigmund Freud's initially perplexing assertion that one must take responsibility even "for the evil impulses of one's dreams. What else is one to do with them?"[45]

Although Popper's faith in falsification may be misguided, he has a valuable lesson to teach. In his formulation, until falsification occurs, our interpretation will always remain fallible, and, therefore, we must remain corrigible.[46] Science is not religion, and neither is law. Crumbling works only for theology. Legal "truths" remain tentative and never graduate to dogma. Whether or not there are true interpretations of the law, there are unjust ones, as Fish shows in his damning critique of Scalia, and it is evil to disingenuously claim that you have no choice in adopting them.

NOTES

1. See Stanley Fish, this volume; and Bernhard Schlink, this volume. All further Fish and Schlink references are to these essays.

2. Immanuel Kant, *Critique of Pure Reason,* trans. and ed. Paul Guyer and Allen W. Wood (Cambridge: Cambridge University Press, 1998), 26–68. Kant refers to this as the problem of stupidity.

3. Jeanne Lorraine Schroeder, *The Four Lacanian Discourses or Turning Law Inside-Out* (Abingdon, U.K.: Birkbeck Law Press, 2008), 130.

4. Jacques Lacan, *The Seminar of Jacques Lacan: Book XVII, The Other Side of Psychoanalysis,* ed. Jacques-Alain Miller, trans. Russell Grigg (New York: W. W. Norton, 2007).

5. Jacques Lacan, "The Instance of the Letter in the Unconscious, or Reason Since Freud," in *Jacques Lacan, Écrits,* trans. Bruce Fink (New York: W. W. Norton, 2006), 412.

6. Slavoj Žižek, "Philosophy, the 'Unknown Knowns,' and the Public Use of Reason," *Topoi* 25 (2006): 137.

7. This is expressed as S/s (i.e., a signifier stands over a signified). See Lacan, "Instance of the Letter," 414n6.

8. Bruce Fink, *Lacan to the Letter: Reading Écrits Closely* (Minneapolis: University of Minnesota Press, 2004), 113.

9. Jacques Lacan, *The Seminar of Jacques Lacan: Book VII, The Ethics of Psychoanalysis*, ed. Jacques-Alain Miller, trans. Dennis Porter (New York: W. W. Norton, 1992), 12; emphasis added.

10. Fink, *Lacan to the Letter*, 90n10.

11. 11. Ibid., 88.

12. District of Columbia v. Heller, 554 U.S. 570 (2008).

13. Richard Tursman, *Peirce's Theory of Scientific Discovery* (Bloomington: Indiana University Press, 1987), 13; Jeanne L. Schroeder, "Abduction from the Seraglio: Feminist Methodologies and the Logic of Imagination," *Texas Law Review* 70 (1991): 109.

14. Jeanne Lorraine Schroeder, *The Vestal and the Fasces: Hegel, Lacan, Property, and the Feminine* (Berkeley: University of California Press, 1998), 101; Schroeder, "Abduction," 179–81.

15. Arthur Conan Doyle, *The Sign of Four*, ed. Christopher Roden (Oxford: Oxford University Press, 1993), 10.

16. Thomas A. Sebeok and Jean Umiker-Sebeok, "'You Know My Method': A Juxtaposition of Charles S. Peirce and Sherlock, in *The Sign of Three: Dupin, Holmes, Peirce*, ed. Umberto Eco and Thomas A. Sebeok (Bloomington: Indiana University Press, 1983), 11, 21.

17. Slavoj Žižek, *For They Know Not What They Do: Enjoyment as a Political Factor* (London: Verso, 1991), 229.

18. Immanuel Kant, *The Metaphysics of Morals*, trans. and ed. Mary Gregor (Cambridge: Cambridge University Press, 1996), 196.

19. Schroeder, "Abduction," 180–81 (citations omitted).

20. Jacques Lacan, *The Seminar of Jacques Lacan: Book XX, Encore, On Feminine Sexuality, the Limits of Love and Knowledge, 1972–1973*, ed. Jacques-Alain Miller, trans. Bruce Fink (New York: W. W. Norton, 1998), 48.

21. Schroeder, "Abduction," 184.

22. Umberto Eco gives as an example of a meta-abductive theory Leibniz's proposition that since God created "both things and minds," he "has engraved in our soul a thinking faculty that can operate in accordance with the laws of nature" (Eco, "Horns, Hooves, and Insteps: Some Hypotheses on Three Types of Abduction," in Eco and Sebeok, *Sign of Three*, 198, 218).

23. Schroeder, "Abduction," 183.

24. As I state elsewhere: "If man could actually see into the mind of God and know the Ethical law, he would no longer be self-legislating (i.e., free). He would be submitting himself to an external force. In Kant's metaphor, 'Man would be a marionette or an automaton'" (Schroeder, *Four Discourses*, 83 [quoting Immanuel

Kant, *Critique of Practical Reason*, trans. T. K. Abbott (Amherst, N.Y.: Prometheus Books, 1996), 123]).

25. Karl R. Popper, *The Logic of Scientific Discovery*, 2nd ed., trans. Karl R. Popper et al. (New York: Harper Row, 1968).

26. Daubert v. Merrill Dow Pharmaceuticals, Inc., 409 U.S. 579, 593 (1993).

27. Popper, *Logic of Scientific Discovery*, 19–20, 34. More specifically, he identifies two purposes—how does knowledge grow and how is science unique—but he considered them so intertwined as to be two sides of the same coin.

28. Oliver Wendell Holmes Jr., *The Common Law* (Boston: Little Brown, 1881), 1.

29. David Hume, *A Treatise on Human Nature: Being an Attempt to Introduce the Experimental Method of Reasoning into Moral Subjects*, vol. 1, ed. T. H. Green and T. H. Grose (London: Longmans, Green, 1874), 388–94.

30. By only using induction negatively, he, in effect, made it identical to deduction. See Karl R. Popper, *Objective Knowledge* (Oxford: Clarendon Press, 1972), 8–39. See also Schroeder, "Abduction," 161–63.

31. Popper, *Logic of Scientific Discovery*, 31.

32. Karl R. Popper, "Normal Science and Its Dangers," in *Criticism and the Growth of Knowledge*, ed. Imre Lakatos and Alan Musgrave (Cambridge: Cambridge University Press, 1970) 51.

33. Popper, *Logic of Scientific Discovery*, 31.

34. For a brief introduction to contemporary philosophy of science and law, see David S. Caudill and Richard E. Redding, "Junk Philosophy of Science: The Paradox of Expertise and Interdisciplinarity in Federal Court," *Washington and Lee Law Review* 57 (2000): 685; and David S. Caudill, *Stories about Science and Law: Literary and Historical Images of Acquired Expertise* (Farnham, U.K.: Ashgate, 2011).

35. See W. V. O. Quine and J. S. Ullian, *The Web of Belief*, 2nd ed. (New York: Random House, 1978), 65, 89–91.

36. Imre Lakatos, "Falsification and the Methodology of Scientific Research Programmes," in Lakatos and Musgrave, *Criticism and the Growth of Knowledge*, 51, 57, 96, 119 (footnotes omitted).

37. Schroeder, "Abduction," 169.

38. Paul Feyerabend, *Science in a Free Society* (London: Verso 1978), 13–16, 186, 212–13.

39. Richard J. Bernstein, *Beyond Objectivism and Relativism: Science, Hermeneutics, and Praxis* (Philadelphia: University of Pennsylvania Press, 1983), 72. Feyerabend denies that he goes quite so far, while admitting that he might have used the expression as a joke (*Science in a Free Society*, 186).

40. Alain Badiou, "The Ethics of Truths: Construction and Potency," in *Infinite Thought: Truth and the Return of Philosophy*, ed. and trans. Oliver Feltham and Justin Clemens (London: Continuum, 1990), 58, 62.

41. United Housing Foundation, Inc. v. Forman, 421 U.S. 837 (1975).

42. In fact, the legislation generally uses the term *shares*, not *stock*, to refer to the interests. See New York—McKinney's Housing Finance Law §31.

43. The Supreme Court subsequently confirmed this when it rejected the argument that sometimes stock (i.e., equity) was not a security. See Landreth Timber Company v. Landreth, 471 U.S. 681 (1985).

44. David Gray Carlson, "Hart *avec* Kant: On the Inseparability of Law and Morality," *Washington University Jurisprudence Review* 1 (2009): 29. In the words of Umberto Eco, he must have "the courage of challenging without further tests the basic fallibilism that governs human knowledge" (Eco, "Horns, Hooves, and Insteps," 220).

45. Sigmund Freud, "Some Additional Notes upon Dream-Interpretation as a Whole," quoted in Ernst Levy, "Responsibility, Free Will, and Ego Psychology," *International Journal of Psychoanalysis* 17 (1961): 260.

46. As Popper notes, if you do not criticize yourself, others will be happy to do it for you (*Logic of Scientific Discovery*, 16).

4

Law against Justice and Solidarity
Rereading Derrida and Agamben at the Margins of the One and the Many

Michel Rosenfeld

DERRIDA, AGAMBEN, AND KEY OTHERS CONFRONTING THE GAPS BETWEEN LAW, JUSTICE, AND SOLIDARITY

Law and justice are in crucial ways against nature as well as against solidarity. As David Hume famously proclaimed, justice is an "artificial virtue"[1] in contrast to the social bonds of family and community that are affectively grounded in solidarity and manifestations of mutual sympathy.[2] Law is also artificial much in the same way as justice. Indeed, the law that governs legal relationships sharply differs from other laws, such as the laws of physics or the laws of nature. Whereas the latter are internal and inextricably linked to their subject matter, legal norms are for the most part external in relation to those they govern, and in an important sense even against those subjected to their force.[3] Law is also against justice, in part because laws are and can be unjust, and in part, as Jacques Derrida has convincingly argued, because law sustains and highlights the impossibility of justice.[4] Indeed, building on Aristotle's insight that justice must be paired with equity and correspondingly generally applicable laws supplemented with equitable exceptions, Derrida demonstrates that justice cannot properly mediate between self and other unless it were to achieve the impossible task of fully encompassing at once the rule and its exception.[5] Furthermore, to this disjunction between law and justice should be added one between the latter two and social solidarity. On the one hand, when self and other are entwined in deep bonds of solidarity in a common communal project in which they are equally invested, questions of justice among them are unlikely to rise to the surface. On the other hand, to the extent that law is conceived as a self-standing normative order propelled by its own inner logic, as it is in Hans Kelsen's positivist vision,[6] it tends to remain too abstract to command heartfelt internalization or commitment sufficient to transcend estrangement and the dominant focus on fear of sanctions. Significantly, Kelsen puzzled over why those subjected to law would commit to a purely formal self-enclosed normative order. And this led him to turn to Sigmund Freud's theories on group psychology in a search for some amalgam between an unconscious drive toward group identity and solidarity and a logical realization that an orderly and unified polity requires adherence to a constitutional hierarchy.[7] Only such a link could properly account for why those subjected to laws would internalize and validate them as their own.

Whereas Kelsen searched for some conjunction between law and solidarity, Carl Schmitt and Giorgio Agamben cast the dynamic between law and solidarity in terms of a disjunction. This becomes manifest in the case of the exception, which for Schmitt arises in cases of emergencies. It is the sovereign who is exclusively empowered to declare the emergency and who triggers the exception that legitimates shedding the shackles of the law and of the constitution in order to leap into the realm of pure politics. Having declared the exception for as long as only he or she deems it warranted, the sovereign exclusively formulates and implements the political agenda projected to best advance the cause of those who count as the regime's friends against the latter's foes.[8] Consistent with Schmitt's vision, law bleeds into politics under the pressure of emergencies, and that highlights the disjunction between the two. At the same time, once the genie of politics spills out of the container that harbors the law, its spread looms as all encompassing, thus apparently stamping all laws with politics. Moreover, whereas Schmitt ties the exception to emergencies, Agamben much more radically links the exception to every law, as for him there is an unbridgeable gap between every piece of legislation and its application.[9] For Agamben, law cannot predetermine its implementation, as the administration of law inevitably leaves a great deal to discretion. In Agamben's view, there is accordingly an unbridgeable disjunction between law and administration. For Schmitt, disjunction emerges as much more fluid given that, at times, law seems to stand in contrast to politics and that, at other times, it appears to spill over into, or to become suffused by, politics.

The disjunctions and spillovers that circumscribe Schmitt's and Agamben's respective legal theories require supplementation for the purposes of presenting law as susceptible of coherence and of legitimacy. Consistent with this, Schmitt turns to political theology and Agamben to an apportionment between allegory, image, spectacle, and symbol, on the one hand, and *oikonomia,* on the other.[10] Significantly, political theology as it emerges in the works of Schmitt and the realm of the symbolic that Agamben couples with *oikonomia* are thoroughly grounded in religion. For Schmitt, politics are deeply rooted in religion, with kings enjoying divinely bestowed powers and historical destiny propelled by miracles. Contemporary secularization does replace theistic religion, but politics retains its traditional *modus operandi* with the divinely backed king replaced by the charismatic leader and miracles giving way to magic.[11] Much in a similar vein, Agamben locates the origin of contemporary politics in Christian theology's account of the mystery bound up in the relationship between the immutable unity of God and the plurality of the Holy Trinity resulting in the unfolding in historical time of divine providence and grace as it pertains to human beings.[12] Originating in the theology in question and still in full force at present is what Agamben posits as an immutable political-constitutional-legal matrix that separates the sovereign from those who govern and the legislator's law from the actual conduct of the affairs of the polity through an *oikonomia.*[13] Strikingly, although historically moored in Christian theology, the matrix unveiled by Agamben is apparently so hardwired as to become impervious to the abandonment of Christianity or the repudiation of all religion.[14]

Derrida's conception of an unbridgeable gap between law and justice in the necessary but always frustrated pursuit of solidarity among self and other is mirrored in Agamben's account of an insurmountable gulf between law and administration. For Derrida, law must call for justice, and solidarity can only be genuinely achieved through justice, which renders the deconstructive quest for an ethical reconciliation of the singular, the universal, and the plural akin to the tragic fate that befell Sisyphus as incarnated in Albert Camus's celebrated account.[15] For Agamben, in contrast, the nexus between law, justice, and solidarity may be as elusive and problematic as it is in the case of Derrida, but it becomes masked by the ceremonial spectacle of the Christian unity of God in its mysterious harmony with the Holy Trinity, on the one hand—thus suggesting an imaginary reconciliation of the singular, the universal, and the plural—and obfuscated by the workings of administration that escapes from (the sight of) law and justice, on the other hand. Is the passage from Derrida to Agamben one from painful truth and despair to artifice, spectacle, and the dulled comforts of ordered administration besides or beneath law and justice? In terms of the challenges posed by law, justice, solidarity, and the relationship between the singular, the universal, and the plural in contemporary polities, does the vision laid out by Agamben represent progress over that elaborated by Derrida? Or does Agamben's reconstruction ultimately lead to a regression in relation to Derrida's deconstruction? Finally, do Derrida's and Agamben's respective contributions point to further, potentially more fruitful, ways to reconcile the singular, the universal, and the plural within a common horizon that could afford greater linkage between law, justice, and solidarity?

To better explore these questions, Derrida's and Agamben's contributions to legal theory are analyzed in Part 1 in relation to the most relevant principal currents of legal theory against which they are set. Part 2 investigates in greater depth the insights and shortcomings of Derrida's and Agamben's contributions to our grasp of the relationship between law, the singular, the universal, and the plural, and also explores whether Agamben can be said in some meaningful sense to be Derrida's successor within the realm of critical approaches in legal theory. Finally, Part 3 focuses on whether Derrida's and Agamben's contributions can be accounted for and adapted in order to aim for a better integrated account of the relationship between law, justice, and solidarity in its confrontation with the dynamic tension between the singular, the universal, and the plural. Moreover, the latter inquiry is undertaken within the ambit of a pluralist, as opposed to a monistic or a relativistic, normative approach.

PART I: SITUATING DERRIDA AND AGAMBEN WITHIN THE LANDSCAPE OF CONTEMPORARY LEGAL THEORY

The Difficulties in Placing Derrida and Agamben within the Streams of Modern Jurisprudence

Derrida's writings on law and justice are situated within his own deconstructive enterprise, and they highlight his increasing turn toward ethics.[16]

Derrida, however, does not directly engage with contemporary legal theorists. Much the same is true for Agamben, though he studied law and engaged with Schmitt.[17] Although both Derrida and Agamben have had influence on legal theorists on both sides of the Atlantic and beyond, their impact on legal theory as a whole has been rather modest. One reason for this is that the writings of both authors are rather dense and complex, rendering them difficult to approach for most legal theorists. Consistent with this, the present undertaking does not attempt to actually locate Derrida's and Agamben's respective contributions within the history of contemporary jurisprudence. Instead, I propose to engage in a counterfactual reconstruction seeking to situate the two of them where they might best fit in the unfolding of twentieth- and early twenty-first-century jurisprudence in both the Anglo-American and the Continental European traditions. In other words, the focus here will be on the questions within contemporary jurisprudence to which Derrida and Agamben can be read as providing answers, on the further salient questions that their contributions can be interpreted as raising, and on the conflicts, contradictions, and tensions that these contributions may illuminate, solve, advance, exacerbate, or redirect. Because of the present concern with overall trends, the references to the relevant jurisprudence are selective and are dealt with for the most part in broad strokes.

In addition to placing Derrida's and Agamben's contributions relevant to jurisprudence within the already mentioned broad framework carved out by Kelsen and Schmitt, they can also be fruitfully associated with notorious turning points in the trajectory of jurisprudence during the last several decades. In Derrida's case, as I have argued elsewhere,[18] deconstruction can be persuasively envisioned as becoming embraced by law within complex contemporary legal systems and particularly within the American one rooted in the common law and engaged in a broad-ranging, often ethically charged, interpretation of a written constitution.[19] Specifically, Derrida and deconstruction irrupted into the American jurisprudential scene in the late 1980s, when Derrida presented his *Force of Law* at the Cardozo School of Law in New York City,[20] and when a panel on deconstruction and the law was held at a critical legal studies (CLS) annual meeting in Washington, D.C.[21] From a theoretical standpoint, moreover, Derrida's deconstructive methodology and ethical quest that centered on justice assumed a notable place in American jurisprudential discourse at a time when CLS was running out of steam and as its former adherents and sympathizers were in search of sequels or alternatives. Derrida and deconstruction thus joined critical feminist theory[22] and critical race theory[23] as heirs to CLS, poised to leap beyond its limitations.[24]

Situating Agamben in terms of the various currents of contemporary jurisprudence, on the other hand, is at once easier and more difficult. It is easier in that, as already mentioned, Agamben directly responds to Schmitt regarding the state of exception. Agamben thus in effect rethinks Schmitt's conception of law as subsumed within political theology and recasts it by sundering law's potential for efficacy from its claim to legitimacy. Law's efficacy derives from its functioning as *oikonomia*, meaning, in the context of ancient Greece, the practical successful management of the household, or, transposed to the confines of the modern polity, meaning administration guaranteeing the orderly steering of the bureaucratic state. Law's legitimacy, in contrast, originates in the religious mystery surrounding the Christian Holy Trinity and, as alluded to above, links to *oikonomia* through the projection of divine grace and divine providence toward the realm of human affairs. In the contemporary era, as the divine is substituted, or even in some circles eradicated, by secularism, the Christian Trinity retains its legitimating force, for Agamben, but this time as an image of mystery, splendor, sumptuous spectacle, and symbol of the transcendent amalgam of the unity and universality of God, and the plurality and individuality of the (now abstracted) Christian Trinity. Going beyond his historical link to Schmittian jurisprudence, Agamben promotes a theory that, in an important sense, purports to be equally valid for any period following the advent and the implantation of Christianity. At the same time, Agamben tackles challenges to his theory that are seemingly posed by competing contemporary accounts of law's legitimacy. Thus, for example, Agamben argues that Jürgen Habermas's discourse theory of law grounding legitimation on communicationally generated consensus does not do away with the need to combine divine origin and *oikonomia*. Indeed, as Agamben sees it, Habermasian consensus points to the glory and acclamation of the people who embody the contemporary iteration of divine intervention.[25] In other words, what appears as rationally produced consensus among communicationally engaged, self-governing, and politically engaged free and equal human beings depends on an instantiation of glory, both divine and human, of the Father and of the Son, and of acclamation of the people as substance and as communication.[26] Habermas may give primary or exclusive emphasis to communication as the basis for legitimation, but Agamben sees the communication in question as but one plausible means to account for the glory and acclamation transmitted by the people as substance.

Ascribing a particular place to Agamben's jurisprudence within the history of contemporary jurisprudence, on the other hand, is made especially difficult by virtue of two principal factors. First, Agamben's purportedly valid jurisprudence throughout the reign of Christendom and through all its sociocultural by-products defies attempts to anchor it in one contemporary school or current rather than in any other. And second, given the density of Agamben's thought and of his dearth of direct engagement with many of his contemporaries, there does not seem to be any obvious place for him to occupy in the succession of jurisprudential trends and debates. With this in mind, as announced above, I proceed with a counterfactual reconstruction: If we had to find a place for Agamben in the unfolding history of contemporary jurisprudence, where would that place be? To which problems, questions, and responses marking contemporary jurisprudence might Agamben's theory make the most notable possible contribution? The most fruitful hypothesis, which I attempt to buttress, is that Agamben is best regarded as providing a reconstruction that replaces or supplements Derrida's deconstruction. Moreover, to better appreciate the import of my hypothesis, it is first necessary to place both Derrida's and Agamben's respective jurisprudences within the broader jurisprudential undertakings of their contemporaries.

Derrida's irruption on the American jurisprudential scene took place, as already mentioned, at a time when the main thrust of the CLS movement was waning. His appeal, in that context, was propelled by the combination of two principal elements: his deconstructive approach to texts and the comprehensive intertextuality it relied on; and the ontological and ethical implications stemming from his confrontation with the necessary but impossible task of reconciling law and justice. CLS's scope and range was wide and diverse, and its adherents drew from a multiplicity of theoretical sources.[27] What drew together the otherwise diverse and highly heterogeneous body of work produced by the CLS movement was a discrete critique of various fields of law purporting to instill order and doctrinal coherence through the uncovering of contradictions, inconsistencies, and the perennial indeterminacy of law. In CLS's view, this indeterminacy allowed judges and others in charge of interpreting the law to operate under a façade of objectivity and respect for rights and standards of justice while in fact engaging in politics and producing outcomes that invariably served the purposes of the powerful. What Derrida's deconstructive approach to texts was poised to contribute to CLS's "trashing"[28] of legal texts was a systematic approach rooted in intertextuality going all the way down, which posited that all interpretations are always subject to revision and that they all inevitably comport ambiguities, aporias, and a seemingly endless stream of actual or potential connotations.

The CLS movement had virtually exhausted itself in the United States by the end of the 1980s because after having completed dazzling unmaskings of the pretenses of discrete fields of private law, such as contracts and torts, and of public law, such as constitutional and criminal law, its proponents stood on the ruins of the bodies of law they had debunked without seeming to be able to suggest any constructive alternatives. At that point, some critical voices suggested that CLS had gone too far. Thus, for example, critical race scholars argued that in spite of law's indeterminacy and susceptibility to being politicized, African Americans were palpably better off thanks to application of the U.S. civil rights laws than they would have been in the latter's absence.[29] Significantly, whereas some critical theorists may have somewhat pulled back from CLS's most radical conclusions, Derrida can be understood as starting where they left off in search of a new path to a more constructive enterprise. This he managed by supplementing deconstruction as a methodological instrument with deconstruction in its ontological and ethical dimensions. Legal texts may be deconstructed endlessly, but law always stands between self and other, each of whom emerges as ontologically indissoluble and as ethically charged to keep pursuing the impossible by using law to do justice—understood as requiring giving the other's due, consistent with the latter's radical and irreducible singularity.[30]

Deconstruction's ethical command to use the law to seek justice entrusts law with a constructive mission that CLS proponents did not provide for, but has not thus far revealed in what that constructive mission might actually consist in, or in what it might result. Consideration of these two crucial issues are addressed in Part 2. Before turning to that task, however, it is necessary to engage further with Derrida's and Agamben's jurisprudential precursors and to attempt some elucidation of the place of our two protagonists' contributions in the broader theoretical landscape of contemporary jurisprudence.

The Precursors of Derrida's and Agamben's Legal Theory

From a bird's-eye perspective, the Kelsen-Schmitt confrontation that framed twentieth-century Continental European jurisprudence finds an echo in the Anglo-American setting. Indeed, on the one hand, the positivism of

H. L. A. Hart shares much with the positivist vision of Kelsen. In both cases, law emerges as a sui generis self-sustained normative order that becomes distinct and particularized through a procedural pedigreed process. For Kelsen, it is the constitution or *Grundnorm* that sets the bounds of the self-contained legal order by specifying how valid laws can be enacted and what counts as a valid law;[31] for Hart, it is the rule of recognition that performs an equivalent function.[32] On the other hand, one can detect definite affinities between Schmitt's jurisprudence and what may be reconstructed as CLS's overriding jurisprudence.[33] As already noted, for Schmitt law becomes subsumed under political theology, with charisma replacing religion in the age of secularism. CLS, for its part, replicates in its own way the Schmittian move from law to politics, but leaves recourse to religion or charisma aside.

Neither law viewed as a self-standing normative order nor law as politics bereft of God or charisma looms as normatively attractive or persuasive from the standpoint of those subjected to such law and to its sanctions. In other words, law hardly emerges as appealing, substantively legitimate, or just if it is reducible to either consistent, orderly enactment or to mere politics. As already mentioned, Kelsen was intrigued by people's inclination to obey the law and looked to Freud for how something deep in the human psyche could account for commitment to lawfulness.[34] Positivism itself does not yield any clue as to why people should find the law legitimate or just and why they should obey it but for fear of sanctions. Furthermore, if law is reducible to politics, thus enabling the powerful to impose their will over the powerless, then it appears to be little more than a tool of oppression.

Those who espouse a positivistic account of law may seek to find legitimacy in democracy to the extent that they operate within a legal system that institutionalizes democratic lawmaking. In that setting, law is the product of the constitutionally empowered legislator, and it appears legitimate because it embodies the will of the citizenry's majority. As often pointed out, however, claims to legitimacy based on the will of the majority can be problematic, particularly in multinational, multicultural, or religiously diverse polities in which majorities may be prone to oppressing, or trampling on the rights of, minorities.

The impasse between positivism's positing law as *mere* law and law as *mere* politics after erosion of the friend-foe divide and the fading of charisma need not necessarily result in a dead end. This follows from a consideration of alternative contemporary jurisprudential theories that offer different perspectives on law and on its sources of legitimacy. For present purposes, it suffices to focus on a particular cluster of such theories, as the latter added to those flowing directly from Kelsen and Schmitt considered thus far provide a fair representation of the jurisprudential landscape into which Derrida's and Agamben's contributions may be most usefully integrated. The most significant theories in question include those that envisage the legitimation of law in terms of contract or consensus; those that embrace a moral justification of law, thus for all practical purposes siding with natural law in its perennial confrontation with positivism; the law and economics theory that justifies laws in terms of their propensity to contribute to wealth maximization; and the theory of law as a self-propelling autopoietic system that is normatively closed and that as such bears some noteworthy affinity to positivism.

Rawls and Social Contract–Based Legitimation

Social contract–based legitimation of law is grounded on the premise that all individuals subjected to law are free and equal and that all obligations to obey the law are self-imposed, either directly or indirectly. Drawing on Immanuel Kant and Jean-Jacques Rousseau and adapting classical social contract theory for contemporary use, John Rawls offers a hypothetical social contract procedure as the means to construe principles of justice that provide criteria of legitimation for law.[35] Rawls's hypothetical social contractors operate behind a "veil of ignorance"[36] and reach agreement on two principles of justice—the equal liberty principle and the difference principle.[37] Moreover, based on this, the hypothetical social contractors further agree on "the basic structure"[38] and the "constitutional essentials"[39] of a just society. Whereas Rawls's contractarian approach does not guarantee the justice of every single law, it does provide for unanimous consent for the lawmaking process as well for enshrining fundamental rights, thus overcoming the legitimating shortcomings of positivism linked to democratic lawmaking. Indeed, if the basic structure and constitutional essentials of a given polity are unanimously agreed to and if these provide for a combination of democratic laws and antimajoritarian fundamental rights guarantees, then the resulting legal regime must be deemed just overall, notwithstanding that an occasional law standing alone would manifestly fail to garner unanimous consent.

Rawls's contractarian approach has been widely criticized, however, especially on the grounds that his veil of ignorance does not make for neutrality among actual interests bracketed away and thus not subject to consideration by the hypothetical contractors.[40] Thus, for example, the veil of ignorance favors the risk averse and privileges individualism over communitarianism.[41] To the extent that it is biased and that its biases are hidden from the hypothetical contractors, any unanimous consent by the latter would fail the contractarian ethos, either as not amounting to a genuine consent or as not adequately respecting all involved as being truly free and equal.[42] Furthermore, from a Derridean perspective, even if the veil of ignorance were thoroughly neutral, the mere fact that it hides many of the contractors' most important interests and aspirations from the contractors precludes that the resulting principles of justice treat each of those coming under their sweep in all his or her singularity.

Habermas and Consensus-Based Legitimation

By moving from consent to consensus, by reinforcing the nexus between Kant and Rousseau, and by doing away with any veil of ignorance in the dialogical process that is supposed to yield just laws, Habermas points to a path toward overcoming the shortcomings found in Rawls's theory. Like Rawls's hypothetical contractors, Habermas's participants in an ideal speech situation that is best suited to lead to a consensus are free and equal individuals who relate to one another as strangers seeking to live together in a common just and fair legal regime.[43] Unlike Rawls, however, Habermas allows for each participant in the idealized discourse procedure—whereby all participants benefit from an equal opportunity to present their arguments and all agree to be persuaded exclusively on the basis of the inherent persuasive force of the arguments before them—to bring all "non-metaphysical" interests to the table.[44]

Habermas asserts that there have been three postmetaphysical paradigms of law that have purported to harmonize legal and factual equality. These are the liberal-bourgeois paradigm, which provides for equal formal rights but promotes factual inequality; the social-welfare paradigm, which is meant to remedy the factual inequality of the preceding paradigm but in so doing reduces welfare recipients into passive clients dependent on state welfare bureaucrats; and, finally, the proceduralist paradigm, which is supposed to overcome the shortcomings of its two predecessors.[45] Indeed, under the proceduralist paradigm everyone subjected to a law is in essence both its author and someone who has willingly embraced it as being just. Moreover, consensus, as Habermas understands it, means agreement *on the same grounds* among all those involved (as opposed to compromise in relation to which those who agree could each do so on different grounds).[46]

Stressing the inadequacies of mere formal legal equality and of bureaucratically administered welfare, Habermas reframes Kantian universalism and the predominance of the right and the just over the good. Habermas does so by making the process whereby the categorical-imperative and just legal regimes are established thoroughly dialogical rather than ultimately monological as Kant does.[47] In other words, whereas for Kant the categorical imperative can be deduced by each individual who uses reason, for Habermas what ought to count as universal in morals or normatively valid for all within the polity in the case of law can only be arrived at as the collective product of a dialogically fair process. To this, moreover, Habermas links Rousseau's concept of the citizen as being at once (part of) the ruler and (part of the) ruled, thus only obeying laws that are self-imposed.[48]

Habermas's dialogical consensus coupled with his insistence on vigorous and thoroughly engaged self-government seems to share much in common with Derrida's account of the relation between law and justice. There is, however, one glaring difference between the two: Habermas posits his discourse-theory of law and morals as sketching a firm path to justice, whereas Derrida insists on the latter's impossibility. Viewing the matter more closely, leaving aside Habermas's contestable commitment to the priority of the right over the good, there are three important criticisms that can be leveled at his dialogical proceduralism.[49] First, Habermas excludes metaphysical perspectives, including religious ones, and thus the dialogical process cannot be universal ex ante. Second, whether the dialogical process would yield a consensus in any particular instance seems purely contingent, unless one assumes that the parties to the dialogue would be bound by reason to reach such consensus (in which case reason and not any intersubjective process would determine what is just and the legitimacy of law). And third, as made manifest by certain feminist critiques,[50] Habermas's procedural paradigm arguably fails to provide a level playing field for all the nonmetaphysical perspectives it invites into the dialogical forum.

Consistent with the three above criticisms of Habermas's proceduralism, both he and Derrida concentrate on the need to reconcile the universal (which for Habermas is embodied in Kantian universalizability) and the individual as free and equal. In the end, Habermas offers a manifestly contestable reconciliation, whereas Derrida concludes that such reconciliation is bound to fail but must nonetheless be steadfastly pursued.

There are also aspects of Habermas's theory that seem relevant from the standpoint of Agamben's contribution. These include Habermas's second legal paradigm, the social-welfare one, and the dynamic relationship that he conceives as emerging from the confrontation between system and lifeworld. Habermas's social-welfare legal paradigm relies on bureaucratic administration to ensure the distribution of goods and services required to secure the basic welfare of the citizenry. The administration in question certainly seems to share much in common with Agamben's notion of *oikonomia*. What is particularly noteworthy in this connection is Habermas's above-mentioned criticism of the social-welfare legal paradigm as reducing the citizenry into passive clientism, thus depriving welfare recipients of autonomy and dignity. Bureaucratic administration seems indispensable in any modern polity, however, and it must therefore stay in place even after full transition to the proceduralist paradigm. One way that one can imagine the legitimation of bureaucratic administration under the proceduralist paradigm is through the subjection of the administrative state to constitutional safeguards and constraints.

To better grasp how bureaucratic administration may be reconciled with self-government, it is necessary to take a closer look at Habermas's understanding of the dynamic between system and lifeworld. In modern complex societies, according to Habermas, bureaucratic administration and the economy operate as self-regulated systems steered by administrative power and monetarization, respectively. Standing against these systems is the lifeworld, which provides an entirely different kind of integration. The lifeworld endows a collectivity with meaning by providing "a social integration based on mutual understanding, intersubjectively shared norms, and collective values."[51] The lifeworld, moreover, can integrate the operative systems within a normatively integrated meaning-endowing framework, but as systems expand, they can threaten to "colonize" the lifeworld.[52] To combat "colonization," the lifeworld must be adapted and geared to constraining the undue expansion of systems so as to preserve meaning and normative coherence.[53] Thus, for example, as global capitalism exacerbates income inequality, the state must deploy welfare policies designed to reduce income inequality. Consistent with this, through use of the proceduralist paradigm in law, the contemporary polity must rein in and subsume under the norms inherent in its appropriately adapted lifeworld the seemingly ever-expanding system of bureaucratically led administrative coordination. What follows from this in relation to Agamben is that whereas he conceives *oikonomia* as standing on its own, for Habermas the economy and the administrative system cannot aspire to meaning or to normative validity unless they can be subsumed under the ethos of the polity and made to conform to the dictates of the dialogical process that yields the proceduralist paradigm of law.

Dworkin's Substantive Liberal Egalitarian Conception of Law's Integrity

Standing against positivism, critical legal studies, and all process-based theories, including Rawls's, Ronald Dworkin articulates a theory of law's coherence, integrity, and legitimacy that is substantive in nature and that posits that law is only ultimately meaningful to the extent that it is grounded in a particular political philosophy and corresponding morality.[54] Through his criticism of Hart's positivism, Dworkin evokes the core traditional natural law conviction that legitimate law is inextricably tied to morality.[55] But whereas natural law relies on divine prescription or reason as the source of morally grounded legitimate law, Dworkin embraces a political philosophy firmly grounded in the Enlightenment. More specifically, Dworkin promotes a particular conception of an Enlightenment-based political philosophy, namely, a liberal egalitarian one built on the proposition that all persons are entitled to equal concern and respect.[56] This difference between traditional natural law theory and Dworkin's theory is crucial in that the former is by its own terms universal in nature and scope—we are all the children of God and/or we all possess reason—whereas Dworkin's theory is inevitably contestable as it is admittedly tied to Enlightenment values and as it stands against many competing existing liberal conceptions, such as the libertarian one.

Dworkin attacks the mere law approach of positivism and the reduction of law to politics of CLS through his use of the distinction between principle and policy. As he specifies, "Arguments of principle are arguments intended to establish an individual right; arguments of policy are arguments intended to establish a collective goal."[57] Dworkinian principles are supposed to constrain legal rules and to guide collective aims embodied in policies pursued through laws. One important question that Dworkin's distinction between principle and policy leaves unanswered is why his liberal egalitarian political philosophy and moral outlook should be preferable to any of the other existing competing conceptions of the good. Dworkin does not provide any full or satisfactory answer to this question, but he tellingly asserts that the US Constitution happens to enshrine fundamental liberal rights as legally binding constitutional rights.[58]

Dworkin and Derrida share in common their rejection of CLS's purely negative conclusions and an unshakable conviction that law must be inextricably linked to justice. Beyond that, however, they emerge as sharp opposites. This is perhaps best exemplified by their diametrically opposed views on the interpretation of texts. As against Derrida's inexhaustible intertextuality, Dworkin has famously defended throughout his entire career that there is a single right answer for every hard and highly contested legal case.[59] Put in its best light, Dworkin's highly contested conclusion implies an alignment between his political philosophy, his morality, his distinction between principle and policy, and the heuristic intervention of an imagined suprahuman all-knowing judge whom he names Hercules.[60] In short, from a Derridean perspective, Dworkin's quest is indispensable, but his positing the contestable as universal and his repression of all singularity through the imposition of a fictitious demigod's legal interpretive diktat is a reminder of the road not to take.

Dworkin's positing the contestable as a manifestation of something that takes the place of the universal within the American polity can be plausibly interpreted as bearing a significant affinity to Agamben's appeal to glory and acclamation as complementing the administrative characteristics of *oikonomia*. As noted, Dworkin draws on one ideology among the many deriving from the Enlightenment and then ties it to the US Constitution, which is widely acclaimed and at the very center of American glory. Arguably, moreover, Dworkin's Hercules magically ensures the right ordering and alignment of law and justice through the guarantee of infallible interpretation. Is this comparable to Agamben's reliance on the Holy Trinity for purposes of endowing *oikonomia* with providence and grace? Are Dworkin and Agamben equally resorting to artifice to cover up, respectively, the contradictions and limitations of the Enlightenment and the mirage of a self-standing administration?

The last two jurisprudential theories that bear significant relevance to the present analysis are the law and economics theory and the autopoietic theory of law. Both of these theories most obviously relate to Agamben's concept of *oikonomia*, though they may also be regarded as having broader connotations that may also be useful in relation to Derrida.

Law and Economics versus Oikonomia   In contrast to positivism, which purports, above all, to tackle law as it is, law and economics is a normative theory. In its most encompassing version, law and economics proclaims that the purpose of law is wealth maximization and that wealth maximization provides the best means to equal freedom allowing each individual to pursue ideals and self-interest.[61] Moreover, based on the assumption that human beings are self-interested and instrumentally rational, Posner, the leading figure in the law and economics movement, posits that economic science can provide an objective evaluation and interpretation of laws in its dual capacity as a positive science capable of explaining the behavior of rationally self-interested individuals and as a prescriptive science oriented toward wealth maximization.[62] Consistent with this, if an open-ended law can be interpreted in many different ways, law and economics requires that the interpretation best suited to promote wealth maximization be adopted. In short, consistent with Posner's theory, law should serve the economy by channeling human nature to wealth maximization, which will leave all in the best possible position to achieve self-realization and self-fulfillment.

Economy for Posner seems quite close to what *oikonomia* represents for Agamben. To be sure, "economy" is not synonymous with *oikonomia*, but the parallels are quite striking. In its early historical understanding, *oikonomia* meant the prudent ordering or management of the household; in the modern prescriptive sense invoked by Posner, the economy is the prudent management, preservation, and increase of a polity's resources with a view to maximizing wealth in order for the society involved to achieve the best possible order and harmony. In the modern context, *oikonomia,* in Agamben's view, connotes administration rather than economy. But, consistent with Habermas's distinction above, both the contemporary economy and bureaucratic administrative function as self-enclosed and self-sufficient systems that remain distinct from the particular lifeworlds with which they share a common social space.

If the systemic aspects of economics and administration are brought to the fore, then Posnerian law ideally would tend to dissolve into economics, whereas law in Agamben's account would become reduced to administration. More precisely, even if law's only purpose were to serve the economy, it would not entirely disappear, as wealth-maximizing would require a functioning law of contracts and of property. Law's validity and legitimacy, however, would be entirely dependent on its advancing wealth maximization. Accordingly, within a law and economics ideal, reducing law to economics would be coherent and self-justified as fitting within the overall objective of achieving wealth maximization, which itself looms as justified as the supposedly best available means to ensure individual self-realization and self-fulfillment. In contrast to this, the passage from law to administration in

Agamben's conception seems doubly contingent. First, it is not apparent whether the *specificity* of the law involved has any impact on the resulting administrative bureaucratic particulars; and second, it seems that no particular administration is inherently more legitimate or just than any other to the extent that the glory and acclamation that provide it with a source of legitimation are external to, independent of, the specific administrative regime in play.

It is obvious that the desirability of linking the legitimacy of law to wealth maximization is highly contestable, as is Posner's libertarian political philosophy. But more important for immediate purposes, law's legitimacy cannot be systematically conceived or assessed exclusively in terms of economics. To his credit, Posner himself has recognized this, and emphasized the limits of the economic theory of law in a discussion on whether a constitutional right to abortion is warranted. Indeed, it is not only impossible to determine whether such a right would be wealth maximizing, but it would be altogether meaningless to ascribe a "cost" to the aborted fetus.[63] What follows from this is that the economy may be a self-contained system, but law cannot be comprehensively and systematically understood or legitimated in terms of economics. That, in turn, results in a comparative advantage for Agamben's theory, as bureaucratic administration may be systemically self-contained and a society with an *oikonomia* would clearly seem better off than one without (assuming, for the sake of argument, that the latter would be plausible).

Luhmann's Legal Autopoiesis and Oikonomia   Inasmuch as Agamben's *oikonomia* is systematic and self-contained, it seems useful to explore how it stacks up against Niklas Luhmann's theory of law as an autopoietic system.[64] Luhmann's theory shares with legal positivism the conviction that the validity of legal norms is not dependent on extralegal norms. Contrary to positivism, however, Luhmann's theory avoids reliance on subjective and contingent factors in favor of systemic self-referential structural elements that are self-contained in their functioning. Specifically, Luhmann's autopoietic theory regards law as a normatively closed subsystem of the social system that creates and reproduces elements through communications.[65] In other words, legal autopoiesis is supposed to result in a legal system that remains operationally severed both from extralegal norms and from arbitrary subjectivity by relying on self-referential circularity as the foundation of law. Placed in its broader context, as society becomes more complex, it requires greater social differentiation, and the legal autopoietic system, which Luhmann characterizes as environmentally and cognitively open but normatively closed, serves to stabilize expectations.[66]

Luhmann's autopoietic theory tackles law at such a high level of abstraction that it is difficult to get a workable handle on it.[67] The systematicity of law can be perhaps better grasped by reference to the analogy drawn by Luhmann between autopoietic economics and autopoietic law.[68] The key to the autopoietic economy is monetarization. In broad terms, the economic system is open to needs, products, services, and so on, but closed in that it converts all economic transactions into the system of monetary exchanges. In the context of a market economy, everything that comes within the purview of the market must be quantified by being ascribed a monetary value.

What is important to retain from Luhmann's theory, for our purposes, is that a complex contemporary society cannot do without an economy that systematically spreads monetarization or without a legal system that systematically provides for stabilization of expectations—in the sense that one can enter into a contract requiring future performance by another party and inevitably face *factual* uncertainty concerning that performance, but not *legal* uncertainty, as the law provides either for performance or for a remedy in case of a failure of performance. It seems warranted to consider Agamben's concept of administration embodied in *oikonomia* as systematically analogous to Luhmann's legal or economic autopoietic system. Moreover, if that analogy were to hold, then arguably Agamben's recourse to the Holy Trinity, glory, and acclamation would be superfluous or purely contingent and external to law. Thus, for example, trial by ordeal makes no sense without belief in Divine intervention in human affairs, but Luhmannian systematic monetarization or stabilization of expectations, and presumably Agamben's administration, loom as completely independent not only from any divine presence but also from any conception of the good that may yield a Habermasian lifeworld.

Another consequence that follows from Luhmann's autopoietic theory of law is that there is no valid connection between law and justice, or more precisely, between justice according to law, that is, justice as reducible to the consistent application of the law, and justice above law, that is, justice pursuant to pertinent moral theories, political philosophies, or conceptions of the good. If Luhmann is right, then Derrida's quest to seek justice through law is not only impossible but also ultimately meaningless. Indeed, if law is a normatively closed system, it is meaningless and completely unproductive to try to assess it in terms of the norms pertaining to other normatively closed systems, such as morals.[69]

Luhmann's autopoietic theory of law is highly contested,[70] as law's normative closure seems questionable, at least in relation to certain areas of law. Thus the focus on stabilization of expectations may be paramount in certain areas of private law, such as contract, but not in others, such as criminal law or constitutional law, where the immorality of discrimination on the basis of sex would trump maintaining stable expectations relating to long-established sexist laws. Moreover, law's separate systematicity as conceived by Luhmann may not hold as compared to the systematicity of a monetarized economy or a rational bureaucratic administration. In the end, Luhmann as well as the other theorists discussed provide insights that shed light on the contributions of Derrida and Agamben, either through significant affinities or oppositions, as intellectual precursors or conceptual foes, and as sources of inspiration or as foils. Keeping that in mind, it is now time to examine in greater detail the respective contributions of Derrida and Agamben.

PART II. FROM DERRIDA'S DECONSTRUCTION
TO AGAMBEN'S RECONSTRUCTION

Derrida's Deconstruction: Methodological and Ethical

Derrida's theory of law as deconstruction features two key components already briefly discussed: the methodology of deconstruction applied to legal texts; and, deconstruction in its ontological and ethical dimensions centered on the irreducible singularity that permeates the relationship between self and other and that between law and justice. To understand how these components may factor into a cogent theory of law—and, in Derrida's case, given his emphasis on the ethical dimension of deconstruction, into a broader normative theory that embraces both law and morality—it is necessary from the outset to place the latter within the dynamic between the universal, the singular, and the plural. All moral and legal theories that postulate that all human beings are in some important sense essentially equal, including Derrida's theory in its ontological dimension, must contain some relevant conception of the universal and of the individual. It is the individual who is the subject of equality, and the equality that binds all individuals together must project a universal dimension. Moreover, inasmuch as particular legal regimes are meant to rule within the nation-state (or within supranational polities that encompass less than all of humanity) and that laws within a polity are the product of democratic majorities, legal theories must account for the plural. The plural, in turn, can consist of the people as distinct from other peoples, the majority and various minorities, as well as various communities that divide along the lines of ethnicity, language, culture, religion, and ideology.

As Derrida emphasizes, law is inextricably linked to violence.[71] Law is most notoriously and objectionably violent when it is applied unjustly against someone. Consistent with this, inasmuch as Derrida believes that justice through law is impossible, all implementation of law must result for him in the perpetration of unjust violence against all those who find themselves constrained by the workings of law. If this were the end of the matter, the import of Derrida's insight would add little to that of CLS and would amount to the conclusion that the powerful under law (whether the government or the powerful interests behind the latter) do violence to the powerless under law. Derrida, however, does not merely link violence to law while simply excluding justice from the entire domain of legal relations. As I have shown, for Derrida every use of law carries an obligation to aim for justice, and although justice will inevitably remain unfulfilled, the unfailing duty to pursue it remains unchanged so long as law mediates intersubjective dealings among human beings. Does this mean that Derrida posits law's irremediable failure as a tragic and inescapable aspect of the human condition?

Although all elements of tragedy cannot be removed from Derrida's perspective on the relationship between law and justice, it does make a difference whether one considers that all laws are equally unjust as opposed to some laws being manifestly more unjust than others. Derrida's theory comes closer to that latter position, but before considering this any further, it is necessary to take a closer look at the dynamic between law, violence, and justice and to spell out in somewhat greater detail Derrida's conception of the nexus between the universal, the singular, and the plural.

Polities that function pursuant to the rule of law grant the state a monopoly over the legitimate use of violence. Laws, moreover, are violent in that they constrain those subjected to them. Laws typically allow for taxing, fining, and imprisoning those under their sway and thus do violence against the latter. Laws can also enable and lend support to those subjected to them, and that is the case for those who rely on laws to safeguard their property or secure their rights under contracts they have decided to enter into. But even when they are enabling, laws are at the same time constraining, as the failure to abide by the property rights of others or to fulfill contractually assumed obligations subject those responsible to legally established remedies or sanctions. Accordingly, all laws entail doing some violence to those within their sway, but not all the violence involved seems equally unjust. Thus, for example, a law commanding racial apartheid is certainly much more unjust than a law ordering thieves to restitute the stolen property in their possession to those they have stolen it from. One may argue that the apartheid law is unjust and hence perpetrates unjustified violence, whereas the property restitution law is just and therefore commands justified violence. Conceivably, the above restitution law may in fact be unjust in whole or part—stealing a loaf of bread to feed one's starving child from an exploiting bakery chain that does not reinvest in the local community may be arguably morally justified and the law that prohibits it therefore arguably unjust—but it would still be reasonable to insist that the apartheid law is more unjust and hence more unjustifiably violent than the restitution law.

Derrida's account of the relationship between the universal and the individual draws on two clashing philosophical traditions that frame his understanding of the relationship between law and justice. The first of these is that of Kant,[72] whereas the second is that of Nietzsche and Heidegger.[73] In a nutshell, Derrida's conception of justice as necessary but impossible combines Kantian universalism with the categorical imperative understood as requiring treating others exclusively as ends in themselves. Living in accordance with the categorical imperative as thus construed is impossible as a matter of *practical reason* because life is inconceivable without treating at least some others at certain times as means. This is perhaps most obvious in a capitalist society where the success of the market depends on treatment of others as means to the achievement of one's economic designs, but is also the case in all other settings in which inevitably others must figure as means to one's survival and well-being. For Derrida, however, this Kantian reading of the categorical imperative as requiring the impossible must be supplemented by the Nietzschean/Heideggerian insight that the living and constantly evolving experience that confronts us in all its complex diversity and vitality can never be neatly captured, much less grasped by reason. Consistent with that, one can never treat the other adequately as an intrinsic end because we cannot account for the other in all its singularity. In other words, in this Derridean perspective, treating the other ethically and with the full justice that an individual is due requires the impossible-to-achieve command to never treat the person in question as a means, as well as the impossible-to-attain knowledge of the unique singularity of the other in all its diversity so as to grant to the latter full justice consistent with full dignity as an autonomous being.

This double impossibility to do justice does not exempt the duty to strive for it, according to Derrida's account. The Kantian impossibility revealed through practical reason should be understood as a stern reminder that whereas we are always bound to fail fully satisfying the categorical imperative, we should persistently strive to approximate it as much as possible and condemn those who patently refuse to do so. Thus, for example, an employer cannot avoid treating his or her employees as means in the furtherance of the relevant enterprise's objectives, but this can be done by awarding decent wages to one's employees and treating them with respect as opposed to exploiting them and needlessly trampling on their dignity. The Nietzschean/ Heideggerian impossibility, on the other hand, does not foreclose constantly striving to better account for the other's singularity and thus aiming at improved though ultimately incomplete and insufficient justice. Accordingly, it seems clearly preferable to take into account the values, interests, convictions, and objectives of others as much as possible rather than ignoring them or remaining largely insensitive to them.

That Derrida understands the double impossibility in question as imposing an inexorable ethical obligation to strive for the impossible in terms of both the universal and the singular is evidenced not only by his conception of the relation between law and justice but also by his analysis of the dynamic between self-regarding and other-regarding friendship[74] and of that between conditional and unconditional forgiveness.[75] Perhaps the most salient example of Derrida's comprehensive ethical approach, for present purposes, is his insistence on the dichotomy between majoritarian democracy and the "democracy to come" (*la démocratie a venir*).[76] Rationally pursuing the will of the majority is certainly preferable to nondemocratic forms of government, but it is insufficient, as it does not allow for full respect for the irreducible singularity of each person and with leaving sufficient room for such singularity to flourish.[77] In other words, democracy is ultimately impossible for Derrida because self-rule through majority-based decisions cannot ever culminate in "the democracy to come," which requires self-rule for every person according to what irreducible singularity requires.

Derrida is not alone in seeking to negotiate the gap between the universal and the singular. So do Kant, Rawls, and Habermas, among others. But whereas the latter three philosophers privilege identity over differences among individuals, which allows them to advance an ethics of identity,

Derrida's uncompromising commitment to irreducible singularity in all its diversity and complexity compels him to embrace an ethics of difference.[78] Indeed, Rawls seeks to bridge the space between the universal and the singular by defining justice for the "basic structure" of society and by specifying "constitutional essentials," whereas Habermas does the same by fostering consensus among all individuals who share moral capacity on what is "universalizable." For Derrida, in contrast, no configuration of common identity can ever suffice, as it necessarily leaves out differences that must be properly factored in order to give singularity its ethical due.

As noted above, consistent with Derrida's ethics of difference, some laws emerge as clearly less unjust than others, and majority democracy is closer to the democracy to come than an authoritarian dictatorship would be. But what about the large number of instances where there is no clear demarcation between various laws that aim for justice or democratic policies that seek to address individual needs? For example, neither equal treatment nor affirmative action can fully achieve race-based or gender-based justice. Should a Derridean therefore be indifferent among laws or policies that defy clarity in relation to the seemingly inexhaustible number of differences associated with individual singularity?

Derrida is anything but indifferent, and his unrelenting commitment to the pursuit of justice and democracy strongly suggests that the best that one can do is to pursue intractable and uncertain decisions affecting justice with authenticity and good faith. In other words, one should choose among alternatives that are not obviously better or worse than one another by doing the best one can with the intention of advancing justice. This approach bears some significant resemblance to Sartre's existential philosophy relying on authenticity as the means to avert "bad faith" and conformity with injustice and oppression.[79] Derrida acknowledged having been influenced by Sartre.[80] What approximates Derrida's commitment to singularity to Sartre's existential leap is the need to act solely on intuition and good faith, as no guidance from preexisting established norms can be counted on in an ever-changing, endlessly diverse normative setting. What separates Derrida from Sartre, on the other hand, is Derrida's Kantian universalism discussed above.

Because of his special concern for singularity and consequent commitment to an ethics of difference, Derrida nurtures an unbridgeable gap between his Kantian conception of the universal and what approximates an existential thrust toward the singular. In Derrida's case, however, reliance on authenticity and good faith is insufficient. This is not only the case where no guidance is available to decide among plausible alternative options in order to approximate justice. It is also more important in the case where individuals are engaged in seemingly irresolvable conflicts against one another. In such situations, accommodating the singularity of one of the antagonists seems bound automatically to detract from the singularity of others. This latter problem is perhaps best illustrated by Derrida's reaction to global terrorism as exemplified by the attacks on September 11, 2001.[81] In a nutshell, Derrida condemns the 9/11 terrorist attackers as perpetrating what amounts to an act of pure violence without meaning or future and thus remaining outside the ambit of intertextual exchange, which is indispensable in the ethical quest to further vindicate the singularity of the other.[82] Particularly, inasmuch as Derrida acknowledges that traditional terrorism at the level of the nation-state—such as ETA in Spain or the IRA in the UK—is meaningful (even if subject to condemnation),[83] his conclusion regarding global terrorism is altogether unconvincing. Indeed, global terrorists certainly have a message, an ideology, and objectives. Moreover, viewed retrospectively, the 9/11 attackers certainly had a "future," as evinced by the various changes involving increased security, decreased liberty, and ever-more-onerous restrictions affecting air travel as well as many other costly measures that have been adopted in numerous countries hit or threatened by terrorist violence.

Derrida strongly condemns global terrorism, but his condemnation appears squarely inconsistent with his ethics of difference and its requirement to honor singularity all the way down. In sum, Derrida's ethics is superior to its existentialist counterpart because of his Kantian universalism. However, because he allows for an unbridgeable gap between the universal and the singular, Derrida's ethical commitment to honor all singularity opens him up to the same criticisms that afflict the existential leap. The gesture may be authentic, but it may be as likely to somewhat advance justice as to somehow set it back. Finally, Derrida's ethics of difference and its fixation on singularity does not leave much room for the plural. And that leaves his deconstructive ethics at a loss when it comes to filling the gap between the universal and the individual.

Agamben's Reconstruction: The Twin Pillars of Glory and Administration

Casting Agamben as providing a reconstruction that complements and/or transcends Derrida's deconstruction of law might well seem oddly paradoxical. Indeed, as discussed above, Agamben's theory rests in a crucial sense on an immovable disjunction, namely, that between law and administration. Is it not, accordingly, better to characterize Agamben's gap between law and administration as a displacement of Derrida's gap between law and justice, with both of these gaps bearing a strong analogy from a deconstructive standpoint?

Upon closer examination, Agamben's disjunction takes on an entirely different meaning if viewed in terms of what is for him the crucial juxtaposition between the realm of theology and that of the orderly conduct of human affairs. What emerges as central for Agamben is the role of Christian theology as determinant in shaping the deep structure of legal/administrative systems, including contemporary ones notwithstanding the latter's self-understanding as being purely secular.[84] Before tackling the particulars of Agamben's theological paradigm and evaluating how it may advance the quest for legitimacy of contemporary legal regimes, it is necessary briefly to highlight the important differences that separate Agamben's theological conception of law from Schmitt's. Besides their differences concerning the state of the exception discussed above, Agamben objects to Schmitt's political theology as failing to account for Christian theology's division between God's sovereign power and the government of the economy as delineating two separate paradigms that frame a "bi-polar" system.[85] As Agamben sees it, by refusing to separate the sovereign from government, Schmitt eliminates all nonpolitical elements in governance and law, thus privileging peoplehood, race, culture, and religion and confining legitimacy to the friend-foe spectrum.[86]

Among the most notable consequences that follow from Schmitt's brand of political theology is the rejection of pluralism as well as that of liberal democracy's separation of powers. Accordingly, Schmitt can be viewed as, above all, standing for a transition from the divinely anointed Christian monarch to the modern charismatic leader who exerts authoritarian power as the "Führer" or "Duce" of a given people with a unique common destiny.[87] The broad friend-foe political framework embraced by Schmitt (at least in its secularized iteration) excludes not only pluralism but also universalism. Consistent with this, the source of Schmittian legitimacy is the collective singular and, for our purposes, the legitimacy involved looms as circular in that the law of a people emerges as legitimate to the extent that it is that people's law.

Christianity is a universal religion in its scope and self-understanding. Schmittian Christian political theology may thus be considered to comport a universal dimension that disappears upon its secularization. Agamben's theological theory steeped in Christianity also projects a universal dimension, and one of the important questions that this raises is whether unlike in the case of Schmitt, in Agamben secularization does not have to precipitate a fall from universalism. At least, upon first impression, it is quite plausible that in Agamben's case secularism need not displace universalism. Indeed, whereas for Schmitt the source of legitimacy of the divinely anointed monarch is the universal God and in that of the modern polity, a particular nation, ethnic group, or other community of friends, for Agamben the relation between the Christian Deity and the *oikonomia* is structural and systemic, as is its counterpart in the secularized polity.

The key to Agamben's conception of legitimation is the dynamic between theological conjunction of the relationship between God and humans and the disjunction between the sphere of the transcendent and that of the immanent wherein government and *oikonomia* unfold. Within the Christian vision that Agamben lays out, legitimation, the universal, the singular and the plural all neatly align into a coherent whole. Moreover, the guarantor of this legitimate order is God (even if he remains absent within the realm of the *oikonomia*) and true religion. Accordingly, the key question that secularization raises in terms of legitimacy, on the assumption that the structural and systemic interplay between law and administration remains the same, is whether the relationship between the universal, the singular, and the plural can be meaningfully harmonized, with each among these receiving its due. In other words, can the kind of legitimacy regarding law and administration guaranteed by Christianity endure the latter's demotion from *the* true religion to one contested conception of the good among many?

To be in a position to consider this last question properly, it is imperative to mark a sharp distinction between structural ordering, systemic functioning, acquiescence, and acclamation, on the one hand, and legitimation and persuasive normative justification, on the other. Even if we were fully to agree with Agamben's account of the workings of the relationship between law and administration from medieval Christianity to the present, the kind of legitimation that has been available in the context of Christian hegemony is no longer available in our contemporary religiously and ideologically diverse political environment. Because of this, either Agamben's factual account is equally compelling whether one can count on a God absent from administration or no God at all, in which case, Agamben's legal theory comes close to Luhmann's autopoietic one from the standpoint of legitimation: functionally and systemically, modern society requires the operation of a complex legal regime that cannot be further legitimated in terms of justice or of broader normative commitments. Or else, in view of the lapse of its Christian source of legitimation, Agamben's theory must be paired with a contemporary persuasive equivalent or, in the absence of the latter, be cast as standing for the proposition that the necessary nexus between law and administration present in every contemporary polity is beyond legitimation. In the latter eventuality, Agamben's gap between law and administration would bear, after all, an uncanny resemblance to Derrida's gulf between law and justice.

Agamben's legal theory derives from his assertion that Christianity separates God from His government of the world.[88] For the world to be well governed, it is necessary that God remain disempowered,[89] thus separating the transcendent order of the Kingdom of God from the immanent order of the government of human bodies (including the body politic) and souls.[90] Although God the Father and God the Son are one (together with the Holy Spirit) ontologically, it is the passion of Jesus that manages the *oikonomia* in pursuit of salvation through providence.[91] It is through history that Jesus as his Father's vicar acts and governs in the latter's name[92] to bring about divine grace upon the governed humans.[93] Providence, however, must confront the "nature of things," which are contingent and inhere within the immanent economy, thus making what appears marginal the very core of what is subjected to the act of governing.[94] In short, even divinely inspired governance must be carried out by (from a practical standpoint) an agent who must administer the contingent in his deployment of providence in the pursuit of salvation, and all that for the glory of God, the Father.[95] As Agamben puts it, the economy of salvation that Jesus institutes on earth is undertaken for the glorification of the Father and is hence an economy of glory.[96]

In the above account, God is omnipresent but remains completely inactive in the administration of human bodies and souls. Agamben specifies that the machine of government functions as a theodicy wherein the sovereign presence is symbolized by a supervising eye, the government, by a hand that leads and corrects, and the judgment (or judicial power) by the word that judges and condemns.[97] Notably, this theodicy is structured and functions like the modern state built on the rule of law.[98] The secular legislator thus becomes the vehicle of the transcendent, whereas the executive power becomes the administrator that gives life to the law by adapting it to creating order amid the unmanaged particularities and contingencies that happen to inhere within the polity. Moreover, Agamben insists that even glory has not disappeared from the modern rule-of-law state. Glory in that state may no longer be proclaimed in relation to God, but it is nonetheless directed to the people as sovereign. This secular form of glory is an acclamation expressed through public opinion, and it is to be understood as the manifestation of the people's consensus in relation to the *oikonomia* that brings them order and that furthers their destiny.[99] Modernity may push the transcendent divine pole of the bipolar theological government and administration model completely out of the picture, but Agamben insists it does not thereby eliminate the theological model itself.[100] On the contrary, in some important sense, atheism completes the theological model in question by taking it to its logical conclusion. In Agamben's words, "God has made the world just as if it were without God and governs it as though it governed itself."[101]

Before I examine Agamben's account in terms of legitimation, two additional points are in order. First, Agamben observes that the theological idea of a natural order of things is also present in modern economic theory, as dramatically illustrated by Adam Smith's postulation that the economic market's functioning is guaranteed by the workings of an "invisible hand."[102] And second, Agamben suggests that glory is best understood in terms of the void, given that the key conjunction between the king's majesty and his necessary idleness for purposes of governance is the image of an empty throne.[103] This suggests that both the expression of glory and the targeted object of one's glorification are completely open-ended, as presumably anything may suffice to overcome a pure void.

One plausible way to account for Agamben's theory involves interpreting his Christian model as figuring as an exemplary allegory of the structure and function of all legal systems and their inevitable devolution into administration. In that case, from the standpoint of legitimation, Agamben would be highly reminiscent of Luhmann. All societies require an administered *oikonomia*, and as long as order is preserved and the citizenry maintains its acclamation by glorifying some contingent being or entity, it is pointless to search for any further source of justice or legitimacy. On the other hand, one can read Agamben's account of the Christian paradigm in its own context wherein it is inextricably linked to the acceptance of Christianity as the true religion. The main virtue of this latter reading is that it yields a rich and illustrative counterfactual that allows for a deeper and more thorough critical understanding of the problem of legitimation in secular contemporary rule-of-law polities.

From within Christianity, legitimation of the Christian *oikonomia* with

Jesus as the vicar of God the Father is self-referential and self-explanatory. The creation is, after all, God's design, and he is the source of all truth and justice throughout the world. Moreover, the bipolarity of the Christian *oikonomia* may owe to certain peculiarities of the Christian narrative (as presented by Agamben), such as the concern with reconciling providence, grace, and human free will, but does not detract from its truth and justice. What is more interesting from the present standpoint, however, is how the Christian *oikonomia* exemplifies how the universal, the singular, and the plural can be harmonized. Ontologically, the Holy Trinity is unified and embodies the universal. On the other hand, as embodied, Jesus becomes an individual with a history, and he stands as a bridge between the individual and the universal, of which he ontologically forms a part. He also partakes in the plural in a variety of ways. Indeed, Jesus in his historical dimension is a Jew who lives in the land of Judea. Also, as a vicar of God the Father charged with the governance of human bodies and souls, Jesus confronts plurality framed by the contingent immanent factors that make up the "nature of things" that must be managed in each realm and for each generation.

Jesus as one with God and the Holy Spirit, as a Jew, and as an individual who was crucified incarnates at once the universal, the plural, and the singular. But what happens to the universal, the singular, and the plural and to the quest for their harmonization and legitimation once Jesus and Christianity have been rendered inoperative within the bounds of the secular rule-of-law state and of its godless *oikonomia*?

What remains in the secular context, consistent with Agamben's account, is the separation between sovereignty and governance and the need for acclamation in recognition and affirmation of glory. Without the reassuring presence of a universally shared religion, however, it seems that acclamation and glory become most problematic. This, as Agamben underscores, is attested by the glorification of Mussolini and fascism in Italy during the 1930s and by the rift between the Duce and Pope Pius XI, as praise and acclamation shifted from the Christian faithful to fascist militants.[104] Moreover, what about the *oikonomia* without Christian providence, grace, or salvation? As already emphasized, neither the economy as a system nor bureaucratic administration can guarantee *good* governance. Likewise, the sole realization of order over the "nature of things" in a polity by no means suffices to ensure justice or legitimacy.

What Agamben's model calls for once Christianity or any other equally sweeping conception of the good fails to garner widespread consensus within a polity is: first, a basis for acclamation that may be subject to legitimation consistent with the coexistence of a plurality of conceptions of the good; and second, the means to differentiate between good and bad administrative governance in light of the unbridgeable gap between law and administration. In the end, Agamben's invocation of acclamation and administration can be interpreted as providing a path toward reconstruction when set against Derrida's deconstructive engagement with the insurmountable gap between law and justice. Moreover, as Agamben's model fails to offer a satisfactory solution to the contemporary challenges posed by the quest for justice, Agamben's reconstruction is best posited as a complement to, rather than as a replacement of, Derrida's deconstruction. Tellingly, both Derrida's and Agamben's respective theories suffer from the same crucial lack. In Derrida's case, as noted above, there is no cogent criterion for distinguishing more relatively unjust laws from relatively less just ones. This bears a striking resemblance to Agamben's lack of criteria to distinguish normatively acceptable acclamations and glorifications from pernicious ones and relatively better administrative governance from relatively worse ones.

PART III. PLACING DERRIDA'S AND AGAMBEN'S INSIGHTS UNDER A PLURALIST LENS: CAN LAW, JUSTICE, AND SOLIDARITY BECOME MORE CLOSELY ALIGNED?

Derrida's deconstructive model with its insurmountable gap between law and justice makes room for the interplay between the universal, which it casts in Kantian terms, and the individual, who emerges in existentialist garb, but, as already noted, it apparently leaves no room for the plural. Agamben's reconstructive model, on the other hand, once detached (ontologically as opposed to structurally or systematically) from its Christian matrix, makes room for the plural and the individual, but not the universal. Indeed, those who acclaim and who glorify always constitute a collective unit that is distinguishable from others, whereas the inevitable presence of the contingent and of the particular in any unit to be administered by an *oikonomia* presupposes an interaction between distinct individualities. At the same time, as God the Father is replaced as the one to be glorified by a king, president, dictator, or other personifier of the sovereign, the polity involved loses all perceptible links to the universal.

Standing out from Derrida's deconstruction are necessity coupled with impossibility and the lack of room for plurality. From Agamben's reconstruction, on the other hand, what comes to the fore is the seemingly purely contingent emotional collective acclamation coupled with a necessary systemic administration impervious to normative justification, a combination resulting in no link to the universal. The challenge at hand, therefore, is to inquire whether departing from the insights of Derrida's deconstruction and Agamben's reconstruction as they relate to law, justice, and administration, there may be any plausible path toward integration and reconciliation of the universal, the singular, and the plural.

Contested versus Uncontested Universals

Before I explore how to proceed in light of Derrida's and Agamben's respective theories, it is necessary to draw attention to an important distinction regarding the concept of the universal. It is not the same thing to claim universal validity for a normative proposition or to assert that the latter should extend to humanity as a whole at all times and places than to be able to demonstrate that a normative proposition is universally valid. Kant, Rawls, and Habermas, for example, propose norms that are meant as universal and as universally applicable, but which, as discussed above, are vigorously contested. Similarly, Catholicism is a religion that is universal in its scope, and, as Pope Benedict XVI emphasizes, it promotes universal truth, since Catholic faith is understood as fully coinciding with human reason. However, one need only refer to the issue of the legality and moral permissibility of abortion, both of which happen to be consistent with secular and certain religious worldviews, to underscore that the pope's claim to universality is contestable.[105] Moreover, whether any moral or legal norm is truly demonstrably universal is certainly a matter of dispute that need not be pursued here. Suffice it, for present purposes, to postulate that certain norms, and in particular the inherent moral equality of all human beings, will be (counterfactually) treated as if universally valid in the context of the present inquiry (although obviously not accepted as such in ancient Greece, under feudalism, or in the age of American slavery). The justification for this counterfactual ascription of universal validity is twofold: first, the norms involved are uncontested by those theorists who are heirs of the Enlightenment and committed to the essentials of contemporary democratic constitutional rule; and second, the ascription in question accentuates the distinction between conceptions of the universal that are best regarded, within their proper context, as uncontested, and those, like Rawls's two principles of justice or Habermas's communicative ethics, that are cast as universal but remain widely contested. In short, this distinction can be encapsulated in the contrast between an "uncontested universal" and a "contested universal."

All the theories discussed above that appeal to, or make room for, a universal, including Derrida's and Agamben's so long as it remains squarely attached to Christian theology, are connected to a contested universal. Proponents of these different contested universals as well as proponents of conceptions of the good that do not appeal to the universal—for example, a tribal religion or ethnic based nationalism—are bound to disagree on what constitutes legitimate law, true justice, or valid morality. Accordingly, both on the level of theory and on that of factual embrace of religion, morality, political agenda, or ideology, there is no consensus in contemporary polities that adhere to constitutional democracy. Furthermore, this lack of consensus opens the way to two plausible alternatives: a struggle among competing contested normative outlooks with no reasonable basis for a consensus on legitimate law or justice; or a quest for accommodation of the relevant competing conceptions of the good within a more broadly encompassing normative framework that would make room for some workable harmonization of the universal, the singular, and the plural.

Comprehensive Pluralism as the Contested Universal of Choice

Based on the belief that the pursuit of this latter alternative is clearly preferable, pluralism in its normative dimension emerges as the optimal choice as compared with liberalism or other available monistic or relativistic approaches.[106] Taking the inherent moral equality of all human beings as an uncontested universal,[107] the commitment to normative pluralism results in the endorsement of a contested universal, as explained below. Normative pluralism, however, puts forth a contested universal that is distinguishable from most of its counterparts. Indeed, ordinarily the embrace of a contested universal must be done to the exclusion of all competing contested universals. Pluralism, in contrast, is dependent for its own coherence and viability on significant accommodation of other contested universals. Thus, for example, liberalism or Catholicism seems best served by elimination, respectively, of illiberalism or of secularism and all non-Catholic religions. On the other hand, if all nonpluralist conceptions of the good were eliminated, pluralism would become completely superfluous. Accordingly, pluralism is more encompassing of competing conceptions of the good than its nonpluralist counterparts, and that enables pluralism to enhance the insights of Derrida's deconstruction and Agamben's reconstruction while mitigating the effects of their respective shortcomings.

As I have made the case for pluralism—namely, for a particular version of it that I have named "comprehensive pluralism"—extensively elsewhere,[108] I shall limit the present discussion to the minimum necessary to address the pertinent issues concerning Derrida and Agamben. With this in mind, it appears at first sight quite plausible that pluralism might provide ways to introduce a plural dimension in connection with Derrida's deconstruction. But, by the same token, it would seem that pluralism would be a poor candidate for finding a suitable universal dimension that might be added to Agamben's reconstruction. Upon further inquiry, however, it turns out that comprehensive pluralism, when properly understood, sets out a dynamic that links together a universal and a singular dimension to its more conspicuous anchoring in a far-reaching plural dimension.

In the broadest terms, comprehensive pluralism embraces as universally valid the proposition that all persons are inherently morally equal. Moreover, comprehensive pluralism interprets the equality in question as including a prima facie entitlement for each person individually or in conjunction with others to embrace and pursue a conception of the good chosen for achieving self-realization and self-fulfillment. Consistent with this, comprehensive pluralism conceives the moral equality of persons as encompassing an *ex ante* presumption of moral equality among all conceptions of the good embraced by one or more persons within the relevant polity. Whereas moral equality itself is presumed to be an uncontested universal, the presumptive equality among conceptions of the good is acknowledged to amount to a contested universal. Furthermore, in what also figures as a contested universal, comprehensive pluralism postulates that peaceful accommodation of as many competing conceptions of the good as best as possible is categorically normatively preferable to any plausible monistic or relativistic alternative. In other words, moral equality as understood by comprehensive pluralism would be frustrated if one contested conception of the good were allowed to officially prevail over all others, or if a systematic adoption of relativism would leave ideologically diverse polities in a permanent war of all-against-all among proponents of competing conceptions of the good.

In its operating dynamic, which unfolds as an ongoing dialectic with no ultimate resolution,[109] comprehensive pluralism is thoroughly pluralistic in its aims, but it also combines a partially monistic dimension and a partially relativistic one. It is partially monistic in its confrontation with other conceptions of the good in the competition to ascend to a (contested) universal status. Thus, for example, pluralism may compete with liberalism and Catholicism to establish a pluralist as opposed to a liberal or a Catholic normative order while aiming to be inclusive of liberalism and Catholicism in its pursuit of accommodation of as many conceptions of the good as best as possible. Conversely, to accommodate other conceptions of the good within its normative purview, it must "relativize" the latter to some degree. Thus, for instance, Catholicism cannot be incorporated consistent with its self-perception as universal given its believed complete overlap between Catholic faith and human reason. The very fact that other conceptions of the good that reject Catholicism must also be included in the pluralist polity implies that neither the Catholic nor the non-Catholic perspectives in question can be given the ultimate say in the normative realm. Consistent with this, a Catholic absolute proscription on divorce on religious, moral, and legal grounds could not be extended to an entire polity also made up of Jews, Muslims, Protestants, and many others espousing various secular ideologies, all of which allow for divorce. Within the ambit of a pluralist normative order, peaceful coexistence between Catholics and non-Catholics would be accommodated as best as possible. That would mean that Catholics could act against divorce within their own religious community—for example, by not recognizing secular divorces religiously and by refusing to perform a religious marriage if a would-be spouse is a divorcee—but could not act beyond the bounds of their own religious community to prevent the state from granting secular divorces or to limit other religions from granting religious divorces within their own communities of faith.

Whereas the preceding example seems relatively straightforward, other clashes between competing conceptions of the good may present much more daunting challenges to the pluralist, particularly when inclusion of one such conception can only be achieved at the expense of exclusion of some other such conception. These difficulties can be left aside here, however, as it is the dynamic mode of functioning of comprehensive pluralism that provides the key to understanding how a pluralist gloss may usefully recast any plausible nexus between Derrida's deconstruction and Agamben's reconstruction. In brief, the ongoing dialectic launched by comprehensive pluralism brings together in a constantly evolving trajectory a universal, an individual, and a plural dimension. Comprehensive pluralism's (contested) universal dimension is encapsulated in its fixed set of norms that it must deploy to pursue and advance its aim of peaceful coexistence among the greatest possible number of conceptions of the good. Its individual dimension, on the other hand, is defined by its incorporation of the (uncontested) proposition that all humans are inherently morally equal, together with endorsement of the proposition that each individual is equally morally worthy as the actual or potential possessor of, or adherent to, a particular conception of the good. Finally, comprehensive pluralism's plural dimension is principally twofold: first, it seeks to optimize conditions for the flourishing of the plural; and second, it depends for its very viability on the survival of the plural.

To complete this highly schematic account of the dynamics of comprehensive pluralism, it is worth briefly concentrating on its mechanics and potential as employed in the context of actual polities. At any time in an actual polity, certain conceptions of the good happen to be privileged while others are disadvantaged, discriminated against, or suppressed. From a pluralist standpoint, this requires a twofold operation: first, the field must be leveled and all privileges revoked in a process of equalization among all competing conceptions of the good; and second, the institutional order must be refitted to accommodate the now-equalized conceptions of the good as much and as best as possible under the aegis of those norms that pluralism casts as universal—including tolerance, maximum liberty within communities, and the highest possible mutual respect and deference among different communities. Moreover, this twofold operation can be used not only for institution-setting purposes but also for counterfactual critique and justificatory purposes. Indeed, an actual situation displaying grave inequalities among competing conceptions of equality can be productively critiqued from the vantage point of what the pluralist ideal would require. On the other hand, an actual situation that, while acknowledged imperfect, may seem the closer to the pluralist ideal than any realistic alternative, could be thus justified in terms of its susceptibility to further perfectibility toward a somewhat closer approximation to the pluralist ideal.

Derrida's Deconstruction in Pluralist Perspective

It is the application of this pluralist dynamic process combining counterfactual critique and justificatory potential toward further perfectibility that can accentuate links between Derrida's deconstruction and Agamben's reconstruction. This process can also address lacunae as well as potential advantages that arise in connection with tracing the trajectory of the narrative that takes us from Derrida to Agamben. Starting with Derrida's deconstruction, the focus on the pluralist dialectic leads to two distinct mutually reinforcing insights. As already briefly indicated above, pluralism can supply the missing plural dimension to better handle deconstruction's conception of the nexus between law and justice. In addition, deconstruction's emphasis on the unbridgeable gap between law and justice reinforces both the sustained need for the continued operation of the pluralist dynamic process and the reminder that the pluralistic dialectic never ascends toward any ultimate resolution. As against Derrida's Kantian universalism, pluralism offers a universalism of its own grounded on the norms that are essential to the constitution and preservation of a pluralist legal and moral order. Although there are differences between these two conceptions of the universal, they are both similar in the crucial respect that is relevant for present purposes, namely, adhesion to the proposition that all persons are inherently morally equal. Moreover, there is also a key confluence between deconstruction and pluralism relating to the individual's irreducible singularity. Pluralism focuses on conceptions of the good and allows for each individual to devise or choose to adhere to one's own. To be sure, most conceptions of the good are collectively created and managed and, to a large extent, individuals are born into, or educated consistent with, particular conceptions to which they are most likely to adhere in whole or part. Nevertheless, and particularly in a pluralist-in-fact setting that is ideologically and religiously diverse, multicultural, and thus open to many competing conceptions of the good, an individual can choose to partake in more than one conception of the good—for example, one can be a nationalist Catholic feminist environmentalist—and to singularize commitments and goals to the point of occupying a unique position that can never be fully accounted for by any prevailing law- or society-wide political or moral order.

The combination of the pluralist universal and of the fact that singularization in relation to conceptions of the good is necessarily mediated through partaking in collectively articulated normative orientations that are plural in nature allows for partially filling the gap between law and justice that Derrida leaves wide open. Indeed, whereas for Derrida the only available means to handle the gap in question is through an existential leap, the pluralist can rely on principled choices. One of these choices is between more-pro-pluralist and more-antipluralist laws; another is based on consideration of the plural collective commitments of individuals that furnish a partial common currency in the realm of normative dealings among a multiplicity of ultimately irreducible singular human beings. A clear illustration of this important difference between Derrida and pluralism is provided by the case posed by global terrorism. As discussed above, Derrida characterized the 9/11 terrorists as purveyors of violence without meaning or future, but as already pointed out, those attacks did not in fact lack meaning or a future.[110] From a pluralist standpoint, however, the global *jihadist* conception of the good that motivated the 9/11 attacks is not hard to assess, as it ranks by far as the most antipluralist one among all those that enjoyed a significant position in the Western democracies targeted by Al Qaeda. And as a consequence, even if the 9/11 terrorists had had a set of valid grievances, their own ideology and the shockingly violent ways in which they sought to vindicate it unmistakably emerged as far more unjust than any of the real or imagined injustices against which they rallied. In the end, even if pluralism provides the means to achieve principled decisions for selecting less unjust laws over more unjust ones, Derrida's insight that the gap between law and justice is ultimately unbridgeable remains exemplary for the pluralist. Indeed, not only does the choice of the least unjust legal alternative achieve only relative justice, leaving many injustices untouched, but also, given the dialectical nature of pluralism, it is almost certain to give rise to new injustices that will pose novel legal challenges.

Agamben's Reconstruction in Pluralist Perspective

Turning to Agamben's bipolar order, pluralism can, at least in part, remedy its identified two principal shortcomings in a post-Christian setting: the lack of a universal dimension and the absence of a criterion of good governance. Separating the sovereign to be acclaimed and glorified from the government has a major virtue. Even in the paradigmatic case of God the Father and his vicar Jesus, human contingency among the governed (or in religious parlance, sinning among the humans under administration) remains inevitable. Accordingly, perfection, justice, and legitimacy can find optimal expression in the personification of the sovereign who remains neatly uncompromised by the vicissitudes of governing. Ironically, however, in a thoroughly secular setting, where the universal guarantee provided by God the Father is categorically withdrawn, the virtue in question can easily turn into a major vice. To put it bluntly, a framework that allows for replacing God the Father with Adolf Hitler, Benito Mussolini, or Joseph Stalin seems to call for downright rejection. Nevertheless, with pluralism in mind, one can avoid the pitfall by construing Agamben's theory as requiring glorification and acclamation of someone worthy of such commitment because of possessing a universal dimension opening a path to legitimacy and to perfectibility. To the extent that pluralism embodies a (contested) universal, any sovereign who adheres to pluralism's core norms would thus foreclose subjection to authoritarian tyrants. But as core norms standing alone are not likely to suffice for purposes of garnering the requisite degree of acclamation and glorification needed to keep a polity sufficiently glued together to function smoothly, something additional would be required. And recourse to pluralism may prove helpful again.

In contemporary democracies, the sovereign is "the people," or more particularly, the people of a given nation-state or of a transnational political unit, such as the European Union. In the United States, it is the "We the People" that has given itself the US Constitution who counts as the sovereign. The American people, moreover, have evolved throughout several waves of immigration, the abolition of slavery, the grant of the vote, and full constitutional equality to women, and many other important changes.[111] Given all these major shifts in the nature and composition of this "We the People," it is best conceived as a collective subject under constant construction that is deployed through the "imagined community" known as the American nation.[112] The American people and all other contemporary peoples can be imagined in many different ways and thus remain at bottom relatively amorphous and malleable much like Agamben's empty throne that figures for him as the symbol of glory.[113] Any plausible image of a people must take into account history, culture, tradition, and in most cases religion and other ideological commitments. These ingredients, however, can be combined in many different ways. The American people, for example, have been marked by slavery and its abolition, and greater emphasis may be placed on images that enhance lingering racial divisions or on contrasting images that accentuate elements of racial healing. More generally, an imagined sovereign people or the person and/or institutions that symbolize it may be depicted in ways that are more or less congruent with pluralism and its (contested) universal norms. As Agamben emphasizes, in modern democracies acclamation is expressed through public opinion,[114] and formation and transformation of the latter certainly seems amenable to pluralist influence.

Turning to the question of good governance, one can agree with Agamben that there is an insurmountable gap between law and administration yet insist that pluralism may be helpful in guiding the functioning of the bureaucracy. All *oikonomia* involves an element of contingency and hence of unpredictability as far as the bureaucratic administrator is concerned.

Beyond that, however, there are both internal and external mechanisms that can constrain or guide the administrative system. Internally, some maintain that the administrative state veers to professional expertise, making it thus, by and large, apolitical.[115] Inasmuch as administrative governing is a matter of expertise, efficiency emerges as the proper criterion of good governance and should remain uncontroversial and consistent with pluralism. Others, on the other hand, consider administration thoroughly political and "expertise," in fact, oriented toward certain (usually powerful) particular interests to the detriment of others. Consistent with this latter position, pluralism can serve as a criterion that sets more inclusive administrative policies as more likely to foster good governance than less inclusive ones. Finally, the fact that the administrative system may not be externally governed does not mean that it may not be externally constrained. As the above discussion of Habermas's distinction between "system" and "lifeworld" suggests, normative constraints can be invoked to limit undue expansions of seemingly runaway administrative bureaucracies.[116] Also, as is quite common in modern democracies, constitutional norms, such as due-process clauses, are widely used to constrain administrative rule, and nothing prevents these norms from conforming to pluralist essentials.

As in the case of Derrida, the contemplated interplay between Agamben's theory and pluralism can be considered potentially mutually enriching. As far as the nongoverning sovereign ruler is concerned, Agamben reminds the pluralist that the community of communities within the polity that makes room for a plurality of perspectives must be susceptible of being imagined in a way that garners sufficient genuinely felt acclamation despite entrenched intercommunal differences. Also, Agamben's reference to the empty throne metaphor should prompt the pluralist not to lose sight that the sovereign people's projected image remains constantly subject to adjustment in conformity with the unfolding of the dialectic of pluralism. Finally, Agamben's focus on the gap between law and administration and the contingency that it underscores reinforces the pluralist's realization that the task is endless, as each instance of pluralist governance will inevitably generate new problems that will require further administrative shifts and adaptations.

CONCLUSION

As understood through the preceding analysis, Derrida's deconstruction followed by Agamben's bipolar reconstruction, particularly as recast in terms of the normative vision grounded in comprehensive pluralism, carve out a cogent and potentially very fruitful account of the questions of law's legitimacy and of its relationship to justice. Derrida's methodological deconstructive intertextual approach to law underscores that there is no definitive interpretation of any legal text both because the latter is open to a multiplicity of often contradictory meanings and because it inevitably remains open to further connotations projected into the future and to reconfigurations of significant portions of its past, due, among others, to reinterpretations of history. All textual interpretations are intersubjective, and pluralism, mindful of Derrida's deconstruction, urges that pursuit of the most inclusive ones be prioritized. Derrida's ethical deconstruction, on the other hand, commands relentless pursuit of ever elusive justice. The pluralist dialectic, in turn, allows for a nonlinear conjunction between a temporary victory of the (relatively) more just over the less just and concurrent acceptance of the impossibility of ever overcoming injustice. Because of his lack of emphasis on the plural, Derrida's methodological and ethical universe appears lonely and tragic. Agamben's reconstruction, in contrast, reintroduces the plural in all its glory and sumptuous imagery. We must be governed, and that entails harsh bureaucratic systemic administrative rigors coupled with the messy travails caused by inevitable irruptions of human contingency. To live through the drudgery, inconveniences, inequities, and frustrations of administration, the polity's citizenry must find a distraction in a sumptuous spectacle worthy of common bonding prompting acclamation and glorification. As I have shown, in the post-Christian universe, Agamben's reconstruction easily seems arbitrary, but that can be mitigated through recourse to pluralism's universal norms and to the pluralist criterion for distinguishing between more- and less-inclusive governance.

From the standpoint of the relationship between law, justice, and solidarity, the conjunction of Derrida's deconstruction, Agamben's reconstruction, and pluralism presents a rather complex and seemingly fractured picture. Law emerges as legitimate partly as it is "our" law inasmuch as we interpret it for Derrida, as we derive it from our acclaimed sovereign for Agamben, and as we make it as inclusive of all of us as possible for the pluralist. On the other hand, law remains at least somewhat repressive and alienating for Derrida because it always falls short of justice, for Agamben because it does not afford protection from the arbitrariness of administration, and for the pluralist because it is never sufficiently inclusive while always provoking new instances of exclusion. Turning to justice, it can never be achieved for Derrida; it fades in the case of Agamben—either because in the Christian world what depends on God and on Jesus his vicar must be considered inherently just or because in the post-Christian world there seems to be no reliable measure of justice to gauge the by-products of acclamation and administration; and it is partial, temporary, and open ended in the case of pluralism, where what predominates is an interminable confrontation between the more just and the less just without ever reaching full justice. Finally, in none of the three cases under consideration is the place of solidarity unequivocal. In the case of Derrida, what seems to predominate is the coexistence of elements of solidarity and alienation inasmuch as law is a gesture toward justice in relation to the other and a concurrent manifestation of injustice in its failure to account fully for the singularity of each person who happens to be under its sway. For Agamben, in contrast, the connection between law and solidarity seems purely contingent, if it exists at all. Indeed, in Agamben's account, solidarity looms as strongly present among those who acclaim and glorify and may link indirectly to law regarded as the product of the sovereign. On the other hand, there seems to be no inherent connection between genuine solidarity and bureaucratic administration. In pluralism, solidarity is related to law and justice, but again not in a straightforward or unchanging way. Above all, pluralist solidarity looms as divided between the sphere of intercommunal interaction and that of intracommunal dealings. The community of communities that encompasses the polity as a whole cannot function harmoniously without some degree of society-wide solidarity. Yet the latter solidarity is at once both sustained and countered by the more intense solidarity that binds distinct groups within the polity intracommunally. Without intercommunal solidarity, intracommunal life may not be peacefully sustained, but allegiance to the community of communities may well require sacrifices resulting in limitations regarding intracommunal life.

In the last analysis, combining the insights of Derrida, Agamben, and pluralism does not lead to a clear, neat, unique persuasive resolution of the thorny issues that the relation between law, justice, and solidarity poses to contemporary legal theory. Nevertheless, the combination in question yields valuable insights and confirms that the pursuit and better understanding of how law, justice, and solidarity may stack against one another are worthy endeavors deserving of ongoing attention. If there is one lesson that emerges from the preceding discussion, it is that what may be most important is to focus on the process whereby the actual quest for harmony between law, justice, and solidarity unfolds over time. Indeed, it seems rather unlikely that we will succeed anytime soon in predicting or imagining a set of realizable conditions that would secure a stable harmony among these three terms that have posed serious dilemmas throughout modern times.

NOTES

1. See David Hume, *A Treatise of Human Nature* (1740), ed. L. A. Selby-Bigge (Oxford: Clarendon Press, 1896), 477–83: "Justice, whether a natural or artificial virtue" (3.2.1).

2. Ibid., 455–76: "Of virtue and vice in general" (3.1)

3. Law's artificiality is most obvious from the standpoint of legal positivism. But even under natural law approaches, be they grounded in divine origin or reason, law often stands out against human will and human nature as exemplified in the Old Testament by the juxtaposition of Cain's murder of his brother Abel with the Ten Commandments' prohibition against murder.

4. See Jacques Derrida, "Force of Law: The 'Mystical Foundation of Authority,'" in *Deconstruction and the Possibility of Justice*, ed. Drucilla Cornell, Michel Rosenfeld, and David Carlson (New York: Routledge, 1992), 3–67.

5. See Michel Rosenfeld, "Derrida, Law, Violence, and the Paradox of Justice," *Cardozo Law Review* 13, no. 4 (1991): 1267.

6. See Hans Kelsen, *Pure Theory of Law*, 2nd ed., ed. M. Knight (Berkeley: University of California Press, 1967).

7. See Hans Kelsen, "The Conception of the State and Social Psychology with Special Reference to Freud's Group Theory," *International Journal of Psychoanalysis* 5 (1924): 1–38.

8. See Carl Schmitt, *Political Theology*, ed. George Schwab (Chicago: University of Chicago Press, 2006).

9. See Giorgio Agamben, *State of Exception*, ed. Kevin Attell (Chicago: University of Chicago Press, 2005), 24–31.

10. Compare Schmitt's *Political Theology* to Giorgio Agamben, *The Kingdom and the Glory: For a Theological Genealogy of Economy and Government*, ed. Lorenzo Chiesa and Matteo Mandarini (Stanford, Calif.: Stanford University Press, 2011).

11. Schmitt, *Political Theology*.

12. See Agamben, *Kingdom and the Glory*, 109–43.

13. Ibid.

14. Ibid., 286–87.

15. See Albert Camus, *The Myth of Sisyphus*, ed. Justin O'Brien (New York: Vintage, 1955).

16. See Michel Rosenfeld, "Derrida's Ethical Turn and America: Looking Back

from the Crossroads of Global Terrorism and the Enlightenment," *Cardozo Law Review* 27 (2005): 815–45.

17. See Agamben, *State of Exception*.

18. See Michel Rosenfeld, *Just Interpretations: Law between Ethics and Politics* (Berkeley: University of California Press, 1998), 29–32.

19. This linking of Derrida's deconstructive approach to texts and to ethical issues arising from the encounter between self and other to the common-law approach is in no way contradicted by Pierre Legrand's claim in his contribution to this volume that Derrida's conception of law was thoroughly and exclusively steeped in French law. Even if that were conceded, Derrida's approach to the interpretation of texts, his insights into the dichotomy between law and justice, and his ontological and ethical concern with doing justice to the other in all his or her singularity all mesh very well with the intertextual proclivities and interweaving of legal and ethical strands typical within common-law adjudication.

20. See Derrida, "Force of Law," in Cornell, Rosenfeld, and Carlson, *Deconstruction*, 3–67.

21. I was one of the panelists at this panel on Derrida, which was one of the best attended at the 1988 annual CLS meeting.

22. See, e.g., Carrie Menkel-Meadow, "Feminist Legal Theory, Critical Legal Studies, and Legal Education or 'The Fem-Crits Go to Law School,'" *Journal of Legal Education* 38, nos. 1–2 (1988): 61–85.

23. See, e.g., Kimberlé Crenshaw, "Race, Reform, and Retrenchment: Transformation and Legitimation in Antidiscrimination Law," *Harvard Law Review* 101, no. 7 (1988): 1331–87.

24. Consistent with what was already mentioned, it bears emphasizing again that in terms of *actual* influence in the American jurisprudence community, Derrida and deconstruction enjoyed a scant presence in comparison with critical feminist and critical race theory.

25. See Agamben, *Kingdom and the Glory*, 258–59.

26. Ibid., 259.

27. See, e.g., Duncan Kennedy, "Form and Substance in Private Law Adjudication," *Harvard Law Review* 89 (1976): 1685–779.

28. See Mark G. Kelman, "Trashing," *Stanford Law Review* 36, nos. 1–2 (1984): 293–348.

29. See Crenshaw, "Race, Reform, and Retrenchment."

30. See Rosenfeld, *Just Interpretations*, 18–32, for a more extended discussion of these points.

31. See Kelsen, "Conception of the State."

32. See H. L. A. Hart, *The Concept of Law* (Oxford: Oxford University Press, 1961), 92–93.

33. Because individual members of the CLS movement professed allegiance, in

whole or in part, to a wide variety of theoretical movements from Marxism to existentialism, poststructuralism, and pragmatism, among others, the reconstruction undertaken here focuses on similarities that span most CLS contributions while disregarding differences and nuances among the various contributors to the movement.

34. See Kelsen, "Conception of the State."

35. See John Rawls, *A Theory of Justice* (Cambridge, Mass.: Harvard University Press, 1971), 12.

36. Ibid., 136–42.

37. Ibid., 60–65.

38. Ibid., 7.

39. See John Rawls, *Political Liberalism* (New York: Columbia University Press, 1993), 139–40.

40. See Michel Rosenfeld, *Law, Justice, Democracy, and the Clash of Cultures: A Pluralist Account* (Cambridge: Cambridge University Press, 2011), 32–34.

41. Ibid.

42. Partly in response to his critics, Rawls reframed his contractarian approach by narrowing the relevant domain for unanimous consent from that of comprehensive justice to that of political justice. See Rawls, *Political Liberalism*. However, this narrowing of the relevant domain of justice did not solve the problem of neutrality or eliminate the privileging of certain interests or conceptions of the good over others. See Rosenfeld, *Law, Justice*, 62–67.

43. See Jürgen Habermas, *Between Facts and Norms: Contributions to a Discourse Theory of Law and Democracy*, trans. William Rehg (Cambridge, Mass.: MIT Press, 1996), 415–16.

44. As Habermas seeks to establish a "post-metaphysical" legal regime that reconciles legal and factual equality, he leaves no room within his discursive process for the introduction of religious dogma or religious ideology. See Rosenfeld, *Just Interpretations*, 136.

45. See Habermas, *Between Facts and Norms*, 418–19.

46. Ibid., 459–60. Habermas specifies that consensus is always required in morals, but that compromise might sometimes suffice in law (460). Consensus requires that what is being agreed to be *universalizable*, and that is imperative in the realm of morals that extends to all human beings at all times (109). Legal regimes, on the other hand, mostly apply to single polities. Accordingly, morality must generate consensus among proponents of all ideologies, whereas law must only do so among proponents of those ideologies present within the relevant polity. Thus, for example, morality must seek consensus equally compatible with all the world's religions, whereas a country that does not have a single Buddhist or Muslim need not adopt legal norms that would garner the consensus of adherents to the latter religions. For present purposes, the distinction between consensus and compromise

can be ignored to the extent that from a Habermasian perspective all legal systems must be consistent with morality and that, for practical purposes, they must garner the agreement for the same reasons of all those within the bounds of a particular legal domain.

47. See Jürgen Habermas, *Moral Consciousness and Communicative Action*, trans. Shierry Weber Nicholsen and Christian Lenhardt (Cambridge, Mass.: MIT Press, 1990), 195, 203–4.

48. See Jean-Jacques Rousseau, *The Social Contract*, ed. Charles Frankel (New York: Hafner, 1947), 16–17.

49. For an extended discussion of these three criticisms, see Rosenfeld, *Just Interpretations*, 136–48.

50. See ibid., 138–44.

51. Jürgen Habermas, *The Postnational Constellation: Political Essays*, ed. Max Pensky (Cambridge: Polity, 2001), 82.

52. See Jürgen Habermas, "Further Reflections on the Public Sphere," in *Habermas and the Public Sphere*, ed. Craig Calhoun (Cambridge, Mass.: MIT Press, 1992), 421–61.

53. For a more extensive account of the dynamic between system and lifeworld in the context of globalization, see Rosenfeld, *Law, Justice*, 276–78.

54. See Ronald Dworkin, "The Forum of Principle," *New York University Law Review* 56 (1981): 478.

55. See Ronald Dworkin, *Taking Rights Seriously* (London: Gerald Duckworth, 1977), 40–45.

56. See ibid., 180–83.

57. Ibid., 90. This articulation seems to imply a natural rights theory in the tradition of Locke rather than a natural law one. Strictly speaking, Dworkin bears affinity to these two traditions without falling squarely within either. An individual right may be an inalienable one in the Lockean mold or one deriving from a moral principle, such as the inherent dignity of all human beings.

58. See ibid., 184–205.

59. For a discussion and critique of Dworkin's "one right answer" thesis, see Michel Rosenfeld, "Dworkin and the One Law Principle: A Pluralist Critique," *Revue Internationale de Philosophie* 59 (2005): 363–92.

60. See Ronald Dworkin, *Law's Empire* (Cambridge, Mass.: Harvard University Press, 1986), 239, 264–66.

61. See Richard Posner, *The Problems of Jurisprudence* (Cambridge, Mass.: Harvard University Press, 1990), 382.

62. Ibid., 353–67.

63. See Richard Posner, *Overcoming Law* (Cambridge, Mass.: Harvard University Press, 1995), 22.

64. See Niklas Luhmann, *Essays on Self-Reference* (New York: Columbia University Press, 1990); and Luhmann, "Operational Closure and Structural Coupling: The Differentiation of the Legal System," *Cardozo Law Review* 13 (1992): 1419–41.

65. See Luhmann, *Essays on Self-Reference*, 3.

66. See Niklas Luhmann, "The Unity of the Legal System," in *Autopoietic Law: A New Approach to Law and society*, ed. Gunther Teubner (Berlin: W. de Gruyter, 1988), 27.

67. See Rosenfeld, *Just Interpretations*, 93.

68. Luhmann, *Essays on Self-Reference*, 230–31.

69. At a public discussion that I attended at Cardozo in the fall of 1992, Derrida and Luhmann profoundly disagreed on this point, with little common ground between them on the subject of the relation between law and morals.

70. See Rosenfeld, *Just Interpretations*, 109–12.

71. See Derrida, "Force of Law," in Cornell, Rosenfeld, and Carlson, *Deconstruction*, 5–6.

72. See Jacques Derrida, *Voyous* (Paris: Éditions Galilée, 2003), 167–94.

73. See Jacques Derrida, *Margins of Philosophy* (Chicago: University of Chicago Press, 1982), 109–36.

74. See Jacques Derrida, *Politiques de l'amitié* (Paris: Éditions Galilée, 1994).

75. See Jacques Derrida, *On Cosmopolitanism and Forgiveness*, ed. M. Dooley and M. Hughes (London: Routledge, 2001).

76. See Jacques Derrida, "Deconstructing Terrorism," in *Philosophy in a Time of Terror: Dialogues with Jürgen Habermas and Jacques Derrida*, ed. Giovanna Borradori (Chicago: University of Chicago Press), 120.

77. See ibid., 130.

78. For a more extended discussion of the contrast between ethics of identity and ethics of difference, see Rosenfeld, *Law, Justice*, 290, 295–97.

79. See Jean Paul Sartre, *Being and Nothingness*, ed. Hazel E. Barnes (New York: Pocket Books, 1966), 86n10.

80. See Jacques Derrida, "'Il courrait mort': Salut, salut," *Les Temps Modernes* 587 (March–May 1996): 7–54.

81. For an extended discussion and criticism of Derrida's position, see Rosenfeld, *Law, Justice*, 255–56.

82. See Derrida, "Deconstructing Terrorism," 147.

83. See ibid., 103 (nation-state terrorists claim to be responding to state-perpetrated terrorism and have national liberation objectives).

84. See Agamben, *Kingdom and the Glory*, 284–85.

85. Ibid., 66–67.

86. Ibid., 74–77.

87. In spite of Schmitt's actual political trajectory within the confines of Adolf

Hitler's Nazi regime, his political theology theory of law based on the friend-foe divide need not be confined to a fascist or otherwise authoritarian regime. Indeed, as long as the "we/they" logic is operative, the nature of friend and foe and the mode of association among friends appear to remain fairly open. Since the present focus is on Agamben and his appraisal of Schmitt, the broader contours of Schmitt's theory are not further addressed.

88. See Agamben, *Kingdom and the Glory*, 54.
89. Ibid., 106.
90. Ibid., 46, 82.
91. Ibid., 47.
92. Ibid., 138.
93. Ibid., 137.
94. Ibid., 118–19.
95. Ibid., 202.
96. Ibid.
97. Ibid., 130.
98. Ibid., 142–43.
99. Ibid., 170.
100. Ibid., 284–85.
101. Ibid., 286.
102. Ibid., 282–84.
103. Ibid., 242–45.
104. Ibid., 192–93.
105. See *Pope Benedict XVI's Legal Thought*, ed. Marta Cartabia and Andrea Simoncini (New York: Cambridge University Press, 2015), 3–9 (referring to the pope's view that Catholic faith and reason coincide in affirming universally valid morality and law); and Christopher McCrudden, "Benedict's Legacy: Human Rights, Human Dignity, and the Possibility of Dialogue" in ibid., 164–65 (pointing to "major tensions between the Catholic Church and several secular human rights positions, including those on abortion").
106. For a comparison of the key differences among pluralism, monism, and relativism, see Rosenfeld, *Just Interpretations*, 206.
107. This postulation does not imply, as noted above, that the proposition in question is uncontestable. Instead, the assumption is that this proposition is uncontested among those who address the legitimacy of law in the context of contemporary constitutional democracies.
108. See Rosenfeld, *Just Interpretations*, 213–24; and Rosenfeld, *Law, Justice*, 297–308.
109. Each particular situation requires first an equalization of all competing conceptions of the good struggling against one another followed by the most in-

clusivist possible accommodation of as many of them as possible. The resulting configuration will result inevitably in the generation of further conflicts, however, thus requiring a new round of pluralist equalization and accommodation. This dialectic, moreover, is not envisioned as culminating in any final resolution. For a more extensive discussion of the contrast between this pluralist dialectic and Hegel's, see Rosenfeld, *Law, Justice*, 42–51.

110. See Derrida, "Deconstructing Terrorism," 147.

111. See Michel Rosenfeld, *The Identity of the Constitutional Subject: Selfhood, Citizenship, Culture, and Community* (Oxon: Routledge, 2010), 34–35.

112. See Benedict Anderson, *Imagined Communities: Reflections on the Origin and Spread of Nationalism* (London: Verso, 1991) (characterizing the modern nation that, unlike families or tribes, is made up of strangers as an "imagined community").

113. See Agamben, *Kingdom and the Glory*, 245.

114. Ibid., 255.

115. See Michel Rosenfeld, "Constitutional versus Administrative Ordering in an Era of Globalization and Privatization: Reflections on Sources of Legitimation in the Post-Westphalian Polity," *Cardozo Law Review* 32 (2011): 2339, 2348–51. The following discussion draws on the analysis developed in this article.

116. See Habermas, *Postnational Constellation*, 82.

Derrida and Dissimulation

5

Jacques Derrida Never Wrote about Law

Pierre Legrand

From the 1970s on, the reception of Jacques Derrida's work in the Anglophone world and in the common-law tradition in particular has prompted compelling narratives and continues to feature eminent exemplifications.[1] Aware of the theoretical shortcomings of the dominant positivist versions of law obtaining in their countries, many of the common-law lawyers who sought to invest themselves in critical interpretive projects saw in Derrida's texts, mostly as they were becoming available in English (although some individuals could read French), crucial themes that they purported to enlist in their pursuit of deviant scholarship, for example, as regards strategies of interpretation. However, even as critical engagement was deepening in the common-law world, the preoccupation with Derrida's work was discernibly accompanied with a forgetting that Derrida's texts in English were but translations, that is, in Derrida's own words, "transformation[s],"[2] and arguably distortions. An illustration concerns the constant reference to "free play" among Derrida's Anglophone discussants, with hardly any realization that the expression arose out of an unjust translation of "jeu" in the English version of Derrida's famous contribution to the celebrated 1966 Johns Hopkins conference.[3]

Interestingly, one of Derrida's distinguished mediators, Gayatri Spivak, who translated what perhaps remains Derrida's best-known book, proceeded to demote the French text by challenging "the absolute privilege of the original" and claiming "the freedom of the absence of a sovereign text." Arguably vindicating Derrida's own critique of origins, she asked: "Why should that act of substitution that is translation be suspect?" And, she said, "Why should the translator's position be secondary?" Spivak left Derrida's interpreters with a further question: "Where does French end and English begin?"[4] In the case of law, common-law lawyers implemented a bold version of Spivak's claim. Ignoring the fact that Derrida had never written in English and that he had therefore never written about *law* properly speaking, they opined that when found in translation the word *law* could readily be taken to mean "law." To adopt and adapt an analyst's rendition of what happened to Derrida's work in the English language generally, common-law lawyers "remove[d] what is foreign and transform[ed] it into the context to which it was foreign."[5] Is it too much to say that, greater fidelity having been shown to local knowledge than to the authority of the original text, the common law's "Derrida" is in fact the outcome not of what common-law lawyers have taken *from* Derrida but of what they have done *to* Derrida?[6] With hindsight, Spivak's interrogations therefore suggest at least another: "Did this growing thematization of translatability, this challenge to the status of the original, license the interpretive freedom and free-for-all that erupted around Derrida's work in the second half of the 1970s?"[7]

In this essay, I expose Derrida's determined pledge to the French language that informed all his work, an engagement having entailed important consequences for his understanding of the legal. I thus challenge every single interpretation of Derrida in English translation whenever Derrida's readers have reflexively assumed that the word *law* meant "law" as usually understood in the Anglophone world. In fact, in Derrida's work *law* never carried that meaning, for Derrida was only ever acquainted with *droit* or *loi*. And since he always wrote in French, he never had anything in mind but *droit* or *loi*. Specifically, Jacques Derrida never wrote about law, and his "law" persistently remained anchored to key epistemic tenets regulating French legal culture under the sway of the most adamant positivism (a fact that common-law lawyers unfamiliar with the French model have conspicuously failed to appreciate). Yet, as I show, out of the impressive Derridean toolbox featuring a dazzling array of daring philosophical and literary interpretive designs, it *is* possible to structure a theory of law epitomizing a post-positivistic understanding of the legal radically different from the governing epistemic assumptions obtaining in France that Derrida himself assimilated. In typical Derridean fashion, such theory would intervene obliquely: while there would obtain a humanist understanding of law, a limited role for the posited would continue to prevail.

On August 19, 2004, the French newspaper *Le Monde* featured the text of an encounter with Derrida that had taken place about four months earlier. At the time of the interview, Derrida knew that he was terminally ill. He died in October, which makes the parts of the conversation devoted to survival—ever a paramount motif in Derrida's work—particularly poignant.[8] Even during what was to be his last recorded interview—and perhaps because he sensed that there might not be further opportunities to express himself publicly, at least in France[9]—Derrida was at pains to emphasize, as he had often done in the past,[10] his abiding love for the French language. Not only did he envisage himself as being situated in language—"my own presence to myself has been preceded by a language"[11]—but Derrida always regarded *philosophy* as being positioned in language. He felt that the articulation of philosophical thought was intimately related to the language in which it was expressed, that philosophy was affected by language (a view evoking the "Whorfian" stance that he held against the dominant philosophical attitude that refuses to pay much attention to the language of philosophy, as if philosophy somehow operated irrespective of language).[12] The significance that Derrida attached to language suggests how a proffered *commitment* on his part to a language, such as his pledge of allegiance to French, must be received as being especially meaningful. Indeed, "*Jacques Derrida is (was) a French philosopher.* To call him a philosopher without qualification is to miss an extraordinary richness."[13] Yes: "Derrida [wrote] in French, and *this ought not to be effaced by any commentary.*"[14]

Language was the bedrock of Derrida's intellectual project. He maintained that "[our] historico-metaphysical epoch *must* finally determine as language the totality of its problematic horizon" (which, incidentally, is not to say, pace some of Derrida's detractors, that there is nothing beyond language, but to assert that without language no "reality" can appear to one and no "understanding" of it can be had by one).[15] Famously, Derrida claimed that no text is fully extricable from the myriad discourses that inform it, in effect that nothing is meaningfully accessible unless the embeddedness of discursive formations is taken into account.[16] Having declared to his *Le Monde* interlocutor that "the experience of language" is "vital,"[17] Derrida formulated his devotion to French in riveting terms (a fidelity that he carefully refused to extend to France, thus revealing aspects of his discomfort with Frenchness): "I love what has constituted me into what I am, the very element of which is language, this French language that is the only language I was ever taught to cultivate, the only one also for which I can say I am more or less responsible."[18] He added: "I suppose that . . . I love this language like I love my life, and sometimes more than one or other native French love it, . . . I love it as a foreigner who has been welcomed, and who has appropriated this language as the only possible one for him. Passion and escalation. All the French of Algeria share this with me."[19]

The reference by Derrida to his North African roots is hardly accidental. As he often explained, to express oneself in French in El Biar, on the outskirts of Algiers, in the 1930s and 1940s, was very much to speak the language that effectively *dominated* the local political, economic, and cultural life, to use the language of the French colonizers of Algeria, a language that had come from elsewhere, from the *métropole*, from the "Capital-City-Mother-Fatherland."[20] It was to adopt another language, someone else's language, so that one did not resort to a language that one could genuinely call one's own—an aporia that Derrida asserted pithily: "I have only one language and it is not mine."[21] With the fierce sense of appropriation that is perhaps characteristic of those who are in search of cultural identity, it is precisely that heterogeneity that Derrida craved to domesticate all his life.

Derrida's relationship to French, which he idealized, was "irreducibly idiomatic."[22] He confessed: "My attachment to the French language takes forms that I sometimes consider 'neurotic.'"[23] For example, Derrida was possessed with a strong aspiration to linguistic acculturation. This meant a compulsion to lose his Algerian accent, a local residue he regarded as a shameful badge of provinciality (a view he extended to every other accent): "I am not proud of it, I make no doctrine of it, but so it is: an accent—any French accent, but above all a strong southern accent—seems incompatible to me with the intellectual dignity of public speech. (Inadmissible, isn't it? Well, I admit it.)"[24] Even though in his work he relentlessly decried every claim to purity as abusive and maintained that what seemed pure had always already been compromised,[25] Derrida styled his demand for "pure French" as being "inflexible" and saw himself as "the last defender . . . of the French language."[26] In fact, not only did he seek to master French, Derrida wanted to *improve* it: "To leave traces in the history of the French language—that is what interests me. I live off this passion."[27] Having ascertained that he felt "lost, fallen, and condemned outside the French language,"[28] Derrida proclaimed: "I only ever write in French and ... I attach great importance to this fact."[29] He added: "I write in a language that I insist on keeping very French."[30]

Although acutely aware that one never speaks one language only,[31] Derrida nonetheless insisted on his "monolingual obstinacy."[32] In an exchange with a French journalist, he made his position clear: "I am very monolingual, very Francophone."[33] In the same vein, while he accepted that nothing was untranslatable, "if only one is prepared to take one's time,"[34] for Derrida translation could only happen "in the loose sense of the word 'translation'"[35]—and "the excellence of the translation [could] do nothing about it."[36] As he noted, the metaphor of the Tower of Babel connects the ideas of "structure" and "language,"[37] and it is indeed the very structure of language that is at stake. Language's irreducible indefiniteness foiling any attempt to bear witness in language 2 to the precise meaning that the word being translated carries in language 1 (either the new word loses some of the significance or adds semantic content so that, for example, "'Peter' ... is not a *translation* of Pierre"),[38] Derrida maintained that "for the notion of translation we will have to substitute a notion of *transformation*: a regulated transformation of one language by another, of one text by another."[39] Strictly speaking, then, "translation is another name for the impossible,"[40] "[a] debt that one [cannot] discharge,"[41] which is no doubt why Derrida referred to "quasi-translations."[42] For him, there could be no dialogue.[43] Indeed, incommunicability is inevitable, and "there are only islands."[44] Thus, Derrida exclaimed, "What guides me is always untranslatability."[45]

No doubt as a consequence of his decision "[to] try to assume all [his] Francophone responsibilities,"[46] Derrida offered further protocolar advice in one of his inexhaustible sentences: "We must begin *somewhere where we are*," "in a text where we already believe ourselves to be."[47] One cannot be surprised to find in this injunction echoes of Martin Heidegger (1889–1976). Although having marked his distance from the German philosopher's totalizing (and totalitarian) thought,[48] Derrida held that Heidegger's work was "extremely important," that it constituted "an unprecedented, irreversible advance."[49] And he claimed that "nothing of what [he] [was] attempting would have been possible without the opening of Heideggerian questions."⁵⁰ In line with his notions of "fore-having" (*Vorhabe*), "foresight" (*Vorsicht*), and "fore-conception" (*Vorgriff*), which indicate that only within the pregiven sign-system within which one is framed can one ever ascribe meaning,⁵¹ Heidegger had explained in his early correspondence that "[he] work[ed] concretely and factically from [his] 'I am'—from [his] spiritual and in particular factical origin—[from his] environment—[from his] life as a whole [*Lebenszusammenhängen*], from what [was], from there, accessible [to him] as living experience, from that within which [he] live[d]."⁵² Starting, then, from the fact that, as Derrida put it, "philosophical nationalities have been formed,"⁵³ and from the further fact that he emphatically styled himself a *French-speaking* philosopher, and a staunchly monolingual one at that, commencing, in other words, from where he, Derrida, was, from where he read and wrote, from the language within which he believed himself to be, one of his principal translators was prompted to ask whether Derrida could in effect be conveyed beyond French: "The question arises—and it is a serious one—whether [Derrida's] essays can be read in a language other than French."⁵⁴ Quite apart from the challenging reflection concerning cross-linguistic transmissibility of meaning that it pointedly invites, this expression of doubt prompts two findings of immediate interest to my argument here.

First, Derrida would have been primordially preoccupied with *droit* and *loi*, two French words that can be said, when taken together, to approximate optimally, but certainly not replicate, the meaning of the English word *law*.⁵⁵ Second, to the extent that Derrida was at all concerned with "law," this English term, which as a word that he could "never inhabit" could only have been *uncanny* and thus of limited significance to him,⁵⁶ would have been open to apprehension for him exclusively through the diffractive prism of French. In effect, "law" could only ever have had meaning for Derrida as a variation on *droit/loi* and not *as such*.⁵⁷ As Derrida himself appreciated, any translation process, even as it carefully purports to convey meaning, is doomed to errancy and to disadjustment, to a lack of justness vis-à-vis the text in translation. As whatever understanding Derrida would have had of "law" would have taken place through the French language, it would therefore have been at irrevocable variance with, say, the understanding of an Anglophone lawyer socialized into English law—both because it would have been affected by Derrida's prejudgments, predispositions, and predilections, all traceable to French legal culture and to French culture *tout court*, and also because it could only have possibly attended to a fraction of the extensive semantic range of "law" familiar to a London barrister or a Cambridge law professor.

It is simply not reasonable, then, to assume that as Francophone an intellectual as Derrida, steeped in a language where *droit* and *loi* inevitably carry resonances profoundly characteristic of the nomothetic legal culture that bred them, would have found himself in a situation allowing him to ascribe *unaffected* (and *unaffecting*) meaning to "law" as the typical product of an idiographic legal culture such as prevails in England or in the United States. Here, the French language is shown to act as much as a "right of way" allowing "law" to reach Derrida-the-Francophone-philosopher in translation as a "barrier" preventing the English word from getting to its destination unimpeded—the issue of how much of the economy of the English term could ever be rendered in French inevitably remaining a matter of speculation.[58] There is a "differend" following from inscription-in-language, which is inscription-in-situation. One crucial point to be emphasized is that this differend is unbridgeable. Indeed, lest one accept the presence of radically different linguistic singularities and come to them as sites for the exploration of incommensurable dissensus, one risks falling for glib readings harking back in one form or another to the specious idea of universalism—precisely the kind of highly underwhelming result against which Derrida's work incessantly seeks to warn us.

To apply oneself to the matter of Derrida's comprehension of "law," to probe the connections between Derrida *and* law, thus raises a seemingly insurmountable challenge for anyone wishing to elucidate what the conjunction masks, that is, aiming to acknowledge the "there is" that haunts this formulation as it brings not-together the inscription of a proper noun (*Derrida*) in the French language and that of a noun (*law*) in the English language. Because language pertains to the *effect* of every word, one simply cannot speak of *a history* ("Derrida-and-law"), but only of *histories* ("Derrida" and "law"). Accordingly, the invitation is to address the discord between *two entities that never actually met, that never were fully in one another's co-presence, that only ever dealt with one another through the French language acting as intermediary between them*. Even as they were in contact via the French language—to be understood, then, as a third space where the negotiation between the protagonists was brokered—the *interpretans* and the *interpretandum* remained "*absolutely* irreconcilable," no matter how much readers of Derrida's texts in English show themselves willing to "live them simultaneously and reconcile them in an obscure economy."[59] One can only contemplate limited options, then: either one must attempt to address the differend through the perceiver, Derrida, thus trying to envisage "law" as Derrida himself would have understood it, that is, as a species either of *droit* or of *loi* or as some combination thereof; or else one has to operate through the perceived, *law*, and apprehend the topic with respect to what this word means in the language in which it appears, that is, in English (or in a range of Englishes), subsequently to transpose that configuration to Derrida's work even though he himself ultimately remained foreign to the word.[60] *In effect, there is no other possibility.* In acknowledgment of the fact that this essay is written in English and therefore directed at Anglophone readers, I retain the latter course of action while remaining keen to emphasize that the dynamics between "Derrida" and "law" cannot be reducible to the specific, English, term of the equation through which I have elected to discuss it. Here, "law" very much intervenes synthetically. It is "compromise English."[61] Circumventing the evidence, let us pretend, therefore, that Derrida would have written about *law*.

As Derrida himself acknowledged, the word *law* can point to meaning issuing "from morality, from legality or from politics, even from nature."[62] Two of his well-known texts are especially topical as regards the possible range of imperatives or *doxas*: "The Law of Genre" and "Before the Law."[63] While I accept that this particular understanding remains problematic inasmuch as it purports to operate in closed fashion by keeping other discourses exterior to it, it is to law in the narrower sense, as it aims to concern itself with "matters legal,"[64] that I shall devote the remainder of this argument—which is, perforce, based on Derrida's work *as I read it*, on *my* Derrida.

It is apt to observe at the outset that most commentators who have wanted to address Derrida's relationship with law in its specialized sense have focused on the text of his well-known opening address at Cardozo Law School's conference "Deconstruction and the Possibility of Justice," delivered in October 1989 as "Force of Law: The 'Mystical Foundation of Authority.'"[65] This is so although Derrida himself was at pains to observe that his work had often foregrounded law.[66] "Deconstruction" is, to be sure, the crucial motion around which Derrida has always articulated his hypercognitive desedimentation and dehierarchization practice. Unwilling to confine deconstruction to a forum that would be its "proper place," Derrida surmised that "if, hypothetically, it had a proper place," it would be "more at home in law schools, . . . than in philosophy departments and much more than in the literature departments where it has often been thought to belong."⁶⁷ For him, "law is essentially deconstructible,"⁶⁸ which is to say that he thought there was nothing more deconstructible than law.

One reason for the special relevance of law to the deconstructive enterprise would have to do with the fact that "deconstruction is not, should not be only an analysis of discourses, of philosophical statements or concepts, of a semantics; if it is going to matter, it has to challenge institutions, social and political structures, the most hardened traditions."⁶⁹ And law, as "a profoundly traditional practice," as a narrative that "rests upon mountains of inherited tradition, preserved, referred and deferred to by highly developed institutions and practices of tradition-maintenance,"⁷⁰ as also "that [which] exposes us to our own blindness or the limits of our historicality," as therefore an "unmasking of the present," as ultimately "the voice out of the past whose task is . . . to torment and scourge,"⁷¹ as all of *that*, law, then, is an evident focal point for the deconstructive challenge—which is about exposing what lies within law about which law has lied (even to itself), that which law, for an array of institutional reasons, has "officially" sought to deny or repress. It is this hidden or other side of law that the Derridean toolbox allows one to capture through what I style an *inventive* approach. Etymologically, *invention* refers simultaneously to discovery and creation. This notion thus appears the least inapt to render the archivistic process at work as it involves at once disclosive and ascriptive dimensions: the analyst works with the texts that are there and reveals their meaning, but it is he who reads those texts in order to make them meaningful.⁷²

In the end, Derrida's equipment permits one to think thoughts that would be more thoughtful than the thinking that goes under the name "positivism," which, in its various declensions, holds that what counts as law is what has been posited as law, ultimately by the sovereign—"positivists," the vast majority of legal academics, being concerned with legal technique and with rationalization of legal technique; fostering "legal dogmatics" through the organization of the different rules adopted by the sovereign in the form of an orderly, coherent, and systematic representation; seeking to offer an interpretive commentary of the legal provisions in force that would be judicious and rational, that would explain their reach and their potential, that would eliminate or reduce their apparent flaws, obscurities, gaps, or contradictions; pursuing fixity of meaning; and adhering to a brand of writing purporting to present itself in an unproblematic and unsituated mode, seeking to deny any political commitment or personal investment (thus, wanting to show itself as being simply "there" rather than as having arrived where it is through processes of contestation with alternative practices). By way of a strategy of invagination (a folding of law back on itself, as one can do with a glove) and by dint of a careful mode of phenomenological attention allowing for a letting-be of law as world, Derrida renders possible the uncovering of law's other language, which can make it feasible for one to hark back to law speaking a different language than the purportedly descriptive, propositional language that has usually been heard from positivists united. But this other language that, pace positivism's enclosing juricentrism, reveals the law's constitutive and exuberant heterogeneity is not outside the law. It is still emphatically law's language; indeed, it is arguably more authentically law's language than the thin or superficial linguistic configuration to which positivism has held law. It is hyperlaw rather than counterlaw. It is *excessively* legal.

Note that the Derridean understanding would be to the effect that law conceals a difference *within* in that the possibility of another language-of-law being spoken is inscribed *within* law itself, which means that the other is within the self, that it is present although invisible, not unlike a phantom. After Derrida, one can say that there is a "logic of haunting" at work when it comes to a law-text.[73] Because "[the law] ghosts,"[74] since "it is spectral structure that *makes the law* here,"[75] law's interpreters have to attest to this otherness and proceed to act *differentially*. While positivism has asserted law's autonomy, one can mobilize Derrida to account for "law" as heteronomy. Interpreters must, in other words, make themselves suspicious of anything that would affirm itself along the lines of a pure, detachable, and separate legal identity. Rather, they have to turn themselves into "hauntologists." Instead of incessantly asking what law "is" (and answer tautologically that it is what is posited as law by the law through the law-making authorities positing the law), law's interpreters require, if only for authenticity's sake, to engage in an exigent mutation of their thinking having law as its object. They need to elicit what law exists *as* or writes *as* or speaks *as*, that is, to show awareness of law's constitutive nexus of relations to space, to place, to situation, to time also, to reveal attentiveness to law's embeddedness in a multiplicity of intensities and in a plurality of forces, to law *as* discourse encumbered with proliferating spatiotemporal precedence. In other terms, they must abandon ontology and, through an exercise in the resignification of the legal, practice "hauntology."[76]

"Spectrality" is a recurring motif in Derrida's work. In fact, the phantom incarnates (so to speak!) Derrida's thought. It is arguably one of his most profound and central ideas. It is the notion that undergirds much of Derrida's writing as it bears witness to his primordial intuition that any "reality"—including, then, law and law-texts—is multiple, indefinite, and complex: "The spectral logic is de facto a deconstructive logic."[77] In other terms, "[the specter] regularly exceeds all the oppositions between visible and invisible, sensible and insensible. A specter is both visible and invisible, both phenomenal and nonphenomenal."[78] Being less than full presence and more than absence, the phantom makes the distinction between the factual and the fictional fuzzy. Critically, the phantom is not exterior to the text but pertains to its very constitution.

I shall return to the matter of law's spectrality presently. But there is at least one other reason, according to Derrida, that would prompt deconstruction spontaneously to focus on law, and this concerns the fact that lawyers stand at the interface of an array of pivotal tensions whose problematic terms, even as they prove as contradictory as they show themselves to be indissociable, ceaselessly inform legal discourse. Consider the following dyads, which refer to the brand of oppositions that lawyers reflexively approach as binary structures not allowing room for the presence of a third term—unless, perhaps, under the auspices of a dialectical resolution à la Hegel—and that lawyers have indeed come to regard as marking "natural" delineations: law/nonlaw, positive law / natural law, legislative text / judicial decision, interpretation/transformation, certainty/discretion, private/public, equality/individuality, and so forth. Arguably, though, as it frames itself through the various techniques from which it has become inseparable—it *is* definition, formulation, classification, composition, arbitration, adjudication, legislation—law must contend with the incessant restlessness attendant on the interaction between concepts or categories that simply do not feature the discrete contours, the sharp distinctions, the clear edges that are sought and assumed by lawyers (whether in good faith or not). One of deconstruction's main messages is precisely that concepts are in effect undelineated and categories unframed, that *there are no unquestionable borders*. The point is not, contrary to what a hasty reading of Derrida might suggest, that the law can operate without distinctions or in the absence of demarcating boundaries. Rather, deconstruction's target is the idea that neat partitions can present themselves so that one could proceed to ground clear and fixed topologies on them. The assumption of foundational alignments, claims Derrida, is at best a metaphorics instantiating wishful thinking, an illusion of reassuring certitude in which deconstruction cannot find solace as it denies "the transcendentality or logical superhardness of the barrier that marks off the conceptual purity of X from everything that is not-X."[79]

For Derrida, there exists an insurmountable indecidability inhering to the very idea of "concept" or "category" or "definition" always already challenging *any* approach based on the sustainability of binary distinctions and undermining *any* order founded on the mastery of classificatory meaning. Indeed, Derrida's insights would lead one to take the instability, the "play," that he addresses as referring, seriously, to a constitutive feature of law, to something that is inscribed, if in white ink, into the very fabric of the law, *as* law. Importantly, the "play" would not intervene from an Archimedean standpoint and is certainly not something that would be "injected" into law or attributed to law by some mischievous deconstructor. Rather, this intrinsic characteristic—think, perhaps, of a "virus"[80]—is, in Derridean terms, immanent to the processes whereby a text like law manifests itself. In the (paradoxical) name of probity, the play of the text would always already subvert any claim made in support of law's conceptual or categorical or definitional purity and would entail that there is always interpretive room for action, interpretive scope for activity, interpretive latitude.

Bearing in mind the oft-repeated accusations of nihilism castigating Derrida's perceived self-indulgence and deconstruction's assumed whimsy, it is important to note that in his work "the value of [law] (and all those values associated with it) is never contested or destroyed . . . , but only reinscribed in more powerful, larger, more stratified contexts."[81] It is not, then, that Derrida's analyses of textuality or of the legal would direct one to seek to forget (legal) tradition but that they would foster through an exacting anamnesis the recall of what law-as-tradition has wanted to forget about itself as it has been repressing all memory of the impurity of its condition while its positivist exponents, whether out of arrogance or fear, chased after the chimera of the *distinctively legal*—it being clear, in any event, that "this amnesic loss of consciousness [has] not happen[ed] by accident."[82] Subtracting itself from law's self-constituted memory that it inherits at the same time as it asserts this inheritance, deconstruction must ascertain and excavate—or *invent*—that which haunts and constitutes law, any law, in its singular uniqueness. Again, deconstruction's motion is *for* hyperlaw. According to Derrida, the notion of "presence" is thus to be approached as being much more complicated than what lawyers have superficially been accepting. Pursuing the re-presentation of the presence of law "in the form of a presence adequate to itself,"[83] an interpreter making use of Derrida's instruments would argue that "the [law] [is] not reducible . . . to the sensible or visible presence of the graphic or the 'literal,'"[84] that "whether in the order of spoken discourse or written discourse, no element can function as a sign without referring to another element which itself is not simply present,"[85] that "this sequence results in each 'element' . . . being constituted on the basis of the trace within it of the other elements of the chain or system."[86] Consequently, there would be a *built-in* dimension to law, a "structural necessity that is marked in the [law],"[87] that would operate tacitly or at least in a manner that could not be graphically visualized in the way the words on a page can be. That "operator"—let us refer to it as "culture"—while not as readily conspicuous as expressed words, leaves a range of constitutive traces within law: historical, epistemological, ideological, social, political, economic, psychological, linguistic, and _____ (fill in the blank), each of them a singular trace, a different trace, all of them ascertainable traces showing that the law is not/cannot be autarkic or "[m]onogenealog[ical],"[88] that even as it is said to be founded on an unconditional point of departure, a textual "ground," law remains but an unreflected conditionality, a self-posited, self-authenticating, and therefore *contingent* event.

In the way in which he permits a *radical* complexification of the law—it is traces *all the way down* so that "there is no atom," which means an "excess of signifying possibilities preceding the text" entailing that no reader of law can ever hope to capture the infinity of law's constitutive network[89]—Derrida fosters the adoption of a resolutely antipositivist stance. Resorting to the array of Derridean tools leads one to appreciate that there is infinitely much more to law than its positivity. In other words, within law, within the positivity of law, *as* law, as the factical concretion of each law, there is the trace, and indeed there is a general economy of traces, "more than one specter,"[90] so that law exists *as cultural text*, that it is always already plural (that it is unimaginable as anything else). In turn, this re-presentation of law allows for a full range of "deconstructive discourses [say, epistemological, ideological, political, and so forth] as they present themselves in their irreducible plurality."[91] In Derrida's language, then, law-as-it-exists is haunted by discursive traces forming complex intertwining and, strictly speaking, never-ending semiotic chains, and it is *that* that law's-interpreters-as-hauntologists are to invent (etymologically speaking) as they revisit the law with an affirmed concern for its spectrality—all the while challenging received ideas such as origin and finitude: there is, in theory at least, no first or last trace. Since one can always take one further step, there is an ever-nextness to the trace that means, crucially, that "there is no absolute origin of sense in general."[92]

Because Derrida's approach to texts shows law to be formed of such interconnecting textual layers, law cannot usefully be envisaged as having an ultimate foundation that would allow it to be apprehended as emanating from some vanishing point. Rather, law consists of an "endless multiplication of folds, unfoldings, foldouts, foldures, folders, and manifolds."[93] One seeking to account for law cannot therefore usefully re-present it as the *distinctively legal*, as a pure entity. There is, to borrow an expression from J. Hillis Miller, the "uncanny inherence" of the trace to the law.[94] The array of traces that haunt law entails that law exists *as* something other than "only law" or that *law can only be law as "not-only-law."* On account of the trace, otherness is inscribed within the legal along the lines of a virus (if one wants to return to Derrida's imagery). For a text to exist *as* law is, indeed, for it to harbor this otherness within (which is not to say that it finds itself submerged in otherness): *legality is trace-affected*. In fact, the trace is always already at home within its host, and so much so that it is *of* the host. In an attempt to capture this point, one could perhaps refer to the "of-ness" of the trace. For the host, there is no escape from the trace: "It is of no avail to show it the door, because it has long since been roaming around invisibly inside the house. The task is to catch sight of and see through" the trace,[95] what Derrida calls "the stranger at home."[96] Law exists—that is, writes and speaks—*as* an interface of heterogeneous traces; it exists *as* the social writing/speaking legally, *as* the political writing/speaking legally, *as* the economic writing/speaking legally, and so forth—it exists, in sum, *as culture* writing/speaking legally.[97] In effect, the law text exists *as* "what is spun, woven,"[98] which is what the words *textile* and *texture* in effect bring to mind. Over against Hans Kelsen and his seemingly innumerable disciples, law does not count only as that which is posited and cannot reasonably be taken to be counting only as that which is posited.[99] The pressing Derridean invitation to lawyers is, in sum, to rethink law's "as-ness."

Derrida's philosophical and literary insights, as they encourage the dismantling of positivism's hegemonic distortions, prove as bracing as they are compelling. Yet, even as his intuitions allow for "the non legal or pre-legal origin of the legal" as a primordial feature of what law exists *as*,[100] and thus for the priority of otherness, and even as his discernment manages to surmount the sterile Cartesian dichotomy between subject and object through the notion of (the invention of the) trace, Derrida's reading of law finds itself being indebted to some of the central tenets of positivism, specifically to the singularly hermetic, postcodification, *Napoleonic*, type that persists unchallenged within French jurisprudence. Perhaps this paradox befits a philosopher having so painstakingly heightened sensitivity to the aporia, that is, to the blockage, to the impasse (the Greek *aporos* refers to what is impassable), to the "non-road."[101] But there is more: Derrida studied and taught in France for over fifty years, a country where what counts as law continues to be bounded in rigorously positivist terms, intellectual order being prized above all else, analytic studies toward the realization of an exhaustive and coherent conceptual system being held in the highest regard,[102] "critical" work being largely reduced to the exposition of the state's laws in "connivence" with the state itself,[103] the dominion of the statute being unceasingly extolled, and adjudication being almost just as incessantly scorned and apprehended along the lines of a seemingly necessary evil.[104] Not only is French law positivized, then, but it is deemed a brand of knowledge that ought to operate strictly formalistically—an understanding that, as Roberto Unger has indicated in his influential critique of formalism, must be contingent on "[a] conception of intelligible essences," the point being, for example, that "to subsume situations under rules, and things under words, the mind must [assume that it is] able to perceive the essential qualities that mark each fact or situation as a member of a particular category."[105] A good illustration of the classificatory certainty or categorical confidence with which French minds apprehend the law is the *Tribunal des conflits*, a jurisdiction that meets occasionally to assign complex cases either to private-law or public-law courts, the underlying assumption being that a case, any case, is ascertainably private *or* public, that it *must* be either, and that it *cannot* be both. While more relaxed positivisms have emerged within the common-law world—I have in mind, for instance, "inclusive legal positivism" whereby under certain circumstances morality may be validated as a positive source of law[106]—these remain positively unknown in France.

To be sure, Derrida traveled widely.[107] But, while he was not trained as a French lawyer, it appears implausible that his conception of law, especially as it took shape in the early years of his intellectual life,[108] would have remained immune to the relentless dogmatism presiding over legal discourse in France. Indeed, a specific mélange of Kelsen's *Pure Theory of Law*,[109] Roman-inherited *scientia juris*,[110] a centuries-old *mos geometricus* whereby law's leading exponents aim to put it on an epistemic par with geometry,[111] not to mention a fixation on Ramist methodology,[112] is still the only configuration of the legal deemed worthy of consideration (no matter how much this supposedly sophisticated view of law can be said to consist, in effect, of scraps of technical or conceptual information locked in ancestral analytic dichotomies whose intellectual authority seems largely indebted to persistence through an age-old and self-perpetuating (and profoundly chauvinistic) recycling process involving academics, their disciples, their disciples' disciples, and so forth).[113]

It is not that every French lawyer has deliberately and publicly committed to Kelsenism on the occasion of a solemn ceremony after being educated at length regarding the fine points of *Pure Theory of Law*. Rather, the dominion of French Kelsenism—the relentless epistemic drive for enhanced terminological clarity, improved logical consistency, and reinforced systematic coherence, that is, for optimized positivization, or for a purer posited law— is a diffuse and insidious affair. In the words of a noted commentator, "if the self-proclaimed 'disciples' of Kelsen are rare in France, . . . with very few exceptions there is no problem in legal theory today that would be formulated while making abstraction of the particular sense with which the Pure Theory of Law has invested traditional concepts of legal thought."[114] Speaking of Kelsen, a French philosopher of law thus writes that "there is no longer any point being discussed in our discipline over which does not stretch nowadays the shadow of his Pure Theory."[115] Likewise, in an encomium marking Kelsen's honorary doctorate from the Sorbonne, a French constitutional lawyer said that "after him, one can no longer write or speak of the law without feeling the hold of his thought."[116] In one form or another, Kelsenism asserts itself with every French yearning for "pure law," for arguments that would be "incontestably neutral," and for the purported eviction of facticity (and its unruly indefiniteness).[117] And in a country where it is still forcefully claimed that each lawyer is a "child of Domat"—the famous seventeenth-century writer who defended the view that legal reasoning had to model itself on geometrical reasoning[118]—such strivings are recurrent. This is why I argue that, when it came to law, Derrida's determined Francophony could not have escaped the very long reach of Frenchness-at-Law—no matter how innovative and cosmopolitan he was in so many other ways. Even allowing for a substantial measure of nomadism, the idea of noninscription in legal space and, indeed, of nonlocation in legal time is untenable: to be Derrida writing about law was to *be* Derrida-the-Francophone-at-Law and was to be *Derrida-in-Frenchness-at-Law-in-the-Second-Half-of-the-Twentieth-Century*. Without situating Derrida within Frenchness at that time, within French legal culture at that time, and therefore within so-called French "scientific" positivism at that time, the classical side of his understanding of law—it has rightly been said of Derrida that "among the last generation of continental philosophers [he] stands out as the most legalistic of thinkers"[119]—would become very awkward indeed to justify.

Derridean instruments allowing for a signal contribution to the hauntology of law, to what law exists *as*, to the intrinsically heteronomic "as-ness" of law (it exists *as* culture speaking legally; it is a cultural form incorporating a labyrinthine assemblage of traces, of "influences, filiations, or legacies"),[120] do not prevent Derrida himself from considering law to be also that which *laws* (if I may be allowed to coin a verb out of a noun, with a nod to Heidegger) because it has been authoritatively posited as law irrespective of anything that it otherwise exists as. There being express evidence that Derrida was aware of Kelsen,[121] one can identify two principal axes inclinating aspects of Derrida's thought about law along unmistakably positivist lines,[122] about law-being-law-because-it-has-been-authoritatively-posited-to-be-law—although it must be observed again that, unlike Kelsen, Derrida never lent credence to the idea of purity, as his "quasi-logic" of spectrality makes emphatically clear,[123] as does indeed his proposed clarification of deconstruction, a brief formula meant to capture the basic gesture of heteronomic commitment: "*Plus d'une langue*, that is, both more than a language and no more of *a* language."[124]

The first manifestation of Derrida's French positivism pertains to his distinction between law and justice. Although of ancient lineage, this idea has more recently been prominently expressed by Kelsen, who, referring to "the dualism of law and justice,"[125] writes that "justice . . . must be imagined as an order different from . . . the positive law."[126] For his part, Derrida formulates this differentiation in terms that are in effect idiosyncratically Derridean. His initial motion is to assert both that law is deconstructible and that it must be deconstructed. The *deconstructibility* of law would emerge from the fact of its intrinsic embodiment in an "as" narrative, a constitutive network of traces whose voice has been relentlessly silenced on the altar of uppercase Law as master-signifier, as "the posited" that, thing-like, is deemed to be visibly, ascertainably "out there," objectively and exclusively identifiable through the deployment of the correct method. The *necessity* of deconstruction would arise on account of this suppression itself, because of the institutionalization of a dominant position not allowing or *out-lawing* all other voices (that I have subsumed under the label "culture"). And it would emerge precisely in the name of the justice that law cannot be, and can never even hope to be, as long as it does not acknowledge the structural presence of that which is not not-law (i.e., the circuits of embedded traces) and the complexity of the interpretive negotiation that must follow from this constitutive fact.[127] Derrida's contrapuntal gesture is to insist that justice is undeconstructible—indeed, that it is the *only* concept that is resilient enough to withstand deconstruction.[128]

Law, for Derrida, pertains to the realm of the calculable. Specifically, it is about claim, obligation, and entitlement,[129] assessed by a third party such as a judge, whose task is to engage in a commutative/distributive exercise that is meant to be kept within strictly *legal* boundaries, within the ambit of an application of *law*. As Derrida envisages justice, it eschews any mediation and concerns the relation between self and other approached as standing face-to-face and as recognizing one's vis-à-vis as *alter ego* (i.e., as another ego just like oneself) or, less self-centeredly, as recognizing oneself as another, as but one source of meaning among others. On this point, Derrida quotes Emmanuel Levinas (1906–1995), one of his main sources of inspiration, who expressly equates "the relation to others" and "justice."[130] On the one hand, then, there is to be found "the calculation of restitution," "calculable equality," "the symmetrizing and synchronic accountability or imputability of subjects or objects . . . that would be limited to sanctioning, to restituting, and to *making law*" (*faire droit*).[131] On the other hand, beyond the realm of the posited, beyond any law, indeed beyond any "economy" and beyond the order of knowledge,[132] as a kind of meta-law, as a Law of law, there would exist justice as what there is that is not there yet, that is always "to-come,"[133] that is infinitely deferred,[134] and as that which, if it exists, exists *in itself* and which "as the experience of absolute alterity is unpresentable."[135] (On this account, Derrida's justice distinguishes itself from any idea of natural law, which claims to precede the posited while purporting to encapsulate both law and justice, that is, to enunciate law as justice and justice as law.)

While the notion of calculability takes one back to that of mathematizable law and shows Derrida to be also a "child of Domat," justice as the "singularity of the an-economic ex-position to others"—as what is at once out of the posited and *stemming from* a position—gestures toward the "incalculability of the gift."[136] And it is precisely because it is "owed to the other, before any contract" that justice is "irreducible in its affirmative character, in its demand of gift without exchange, without circulation, without recognition or gratitude, without economic circularity, without calculation and without rules, without reason and without rationality."[137] There is, and these are Derrida's own words, "a madness" in this—an observation that prompts him to say that "deconstruction is mad about this kind of justice."[138]

Having sketched this opposition between law and justice, Derrida swiftly proceeds, in typical deconstructive fashion, to blunt anything that might come across as too sharp a delineation. Thus, he observes that although heterogeneous to each other, law and justice are not immiscible. Indeed, he claims that their very heterogeneity *requires* their "inseparability" (*indissociabilité*). There cannot be justice except through law and thus by way of legal determinations. And there cannot be any becoming or any perfectibility of law, any transformation of law, that does not call on an idea of justice destined inevitably to exceed it.[139] (Still in contradistinction to the idea of natural law, Derrida's justice, then, assumes neither the effacement of the posited nor an opposition to it.)

This imbrication of law and justice offers an illustration of the logic of supplementation that is a hallmark of Derrida's deconstructive investigations.[140] Law fashions itself as whole, complete, and self-sufficient. It is readily taken to be such by positivists whose *Dogmatik* draws an acute line between law and nonlaw, deeming anything that is not strictly law (such as equity, discretion, and even interpretation) an external appendage—and therefore supplementary *to* law. While Derrida accepts that justice is to be distinguished from law and that it therefore operates supplementarily to it in the sense at least that it differs from it, he takes the view that this "supplement" partakes *of* law on account of the fact that law must comport at the very least a yearning for justice. From this perspective, justice is an other-of-the-law, an out-of-law, an extrinsicism that is intrinsic to law as that-which-law-wants-to-be, which is a part of what-law-exists-as (a constitutive part of what I exist as today is what I want to be tomorrow). This schema illustrates both the indefiniteness between law and any supposed beyond-the-law and the fluidity of any notion of supplementarity as what is neither "present" within nor "absent" from within. Here, justice fills a hole in the law that sees itself as whole (and therefore as just) "on its own."

There is an additional point to be made about Derrida's thoughts on law/justice. What he says about justice being undeconstructible and "deconstruction tak[ing] place in the interval that separates the undeconstructibility of justice from the deconstructibility of [law]," that is, what he observes about deconstruction helping bridge the gap between calculability and incalculability, does not only concern deconstruction as it applies to law but addresses the whole of the deconstructive enterprise.[141] In other words, "deconstruction is justice" not only when it comes to law.[142] Rather, "deconstruction is justice" is to be understood as a generic slogan, which suggests that Derrida's contribution to legal theory is significant in terms of his deconstructive strategy as a whole and that a good understanding of Derrida's apprehension of law is necessary to a sound appreciation of his thought.[143]

The second salient strand of Derrida's French positivism concerns the fact that, aporetically,[144] law and force are structurally imbricated into each other—specifically, force is endogenous to law while being precisely that exogenous threat that law is meant to counter. In Derrida's words, "law is always an authorized force."[145] He adds: "There is no such thing as law . . . that doesn't imply *in itself, a priori, in the analytic structure of its concept*, the possibility of being . . . applied by force."[146] In other words, while force is law's other, law contains within itself the fact of force: "That which threatens law already belongs to law."[147] Drawing on a statement by Pascal,[148] Derrida shows how law cannot usefully be understood apart from the idea of "enforceability."[149] Law cannot operate as law unless it is in force (i.e., unless it has come into force) and unless it is enforced in a context where its coming-into-force or its enforcement call on the mobilization of an institutional machinery pertaining both to the executive and judicial authorities by those who have a monopoly on legitimate/legal force. Derrida's reference to law as "authorized force" is again reminiscent of Kelsen, who claimed that law cannot subsist without force, that law is a mode of organization of force.[150] But I do not wish to dwell on these habitual connotations of the word *force*. Instead, I propose to address another sense in which, according to Derrida, law is force. This other meaning is usually overlooked, although it is tied to the very possibility of law and, beyond it, to the very possibility of language,[151] so that "force" apprehended in this sense is an irreducible feature of law.[152]

On account of its primordial character, Derrida refers to this form of force as "arche-violence," the Greek root *arche* suggesting that the violence in question would have been always already there.[153] Derrida's basic point about violence's inherence revolves around language and addresses the very fact of articulation,[154] which is "appellatio[n]," "classification," and therefore "differen[tiation]."[155] As such, articulation, any articulation, *is* a determination. Now, any determination *is* violent to some extent given that, as an act of meaning-creation, it operates in a moment of decision that, as is the case with any expression of decidability, proves simultaneously inclusive and exclusive (e.g., as I decide to refer to this tree as an oak, I include and exclude certain characteristics). Since every discourse is inescapably an act of articulation, it follows that it is just as inevitably a determination, and it ensues that it is violent. Indeed, only a discourse that would say nothing at all could eschew violence, but then it would make no sense to talk of *that* as a discourse.[156] Thus discourse and violence are to be seen as arising at once as facets of a single event. In Derrida's words, "The structure of violence is complex and its possibility—writing—no less so."[157] This entanglement is emphatically relevant to law (which is not to say that Derrida reduces juridicity to an exclusive interaction between law and violence; as one knows, he allows for justice also).

No matter how much law wishes to circumvent violence, it simply cannot operate only as the inevitable unfolding of the kind of mechanistic process that would deprive it of any and all articulatedness. Irrespective of how technical the legal decision to be made, of how seemingly automatic, any expression of law represents a determination and, as such, shows itself to be violent. No expression of law can be other than the making of a determination, the taking of a *position*—which means that no determination can be other than a reassessment of the tradition. Law is, intrinsically, discursive positionality. Paul Ricoeur helpfully makes this point as follows: "Between the least contradicted rule and its application there always remains a hiatus."[158] Even if the zone of intervention within which the legal official is operating should prove extremely narrow, any determination represents a movement away from the paradigm of generality (whereby the law must apply to all cases identically in the name of equality) toward that of particularity (whereby the law must apply to each case differentially on account of the singularity of individual circumstances), a process that is always conducted by a particular person at a specific time in a given place. This must mean that there is always a moment of decidability, however fleeting, during which a course of action is retained and another is rejected, even if as being wildly implausible. Although it asserts itself as a mere reenactment of a prior law, the legal determination-as-position cannot escape being a decision against an alternative claim—in other words, it cannot avoid being a denial of an alternative source of meaning.[159] Ultimately, the fact is that a legal determination can never appeal to a prior law to hide its constitutive character: *there is no guarantor*.[160] Any purported restatement of a prior law is, structurally, but a reinvention of it. Again, the Latin *inventio* is at once discovery and creation: as the antecedent law is discovered, it is created.

The inherence of violence to law is aptly summarized in these terms: "All law—unlike justice—is dependent on a positing (*Setzung*), and no positing manages without violence."[161] Inasmuch as legal determination is as articulation, which it necessarily is, it embodies arche-violence and indeed reiterates it every time that another legal intervention takes place. To paraphrase Derrida, "[a] [law] without violence would be a [law] which would occur outside the existent."[162]

Note that although it is a contrivance of law in every case, the legal determination cannot be regarded as *pure* violence. Otherwise, it would amount to the utter obliteration of other horizons of meaning to such an extent that alternative standpoints could not even be recognized as *arguments*, as something refutable. In effect, the holding of different positions would become impossible.[163] Granted that the legal decision "belongs to the structure of fundamental violence,"[164] the violence at work, then, is best understood as an "economy" of violence, that is, as modulated violence.[165]

To admit the inescapability of law-as-violence does not leave deconstruction bereft as a dismantlement strategy. By calling into question—by putting *to* the question—the alleged foundations on which law claims to be established, by "interrogati[ng] . . . the origin, grounds and limits of our conceptual, theoretical or normative apparatus,"[166] by lifting the "veil,"[167] deconstruction shows that law, *even* law, is discursively bound to the particular horizon of its writers or promoters and ultimately tied to the necessary perspectivism of egoity. By claiming that law is "constructed on interpretable and transformable textual strata,"[168] deconstruction seeks to mitigate the violence that law-as-established-discourse would otherwise continue to perpetrate on repressed voices in the name of its own reiteration. Again, it is not so much that deconstruction aims to destroy law-as-established-discourse, but that it calls on it to show responsibility in the face of the question put to it, in the face of others, and in the face of justice. Law is thus given an opportunity to justify itself, to account for itself, to reestablish itself in a way that better approximates justice by doing justice to the situation, that is, for instance, to the repressed "others" within the situation, by recognizing them as independent sources of meaning (which is an acknowledgment of the others' being-in-the-world). Confronted with a law that, in the name of its presumed universality, imposes its perspectives on others who are structurally denied status as meaning-creators, deconstruction promotes the reception of all voices in their individuality and thus, assuming the primordial nature of the other as a source of meaning at least equivalent to the self, aims to respect the face of the other as a sovereign face, to avoid its effacement, that is, *to give the other what the other is due.*

Although it purports to minimize violence by countering the aggression of law-as-established-discourse's totalizing presence, deconstruction is, of course, itself a form of violence. But it is not rabid rebellion seeking to overthrow law-as-established-discourse for revolution's sake. It is violence deployed as unfolding, as interruptive reading, in order to avoid the kind of violence that would permanently silence all positions except one. Through a radical questioning of the basis of law-as-established-discourse, deconstruction operationalizes a suspension of law's programmatic agenda suspending the epistemic relevance of otherness (yes, deconstruction "assumes the right to contest, and not only theoretically, constitutional protocols, the very charter that governs reading in our culture").[169] As it ensures that the self-identity of juridicity is neither assured nor reassuring, deconstruction, then, adduces an "infinite demand for justice."[170] It is thus "an impure, contaminating, negotiated, bastard and violent way,"[171] "violence against violence,"[172] violence as counterviolence, but violence *as vigilance.*[173] Pure nonviolence being impossible (a point that takes us back to discourse necessarily being articulation), deconstruction is that which constantly challenges law in the name of justice *for* those who are currently marginalized (and never, of course, the kind of "bad violence" that "does not leave room for the other").[174]

For the positivist, there would be a unique foundational manifestation of authority that would be law's only positive force. Every subsequent expression of legal discourse—for instance, in an adjudicative context—would repose on the posited foundation; in other words, it would simply consist in an act that would repeat or re-pose the foundation. Not only would law be static (in terms of the source of its authority), it would also be "automatic," the result of a legal order operating measuredly, regulatedly, predictably. And law's authority would be a function of this very automatization.

Clearly, law's mode of production, formal structure, rhetorical organization (not least through the development of a system of reference and self-reference), and dissemination of legal knowledge articulate an impressive mise-en-scène. And, no matter how fanciful *ratio scripta*'s scenario (one could refer to an "epistolary fictio[n]"),[175] there seems little merit in doubting the relevance of the posited law as a pertinent and commodious point of departure for the analysis of legal discourse (indeed, there is something like the impossibility of not passing through posited law). Derrida's own French positivism can be apprehended as an acknowledgment of this fact. But even Derrida's concessions to the posited cannot detract from his main philosophical and literary message that law texts cannot usefully be confined to law-as-the-posited, to "*das Gesetzte*" (it is interesting to observe that the German word used to render "the posited," *Gesetzte*, is so close to that which accounts for "statute," *Gesetz*). In this regard, Derrida's argument would be that law inherently exceeds any automation or calculation. It surpasses any possible reduction to a presently posited that would be there as such (to transpose Derrida's words, "[law] transgress[es] the figure of all possible representation").[176] There is that within law, as constitutive of law, as law, "which in no case can be 'posed,'" indeed "that by means of which every position is *of itself confounded*."[177] What undermines the posited by necessarily overcoming it is the trace, which is the inscription of otherness in law and as law. Now, the instantiation of the trace within the structure of law shows law as situated, located, embedded, factical. And law cannot escape the trace, its "idiomatic hereness."[178] The trace is an encrypted imprint of a past that is invisibly and imperceptibly present within law and as law, which positions law. It turns law into a position (even as there are those within law who wish to claim for it a "view-from-nowhere" status). The trace pertains to law "*in the analytical structure of its concept*."[179] When it comes to law, then, "there is the writing + something else that would be there *in addition* . . . , . . . something that the law cannot do without."[180]

The economy of the trace thus demands an interpretive passage from law-is-"*das Gesetzte*" to law-as-"*die Setzung*." Consider Jean-Luc Nancy's claim as he observes that "*Setzung* . . . responds point for point to the dynamic of *différance* by which Derrida designates the infinite motion of finite being as such."[181] In other words, even though finite or posited, law and its meaning is incessantly in movement, which means that any idea of repose is demoted or dis-posed of, reflecting a distrust in positing and in positivity and in positivists and in the positivist *Zeitgeist*, which is thus *ex-posed* as a position on account of the dynamic presence of the traces deposited in the law-text (and de-positing the law-text). In Derrida's own words, "positive law does not make the law."[182] There is "an inadequation between the form and the content of discourse or . . . an incommensurability between the signifier and the signified."[183] As much as *das Gesetzte* is wanted, and as much as it may appear that this is what is on offer, a close examination of law as it exists, of law-as-cultural-text, shows that in effect law can only generate *die Setzung* or, more accurately, *die Setzungen*, that is, positions.[184]

The inherent facticity of law means that law is not, and cannot ever be, a text that would have a finite and fixed meaning. Rather, it is a text, and can only ever be a text, whose meaning is always already deferred (and which, in this respect, is not different from any other text, law's specific brand of normativity not being enough to detract from law as literary genre). Any interpreter is accordingly doomed to an (unceasing) quest for law's meaning. And, as if to complicate matters further, any ascription of meaning to law by its interpreter is an inevitable function of the interpreter's own facticity, which entails that there takes place the imputation of a position to law in this sense also. This observation confirms Derrida's insight that although meaning cannot escape the trace, the trace is not all there is to meaning. In Derrida's terms, the trace does not "saturat[e]" meaning.[185] Just as the trace is inadequate to all that there is, fails to correlate exactly with the "there-isness" of law in its endless ramifications, any writing purporting to capture the law through the trace is itself destined to err, which brings to mind the Derridean figure of "destinerrance." As the interpreter brings the traces into play, there will always be a trace missing: it is a case of n-1 or, rather, of t-1. This situation leads, ultimately, to a relation without a relation. As the interpreter refers to law according to this new form of coherence (rather than in pursuit of formal coherence), he cannot connect with it, that is, with the whole of it. He can only ever stand on the verge of the law, which means that he can only ever write *toward* law. The purported relation between the interpreter and the law becomes, in effect, a *nonrelation*. Still, though, the trace keeps the alienating character of the positivist reduction under check.

After Derrida, authority-*Gesetzte* cannot escape the grip of authority-*Setzung*. In other words, *die Setzung* haunts *das Gesetzte* as law is shown as a matter of *structure* to be a "ghost story."[186] Ultimately, then, Derrida's key lesson would thus be that, even if it can mark a convenient point of departure for legal interpretation, the posited cannot constitute a term of arrival for analysis of *law*.

I have been making three principal claims. First, I have established Derrida's abiding commitment to the French language. Literally, he never wrote about "law." Second, I have emphasized that Derrida's philosophical and literary insights make it possible to revisit the dominant, positivist, understanding of the legal to considerable advantage. Third, I have shown that Derrida's appreciation of "law"—on the assumption that, for convenience's sake, this word is to be retained for present purposes—features not only the brand of deconstructive understanding that is readily associated with him but also an ascertainably positivist facet incorporating salient features of Kelsenism, as one would expect from a French academic expressing interest in matters legal.

I want to suggest one further argument, if briefly, which is that once one has become aware of the French singularity of Derrida's thought on "law," one can marshall this fact beneficially to inform a postpositivist, indeed a humanist, understanding of the legal going beyond the French model. A key insight is supplied by Derrida himself as he observes that "a written sign contains a power of severance from its context,"[187] that it is *iterable*.[188] Aspects of his reflection on the constitution of the legal, therefore, can/must be severed from their French moorings. Interestingly, Derrida's basic guidance is formulated in terms of a law: "My law, the one to which I try to devote myself or to respond, is *the text of the other*, its very singularity, its idiom, its appeal which precedes me."[189] It is, then, this primordial motion in favor of recognition and respect that justifies the move away from the rendition of the legal in tightly formatted descriptive, propositional terms—a reductionist narrative acting as an epistemic obstacle that brings to a halt, that silences, the movement of otherness incessantly at work within the law-text—toward an acknowledgment of law as the nexus of relations out of which it emerges, that it exists as. Qualifying his positivism in significant manner as he defends the necessity of thinking at once both the law and the trace, and of resisting thinking the trace as the nonlaw, Derrida equips one with a strategy that allows for a letting-be of law that is also a letting-emerge-the-world-as-law. Along the way, he shows one that place is not a mere static backdrop to legal meaning but a dynamic constituent of it. In other words, place is not simply a physicalist conception: it is also an existential notion. Law proceeds only in and through place (an assertion that does not entail an essentialist, exclusionary, reactionary, conservative, or immobile understanding of place—one can indeed approach place as source rather than terminus, as that from which something begins in its unfolding, rather than that at which it comes to a stop). It is not that law exists in space but, primordially, that there is no aspatial law. Through the trace, law and place are inextricably enmeshed, which means, incidentally, that law can be constitutive of place in its turn. In the same way as there is no ungrounded language, there is no ungrounded law. For law, for any law, to exist "as law," it must stand forth in terms of an experience of place. It must *dwell*. For those who have German, Derrida's claim, in short, is for *Ortung* in contradistinction to the seemingly relentless drive for evermore *Ordnung* being promoted by positivists. To attend to law in this way is to honor one's debt to the singularity and to the difference that there is, to pledge allegiance to their implacable demand through the law, to agree to be interpellated *thus* by the law-text. Derrida's thought therefore reminds one that positivism is no longer to be understood as holding the exclusive position that positivists have wanted it to occupy. It prompts one to think about the law other-wise, that is, in a way that, as legal thought wises toward otherness, differs from how it has habitually operated. Now, the fostering of thoughts other than what positivism has been thinking means, to that extent at least, a dethronement of positivism.

Yet positivism keeps a place, as it does in Derrida's own thinking. Indeed, one's goal cannot be simply to jettison statutes and judicial decisions as if they had nothing to do with law. Rather, the point is to approach them afresh, that is, to come to them obliquely. The idea is that no formulation of the posited law can safely escape a spectral interpretation and therefore that all formulations of the posited law must be envisaged through the traces that haunt the legal. Yet, in no way can a humanist understanding of law seek to dispense altogether with the usual artifacts such as statutes and judicial decisions. As I have explained, the traces are indeed to be found at work at the heart of statutes and judicial decisions, which must therefore remain one of the principal foci of study for lawyers. But the posited law cannot be something at which interpretation stops. Rather, it must be something from which interpretation begins its *presencing*. The idea is to refuse to take statutes or judicial decisions as a literal given and, through an unceasing movement of oscillation toward and away from the posited, to try to see how they are conditioned and shaped by what haunts them. Ultimately, the governing direction can be expressed thus: "Let us return to the thing itself, that is to say, to the ghost."[190] This call is very important and is, in fact, key.

As there takes place a tracing of the law, the act of interpretation is being conducted as a matter of recognition and respect for the law as it exists (rather than as positivism has wanted it to be). In this regard, Derrida is adamant: "[Reading] . . . cannot legitimately transgress the text toward something other than it,"[191] for there is "the law of the other text, its injunction, its signature."[192] And what is arguably one of the most significant features of any tracing exercise is precisely that in the course of tracing, the interpreter does not reach beyond the law and therefore does not disqualify himself as someone purporting to ascribe meaning to *other-than-legal* discourse. To be sure, to the extent that the traces attest to the instability/interstitiality/interlinearity of the text, that they are taking the text beyond stasis, they can be said to connote a "beyond" of the analytic limits of the hard copy, that is, to suggest a hypertext showing in intertwining fashion discourses interlaced within discourses. Instead of a hardened text, then, there would be a fluid text featuring, for instance, flexibility and recursivity. (Observe that fluidity can act as a powerful trope for feminist sensibility and show tracing as the feminization of the text.) But while the reader gets farther away from what the text is said to declare according to positivist dogma (pure, uncontaminated by other discourses, protected), one gets closer to what the text declares in effect. The reader is not, then, re-presenting the text as being other than itself, as if one were betraying it. Rather, the reader is re-presenting the text as other than itself inasmuch as it is constituted of otherness and therefore exists as something impure.

Deconstruction's commitment to a humanist understanding of law—to an appreciation of its enculturation and of the enculturation of those who study and practice it—must be understood as a critical posture featuring a significant political dimension. As Derrida himself was at pains to underline, "Deconstruction . . . is not *neutral*. It *intervenes*."[193] Not only is it the case that "no deconstruction is . . . apolitical,"[194] but deconstruction is, in fact, "hyper-political."[195] For Richard Bernstein, Derrida's fight against hierarchy, subordination, repression, exclusion, violence—in other words, his objection to the condemnation of otherness or difference (i.e., for present purposes, his struggle against positivism's strategy to proscribe, silence, outcast, exile other discourses, a segregation that is institutionally prescribed and ceaselessly inscribed)—is "primarily" political.[196] Likewise, according to Terry Eagleton, "deconstruction is for [Derrida] an ultimately *political* practice."[197] And Derrida's is uncompromisingly a *subversive* politics, that is, "a disturbance, displacement, or disruption of the status quo . . . that retains enormous potential for resisting the self-assurance of any hegemonic discourse or practice" such as positivism.[198] Consider his claims that "[the law] is always already a trace," that the trace "reintroduces into [law] originarily all the impurity that one had thought to be able to exclude from it," and that "the trace is the relation of the intimacy of the [law] to its outside, the openness to exteriority in general, to the non-proper" (at least according to the traditional understanding of the legal). Contemplate, in sum, Derrida's argument for the trace's suturation to the law-text so that "the same is the same only by affecting itself with the other,"[199] or that, once more, the law is the law only in being affected by the historical, the epistemological, the ideological, the social, the political, the economic, the psychological, the linguistic, and the _____ (fill in the blank)—a strong defense of the "irreducible" character of law-as-difference.[200]

As if these counterpositivist assertions did not generate enough disciplinary dissonance, Derrida's programmatic challenge for the release of law from the shackles of positivism can be extended to the view that everything one alleges to know regarding law manifests itself within a strictly contingent cognitive scheme, indeed within a frame that is doubly contingent on account of law's situatedness, on the one hand, and of the emplacement of law's interpreter, on the other—two "self-referentialities," to write like Niklas Luhmann, making for a variation on the Batesonian theme of the "double bind."[201] Specifically, according to Derrida, no reading of a text—and therefore no reading of a law-text—can ever operate on the basis of rational or objective foundations. Once more, his argument is not that such foundations have been lost but that they were never there. Nor can a law-text ever harbor an exact meaning that would be lying in wait for its reader or indeed conceal a meaning that would be fully available to interpretation.

In core respects, then, Derrida's deconstruction stands for an extolment of values such as indefiniteness and unmasterability, co-specification and unsynthesizability, that positivists reflexively regard as practices of articulation pertaining to a cognitive predicament rather than as supplying the propitious signposts for thought—which they prefer (if illusorily) to associate with the transparency and exhaustibility of meaning. Through the idea of traces gathered, as it were, into the microchip of the law-text (there is "what one could call the *bindinal* economy," "the economy of the tie or of the link"),[202] Derrida's *coup de dé* solicits and encourages one, on account of the motif of spectrality, to do away with the fantasy of the will to power that would have law exist as univocal texts and to promote the law's heteroreferentiality, to foster the rehabilitation of otherness-in-the-law, to show care, to be careful, to display response, to be response-able and responsible, to be *hospitable* vis-à-vis otherness.

I have come full circle, as one does. That so many common-law lawyers should have domesticated Derrida's work on "law" in order to edify their critique of positivism, that Derrida should therefore have been mobilized in earnest to assist beyond France with alternative legal scholarship and with other strategies of interpretation in particular, is not to be regretted. There remains one unfortunate factor, which I have wanted to address: all along, there has been insufficient realization in the common-law world that this process of appropriation was persistently crossing linguistic and legal boundaries in somewhat spectacular fashion without attending to the cultural fact that, in Derrida's own formulation, "it is in French, of a French word that [he] always speak[s]," "in the irredentism of [French's] most untranslatable idiom."[203]

NOTES

1. E.g.: Mark Currie, *The Invention of Deconstruction* (New York: Palgrave Macmillan, 2013), 28–63; Peter Goodrich, "Europe in America: Grammatology, Legal Studies, and the Politics of Transmission," *Columbia Law Review* 101 (2001): 2033–84; Pierre Schlag, "'Le hors de texte, c'est moi': The Politics of Form and the Domestication of Deconstruction," *Cardozo Law Review* 11 (1990): 1631–71; J. M. Balkin, "Deconstructive Practice and Legal Theory," *Yale Law Journal* 96 (1987): 743–86; Clare Dalton, "An Essay in the Deconstruction of Contract Doctrine," *Yale Law Journal* 94 (1985): 997–1114.

2. Jacques Derrida, *Positions*, trans. Alan Bass (New York: Continuum, 2002), 19 (emphasis omitted). For the reader's convenience, I refer to published English translations whenever possible, although I silently modify them on a number of occasions.

3. For a recension of the basic facts concerning this issue (including a reference to Derrida's complaint), see Jeffrey T. Nealon, "Deconstruction and the Yale School of Literary Theory," in *Poststructuralism and Critical Theory's Second Generation*, ed. Alan D. Schrift (London: Routledge, 2014), 389–90.

4. Gayatri C. Spivak, "Translator's Preface," in Jacques Derrida, *Of Grammatology*, trans. Gayatri C. Spivak (Baltimore: Johns Hopkins University Press, 1997), lxxxvi. I deliberately refer to this edition of Spivak's commentary.

5. Ibid., 55.

6. Cf. Joseph F. Graham, introduction to *Difference in Translation*, ed. Joseph F. Graham (Ithaca, N.Y.: Cornell University Press, 1985), 14. Ironically, the common-law lawyer's attitude would broadly accord with Derrida's views on untranslatability to the effect that his French law in French would be, strictly speaking, ultimately untranslatable into common law in English.

7. Currie, *Invention of Deconstruction*, 44.

8. See Jacques Derrida, *Learning to Live Finally*, trans. Pascale-Anne Brault and Michael Naas (Hoboken, N.J.: Melville House, 2007), 22–26, 31–34, 50–52. This

title is taken from the first sentence of the exordium in Jacques Derrida, *Specters of Marx*, trans. Peggy Kamuf (London: Routledge, 1994), xvi.

9. Derrida's last public appearance took place in Rio de Janeiro on August 16, 2004.

10. See, e.g., Jacques Derrida, *Monolingualism of the Other; or, The Prosthesis of Origin*, trans. Patrick Mensah (Stanford, Calif.: Stanford University Press, 1998).

11. Jacques Derrida, *Dissemination*, trans. Barbara Johnson (Chicago: University of Chicago Press, 1981), 340.

12. That "Derrida was . . . teaching philosophy and philosophers . . . that there may be some conceptual and practical problems attendant to the fact that most philosophy is articulated in a given, nonuniversal language," a "lesso[n] that some modes of institutionalized philosophy were not at all anxious to learn," is articulated in Ian Balfour, introduction to "Late Derrida," special issue, *South Atlantic Quarterly* 106, no. 2 (2007): 212. See, e.g., Jacques Derrida, *Points . . .* , ed. Elisabeth Weber, trans. Peggy Kamuf (Stanford, Calif.: Stanford University Press, 1995), 374.

13. Verne Harris, *Archives and Justice* (Chicago: Society of American Archivists, 2007), 72.

14. Marian Hobson, *Jacques Derrida: Opening Lines* (London: Routledge, 1998), 2; my emphasis. According to Hobson, her book can be read as an extended argument on the importance that Derrida's writing held for his own work and on the significance of the fact that that writing was in French (1).

15. Derrida, *Of Grammatology*, 6.

16. The actual enunciation is more cryptic, as Derrida states, "Il n'y a pas de hors-texte," in *De la grammatologie* (Paris: Editions de Minuit, 1967), 227. Translations vary. I favor a close reading and retain "There is no out-of-text." Cf. Derrida, *Of Grammatology*, 158: "*There is nothing outside of the text.*"

17. Derrida, *Learning to Live*, 34.

18. Ibid., 36. For Derrida's reservation regarding France, see ibid., 37.

19. Ibid.

20. Derrida, *Monolingualism*, 41.

21. Ibid., 25. Derrida was still remarking on this paradox in his final interview. See Derrida, *Learning to Live*, 38.

22. Jacques Derrida, "La vérité blessante ou le corps-à-corps des langues," *Europe*, May 2004, 10.

23. Derrida, *Monolingualism*, 56.

24. Ibid., 46.

25. "The dyad [i]s the minimum": Jacques Derrida, *Margins of Philosophy*, trans. Alan Bass (Chicago: University of Chicago Press, 1982), 111.

26. Derrida, *Monolingualism*, 46, 47, 47.

27. Derrida, *Learning to Live*, 37. The most celebrated of Derrida's numerous neologisms earned an entry in the leading French dictionary. See, e.g., *Le Grand*

Robert de la langue française, 2nd ed., Alain Rey, vol. 2 (Paris: Le Robert, 2001), s.v. "différance."

28. Derrida, *Monolingualism*, 56.
29. Derrida, *Points*, 416.
30. Derrida, "La vérité blessante," 9.
31. See Derrida, *Monolingualism*, 7–11.
32. Ibid., 57.
33. Franz-Olivier Giesbert, "Ce que disait Derrida...," *Le Point*, October 14, 2004, http://www.lepoint.fr/actualites-litterature/ce-que-disait-derrida/1038/0/31857.
34. Derrida, *Monolingualism*, 56.
35. Ibid.
36. Derrida, *Specters*, 21.
37. See Jacques Derrida, "Des tours de Babel," trans. Joseph F. Graham, in *Psyche*, ed. Peggy Kamuf and Elizabeth Rottenberg, trans. Joseph F. Graham, vol. 1 (Stanford, Calif.: Stanford University Press, 2007), 191–92. Elsewhere, Derrida observes that "the words *deux, two, zwei* are the same only each in its own language: . . . they remain bound to a language" (*The Beast and the Sovereign*, ed. Michel Lisse, Marie-Louise Mallet, and Ginette Michaud, trans. Geoffrey Bennington, vol. 1 [Chicago: University of Chicago Press, 2009], 178).
38. Ibid., 198.
39. Derrida, *Positions*, 19.
40. Derrida, *Monolingualism*, 57.
41. Derrida, *Psyche*, 199.
42. Jacques Derrida, "What Is a 'Relevant' Translation?," trans. Lawrence Venuti, *Critical Inquiry* 27 (2001): 174.
43. See Jacques Derrida (with Pierre-Jean Labarrière), *Altérités* (Paris: Osiris, 1986), 85.
44. Jacques Derrida, *The Beast and the Sovereign*, ed. Michel Lisse, Marie-Louise Mallet, and Ginette Michaud, trans. Geoffrey Bennington, vol. 2 (Chicago: University of Chicago Press, 2011), 9.
45. Aliette Armel, "Du mot à la vie: Un dialogue entre Jacques Derrida et Hélène Cixous," *Magazine littéraire*, April 2004, 26.
46. Jacques Derrida, *Paper Machine*, trans. Rachel Bowlby (Stanford, Calif.: Stanford University Press, 2005), 140. This text is the English version of an interview with Antoine Spire.
47. Derrida, *Of Grammatology*, 162.
48. See, e.g., Catherine Malabou and Jacques Derrida, *Counterpath*, trans. David Wills (Stanford, Calif.: Stanford University Press, 2004), 54. Indeed, Derrida refuted the ascription of the label "Heideggerian" (*Paper Machine*, 149–50).
49. Derrida, *Positions*, 48.

50. Ibid., 8.

51. Martin Heidegger, *Being and Time*, rev. trans. Joan Stambaugh (Albany: State University of New York Press, 2010), sec. 32, pp. 145–46.

52. Martin Heidegger, [letter to Karl Löwith], in *Zur philosophischen Aktualität Heideggers*, ed. Dietrich Papenfuss and Otto Pöggeler, vol. 2 (Frankfurt: Klostermann, 1990), 29.

53. Derrida, *Margins*, 111.

54. Alan Bass, "Translator's Introduction," in Jacques Derrida, *Writing and Difference*, trans. Alan Bass (Chicago: University of Chicago Press, 1978), xiv.

55. In continental Europe, most legal terms used in modern political philosophy come from a transcription into vernacular languages of words issuing from Roman law and from Roman law's reception in medieval Europe. Although such transcriptions have been accompanied by important inflections of the ancient meanings, translation practices have proved stable enough throughout continental Europe for foundational terms like *jus* and *lex* to find local renditions—such as *droit* and *loi* in French—giving effect to the basic distinction between, very roughly, the legal order (as in "according to French *droit*, three conditions are required for the formation of a valid contract") and the output of the legislative authority (as in "the recent *loi* on immigration aims to curb the arrival of economic migrants"). Thus, *loi* enjoys a narrower extension than *droit*, being one source of *droit* only, albeit traditionally by far the principal one. Where French has two words, *droit* and *loi*, to convey two different ideas, English has settled for amphibology inasmuch as it has long featured exclusively the word *law* to cater to both configurations (earlier, the language had oscillated between *ley*, *lay*, and even *dreit*).

56. Derrida, *Monolingualism*, 57.

57. In his first text expressly devoted to law, Derrida addressed the Frenchness of *loi*. See Jacques Derrida, "Before the Law," trans. Avital Ronell and Christine Roulston, in Jacques Derrida, *Acts of Literature*, ed. Derek Attridge (London: Routledge, 1992), 206.

58. I borrow the formulation of the paradox from Spivak, "Translator's Preface," lxxxvi.

59. Jacques Derrida, *Writing and Difference*, trans. Alan Bass (Chicago: University of Chicago Press, 1978), 293; my emphasis.

60. While my argument does not require me to address the matter of patterning at any length, I accept that "law" does not hold the same meaning for all Anglophone readers within, say, a given geographic area. The opposite contention would be silly.

61. Geoff Bennington and Ian McLeod, "Translators' Preface," in Jacques Derrida, *The Truth in Painting*, trans. Geoff Bennington and Ian McLeod (Chicago: University of Chicago Press, 1987), xiv.

62. Derrida, "Before the Law," 192.

63. Jacques Derrida, "The Law of Genre," trans. Avital Ronell, in Jacques Derrida, *Acts of Literature*, ed. Derek Attridge (London: Routledge, 1992), 221–52; Derrida, "Before the Law."

64. See generally Jacques de Ville, *Jacques Derrida* (London: Routledge, 2011).

65. See Jacques Derrida, "Force of Law: The 'Mystical Foundation of Authority,'" trans. Mary Quaintance, *Cardozo Law Review* 11 (1990): 919. This article also features the French original that was subsequently published in book form as *Force de loi* (Paris: Galilée, 1994). The semantic disjuncture between *law* and *loi* in the two titles is exemplary of the structural impediment I address above.

66. See Derrida, "Force of Law," 929.

67. Ibid., 931. See also Jacques Derrida and Jeffrey Kipnis, afterword to *Chora L Works*, ed. Jeffrey Kipnis and Thomas Leeser (New York: Monacelli, 1997), 167: "Thus architecture, and for similar reasons the law, are the ultimate tests of deconstruction." The words are Derrida's.

68. Derrida, "Force of Law," 943.

69. Derrida, *Points*, 213.

70. Martin Krygier, "Law as Tradition," *Law and Philosophy* 5 (1986): 239, 256.

71. Gerald L. Bruns, *Hermeneutics Ancient and Modern* (New Haven, Conn.: Yale University Press, 1992), 204.

72. For a reflection on "invention," see Jacques Derrida, "Psyche: Invention of the Other," trans. Catherine Porter, in *Psyche*, ed. Peggy Kamuf and Elizabeth Rottenberg, vol. 1 (Stanford, Calif.: Stanford University Press, 2007), 1–47.

73. Derrida, *Specters*, 10.

74. Derrida attempts a translation of the German "es spukt" (ibid., 216).

75. Derrida, *Paper Machine*, 89; my emphasis.

76. The word *hauntology* (*hantologie*) is Derrida's (*Specters*, 10). Studies of Derrida's work on revenants include David Applebaum, *Jacques Derrida's Ghost* (Albany: State University of New York Press, 2009); Michael Sprinker, ed., *Ghostly Demarcations* (London: Verso, 1999); Kas Saghafi, *Apparitions—Of Derrida's Other* (New York: Fordham University Press, 2010).

77. Jacques Derrida and Bernard Stiegler, *Echographies of Television*, trans. Jennifer Bajorek (Cambridge: Polity, 2002), 117.

78. Ibid.

79. Henry Staten, *Wittgenstein and Derrida* (Lincoln: University of Nebraska Press, 1986), 18. See generally Jacques Derrida, "Living On," trans. James Hulbert, in Harold Bloom, Paul de Man, Jacques Derrida, Geoffrey H. Hartman, and J. Hillis Miller, *Deconstruction and Criticism* (New York: Continuum, 2004), 67–70.

80. Geoffrey Bennington and Jacques Derrida, *Jacques Derrida*, trans. Geoffrey

Bennington (Chicago: University of Chicago Press, 1993), 91. The word is Derrida's, who adds that "the virus will have been the only object of [his] work" (91–92).

81. Jacques Derrida, *Limited Inc*, ed. Gerald Graff, trans. Samuel Weber (Evanston, Ill.: Northwestern University Press, 1988), 146. In his text, Derrida applies this sentence to "truth"—which means that it works for law, at least as conventionally understood by the *doxa*.

82. Derrida, "Force of Law," 1015.

83. Derrida, *Margins*, 80.

84. Derrida, *Positions*, 55.

85. Ibid., 23–24.

86. Ibid., 24. As the mark of otherness, Derrida credits the notion of trace (*trace*) to Emmanuel Levinas. See Jacques Derrida, "Differance," in *Speech and Phenomena*, trans. David B. Allison (Evanston, Ill.: Northwestern University Press, 1973), 152.

87. Derrida, *Dissemination*, 223.

88. Jacques Derrida, *The Other Heading*, trans. Michael B. Naas (Bloomington: Indiana University Press, 1992), 10.

89. Derrida, *Points*, 137; Christopher Johnson, *System and Writing in the Philosophy of Jacques Derrida* (Cambridge: Cambridge University Press, 1993), 29.

90. Derrida, *Specters*, 24.

91. Derrida, "Force of Law," 1035.

92. Derrida, *Grammatology*, 65. No invention of traces by law's interpreters can plausibly be dissociated from autobiographical investments.

93. Derrida, *Dissemination*, 270.

94. J. Hillis Miller, "The Critic as Host," in Harold Bloom, Paul de Man, Jacques Derrida, Geoffrey H. Hartman, and J. Hillis Miller, *Deconstruction and Criticism* (New York: Continuum, 2004), 188.

95. Martin Heidegger, "On the Question of Being," trans. William McNeill, in *Pathmarks*, ed. William McNeill (Cambridge: Cambridge University Press, 1998), 292.

96. Jacques Derrida, *Aporias*, trans. Thomas Dutoit (Stanford, Calif.: Stanford University Press, 1993), 10.

97. For leading arguments on law as culture, see Lawrence Rosen, *Law as Culture* (Princeton, N.J.: Princeton University Press, 2008); and Gary Watt, "Comparative Law as Deep Appreciation," in *Methods of Comparative Law*, ed. Pier G. Monateri (Cheltenham, U.K.: Elgar, 2012), 82–103.

98. *Dictionnaire historique de la langue française*, 2d ed., Alain Rey (Paris: Le Robert, 2010), s.v. "texte." In Latin, a *textor* is a weaver (and *texere* is "to weave"). See *Shorter Oxford English Dictionary*, 6th ed., Angus Stevenson, vol. 2 (Oxford: Oxford University Press, 2007), s.v. "textorial."

99. I track Kelsen's pronouncement in the first edition of his *Reine Rechtslehre*

(Vienna: Deuticke, 1934), 64: "Das Recht gilt nur als positives Recht." For an English version, see Hans Kelsen, *Introduction to the Problems of Legal Theory*, trans. Bonnie L. Paulson and Stanley L. Paulson (Oxford: Oxford University Press, 1992), sec. 28, p. 56: "The law [counts] only as positive law."

100. Jacques Derrida, *The Politics of Friendship*, trans. George Collins (London: Verso, 1997), 153.

101. Derrida, "Force of Law," 947.

102. It is not that the French model disconsiders scholarly interpretation, a revered practice boasting Roman ancestry. Indeed, a leading academic like Michel Troper is willing to grant interpretation a measure of relevance as a source of normative meaning. But in order to earn its warrant, interpretation must unambiguously qualify as conceptual, that is, it must address the refinement—the detersion—of legal concepts.

103. Philippe Jestaz and Christophe Jamin, "L'entité doctrinale française," D.1997.Chron.167–75, 172. Such critique of French legal scholarship by French legal scholars remains unique. It is, in fact, so inhabitual that even these academics' subsequent publications fail to sustain it.

104. For (cursory) theorizations of thoroughgoing judicial subordination, see Christian Atias, *Devenir juriste* (Paris: LexisNexis, 2011), 3, who, having introduced "legal rules" ("règles de droit") as "answers" ("réponses"), writes that "the judge is there to ascertain the right answer and to impose it"; Daniel Gutmann, "Le juge doit respecter la cohérence du droit," in Georges Fauré and Geneviève Koubi, eds., *Le titre préliminaire du Code civil* (Paris: Economica, 2003), 109: "The judge must respect the coherence of the law."

105. Roberto M. Unger, *Knowledge and Politics* (New York: Free Press, 1975), 92–93.

106. See, e.g., W. J. Waluchow, *Inclusive Legal Positivism* (Oxford: Oxford University Press, 1994).

107. In 2000, for instance, Derrida spoke in Mainz (Germany), Cairo, London, Puerto Rico, Irvine (California), Helsinki, Uppsala, Frankfurt, Pecs (Hungary), New York, Albany (New York), Chicago, Milan, Trieste, and Murcia (Spain). As extensive biographical notes make clear, this peripateticism repeated itself year after year as of the early 1990s. See [Marie-Louise Mallet and Ginette Michaud], "Repères biographiques," in *Jacques Derrida*, ed. Marie-Louise Mallet and Ginette Michaud (Paris: L'Herne, 2004), 601–6.

108. In a conversation with Michel Rosenfeld published in the Fall 1998 issue of *Cardozo Life*, Derrida said: "My interest in law as an academic discipline started very early." He also asserted that "[he] never acted on [his] dream to really study law." For the transcript, see "An Interview with Jacques Derrida," http://hydra.humanities.uci.edu/derrida/law.html (accessed January 14, 2018).

109. After the first German edition of Kelsen's book had appeared in 1934, the French translation, featuring input by Kelsen himself, was published in 1953 as *Théorie pure du droit*, trans. Henri Thévenaz (Neuchâtel: La Baconnière, 1953). The second German edition dated 1960 was released in French in 1962 (the translation having been revised by Kelsen): *Théorie pure du droit*, 2nd ed., trans. Charles Eisenmann (Paris: Dalloz, 1962). Thévenaz later published a further translation of the second German edition incorporating a number of post-1960 changes: *Théorie pure du droit*, 2nd ed., trans. Henri Thévenaz (Neuchâtel: La Baconnière, 1988).

110. See generally Fritz Schulz, *History of Roman Legal Science* (Oxford: Oxford University Press, 1946); Peter Stein, "The Quest for a Systematic Civil Law," in *Proceedings of the British Academy* 90 (1996): 147–64; Lelio Lantella, *Il lavoro sistematico nel discorso giuridico romano* (Turin: Giappichelli, 1975); Witold Wołodkiewicz, *Les origines romaines de la systématique du droit contemporain* (Wrocław: Ossolineum, 1978); Henry Goudy, *Trichotomy in Roman Law* (Oxford: Oxford University Press, 1910). The contemporary French predilection is epitomized in Jean-Louis Bergel, *Méthodologie juridique* (Paris: Presses Universitaires de France, 2001), 34: "Law is uncontrovertibly a science." Indeed, a leading French theoretician observes that "the assertion of the scientificity of [l]aw . . . has become a truism" (André-Jean Arnaud, *Les juristes face à la société* [Paris: Presses Universitaires de France, 1975], p. 195; emphasis omitted).

111. For a famous sixteenth-century French law professor, "the elements of law, the bases of its maxims and of its fundamental problems are like the points, the lines, and the surfaces in geometry" (François Le Douaren, *In primam partem Pandectarum, sive Digestorum, methodica enarratio* [1561], in *Opera omnia*, vol. 1 [Lucca, 1765], 3). The same idea appears in a late twentieth-century French introduction to legal methodology where the author claims that "ideally, *of course*, the solution to any litigation would be mathematically deduced from clearly defined legal rules" (E. S. de la Marnierre, *Eléments de méthodologie juridique* [Paris: Librairie du Journal des notaires et des avocats, 1976], sec. 91, pp. 193–94; my emphasis). For an analogy between the French doctoral dissertation in law and mathematics, see Philippe Jestaz and Christophe Jamin, *La doctrine* (Paris: Dalloz, 2004), 186.

112. On Ramus, see Nelly Bruyère, *Méthode et dialectique dans l'oeuvre de La Ramée* (Paris: Vrin, 1984); Walter J. Ong, *Ramus, Method, and the Decay of Dialogue* (Cambridge, Mass.: Harvard University Press, 1983).

113. The uncontested prevalence of Kelsenism on the French jurisprudential stage can be shown by the fact that the author of a general introduction to legal theory published in the best-known "pocket-book" series in France confines himself to a discussion of Kelsen. Out of the 128 pages of text (the iconic length of books in the series) and in terms of those pages that one can access electronically, the website Amazon.fr thus informs me that the name "Kelsen" appears 44 times (accessed

November 1, 2015). I can supply a TIFF screen capture confirming this information. Meanwhile, economic analysis of law, critical legal studies, and feminist legal studies are omitted. See Michel Troper, *La Philosophie du droit*, 4th ed. (Paris: Presses Universitaires de France, 2015). "Natural law" is the only other theory benefiting from any kind of entitlement to serious intellectual consideration on the French scene. Like positivism, it applies a paradigm seeking to contain law within a logic of authority—an unsurprising fact in the French context. See Roger Cotterrell, *The Politics of Jurisprudence*, 2nd ed. (London: Lexis Nexis, 2003), 120.

114. Michel van de Kerchove, "L'influence de Kelsen sur les théories du droit dans l'Europe francophone," in Kelsen, *Théorie pure* [1988], 227–29.

115. Michel Villey, "Préface," in J[oseph] Miedzianagora, *Philosophies positivistes et droit positif* (Paris: L.G.D.J., 1970), i–ii (emphasis omitted).

116. Georges Vedel, "Eloge," *Annales de l'Université de Paris* (1963), 552.

117. Atias, *Devenir juriste*, 55.

118. Laurent Aynès, Pierre-Yves Gautier, and François Terré, "Antithèse de 'l'entité,'" D.1997.Chron.229–30, 230. These writers were reacting to Jestaz and Jamin's diatribe ("L'entité doctrinale française"). For samples of Domat's statements on "law-as-geometry," see Jean Domat, *Les quatre livres du droit public* (1697; repr. Caen: Université de Caen, 1989), 1.17.307; Domat, *Les loix civiles dans leur ordre naturel* (Paris, 1689), "preface." On Domat's mathematics, see André-Jean Arnaud, *Les origines doctrinales du code civil français* (Paris: L.G.D.J., 1969), 142–47.

119. Thus began the description of *Derrida and Legal Philosophy*, ed. Peter Goodrich, Florian Hoffmann, Michel Rosenfeld, and Cornelia Vismann (New York: Palgrave Macmillan, 2008) when I visited the publisher's website on April 1, 2008. Later, the word *legalistic* was replaced by *jurisprudential*, which can also be found on the back cover of the published book. Until they closed their doors on September 18, 2011, the booksellers Borders retained the early formulation for their website. I can supply a PDF copy of this text dated July 1, 2011.

120. Derrida, *Paper Machine*, 176.

121. Jacques Derrida, *Who's Afraid of Philosophy?*, trans. Jan Plug (Stanford, Calif.: Stanford University Press, 2002), 46.

122. I draw on Adolfo Barberá del Rosal, "Derrida et le positivisme (juridique)," in *Le passage des frontières*, ed. Marie-Louise Mallet (Paris: Galilée, 1994), 387–90.

123. See Derrida, "Force of Law," 973. Derrida refutes "the sphere of pure, immune law, intact, not contaminable by everything we would want to purify it of" (Jacques Derrida and Elisabeth Roudinesco, *For What Tomorrow . . .*, trans. Jeff Fort [Stanford, Calif.: Stanford University Press, 2004], 150).

124. Jacques Derrida, *Memoires for Paul de Man*, rev. trans. Cecile Lindsay (New York: Columbia University Press, 1989), 15. The words "plus d'une langue" appear in French in the English text. The periphrasis is added to the English version.

125. Kelsen, *Introduction*, sec. 8, p. 16.

126. Ibid.

127. See Derrida, "Force of Law," 943. Law denies its contingency. In Derrida's words, "to be invested with its categorical authority, the law must be without history, without genesis, or without any possible derivation" ("Before the Law," 19). Derrida makes the point more pithily still: "The story of prohibition is a prohibited story" (200).

128. See Derrida, "Force of Law," 945.

129. See ibid., 947, 963.

130. Ibid., 959. The reference is to Emmanuel Levinas, *Totality and Infinity*, trans. Alphonso Lingis (Pittsburgh: Duquesne University Press, 1969), 89: "The relation with the Other, that is, to justice."

131. Derrida, *Specters*, 26.

132. "One cannot speak *directly* about justice" (Derrida, "Force of Law," 935).

133. Ibid., 969.

134. In Derrida's language, justice is caught in the net of "differance," that is, of the infinitely deferred and ever different.

135. Derrida, "Force of Law," 971.

136. Derrida, *Specters*, 26. For the phrase "child of Domat," see Aynès, Gautier, and Terré, "Antithèse," 230.

137. Derrida, "Force of Law," 965.

138. Ibid.

139. I paraphrase Jacques Derrida, *Rogues*, trans. Pascale-Anne Brault and Michael Naas (Stanford, Calif.: Stanford University Press, 2005), 150.

140. See, e.g., Derrida, *Grammatology*, 95–316.

141. Derrida, "Force of Law," 945.

142. Ibid.

143. See Pierre-Yves Quiviger, "Derrida: de la philosophie au droit," *Cités*, no. 30 (2007): 41–52.

144. "Ethics, politics, and responsibility . . . will only ever have begun with the experience and experiment of the aporia" (Derrida, *Other Heading*, 41).

145. Derrida, "Force of Law," 925.

146. Ibid.

147. Ibid., 989.

148. See Pascal, *Pensées*, trans. A. J. Krailsheimer, 2nd ed. (London: Penguin, 1995), sec. 135, pp. 200–1. Pascal's text initially appeared posthumously in 1670.

149. Derrida, "Force of Law," 925.

150. Kelsen, *Introduction*, sec. 30(b), p. 61: "The law is . . . a certain system (or organization) of power."

151. See Derrida, *Writing and Difference*, 21: "Force . . . [is] meaning itself." See

also ibid., 125, where Derrida refers to the fact that force is "embedded in the root of meaning and logos."

152. Ibid.: "'The structural fact thus described . . . appears as a constant.'" Derrida appropriates these words from Jean Rousset (1910–2002), a Swiss literary critic.

153. Derrida, *Grammatology*, 112.

154. See ibid., 148.

155. Ibid., 110.

156. See Derrida, *Writing and Difference*, 147.

157. Derrida, *Grammatology*, 112.

158. Paul Ricoeur, *Freedom and Nature*, trans. Erazim V. Kohak (Evanston, Ill.: Northwestern University Press, 1966), 174.

159. This is not to say, though, that a position spontaneously partakes in originality. It is embedded and, as such, it is "a call for self-conserving repetition," which means that, ultimately, there is "no rigorous opposition between positioning and conservation" (Derrida, "Force of Law," 997).

160. See ibid., 961: "Each case is other, each decision is different and requires an absolutely unique interpretation, which no existing and codified rule can or ought to guarantee absolutely."

161. Werner Hamacher, "Afformative, Strike," trans. Dana Hollander, *Cardozo Law Review* 13 (1991): 1134.

162. Derrida, *Writing and Difference*, 147.

163. Derrida thus writes of "pure violence" that it is "a relationship between beings without face" (ibid., 146).

164. Derrida, "Force of Law," 997.

165. Derrida, *Writing and Difference*, 117.

166. Derrida, "Force of Law," 955.

167. Derrida, *Dissemination*, 316.

168. Derrida, "Force of Law," 943.

169. Ibid., 995.

170. Ibid.

171. Ibid., 1035.

172. Derrida, *Writing and Difference*, 117.

173. Deconstruction's violence can also arise from the fact that it is situated: "What I call 'deconstruction,' . . . is European; it is a product of Europe, a relation of Europe to itself as an experience of radical alterity" (Derrida, *Learning to Live*, 44–45).

174. Jacques Derrida and Maurizio Ferraris, *A Taste for the Secret*, ed. Giacomo Donis and David Webb, trans. Giacomo Donis (Cambridge: Polity, 2001), 92. The words are Derrida's.

175. Jacques Derrida, *The Post Card*, trans. Alan Bass (Chicago: University of Chicago Press, 1987), 232.

176. Jacques Derrida, "Envoi," trans. Peter Caws and Mary Ann Caws, in *Psyche*, ed. Peggy Kamuf and Elizabeth Rottenberg, vol. 1 (Stanford, Calif.: Stanford University Press, 2007), 128.

177. Derrida, *Positions*, 77.

178. Derrida, *Aporias*, 52.

179. Derrida, "Force of Law," 925.

180. Pierre Legendre, *Le désir politique de Dieu* (Paris: Fayard, 1988), 295.

181. Jean-Luc Nancy, *The Experience of Freedom*, trans. Bridget McDonald (Stanford, Calif.: Stanford University Press, 1993), 186.

182. Derrida, *Post Card*, 180. The French is "ne fait pas la loi," an idiomatic expression that could also be translated as "does not rule."

183. Derrida, *Dissemination*, 18.

184. See Barberá del Rosal, "Derrida et le positivisme (juridique)," 390–91.

185. Derrida, "Living On," 67.

186. Derrida, "Force of Law," 1009.

187. Derrida, *Margins*, 377.

188. Using the lemma "iter," which he claims to derive from the Sanskrit *itara*, meaning "other," Derrida coins "iterability," a neologism connoting both "reiteration" and "alterity," that is, repeatability with a difference, which entails that repetition does not cancel singularity. See ibid., 314–21.

189. Jacques Derrida, "This Strange Institution Called Literature," in *Acts of Literature*, ed. Derek Attridge (London: Routledge, 1992), 66.

190. Derrida, "Force of Law," 1009.

191. Derrida, *Grammatology*, 158.

192. Jacques Derrida, "Fidélité à plus d'un," *Cahiers Intersignes*, no. 13 (1998): 262.

193. Derrida, *Positions*, 76.

194. Michael Sprinker, "Politics and Friendship: An Interview with Jacques Derrida," in *The Althusserian Legacy*, ed. E. Ann Kaplan and Michael Sprinker (London: Verso, 1993), 212. The words are Derrida's.

195. De Ville, *Jacques Derrida*, 165.

196. Richard J. Bernstein, *The New Constellation* (Cambridge, Mass.: MIT Press, 1991), 176.

197. Terry Eagleton, *Literary Theory*, 3rd ed. (Minneapolis: University of Minnesota Press, 2008), 128.

198. David Wills, *Matchbook* (Stanford, Calif.: Stanford University Press, 2005), 13.

199. Jacques Derrida, *Voice and Phenomenon*, trans. Leonard Lawlor (Evanston, Ill.: Northwestern University Press, 2011), 73.

200. Derrida, *Limited*, 137.

201. This expression, which Derrida presses into service in a variety of settings,

always in English *dans le texte*, is indebted to Gregory Bateson, who coined the phrase in 1956 as an explanation partaking in the etiology of schizophrenia but more broadly to illustrate the complexities of communication. See Gregory Bateson, *Steps to an Ecology of Mind* (Chicago: University of Chicago Press, 1972), 201–27.

202. Derrida, *Post Card*, 389. Miller reports that there are two meanings of the word "trace" in English that suggest "connection." For Miller, "the trace is a hinge": J. Hillis Miller, "Trace," in *Reading Derrida's* Of Grammatology, ed. Sean Gaston and Ian Maclachlan (New York: Continuum, 2011), 51.

203. Jacques Derrida, "Abraham, the Other," trans. Gil Anidjar, in *Religion*, ed. Hent de Vries (New York: Fordham University Press, 2008), 318, 327.

6

Derrida's Legal Times
Decision, Declaration, Deferral, and Event

Bernadette Meyler

Testimony, the history and theory of sovereignty, the juridico-political form of the death penalty, the politics of life, and the dynamics of perjury all figure in the late seminars of Jacques Derrida.[1] These preoccupations echo those of Michel Foucault's seminars at the Collège de France during the final years of his life, when he examined punishment, sovereignty, governmentality, biopolitics, and truth telling (*parrésia*).[2] Although Derrida rarely considered Foucault's work explicitly,[3] the influence of the topics that troubled Foucault during the 1970s and early 1980s seems evident throughout Derrida's more explicitly political writings from the 1990s until his death in 2004.[4]

To the extent that European critical theory influenced the American legal academy via the critical legal studies movement and its aftermaths, however, it has tended to be Foucault (and, more recently, his inheritance in the writings of Giorgio Agamben) who has affected the discussion of the relation between law and politics and the power relations at the heart of the juridical.[5] Derrida's earlier essay "The Force of Law" spawned some commentary, but his work was largely valued in legal circles for its explication of the indeterminacy of language and for the inversion of binaries, which legal scholars took as a source of ideology critique.[6]

The aim of this essay is to suggest what a return—or simply a turn—to Derrida's later forays into law and politics might contribute to thinking in legal theory beyond what can be derived from Foucault and his inheritors. The key differences, I contend, pertain to time and timing. In particular, Derrida's writings lead us to reconsider the timing of the relation between the subject and the law, whether that subject is declaring independence or awaiting death. Through the vector of time, the trace of the subject—certainly not self-present or autonomous, but a subject nonetheless—is recovered within the juridico-political sphere.[7]

A late interview with Derrida himself—the dialogue with Élisabeth Roudinesco published as *For What Tomorrow*—indicates that it is precisely time that separates Derrida's thought from Foucault's. As Roudinesco glosses the "Cogito" essay's critique, Derrida "reproach[es] Foucault for constituting an event as a structure."[8] Derrida then takes up the point Roudinesco raised:

> What has always left me a little perplexed with Foucault, beyond the debate on the *cogito*, is that while I understand very well the necessity of making divisions, ruptures, and passages from one *episteme* to another, at the same time I have always had the impression that this risked making him less attentive to long sequences. . . . Foucault's typical gesture consists in hardening into an opposition a more complicated play of differences that stretches along a more extended time. To schematize in the extreme, I would say that Foucault sets up as ruptures and binary oppositions a range of more complex differences. For example, the couple visibility/invisibility in *Discipline and Punish*. While I recognize the relative legitimacy of this analysis, according to certain limited criteria, I would be tempted to say that in the evolution of punishments, we shift not from the visible to the invisible but rather from one visibility to another, more virtual one.[9]

One might argue in response that Foucault's schemas are precisely schemas and, as Foucault himself acknowledges, that the historical trajectory Foucault traces is also a conceptual one.[10] Despite this potential quibble with Derrida's diagnosis of Foucault, this passage marks a significant difference between the two thinkers, pointing up the salience of time for Derrida's own analyses and, critically here, his analyses of the juridico-political sphere.

At the conclusion of his first seminar on "the beast and the sovereign,"

Derrida extends his critique of Foucault to the latter's inheritance in Agamben's *Homo Sacer*. Noting that both ignore Martin Heidegger—a crucial figure whenever time is concerned—Derrida questions the extent to which Agamben, like Foucault, posits a "decisive event of modernity."[11] Referring to both Foucault and Agamben, Derrida states that "the difficulties [their texts] encounter . . . compel us . . . to reconsider, precisely, a way of thinking history, of doing history, of articulating a logic and a rhetoric onto a thinking of history or the event."[12]

These discussions of time reveal two views of history—one marked by ruptures and distinct *epistemes* and the other characterized more by hidden continuities and repetitions. These disparate stances on history are not disconnected from Derrida's account of the temporality of the subject. Indeed, in Derrida's work, the subject's temporal experience of the juridico-political pervades historical inquiry. Hence in "Cogito and the History of Madness" itself Derrida critiques both Foucault's domestication of René Descartes as excluding madness from Descartes's own subjectivity and his attempt to make madness "the *subject* of his book in every sense of the word," not realizing that "*nothing* within language, and *no one*, among those who speak it, can escape the historical guilt" of "the act perpetrated against madness."[13] Foucault's treatment of madness is, thus, guilty of a double erasure, eliding the non-self-presence of Descartes's own consciousness and Foucault's own implication within the history he recounts.

Focusing primarily (although not exclusively) on Derrida's later and more explicitly political writings, the remainder of this essay analyzes some of the concepts most salient to Derrida's account of the temporality of the juridico-political. In doing so, it puts into circulation the question of what law might look like if it were based on the premise of a subject who did not wish to escape time and whose time was never his or her own but should only be taken with the utmost seriousness.

Four temporally inflected terms—decision, declaration, deferral, and event—bear a particular weight in Derrida's discussions of the juridico-political and form a sort of constellation. They assist in understanding the Derridean account of political forms like sovereignty and democracy, among other more specifically legal phenomena, like the death penalty. While the precise relationship between the legal and political in Derrida's work is so complex that it would merit another essay, it would be a mistake to separate the two rigorously, as Derrida often dwells on their complicated imbrication. Indeed, it is perhaps the narrowness of the construction of what is properly within the legal domain that has prevented Derrida's later work from being fully recognized in American legal circles.

DECISION

Many of Derrida's late writings circle the decision in the sense Carl Schmitt gave it, attempting to displace the sovereign who decides on the exception.[14] As John McCormick's analysis of "The Force of Law" essay demonstrates, a similar preoccupation appeared already in that piece. As McCormick argues, countering the accusation that, in "The Force of Law," Derrida reveals the decisionism at the heart of his theory—one that is continuous with that of Heidegger and Schmitt—the essay's aim is instead to "point out the authoritarianism latent in Western political philosophy and . . . raise[] the possibility of a justice even *less* decisionistic than the purportedly rational one elevated by the Enlightenment."[15]

Consistent with this account, Derrida's subsequent work often criticizes the temporal structure of the sovereign decision. Hence, in the discussion of the genealogy of democracy toward the beginning of *Rogues: Two Essays on Reason*, Derrida insists on the myth of Zeus's killing of Cronos as the source of a particular vision of sovereignty. As Derrida writes:

> Zeus is first of all a son, a male child and a descendant who, by means of a ruse, but also with the help of his mother, manages to escape time [i.e., Cronos]. . . . It is by winning out over time, by putting an end to the infinite order of time, so to speak, that he asserts his sovereignty. One might take this formulation to the extreme, to the point where it touches the end of time, touches the finitude or the finity of time, touches sovereignty as the instant of a decision that, at the indivisible point of its action, puts an end to time, as well as to language.[16]

In this instance, the sovereign decision is not suspect simply to the extent that it is monarchical. Instead, as Derrida elaborates, "This political theogony or theology gets taken over . . . even by the unavowed political theology . . . of the sovereignty of the people, that is, of democratic sovereignty."[17] Whether the decision of the monarch or the "people," this decision refers back only to itself; it is self-contained, or what Derrida terms "ipsocentric," closing the circle of the self or selves into the micro-circle of the point of decision.

In this chapter, "The Free Wheel," the circle as reduced to the punctum seems not so far from the wheel on which bodies are racked. Another possibility of democracy emerges from the figure of the ellipsis—denoting, as figure, a certain omission, but also invoking the geometry of the ellipse, extending the circle through a new focal point. As the first paragraph of *Rogues* reads, "For a certain sending [*envoi*] that awaits us, I imagine an economic formalization, a very elliptical phrase, in both senses of the word *ellipsis*. For *ellipsis* names not only lack but a curved figure with more than one focus. We are thus already between the 'minus one' and the 'more than one.'"[18] If Zeus cut off time with the figure of a self-present decision, the ellipsis revisits time after its demise. According to Derrida, "The elliptical sending would arrive by e-mail, and we would read: '*The democracy to come: it is necessary that it give the time there is not.*'"[19] In the world after Cronos, there is no time, yet the democracy to come displaces the decision that has supplanted time. On the other side of the sovereign decision, time is not, but must be given.

From another perspective as well, the violence of the sovereign decision is that of time, the time of the deadline marked by the death penalty. In the first seminar on the death penalty, Derrida emphasizes the manner in which that punishment distorts the subject's relation to time; one of the principal cruelties of the death penalty is, he insists, the fact that the subject's death is known in advance (even if not to himself or herself), and that that death is the object of another's calculation. As he writes, "If there is some torture, torturing, cruelty in the process of the condemnation to death, what is most cruel, and the cruel itself, . . . is indeed, beyond anything, . . . the experience of time."[20] The torture consists partly in the insistence on the correspondence between what Derrida designates objective and subjective time. The legal system and its apparatus, in administering the death penalty, maintains a "knowledge of death," which is "a presumed knowledge on the subject of time and of the coincidence between objective time and let us say the subjective time of the subject condemned to death and executed."[21]

The anticipation and knowledge of the time of death is not the only distinguishing temporal feature of the death penalty. As Derrida demonstrates, even those attempting to improve the death penalty and avoid inhumanity insist on time as the crucial feature, reducing the time death takes to an instant. Under Derrida's account, the "two themes" of "instantaneity and anesthesia, the almost intemporal instantaneity and insensibility, non-pain, non-cruelty, even gentleness—are indissociable."[22] The guillotine is presented as conferring a new benefit because of the illusion that it can render death instantaneous—an instantaneity that Albert Camus's "Réflections sur la guillotine" refutes. Reversing the usual logical order—that one must think death and then the death penalty—Derrida suggests that some notion of the death penalty, in its insistence on the moment of death, infects all thought of death: "The simple idea of this limit between life and death organizes all these meditations, whether classic or less classic, even revolutionary, even those of a deconstruction, of a 'destructio' in Luther's or in Heidegger's sense at least."[23]

When punishment is reprieved and the death penalty averted, the gift of the pardon is the gift of time: "The pardon [la grâce] gives time, and the only 'thing' that can be given graciously is time, that is to say, at once nothing and everything."[24] Just as democracy must give the time that is not, the pardon too gives time.

The self-presence of the sovereign decision finds its echo in the illusory limit between life and death; the power over life and death that the sovereign claims to wield here turns out to be a putative capacity to eliminate duration and to stop time. The aspiration to the instant here seems the mirror image of the thought of eternity, that, as Martin Hägglund has shown, Derrida again and again critiqued; operating from different ends of the spectrum, each brings an end to duration.

Sovereignty—whether that of the people or the monarch—insists both on its capacity for instantaneous decision and its ability to decide on and, ultimately, *know* the instant of another's death. In that sense, the overthrow of Cronos could be seen as the origin of the death penalty. By contrast, another nonsovereign decision on the undecidable emerges out of the disassociation of sovereignty and unconditionality.

Returning to Foucault, it is not incidental that Derrida refers to his work several times in relation to the death penalty, mentioning at the end of the first seminar on "the beast and the sovereign" that Foucault suggests "that some decline of the death penalty is principally to be explained by the new advent <of biopolitics> (which Foucault dates to the end of the classical age)"[25] and reading the long opening passage of *Discipline and Punish* describing the execution of Damien the regicide toward the beginning of the seminar on "the death penalty." Foucault's work—and by extension Agamben's—de-emphasizes the death penalty while insisting on the biopolitical constitution of modernity. This shift both displaces the temporal questions that Derrida diagnoses at the heart of the death penalty and generates its own artificial limit marking modernity.

Rather than overwrite the paradigm of sovereignty with another, Derrida insists that the constitutive problems of sovereignty remain, including that of the decision, with its temporal implications. It would be a mistake, however, to construe this diagnosis of the ineradicability of the problem of sovereignty with approval, as Vincent Leitch appears to do in his essay "Late Derrida: The Politics of Sovereignty."[26] In Leitch's view of Derrida:

> A responsible decision stems from the sovereign subject, who makes an impossible mad leap. Such pure decision starkly opposes the ordinary variety, leaving us in a jam (each time permanently). Whereas earlier Derrida dreamt of forgiveness without sovereignty, here he projects an ideal responsibility dependent on sovereignty. What's it going to be? Sometimes a sovereigntist, sometimes an antisovereigntist.[27]

Here Leitch confuses Derrida's insistence that one must not avoid decision—even on the undecidable—with a valorization of the sovereign decision. Whereas the sovereign decision would attempt to impose on the world, or the body of the condemned, a knowledge claimed to be arrived at in advance, the deconstructive decision assumes responsibility without epistemological grounding.

Derrida gestured in this direction in a 1998 interview in South Africa, where he claimed:

> Deconstruction is more and more a way of thinking what responsibility and decision should be. Decision and responsibility worthy of these names should not be controlled by previous knowledge, it should not be programmed. This does not mean that we have given up knowledge. Not at all, on the contrary, we have to know all that we can know. But we should also know and think that between the act of knowledge, between science and the act itself, the decision, there will be a gap, there is a heterogeneity between knowing and doing. . . . Simply, in order for a decision to be a decision it has to go through a moment where, irrespective of what you know, you make a leap into the decision. This leap into the responsibility is an infinite one and you take a decision only in a situation when there is something undecidable, when you don't know what to do.[28]

The notion of the "moment" appears again in this passage, here the moment "you make a leap into the decision." What, one might ask, distinguishes this from the moment of sovereign decision? In one respect, the dislocation of knowledge and action here—the mirror image of the other's knowledge of the condemned man's moment of death—disrupts the unity of the moment of decision. The decision referred to here is not the decision of a subject who is assumed capable of deciding, based on a judgment reached, but rather a taking of a step into the abyss.[29]

In another respect, it may be time itself that differentiates them. As Hägglund points out: "Derrida's argument is that there can be no justice without . . . decisions, which are precipitated by the undecidable coming of time. Justice is thus essentially a matter of temporal finitude, since it is ultimately because of temporal finitude that one has to make decisions."[30] Because the subject is situated in time, failing to decide on the undecidable does not pause movement but constitutes an implicit decision not to act; the decision is not the act of a sovereign taking control of the movement of time and pressing pause but the manifestation of a subject caught, suffering, and enjoying the experience of time.

DECLARATION

A short early prelude to a talk, "Declarations of Independence," points the way toward a version of the democratic people that avoids what Derrida in *Rogues* dubs the "ipsocentric."[31] On one level, the analysis of the Declaration of Independence rehearses the by-now-familiar indistinction of the performative and the constative. Only by the signature of the Declaration does the fact that the Declaration announces come into being; the document's temporality hence "articulates and conjoins two discursive modalities, the to be and the ought to be, the constation and the prescription, the fact and the right."[32] It is only in the name of God, of God as "the name, the best one" of "the instance of judgment, . . . the last instance for saying the fact *and* the law,"[33] that the Declaration can be pronounced. God is the fiction or fable that authorizes the merging of fact and law in the form of the judgment.

A final turn of the essay renders the situation more complicated, however. Derrida asks why Thomas Jefferson, as representative of his fellow revolutionaries, and ultimately of the people themselves, suffered.[34] Apparently he felt wounded at having his text cut. Derrida repeats the story of Ben Franklin consoling Jefferson through another fable, that of a hatter. The first version of the sign for the hatter's store read "John Thompson, hatter, makes and sells hats for ready money." Following the intervention of his friends, there remains only a picture of a hat underwritten with the name "John

Thompson." This story—elliptically furnishing an explanation for the necessity and value of abbreviation—is one to which we never hear a response. This second fable bolsters the legitimacy of a document that turns out to be a source of ambivalence for the designated representative—Jefferson.

As Derrida speculates about Jefferson's response to the story, he states that "I imagine it as strongly undecided. The story [*récit*] reflected his unhappiness but also his greatest desire. Taken as a whole, a complete and total effacement of his text would have been better, leaving in place, under a map of the United States, only the nudity of his proper name; instituting text, founding act and signing energy."[35] The fantasy of the reduction of the Declaration to a signature with a map (sovereignty and territoriality, one might almost say) seems like the reduction of time to the point of the sovereign decision, yet, as it turns out, that reduction is impossible with respect to the Declaration. The Declaration remains both the signature of the representative and a text that was not exactly the one designed by that representative; in the difference between those two things lies a distinction of significance to American—and other—law, a distinction between the social compact supposedly authorizing the polity and its constitution and the meaning of that text itself.

The gap between knowledge and decision is here echoed in the divide between the declaration and what is declared, a divide that carries implications for how we understand founding documents in America and elsewhere. Jacques de Ville has suggested the significance of Derrida's account for constitutional interpretation:

> Constitutional democracy should no longer be viewed in terms of the circular turning of a wheel—the people giving themselves a foundational document in order to rule themselves, giving themselves reason and rights in sovereign fashion. The wheel is also a free wheel, a dissymmetrical contract which does not return to itself. This is indicated by an analysis of the inscription in writing of a constitution, the performative speech act which seems to institute it, its signatures, and its proper names.[36]

Within the U.S. constitutional context, social contract reasoning has proved a powerful underpinning for originalist constitutional interpretation. Derrida's essay on the Declaration of Independence points the way toward the possibility of a form of interpretation that would neither dispense with examination of the putative founding moment nor insist on the closed circle of democracy.[37]

DEFERRAL

Deferral takes us from origin to future, from the undecided response of the founder whose founding may have misfired to the "democracy to come" (*à venir,* punning on *avenir,* or "future") that Derrida dwells on in works like *Rogues* and "Passions."[38] In *Rogues,* Derrida links the democracy to come with *différance* as both deferral and a relation to the other. As deferral, the phrase "suggests the incompletion and essential delay, the self-inadequation of every present and presentable democracy, in other words, the interminable adjournment of the present of democracy."[39] Far from naming a state of affairs that will be actualized in the future, democracy to come designates the deferral within the present of democracy itself.[40]

Later in the essay, Derrida elaborates further on the temporal aspects of the democracy to come, designating five foci of his examination. First, democracy to come "translate[s] or call[s] for a militant and interminable political critique.... But, beyond this active and interminable critique, the expression 'democracy to come' takes into account the absolute and intrinsic historicity of the only system that welcomes in itself, in its very concept, that expression of autoimmunity called the right to self-critique and perfectibility."[41] This historicity, which must not be construed teleologically, frustrates the effort to define democracy either as an abstract philosophical concept or as a particular stage within world history.

Second, "This implies another thinking of the event . . . , which is marked in a 'to-come' that, beyond the future (since the democratic demand does not wait), names the coming of *who* comes or of *what* comes to pass."[42] Here Derrida again insists on the difference between a democracy to come and a simple notion of a democracy that will come to pass in the future. The democracy *à venir,* to the extent that it is possible, is a possibility within the present.

Third, the democracy to come extends beyond the nation-state. Fourth, the democracy to come is connected with justice, which itself is identified with a time "out of joint" and "with the interruption of relation, with unbinding, with the infinite secret of the other. All this can indeed seem to threaten a community-oriented or communitarian concept of democratic justice."[43] Recalling both *Specters of Marx* and "Passions," this fourth point emphasizes that the democratic demand for publicity coexists with the secret of the other and even of literature, and that although the democracy to come conjoins democracy with justice, not all notions of democracy do so.

The connection between law and politics—both haunted by the specter of justice—emerges here as well.

And, finally, fifth, the obscurity of the democracy to come is identified with the political question of democracy itself: "For 'democracy to come' can hesitate endlessly, oscillate indecidably and forever, between two possibilities: it can, on the one hand, correspond to the neutral, constative analysis of a concept. . . . But, on the other hand, no longer satisfied to remain at the level of a neutral, constative conceptual analysis, 'democracy to come' can also inscribe a performative and attempt to win conviction by suggesting support or adherence. . . . The *to* of the 'to come' wavers between imperative injunction (call or performative) and the patient *perhaps* of messianicity."[44] The democracy to come hence both calls on us to realize it and asks us to wait for an event that we cannot anticipate.

Under this account, the subject of democracy is neither a self-present founder or decider nor an individual subsumed within a communitarian unity but instead someone who both responds to the imperative of a democracy to come and is open to whatever events or arrivals may occur. Crucially, the phrase *democracy to come* not only describes but is also addressed to the subject of democracy, who is situated in a temporality from which he or she cannot escape.

EVENT

As I have shown, for Derrida, the democracy to come requires "another thinking of the event." Another than what, or than whose account, we might ask; Alain Badiou, the contemporary philosopher most associated with the event, is certainly a possibility,[45] but I would like to recall here that it is also precisely with respect to the event that Derrida (as glossed by Roudinesco) took issue with Foucault.

Derrida's reflection on the event draws together his critiques of the decision and declaration as well as his response to Foucault and Agamben. In his seminar, "The Beast and the Sovereign," Derrida claimed:

> I'm tempted to think that this singularity of the event is all the more
> irreducible and confusing, as it should be, if we give up that linear
> history which remains, in spite of all the protests they would no doubt
> raise against this image, the common temptation of both Foucault and
> Agamben . . . —if we give up this linear history, the idea of a decisive

and founding event (especially if we try to rethink and reevaluate the enduring and aporetic experience of what "decision" means in the logic of sovereign exception).... To give up the idea of a decisive and founding event is anything but to ignore the eventness that marks and signs, in my view, what happens, precisely without any foundation or decision coming along to make it certain.[46]

Another thinking of the event would hence reject the sovereign decision and the founding moment or the epistemic rupture in favor of something else.

Derrida's late writings often connect the event positively not only with the democracy to come but also with the unconditional, and with the possibility of the unconditional as detached from sovereignty. As Derrida elaborates, the event as he refers to it cannot be confused with a significant moment that has shaped our history—September 11, 2001, for example, or something of the sort. Instead, the event takes the structure of an occurrence that may neither be anticipated in advance nor even be made known in retrospect: the gift, pure hospitality, and the pardon.

As Derrida says with respect to hospitality, the making known of the act of granting hospitality itself reinforces the mastery of the one offering his house or his polity; hence "pure hospitality" might occur only without such a knowledge or decision.[47] Would the grant of citizenship to those born within the territory—even of alien parents—count? Or would something else render this hospitality in the political realm? In any case, the event occurs in the absence of a horizon or teleology, not anticipated and therefore hardly recognized. Rather than being recognized, the event must be read, the secret that a text withholds but relinquishes—at least in part—to the astute interpreter.

Returning to Foucault and the conjunction between power and knowledge, Derrida asks us to think the event as outside the demand for knowledge as power[48] yet nevertheless susceptible to another kind of reason:

To indicate it already in advance, it will be a matter for me of asking whether, in thinking the event, in thinking the coming [*venir*], the to-come [*avenir*], and the becoming [*devenir*] of the event, it is possible and in truth necessary to distinguish the experience of the unconditional, the desire and the thought, the exigency of unconditionality, the very reason and the justice of unconditionality, from everything that is ordered into a system according to this transcendental idealism and its teleology. In other words, whether there is a chance to think or to grant the thought of the unconditional event to a reason that is other than the one we have spoken about, namely, the classical reason of what presents itself or announces its presentation according to the *eidos*, the *idea*, the ideal, the regulative Idea, or, something else that here amounts to the same, the telos.[49]

The "to-come" of this alternative reason Derrida again juxtaposes not only with "the teleology or teleologism that so powerfully governs the transcendental idealisms and rationalisms of Kant and Husserl" and, in their systems, "limits or neutralizes the event", but also with other versions of a "*telos* . . . [that] comes to orient, order, and make possible a historicity," including the "*episteme* in Foucault's sense."[50]

As with the democracy to come, the event is not something that simply happens *to* a subject but might involve the subject's leap as well. In *Rogues*, Derrida gives two related examples of an event, the first "running aground [or] the moment when a ship, touching bottom, gets accidentally immobilized," and the second "*grounding* . . . when . . . the captain of a ship, failing to keep his heading, takes responsibility for touching bottom—and this decision too resembles an event."[51] The initial accident and the captain's acceptance of responsibility for what had not been anticipated both constitute—or at least resemble—events. The latter is reminiscent of the leap taken by the subject deciding on the undecidable, the one who took a step into the abyss without a proper grounding. The event thus pertains to a subject who takes responsibility but does not emerge from a horizon of anticipation and cannot fit into a subsequent judgment based on knowledge. Instead, it names an unconditionality beyond sovereignty and a relation between the subject and what arrives.

The unconditional event, and the unconditionality of the event is not law—any more than, as Derrida tells Roudinesco, pure hospitality presents an unmediated political program—but it provokes law and incites justice. The reason not of the stronger but of the unconditional—reasoned by what we might still call a subject—leaves open the impossible possibility of justice at the heart of law. Against the sovereign decision, the declaration of independence of a democracy to come announces that we must wait, in part, hoping without expectation, in part inciting the elliptical arrival of the event of an unconditional justice.

NOTES

1. Derrida's seminars from 1992 to 1995 considered "Le témoinage"; he turned to "Le parjure et le pardon" from 1997–99, then in 1999–2001 to "La peine de mort," and finally to "La bête et le souverain" (2001–3). List available at http://derridaseminars.org/seminars.html. Several of these seminars have been published in translation. See Jacques Derrida, *The Beast and the Sovereign*, vols. 1 and 2, ed. Michel Lisse, Marie-Louise Mallet, and Ginette Michaud, trans. Geoffrey Bennington (Chicago: University of Chicago Press, 2009, 2011); Derrida, *The Death Penalty*, vol. 1, ed. Geoffrey Bennington, Marc Crépon, and Thomas Dutoit, trans. Peggy Kamuf (Chicago: University of Chicago Press, 2014).

2. The seminars "Penal Theories and Institutions" (1971–72) and "The Punitive Society" (1972–73) examined the operations of punishment, while "Society Must Be Defended" (1975–76) delved into sovereignty with the greatest depth. Governmentality and biopolitics appear in "Security, Territory, Population" (1977–78) and "The Birth of Biopolitics" (1978–79). Truth telling is a concern of several of the final seminars, culminating in "The Government of Self and Others" (1982–83) and "The Courage of Truth" (1983–84). Picador has now finished publishing these and Foucault's other seminars in English.

3. One notable exception is the essay "Cogito and the History of Madness" in *Writing and Difference*, trans. Alan Bass (Chicago: University of Chicago Press, 1978), 31. Toward the beginning of his discussion of the death penalty in the eponymous seminar, Derrida also quotes at length from Foucault's description of the execution of Damien the regicide in *Discipline and Punish* (Derrida, *Death Penalty*, 42–45). He treats the relationship between Foucault's and Giorgio Agamben's writings on biopolitics extensively in the twelfth session of *The Beast and the Sovereign*, vol. 1, 305–34. For a discussion of other instances in which Foucault and Derrida addressed each other's work, see Antonio Campillo, "Foucault and Derrida—the History of a Debate on History," *Angelaki* 5, no. 2, (2000): 113–35.

4. Derrida himself rejected the notion of a "political turn." As Pheng Cheah and Suzanne Guerlac suggest in the introduction to their collection *Derrida and the Time of the Political*, however, there was a "becoming more explicit" of the political in his later writings. See Pheng Cheah and Suzanne Guerlac, introduction to *Derrida and the Time of the Political* (Durham, N.C.: Duke University Press, 2009), 3–4.

5. For example, Bernard Harcourt's *Illusion of Free Markets: Punishment and the Myth of Natural Order* relies heavily on Foucault (Cambridge, Mass.: Harvard University Press, 2011), and the collection *Left Legalism / Left Critique*, which attempts to reconstruct critique in the aftermath of critical legal studies, often refers explicitly to Foucault. See Wendy Brown and Janet Halley eds., *Left Legalism / Left Critique* (Durham, N.C.: Duke University Press, 2002). Likewise, Paul Kahn engages with

Agamben in *Political Theology: Four New Chapters on the Concept of Sovereignty* (New York: Columbia University Press, 2012) and elsewhere.

6. One of the most prominent American legal engagements with Derrida's work, Jack Balkin's 1987 essay "Derrida and Law," suggests that deconstruction should be of interest to lawyers because it "provides a method for critiquing existing legal doctrines," "can show how doctrinal arguments are informed by and disguise ideological thinking," and "offer[s] both a new kind of interpretive strategy and a critique of conventional interpretations of legal texts" ("Derrida and Law," *Yale Law Journal* 96 [1987]: 743, 744). In *Deconstruction and the Possibility of Justice*, the volume in which Derrida's "Force of Law: The 'Mystical Foundation of Authority'" first appeared, several essays similarly take up the notion of indeterminacy. See Drucilla Cornell, Michel Rosenfeld, and David Gray Carlson, eds., *Deconstruction and the Possibility of Justice* (Berkeley: University of California Press, 1992). Reflecting on the influence of deconstruction in the legal academy in 2005, Balkin summarizes the stance on deconstruction taken by many adherents of critical legal studies: "Deconstruction argues that texts are always overflowing with complicated and often contradictory meanings. The predicament that deconstruction finds in texts is not the lack of meaning but a surplus of it. Similarly, the point of deconstructing conceptual oppositions is not to show that concepts have no boundaries, but rather that their boundaries are fluid and appear differently as the opposition is placed into new interpretive contexts" ("Deconstruction's Legal Career," *Cardozo Law Review* 27 [November 2005]: 727).

As the editors of *Derrida and Legal Philosophy* commented in their introduction to the volume, despite the fact that "Force of Law" "swept across the legal academy throughout the common law world and beyond," "Derrida has had very little direct influence on the upper echelons of the US legal academy" (Peter Goodrich, Florian Hoffmann, Michel Rosenfeld, and Cornelia Vismann, eds., *Derrida and Legal Philosophy* [New York: Palgrave Macmillan, 2008], 9, 11). Derrida's later writings in particular have attracted little attention from legal scholars despite the detailed attention they often devote to law, including contemporary American law.

7. Several critics have furnished important accounts of the crucial differences between the work of Foucault and that of Derrida. Campillo's "Foucault and Derrida—the History of a Debate" chronicles the stages in the critiques of one thinker by the other and vice versa, concluding that it is possible to reconcile much of the division by positing simply a distinction in emphasis. As Campillo writes, "Both [Foucault's and Derrida's] views coincide in the claim that philosophical thought ought to think radically the historicity of experience, beginning with the experience of thinking itself. But Derrida believes it necessary to do this by means of a 'quasi-transcendental' analysis of the general or regular conditions of historicity, whereas Foucault believes it necessary to do it by means of a 'quasi-empirical' analysis of the particular or singular conditions of it" (130). Yet Campillo also identifies "one

deeper philosophical difference, that is, a moral difference, a different way of responding to the difference and to the alterity of the other. Whereas Derrida would consider a certain relation to welcoming, hospitality and alliance to be irreducible, Foucault would consider as irreducible a certain relation to violence, hostility and force" (130). Eric Jonas similarly posits that the divide between the two consists in their stances toward alterity and claims that "the Derridean and Foucauldian conceptions of alterity each suffer from inadequacies which require us to postulate a relationship of mutual supplementarity between them" ("Historicity and Alterity: Revisiting the Foucault-Derrida Debate," *Constellations* 22, no. 4 [2015]: 594). While Campillo's and Jonas's emphasis on alterity and the relation of the self to the other in Derrida and Foucault is certainly connected to temporality, Campillo and Jonas do not focus on time as the critical difference.

Others have contrasted Derrida's approaches to specific law-related topics, such as sovereignty, with Foucault's. According to Friedrich Balke, "For Derrida, there is no escape from the structure of sovereignty, nor from that of metaphysics; what he apostrophizes as the coming democracy can never substitute sovereignty, but can only—if at all—differ from it in an inconspicuous, minimal matter. Politics for Derrida means: to mark a difference in the relation to sovereignty . . . . For Foucault, the problem of sovereignty is not founded in a basic metaphysical position, but in the—not at all arbitrary—impact of a model or a discourse that prevents us from thinking of a power that has long ceased to function according to the model of sovereignty" ("Derrida and Foucault on Sovereignty," in *Derrida and Legal Philosophy*, ed. Peter Goodrich, Florian Hoffmann, Michel Rosenfeld, and Cornelia Vismann [London: Palgrave, 2008], 106). David Durst's review essay "The Place of the Political in Derrida and Foucault," treating Richard Beardsworth's *Derrida and the Political* and Jon Simons's *Foucault and the Political*, draws a limited comparison between the two theorists, concluding that "despite their profound differences, the ethico-political projects of Derrida and Foucault converge in many ways on what we could term a common sensibility for the irreducible violence of discourse and the need for an open, aporetic, and agonal democracy. It is the merit of Jon Simons's book *Foucault and the Political* not only to reconstruct in general terms Foucault's oppositional critique of modern (political) rationality but also to throw further needed light on his affirmative theorization of new modes of subjectivity" (Durst, "The Place of the Political in Derrida and Foucault," *Political Theory* 28, no. 5 [October 2000]: 685). Durst identifies these new modes of subjectivity that concerned Foucault with his late writings on "*parrhesia* or truth-telling as speaking frankly to powers that be despite its inherent dangers" (688).

A number of scholars have identified the critical role of time in Derrida's political thought, although again those discussions have not permeated legal scholarship. In *Derrida and the Political*, Beardsworth analyzes Derrida's reflections on time in relation to both Heidegger and Levinas and argues, "For Derrida, in contrast to the metaphysical reduction of the passage of time to presence, reflection upon the political necessitates reflection upon the irreducibility of time. And this, in turn, means enduring the experience of the aporia of law (and) time" (*Derrida and the Political* [London: Routledge, 1996], 101). Likewise, Geoffrey Bennington touches on the temporality of the decision, event, and democracy to come in his essay "Derrida and Politics," in *Jacques Derrida and the Humanities: A Critical Reader*, ed. Tom Cohen (Cambridge: Cambridge University Press, 2001), 193–212. The title of the last chapter of Jacques de Ville's book *Jacques Derrida: Law as Absolute Hospitality* also involves the notion of a "Hospitality towards the future" as implicit in Derrida's critique of law (*Jacques Derrida: Law as Absolute Hospitality* [New York: Routledge, 2011], 192).

Guerlac and Cheah diagnose the centrality of time to Derrida's political thought in the manner perhaps closest to this essay, connecting the subject's experience of time with the political themes that Derrida took up, including hospitality, sovereignty, democracy, and the decision. As they write in their introduction to the volume on Derrida and the time of the political:

> Although Derrida also deconstructs the classical philosopheme of the political in the name of something unconditional and ultrapolitical, "something in politics, or in friendship, in hospitality which cannot, for structural reasons, become the object of knowledge, of a theory, of a theorem," he argues that the unconditional gives rise to a structure of urgency and precipitation, an exigency that forces the reasoning subject to respond in a decision in which what is unconditional and incalculable is necessarily contaminated by the calculations and negotiations we associate with politics. (7)

They further suggest that "all canonical understandings of the political and politics presuppose concepts of time that deconstruction radically puts into question. . . . a radical reposing of the question of time, one that does not take time for granted as a given but that attends to the aporetic giving of time, will necessarily shake up canonical political concepts and categories" (14). This account of the centrality of time to Derrida's political thought also connects back to Jonas's and Campillo's claims about the nature of alterity in Derrida's writings. For Guerlac and Cheah, the subject's relation to time constitutes its relation to alterity:

> Simply put, Derrida's argument is that under conditions of radical finitude, time can be thought only as coming from an absolute other beyond presence. But because the relation to alterity also constitutes the order of presence and experience in general—since presence or experience presupposes persistence in time—any presence is subject to a strict law of contamination by an other that destabilizes, disrupts, and makes presence impossible even as it maintains, renews, and makes presence possible by giving it a to-come. (13)

The aspiration is not to end such time—as eschatological or teleological thought might do—but rather to recognize the consequences of living in time for the nature of the subject and politics. Martin Hägglund helpfully explicates the difference through pointing out the contrast between unconditionality in Kant and Derrida. As Hägglund observes, "For Kant, the unconditional is the Idea of a sovereign instance that is not subjected to time and space (e.g., God). For Derrida, on the contrary, the unconditional is the spacing of time that undermines the very Idea of a sovereign instance" (*Radical Atheism: Derrida and the Time of Life* [Stanford, Calif.: Stanford University Press, 2008], 19).

Cheah's chapter "The Untimely Secret of Democracy," also in *Derrida and the Time of the Political*, further explicates how "the gift of time always already involves a delimitation of the political ontology of sovereignty" and how the Derridean "democracy to come" "cannot be reduced to positive historical forms of democracy even though it has a necessary relationship to them" (74).

8. Elisabeth Roudinesco, *For What Tomorrow . . . A Dialogue*, trans. Jeff Fort (Stanford, Calif.: Stanford University Press, 2004), 10.

9. Ibid., 12.

10. In a session of the seminar "Security, Territory, Population" that was published separately as his essay "Governmentality," Foucault noted that "we should not see things as the replacement of a society of sovereignty by a society of discipline, and then of a society of discipline by a society, say, of government. In fact we have a triangle: sovereignty, discipline, and governmental management, which has population as its main target and apparatuses of security as its essential mechanism" (*Security, Territory, Population*, 107–8).

11. Derrida, *Beast and the Sovereign*, 332.

12. Ibid. The final chapter of Kevin Attell's book *Giorgio Agamben: Beyond the Threshold of Deconstruction* treats Agamben's critique of Derrida's conception of time in terms of the relation between what Attell, following Agamben, calls the contrast between the messianic and the apostolic. Very briefly, whereas the apostolic (or apostolic messianism), espoused by Agamben, connects with an event that has already occurred, the messianic (or prophetic messianism), which Attell attributes to Derrida, pertains to the future. See Kevin Attell, *Giorgio Agamben: Beyond the Threshold of Deconstruction* (New York: Fordham University Press, 2015), 213–54. I register a disagreement with this interpretation below.

13. Jacques Derrida, "Cogito and the History of Madness," in *Writing and Difference*, trans. Alan Bass (Chicago: University of Chicago Press, 1978), 34–35.

14. As Schmitt famously announced, "Sovereign is he who decides on the exception" (*Political Theology: Four Chapters on the Concept of Sovereignty*, trans. George Schwab [Chicago: University of Chicago Press, 2005], 5).

15. John McCormick, "Derrida on Law: Or, Poststructuralism Gets Serious," *Political Theory* 29, no. 3 (2001): 395–423. Bennington makes a similar point in "Derrida and Politics," distinguishing the Schmittian from the Derridean decision

and maintaining that "where the classical theory of the subject (still operating in Schmitt's decisionism, which Derrida discusses at length in *Politiques de l'amitié*) tends to reduce the eventhood of the event of decision by referring it to a subject, Derrida is trying to 'eventize' the decision, and this means it can no longer be quite *my* decision" (202).

16. Derrida, *Rogues: Two Essays on Reason*, trans. Pascale-Anne Brault and Michael Naas (Stanford, Calif.: Stanford University Press, 2005), 17.

17. Ibid.

18. Ibid., 1.

19. Ibid.

20. Jacques Derrida, *Death Penalty*, 220.

21. Ibid.

22. Ibid., 225.

23. Ibid., 238.

24. Ibid., 220.

25. Ibid., 332.

26. Vincent Leitch, "Late Derrida: The Politics of Sovereignty," *Critical Inquiry* 33, no. 2 (2007): 229–47.

27. Ibid., 239.

28. "Justice, Law and Philosophy—an Interview with Jacques Derrida," *South African Journal of Philosophy* 18, no. 3 (1999): 280.

29. Derrida elaborates a further connection between knowledge and sovereignty in another passage from the seminar "The Beast and the Sovereign" critiquing Agamben. Here he says that "the sovereign, if there is such a thing, is the one who manages to get people to believe, at least for a while, that he is the first to know who came first, when there is every chance that it is almost always false, even if, in certain cases, no one ever suspects so" (92).

30. Hägglund, *Radical Atheism*, 41. Hägglund later writes, comparing the decision in Schmitt and Derrida, that "the pivotal difference . . . concerns the 'exceptional' status of the decision. For Schmitt the decision is exceptional because it is an act of indivisible sovereignty that suspends the law and puts an end to debate. For Derrida, on the contrary, the sovereign decision is impossible as such; it can never be *in itself* but is haunted by a structural opening to the undecidable future" (182). While I largely agree with Hägglund, particularly in his diagnosis of the condition of temporality as the source of the specificity of the decision in Derrida, I would part ways from his emphasis on undecidability as dependent on the possibility of an unknown future. Instead, the situation of the undecidable may arise out of two equally compelling readings of a present state of affairs.

Interpreting Derrida as oriented toward the future leads to what I would consider the misreading that Attell, reading Agamben on Derrida, performs. Attell follows Hägglund's "concise definition of the Derridean messianic 'as another name for the relation to the undecidable future'" and writes that "herein lies the basic difference between the Derridean and Agambenian notions of the messianic, for as Hägglund's gloss implies, the Derridean 'prophetic' messianic (as opposed, as we will see, to the Agambenian 'apostolic' messianic) is fundamentally a matter of the aleatory 'to come'" (Attell, *Giorgio Agamben*, 222).

31. Jacques Derrida, "Declarations of Independence," *Caucus for a New Political Science* 15 (1986): 7–15.

32. Ibid., 11.

33. Ibid., 12.

34. It is worth recalling here Derrida's gloss of the effort to achieve death instantaneously in the seminar on the death penalty; there he notes that "time is suffering" (*Death Penalty*, 226).

35. Derrida, "Declarations of Independence," 13.

36. Jacques de Ville, "Sovereignty without Sovereignty: Derrida's *Declarations of Independence*," *Law and Critique* 19 (2008): 108.

37. I have elsewhere attempted to elaborate a form of originalism that would be attentive to both of these points and recognize the tension between a social contract and the constitutional meaning that supposedly results from it. See Bernadette Meyler, "Accepting Contested Meanings," *Fordham Law Review* 82 (2013): 803–26.

38. Derrida, *Rogues*; Derrida, "Passions: 'An Oblique Offering,'" in *On the Name*, trans. and ed. Thomas Dutoit (Stanford, Calif.: Stanford University Press, 1995), 3–34.

39. Derrida, *Rogues*, 37.

40. Again this contrasts with Attell's account of Derrida's messianicity. Cheah's essay "The Untimely Secret of Democracy" helpfully emphasizes both the connection between Derrida's understanding of the subject and the notion of a "democracy to come" and the significance of that notion to the constitution of democracy in the present as a locus of contestation: "Although the untimely is the structural condition of ipseity, Derrida also argues that there is a special affinity between the a-venir and the political regime of democracy. Democracy's untimeliness can be seen in the fact that it is the only inherently plastic political paradigm, the only regime that is open to and welcomes the possibility of contestation and self-contestation. This openness stems from democracy's radically improper character, its lack of self-identity" (80).

41. Derrida, *Rogues*, 87.

42. Ibid.

43. Ibid., 88.

44. Ibid., 91.

45. Badiou reflects on the event in works like his *Being and Event*, trans. Oliver

Feltham (London: Continuum, 2006). Antonio Calcagno helpfully distinguishes Derrida's and Badiou's use of the term in *Badiou and Derrida: Politics, Events, and Their Times* (New York: Continuum, 2007). According to Calcagno: "Both Badiou and Derrida give the event a central role in structuring politics and political thinking. For Badiou, events make politics possible and thinkable. They give both a decidable and intelligible structure to politics while still accounting for indeterminacy and multiplicity. Derrida, unlike Badiou, believes that events themselves are structured by the double bind of possibility and impossibility, radically calling into question the very naming of events or even giving them any definite or set meaning as does Badiou" (2).

46. Derrida, Beast and the Sovereign, 333.

47. In the same context, Derrida emphasizes that teleological thinking would frustrate the eventness of the event. As he observes, "The teleology or teleologism that so powerfully governs the transcendental idealisms and rationalisms of Kant and Husserl is also that which limits or neutralizes the event. Teleologism seems always to inhibit, suspend, or even contradict the eventfulness of what comes, beginning with the scientific event, the technoscientific invention that 'finds' what it seeks, that finds and finds itself finding, and thus is possible as such, only when invention is impossible, that is, when it is not programmed by a structure of expectation and anticipation that annuls it by making it possible and thus foreseeable" (*Of Hospitality: Anne Dufourmantel Invites Jacques Derrida to Respond*, trans. Rachel Bowlby [Stanford, Calif.: Stanford University Press, 2000], 128).

48. Derrida, *Rogues*, 137.

49. Ibid., 135.

50. Ibid., 128.

51. Ibid., 122.

Derrida's Shylock
The Life and the Letter of the Law

Katrin Trüstedt

I

In "What Is a 'Relevant' Translation," a text that was first published in *Critical Inquiry* in 2001, Jacques Derrida unfolds a reflection on the problem of translation that departs from a phrase from Shakespeare's *Merchant of Venice*: "Mercy seasons Justice."[1] This phrase serves as a starting point both for the introduction of an unusual translation and for a general reflection on translation itself. Derrida proposes the translation "Le pardon relève la justice," in which the verb "to season" is translated by "relever" and, as such, related to the movement of translation: "seasoning" is understood in terms of a movement of trans- or sublation. Following Derrida's title, the verb refers to a specific qualification or type of translation: a "relevant" translation.

What distinguishes this type of translation? *Relever* is the term that Derrida had also proposed some decades ago as the translation for G. W. F. Hegel's notion of *Aufhebung*. In using *relever* as the name for the movement of translation, Derrida is thus linking the movement of translation to the transformation of Hegelian *Aufhebung*. A "relevant" translation is one that sublates the translated original in a new medium, that means: negates, elevates, and preserves the original in a new form. Translated back from Derrida's French translation of Shakespeare, "Mercy seasons justice" thus reads: *"Mercy elevates and interiorizes, thereby preserves and negates, justice (or the law)."*[2] With this elaboration, Derrida ultimately suggests that "mercy" is in some way a "relevant"—that is, a transformative and at the same time a true—translation of justice. This translation would thus be limited only in the way every relevant translation is. But what does it mean, that mercy "sublates" justice or, more precisely in this context, the law? What does it mean that the law is in need of sublation? And what would it mean for the law in this very particular, Shylock's, case, to be in need of sublation and to be "sublated"?

The relation of law and mercy that informs *The Merchant of Venice* is usually understood in the context of a larger narrative: the narrative of the opposition between a supposedly "Jewish" obedience to the "letter of the law" and a Christian spirit of mercy, which is regarded as a *sublation*—a negation and elevation—of the Jewish relation to the law. According to this reading, Christian spirit exhibits, as Hegel puts it, "that which fulfils the law but annuls it as law [*aufhebt*] and so is something higher than obedience to law and makes law superfluous."[3] The ever-insisting, quasi-allegorical reading of the play thus frames the opposition of a Jewish law and a Christian mercy in such a way. Take Katharine Eisaman Maus's introduction to the play as an example for this type of contextualization:

> The opposition between the Christians and Shylock seems rooted in religious disparities. Judaism in the play is presented . . . as a sixteenth-century Christian like Shakespeare would have construed it, as a set of dramatically vivid contrasts with Christian norms. The law of Moses, as set down in Deuteronomy and Leviticus, specifies numerous aspects of the observant Jew's life. . . . The Mosaic code places a high value upon justice and emphasizes the importance of *adhering to the letter of the law*. Shylock's Judaism reveals itself . . . in his trust of *literal meanings*, his respect for *observable facts*, his expectation that *contracts will be rigorously enforced*. The typical Christian outlook is different. Christians obtain divine approval not by wearing certain garments, avoiding certain foods, or circumcising their boys, but by believing in Christ's power to save them. The central virtues in this religious system are not justice and

> *scrupulous compliance with the law* but *charity, mercy, and a willingness to believe what seems incredible.*[4]

This opposition between "sticking to the letter of the law" and a "scrupulous compliance with the law" in its "literal meanings," on the one hand, and "charity," "mercy," and "faith," on the other, is of course referring to Paul's famous distinction between a supposedly dead "letter of the law" and a living spirit of internalized law, or love.[5] "The letter kills, but the spirit gives life" (2 Cor. 3:6).[6] Derrida also touches on this opposition in his reflection on Portia's "Mercy seasons justice," even if in passing:

> [Portia] tries to convert him [Shylock] to Christianity by persuading him of the supposedly Christian interpretation that consists of interiorizing, spiritualizing, idealizing what among Jews (it is often said, at least, that this is a very powerful stereotype) will remain physical, external, literal, devoted to a respect for the letter. As with the difference between the circumcision of the flesh and the Pauline circumcision of the heart—there will certainly be a need to look for a translation, in the broad sense, with regard to this problematic of circumcision (literal circumcision of the flesh versus ideal and interior circumcision of the heart, Jewish circumcision versus Christian circumcision, the whole debate surrounding Paul).[7]

What distinguishes the type of translation that Derrida develops in "What Is a 'Relevant' Translation?" is the proximity to this Paulinian model of opposition, sublation, and conversion. Derrida seems to rely on Hegel's *The Spirit of Christianity and Its Fate*, when he characterizes this dynamic as one of *Aufhebung* or sublation: "interiorizing, spiritualizing, idealizing what ... will remain physical, external, literal, devoted to a respect for the letter."[8] Yet he relies on Walter Benjamin when he characterizes it also as a form of translation that accounts for what is lost in the process, and thereby for the element of negativity inherent in it:

> What the translation with the word "relevant" also demonstrates ...
> is that every translation should be relevant by vocation. It would thus guarantee the *survival* of the body of the original (*survival* in the double sense that Benjamin gives it in "The Task of the Translator," *fortleben* and *überleben*: prolonged life, continuous life, *living on*, but also life after death). Isn't this what a translation does? Doesn't it guarantee these *two* survivals by losing the flesh during a process of conversion (change)?

By elevating the signifier to its meaning or value, all the while preserving the mournful and debt-laden memory of the singular body, the first body, the unique body that the translation thus elevates, preserves, and negates (*relève*)?[9]

Although the general idea of a relevant translation that Derrida draws from Portia's phrase is indeed compelling, the particular example that he draws it from, "Mercy seasons justice," is actually not a "relevant translation" in his own terms. To think of Portia's mercy as a relevant translation of justice in Derrida's sense seems to buy into Portia's own problematic description of the central opposition of letter and spirit and misses a possible alternative reading (and deconstruction) of it. In characterizing the act of mercy Portia proposes as a relevant translation of justice, Derrida suggests that this mercy comes only with the type of loss that accompanies every translation as such, and therefore misses the specific losses and costs that Portia's act of translation produces. With his reference to Benjamin, Derrida seems to propose that this translation implies a certain mournful preservation of what is lost. However, Portia's Mercy obscures not only the loss during the movement of translation but actually the aversion of a translation itself, of an interpretation and legal debate of Shylock's case. While Derrida indeed criticizes Portia's strategy, he blames Shylock for resisting and preventing a "relevant" translation. According to Derrida's argument, Shylock, by insisting on the particularity of his pound of flesh, prevents the work of translation and thereby only strengthens his opponents. "By resisting this *transcription*, this transaction *which is a translation*, this relève, Shylock delivers himself into the grasp of the Christian strategy, bound hand and foot."[10] With this insistence, Derrida's Shylock resists not only the Christian strategy but also the whole work of translation itself, the "*labor* [*travail*]," the "*transferential* and *t*ransformational *t*ravail," the "*t*ranslation, as *transaction* and as *t*ransfer."[11] While he grants the problematic elements of the Christian strategy, for Derrida such a refusal of translation cannot be the answer: "In expressing all the evil that can be thought of the Christian ruse as a discourse of mercy, I am not about to praise Shylock when he raises a hue and cry for his pound of flesh and insists on the *literalness* of the bond."[12]

In what follows, I offer an alternative reading of *The Merchant of Venice*, reversing Derrida's reading with his own terms, not least because the question of translation as *Aufhebung* indeed seems poignant with regard to the questions of law and interpretation that this volume poses. In my view,

Shylock's case seems to offer both an account of the violent implications of the *Aufhebung* of law by mercy and an attempt at the deconstruction of the opposition assumed by it. Contrary yet somehow relevant to the setting that Derrida's text suggests, it is in fact Shylock who offers a translation, and it is the Christian call for mercy that prevents it. In this sense, the shift consists of linking the notion of insisting on "the letter of the law" not to any kind of "literal meaning" or a "scrupulous compliance with the law" but to an insistence on the *textuality* of the law. Textuality is here to be understood in Derrida's usual sense—a scripture not restricted to its literalness but on the contrary always open to and in fact in need of interpretation, translation, and sublation, while a "relevant translation" would be one that in some way pays tribute to what was lost in the process. As I would like to show, it is Shylock who, far from insisting on the literalness of his case and thereby refusing its translation, offers such translations. Following this reading will eventually invert the implicated Paulinian opposition of killing and giving life: As Shylock demonstrates, it is not mercy but rather the letter that "giveth life."

2

Against the grain of the traditional dichotomy of a deadening literal Jewish and an enlivening spiritual Christian conception of law, Shylock is first introduced to us as engaged in "lively" practices of interpretation and translation that refer us to an understanding of the "letter of the law" that is anything but deadening. In the third scene of act 1, the Christian merchant of Venice Antonio turns to the Jew Shylock to borrow money from him. Shylock responds to this approach not by immediately accepting or declining Antonio's request but by performing an act of interpretation or translation, in which he offers another, wider context for Antonio's particular issue of money lending, interest, and usury.

> SHYLOCK
> When Jacob grazed his uncle Laban's sheep—
> This Jacob from our holy Abram was,
> As his wise mother wrought in his behalf,
> The third possessor; ay, he was the third—
> ANTONIO
> And what of him? did he take interest?
>
> (1.3.66–73)

In this scene, which introduces Shylock for the first time, it is the Christian Antonio who is unwilling or unable to "translate" and transpose the practices of money lending at hand with regard to another context. In Shylock's response, we are confronted with a translation in the sense of the *translatio* of a metaphor: Shylock articulates the subject of loan and interest with the help of a biblical story of sheep breeding. This metaphorical context also provides a perspective for the two characters who are introduced as the Christian and the Jew: In this story, Shylock evokes the third born not just in the literal sense but as a metaphor for the marginalized, the underprivileged, that is, Shylock himself with regard to the privileged Christian Antonio, who understands neither the metaphorical transaction nor the implications this transaction provides for him or the situation at hand. Apparently neither trained nor interested in any kind of exegetical or translational practice, it is Antonio who in this instance insists on the literalness of his issue: "And what of him? did he take interest?" Shylock responds with a patient deliberation, leading a reluctant Antonio through an exercise of the art of interpretation of the law of usury by relating it to the biblical narrative of the overturning of the succession order.

> SHYLOCK
> No, not take interest, not, as you would say,
> Directly int'rest. Mark what Jacob did:
> When Laban and himself were compromised
> That all the eanlings which were streaked and pied
> Should fall as Jacob's hire, the ewes, being rank,
> In the end of autumn turnèd to the rams,
> And when the work of generation was
> Between these woolly breeders in the act,
> The skilful shepherd peeled me certain wands,
> And in the doing of the deed of kind
> He stuck them up before the fulsome ewes,
> Who, then conceiving, did in eaning time
> Fall parti-colour'd lambs; and those were Jacob's.
> This was a way to thrive; and he was blest;
> And thrift is blessing, if men steal it not.
>
> (1.3.74–88)

This interpretation that Shylock displays, could, I would like to argue, be called a "transaction which is a translation" on more than one level. By way of a transaction, Shylock relates his own practice of lending money against interest to the narrative of the third-born yet skilled shepherd Jacob, who "produces" "interest" in the form of sheep from his work. His exegetical techniques—reading the "letter of the law," that is, its text—are far from any supposed "literalism" or "legalism" that would insist on the singular body of the original; rather, they showcase a particular practice of textual interpretation that explicates the defining ideas of a given nomos through narratives. It is in line with Jewish interpretation, or more precisely with "the project of early midrash," as Julia Lupton has outlined.[13] The precept of the succession order in Deuteronomy—the "Mosaic code" that, as the Norton introduction to *The Merchant of Venice* emphasizes, "places a high value upon justice and emphasizes the importance of adhering to the *letter of the law*"—requires acknowledging the first-born son regardless of circumstances, even if he is the son of the hated wife.[14] Yet Shylock tells a story exactly not of "rigorous enforcement" of or "scrupulous compliance" with this precept. He does not in this sense insist on the letter of the law, but returns to the "letter" in another, contrary sense. Shylock offers an interpretation of the law of usury by embedding that law narratively and relating it to a story of a third born who himself manages to resist the law (here: the order of succession) by a rather questionable practice of sheep breeding.

Shylock's exegesis is in line with the traditional practice of Jewish interpretation, as Pierre Legendre describes it, when he argues that since the Jews miss a pope as the "living voice of the law" to guarantee the truth, the signifier itself is much more radical and autonomous in the Jewish interpretative system. In his assessment, this explains the important role of the fables, that—like the stories of overturning the order of the first born and third born—demand interpretation and produce legal, poetical, and metaphorical meaning.[15] Shylock's take seems to be an act of interpretation of the law that operates as a translation in Derrida's sense: negating, preserving, and elevating the original by relating it to this other narrative. In Shylock's case this kind of "relevant translation" does not operate through a mercy interrupting the legal procedure but through a narrative explication and translation of normative precepts. The relevant translation of justice is not mercy, it seems, but interpretation.

3

The succession order regulated by the book of Deuteronomy that Shylock takes up in his negotiations with Antonio is also a prominent example of one of the great essays on the subject of law and interpretation. Robert Cover uses it in his famous essay "Nomos and Narrative" to describe the practice of interpretation in a way very much in line with Shylock's display of exegesis. And just like Shylock's interpretation gestures toward a "life of the letter," Cover offers an alternative to the Paulinian opposition between the "dead letter" and the living spirit of the law. To explicate the life of the law, Cover highlights the productive tension between the normative order and the narratives that are supposed to elucidate it. With regard to the succession order in Deuteronomy, Cover goes so far as to suggest that, "indeed, all of the stories of the patriarchs revolve [in one way or another] around the *overturning* of the 'normal' order of successions."[16] What makes a Jewish practice of interpretation especially interesting in this context is that both the precepts and those stories overturning them belong to the same corpus of the law as a text. Diverging from the Paulinian tradition, Cover links the engagement with the letter of the law to "life": The letter of the law is the medium of an abundance of interpretations and thereby the medium of jurisgenesis. From this perspective on the law and its interpretation, the letter does not so much "killeth" the law but on the contrary actually "giveth life."[17] The practice of interpretation and the study of the law—the "paideia," as Cover calls it—is for Cover the foundation for a "life of the law" that coincides with, instead of being opposed to, the "letter of the law." In his description, using terms like *legal DNA* and *juridical mitosis*, he combines the paradigm of interpretation with biological terms pertaining to life and the processes of its evolution. According to this description, the paideic practices function as a medium of "jurisgenesis," as the field in which the "legal DNA" is replicated, reproduced, or modified and in which law is engendered. The "life of the law" is thus dependent on the paideic practices of interpretation, which allow for and thrive on difference. The imperial mode, on the other hand, consists of procedures of selection, negation, and restabilization: institutionalizing certain interpretations and cutting off others. The life of the law in this sense requires *both* an abundant proliferation of translations that can produce new law as well as a mechanism that can restrict this proliferation and institutionalize certain interpretations without, however, cutting off the productive movement of translation in such a way that jurisgenesis itself is cut off.[18]

In this dynamic of genesis and regulation, production and restriction, Cover ascribes to the court a special role as a doorkeeper and a governing site, with its procedures of intervening and institutionalizing that regulate and restrain the chaotic growth of the law in all its interpretations. Being in this central position, the court—that is, in this case, the Supreme Court—has the responsibility to face the challenge that the "demands of interpretation"[19] produce: "Confronting the luxuriant growth of a hundred legal traditions, they assert that *this one* is law and destroy or try to destroy the rest."[20] If interpretation follows a similar logic that Derrida ascribes to translation, then the court faces the challenge of asserting one interpretation against another, which is the challenge Derrida poses in the title of his text: "What is a *'relevant'* translation?" To be relevant in the richer sense that Derrida adumbrates, the selected interpretation should, however, not just negate the other options but somehow sublate and preserve them. Following this line of thought, the court has to face not only the demand that it has to decide but also the challenge that this decision has to reflect in some way the contesting normative views of the matter and has to find a resolution that addresses normative variety. Cover criticizes the Supreme Court in *Bob Jones University v. United States*—the paradigm case of his classic essay "Nomos and Narrative"—for failing to face such a more complex challenge. Instead of providing a space for allowing differing interpretations of the text of the law, in order to discuss, weigh, and deliberate their "relevance," and then enforce one while keeping the memory of the other, the court neglected its difficult task and jumped to a conclusion that prevented the challenge of facing other, possibly violent interpretations: "The apologetic and statist orientation of current jurisdictional understandings prevent courts from ever reaching the threatening questions."[21]

Not in its decision, but in avoiding the discussion of and failing to reflect the alternative in the reasoning did the court in Cover's judgment fall short of its difficult task: Without weighing the relevance, however minimal, of the problematic and violent (i.e., racist) interpretation of Bob Jones University, the Court arrested the practice of controversial interpretation to prematurely enforce an existing hierarchy. Moreover, by merely enforcing one interpretation without considering a differing one, the Court also failed to acknowledge the necessary loss of the "original body" of the law in the specific interpretation it enforced. Finally, by referring to public safety and political factors as the main reasons underlying its decision, the Court left the practice of *legal* interpretation behind for arguments *outside the text of the law* that can hardly be challenged (translated, interpreted) in legal terms, thereby arresting the practice of legal debate.

4

Avoiding the practice of interpretation in such a way is precisely, one could say, what happens in the court scene of *The Merchant of Venice*.[22] Instead of facing the challenge of both fostering the "jurisgenerative" process productive of normative meaning and finding a decision that negates and preserves the variety of interpretations in favor of the enforced one,[23] the Court shows itself to be informed by a normative Christian project and hence to be one of the sides it is supposed to assess. Instead of providing the space for the life and growth of differing interpretations, weighing and assessing them, the Venetian court fails to acknowledge its "relevance" by denying controversial textual exegeses, opening the sphere of the law up for political ruses. The Venetian court fails to face its paradoxical task—Derrida elsewhere calls it "impossible yet necessary"—to assert one interpretation against another. This task implies that the decision needs to acknowledge the relevance of each interpretation, including acknowledging what is lost of the law in its interpretation and the court's own precarious legitimacy[24] to make such a decision. Reflecting its own precarious status as a selector for competing interpretations of the law[25] means for the court to select carefully and while making a necessary decision, to protect the overall life and growth of the law.[26] The Venetian court fails to realize this task in the attempt to arrest the act of legal interpretation, to leave the sphere of the law and to aim at something beyond the law (the soul of the subject behind the legal person), outside the law (political strategies), or above the law (mercy, elevating the law). It is an attempt to leave the realm of interpretation and the work of translation behind.

In line with the practice of interpretation with which he was first presented to us, Shylock does in fact challenge the Christian majority to a legal dispute: If they "own" their slaves, why can he not "own" part of Antonio's body?

SHYLOCK
What judgment shall I dread, doing no wrong?
You have among you many a purchased slave
Which, like your asses and your dogs and mules,
You use in abject and in slavish parts
Because you bought them. Shall I say to you
"Let them be free, marry them to your heirs.
Why sweat they under burdens? Let their beds

> Be made as soft as yours, and let their palates
> Be *seasoned* with such viands."
>
> (4.1.88–96)

Contrary to the view that he would cling to a literal interpretation, Shylock initiates an actual legal debate over the right of possession and thereby challenges the other side to show him where and how the law does not allow his claim. He offers possible routes of interpretation: comparing one case to another, as well as relating his particular case to a general norm.

It is remarkable that Shylock himself uses the term *seasoned*, in his challenge. He does so with reference to the context with which Derrida introduces his translation of Portia's "Mercy seasons Justice": the culinary context of flavors. For Derrida, it is the "the first reason to translate *seasons* with 'relève,' which effectively preserves the gustatory code and the culinary reference of *to season*, 'assaisonner': *to season with spice*, to spice. *A seasoned dish* is, according to the translation in the *Robert* dictionary, 'un plat relevé.' Justice preserves its own taste, its own meaning, but this very taste is better when it is *seasoned* or 'relevé' by mercy."[27] In the rhetorical tradition, seasoning in this sense sometimes serves as a metaphor describing the mechanism of a metaphor itself, or of rhetoric as a whole. Plato's famous equation of rhetoric with cooking devalues rhetoric as a nonsubstantial addition (or supplement). Bassanio is the first to introduce the term in this way into the play and linking it to a dangerous supplement:

> So may the outward shows be least themselves.
> The world is still deceived with ornament.
> In law, what plea so tainted and corrupt
> But, being *seasoned* with a gracious voice,
> Obscures the show of evil?
>
> (3.2.73–77)

In this first usage of the crucial term in the play, the "seasoning of the law" indicates quite a different process than the one Portia later aims for: the seasoning of a legal plea in fact obscures its "show of evil." This first use of the term *seasoned*, in line with anti-rhetorical sentiments, seems to haunt Portia's own move when she claims that "Mercy seasons Justice." Her plea for mercy now may also be understood to be obscuring the evil Christian strategy, Shylock's conversion to Christian mercy to be obscuring justice or, rather, the lack thereof. Seasoning the law in this light may be understood as obscuring its cancellation. When Shylock uses the term, it is neither in the sense of obscuring, as Bassanio introduces it, nor in the sense of elevating, as Portia attempts to, but in its "literal meaning" of spicing; yet he uses it in the context of a legal interpretation of the right to own another human being (or part of it). In this context, to have one's "palate seasoned," turns out, however supplementary, to mark the ultimate distinction between being a "slave" and being a "free citizen"—a distinction the Christians have introduced and accepted in their laws, just as much as that between the Christians and the Jews. With this move—reflecting back his right to possess part of Antonio to Antonio's right to own a slave and using the notion of *seasoning* in this way for it—Shylock in some way performs an act of interpretation as seasoning. While Derrida portrays Shylock as the one resisting such acts of translation or interpretation, Shylock could very well be described as engaged in an act of "relevant translation."

It is, on the contrary, the Venetian court that deals with the challenge posed by Shylock by resisting any practice of interpretation. Instead of engaging in negotiations with Shylock's interpretation of contract law (which is certainly questionable), weighing its "relevance," its meaning, its limits, and its losses, discussing equity or the like, Portia simply asserts her claim,[28] only to replace it with another case and to "season" this shift with Christian mercy,[29] not least in the sense of "obscuring" it. When Portia enters the scene dressed up as a supposed expert on the law (also obscured, one could say), Shylock does not simply reject mercy but asks for its status *within* the debate of his case in court. Shylock resists the Christian attempt to leave this debate for a mercy from "above" and insists not on the dead letter of the law but on the continuation of the legal proceedings.[30] Portia says, "Then must the Jew be merciful"; Shylock responds, "On what compulsion must I? tell me that" (4.1.177–79). Shylock's demand for legal reasoning is repeatedly denied. While he himself may have motives for his claim that lie outside the law (revenge), Shylock's insistence is always a request to stay on this side of the law and legal reasoning. When the Christian party repeatedly aims for a subject behind his legal persona, by appealing for mercy or asking for his personal motives, he repeatedly resists this move beyond: "I'll not answer that" (4.1.41). The Venetian court, rather than Shylock, resists the work of interpretation and translation: Instead of engaging in attempts at a responsible translation, the court surreptitiously and in what could be called an "obscured" dodge substitutes a question of criminal law for the civic law issues that Shylock raises by insisting on his bond.[31] Shifting the trial in its constellation from civil to criminal law, from "breach of contract" to "attempted murder" and displacing Shylock from the position of the plaintiff to the accused, Portia does not mainly answer Shylock's supposed Jewish legalism with more legalism, as some commentators have suggested,[32] but in fact grants him the undiscussed bond and by replacing it in the same instance, with another case, she arrests the possibility of any interpretation. Refusing to interpret Shylock's case by replacing the original body unaltered with another one, does not, in fact, seem like a "relevant" translation. Neither elevating nor preserving it, this obscured shift does not even allow for a mourning of what is lost.

The dodge also obscures a weakness of the Venetian law itself, that seems to allow any kind of private contract, even if it involves killing a citizen, while providing a totally unconnected law that not only contradicts this "absolute" freedom of contract but also rests on the political distinction between a citizen and an alien—a distinction that the contract law supposedly does not draw. What would be "relevant" at this point is an interpretation that could "translate" between the two bodies of law. Instead, the Venetian court abandons the order of a juridical process and turns to political and executional powers: Shylock is ordered to beg the Duke—the sovereign political instance—for the mercy that "seasons" justice. Moreover, this dodge is based on a law that apparently nobody knows: Unlike the civil contract law, it is not part of a practiced nomos but originates from a state of exception. Not unlike the case that Cover commented on in "Nomos and Narrative," the decision is legitimated by recourse to external factors (public safety and political reasons). What Portia's dodge does, in terms of Cover's conception, is not protecting the life of the law but "killing" it by arresting any "work of translation" that seems so "relevant" at this crossroad, against Shylock's ineffective attempts to "give it life."

5

When the Christian appeals to his mercy, only to then order him in turn to beg for political mercy himself, Shylock repeatedly answers the calls for "Christian" mercy with calls on their *wit*. Linking the skill of language to that of legal arguments, he thereby insists on a debate "relevant" to the court: When Gratiano says, "Can no prayers pierce thee?," Shylock responds, "No, none that thou hast *wit* enough to make" (4.1.125–26). Bassanio with his misplaced prayers fails to provide anything that would have to be, as Shylock suggests, a "relevant"—that is, witty—translation of his legal case. When Gratiano offends Shylock, "O, be thou damned, inexorable dog," Shylock replies, "Thou but offend'st thy lungs to speak so loud. / Repair thy *wit*, good youth, or it will fall / To cureless ruin. *I stand here for law*" (4.1.121–41).

What it would require to move Shylock in his so far undisputed position, he suggests, is wit. While Bassanio denies Shylock the status of being human for failing to prove spirit (that Bassanio himself in a performative contradiction obviously fails to show), Shylock insists on remaining on this side of the law, which is also the side of wit, that he, Shylock, questions in turn in Bassanio. Relating the legal arguments to "wit" is especially interesting with regard to an understanding of the letter of the law as its textuality. If wit is understood to be opposing a spiritual realm of prayers and itself as immanent to the law and (its) textuality, such an understanding would question the Paulinian opposition of the dead letter of the law and the spirit giving life. Insisting on the letter of the law is in this scenario not deadening but practicing wit and actually allowing for the work of interpretation and translation. Shylock has exhibited his interpretative, "lively" wit from the first scene in which we have encountered him.

In his essay "The Insistence of the Letter in the Unconscious," Jacques Lacan takes up the Paulinian phrase, but (almost in passing) deconstructs it by translating spirit with ésprit, and linking ésprit in a footnote to "wit" and "pun"—the textual form that deals with textual ambiguity per se.[33] The title of the essay—"The insistence of the letter"—presents us with a kind of reversal of the Paulinian phrase that Lacan mentions: It is the letter that "moves," insists, and makes the spirit "live." To prove spirit or *Geist* for Lacan means, by way of translating spirit by esprit and esprit by wit or *Witz*, to prove wit. Wit, however, is not a spirit that can be opposed to the letter but a spirit or life *of* the letter. It seems that a seasoning in Derrida's sense of a "*relevant* translation" would require wit, and in some way correspond to it. "Wit seasons justice" seems to be Shylock's answer to Portia's phrase.

The actual conversion to the Christian merciful "spirit" that happens instead of the (witty) legal interpretation that Shylock was aiming for does not exactly "give life" to Shylock: With "I am not well" Shylock leaves the stage and in some way the play to end. What seems to set this tone throughout is not, I would argue, a lack of Christian spirit, but on the contrary a lack of wit. That holds true even for the protagonist, the merchant of Venice Antonio, who seems not especially vitalized or animated by his Christian spirit and calls himself a "want-wit." In contrast to how Shylock is introduced in the play, displaying his excessive wit, this is how we encounter Antonio for the first time and how the play begins:

> In sooth, I know not why I am so sad.
> It wearies me, you say it wearies you,
> But how I caught it, found it, or came by it,
> What stuff 'tis made of, whereof it is born,
> I am to learn;
> And such a *want-wit* sadness makes of me
> That I have much ado to know myself.
>
> (1.1.1–7)

Not insisting on the letter of the law is what seems to "kill" in this play. Insisting on mercy to "season" justice makes Shylock "not well," while the lack of wit to "work the letter" seems to drain the life of the law as well as of the want-wit Antonio. Insisting on the letter of the law in this play turns out to mean, as my reading has suggested, to insist on the work of interpretation. Shylock does not reject mercy in some kind of blind adhering to a dead letter, but in his insisting on the complex challenge of interpreting what remains debatable, readable, and translatable and what should not be replaced by a supposedly "seasoning" "mercy from above." *The Merchant of Venice* ultimately suggests the possibility of another translation—even if it may never be a fully "relevant" translation, but maybe, rather, a witty one.

NOTES

1. Jacques Derrida, "What Is a 'Relevant' Translation?," *Critical Inquiry* 27 (2001): 174–200.
2. Ibid., 195. In the context of this article, Derrida is not concerned with the complicity and tension between law and justice that is at the center of his essay "*Force of Law*: The "Mystical Foundation of Authority," *Cardozo Law Review* 11 (1990). "Justice," rather, serves as a synonym of what the former article had called "the law."
3. *Hegel's Early Theological Writings*, trans. T. M. Knox (Philadelphia: University of Pennsylvania Press, 1971), 212.
4. Katharine Eisaman Maus, introduction to *The Merchant of Venice*, in *The Norton Shakespeare: Based on the Oxford Edition*, ed. Stephen Greenblatt et al. (New York: Norton, 1997), 1114–15; my emphasis.
5. It is Pierre Legendre's specific twist to point out that this Christian love needs

and evokes Roman law and can thus not confine itself to opposing itself to the (dead) law. Christian love and Roman law, rather, form two complementary institutions.

6. See also Lisa Lampert, *Gender and Jewish Difference from Paul to Shakespeare* (Philadelphia: University of Pennsylvania Press, 2004), 10.

7. Derrida, "What Is a 'Relevant' Translation?," 194.

8. Ibid. For the Hegelian background, see *Hegel's Early Theological Writings*, trans. T. M. Knox (Philadelphia: University of Pennsylvania Press, 1971), 212: "This spirit of Jesus, a spirit raised above morality, is visible, directly attacking laws, in the Sermon on the Mount, which is an attempt, elaborated in numerous examples, to strip the laws of legality, of their legal form. The Sermon does not teach reverence for the laws; on the contrary, it exhibits that which fulfils the law but annuls it as law and so is something higher than obedience to law and makes law superfluous." In the further explication of the contrast of Christianity and Judaism, Hegel does not mention Shylock but, interestingly enough, Macbeth: "The fate of the Jewish people is the fate of Macbeth who stepped out of nature itself, clung to alien Beings, and so in their service had to trample and slay everything holy in human nature, had at last to be forsaken by his gods (since these were objects and he their slave) and be dashed to pieces on his faith itself" (205).

9. Ibid., 199.

10. Ibid.

11. Ibid., 176.

12. Ibid., 198; my emphasis.

13. Julia Reinhard Lupton, *Citizen-Saints: Shakespeare and Political Theology* (Chicago: University of Chicago Press, 2005), 80. Michael Greenstein calls it "a more imaginative mode of interpretation" in "Breaking the Mosaic Code: Jewish Literature vs. the Law," *Mosaic* 27 (1994): 88.

14. "If a man has two wives, one loved and the other hated, and both the loved and hated have borne him sons, but the first born is the son of the hated wife—when he leaves his inheritance to his sons he may not prefer the son of the beloved wife over the elder son of the hated wife. He must acknowledge the first born son of the hated wife and give him the double portion. For he is the first fruit of his loins and to him is the birthright" (Robert M. Cover, "Nomos and Narrative," in *Narrative, Violence, and the Law: The Essays of Robert Cover*, ed. Martha Minow, Michael Ryan, and Austin Sarat [Ann Arbor: University of Michigan Press, 1993], 114).

15. Pierre Legendre, "Die Juden interpretieren verrückt," in *Vom Imperativ der Interpretation* (Vienna/Berlin: Turia + Kant, 2010), 182. Cf. *Law, Text, Terror: Essays for Pierre Legendre*, ed. Peter Goodrich, Lior Barshack, and Anton Schutz (New York: Routledge, 2006).

16. Cover, "Nomos and Narrative," 115; my emphasis.

17. See Stéphane Mosès, *The Angel of History: Rosenzweig, Benjamin, Scholem*, trans. Barbara Harshav (Stanford, Calif.: Stanford University Press, 2009).

18. If the practice of interpretation can be understood in terms of Derrida's idea of translation, this second, imperial mode is somehow in line with how Derrida describes the canonization of certain translations, for example, the way in which his translation for *Aufhebung* has been canonized, against certain odds and to his own surprise.

19. Cover, "Nomos and Narrative," 144.

20. Ibid., 155.

21. Ibid., 159.

22. William Shakespeare, *The Merchant of Venice*, in *The Norton Shakespeare: Based on the Oxford Edition*, ed. by Stephen Greenblatt et al. (New York: Norton, 1997).

23. Cover, "Nomos and Narrative," 110.

24. According to Cover, an imperial law structurally rests on overturning or repressing another law, an overturning that—as Derrida has shown in *Force of Law* in his reading of Benjamin's *Critique of Violence*—can be legitimized only by itself and retrospectively.

25. According to Ronen Reichman, the stakes for judicial (as well as legislative) decision making is extremely high in the Talmudic legal discourse, and compared to this standard, the court scene in the *Merchant* seems especially problematic. See Ronen Reichman, "Aspects of Judicial and Legislative Decision-Making within the Talmudic Legal Discourse," in *Talmudische Tradition und moderne Rechtstheorie: Kontexte und Perspektiven einer Begegnung*, ed. Karl-Heinz Ladeur, Ino Augsberg, and Mohr Siebeck (Tübingen: Mohr Siebeck, 2013).

26. Cf. Ino Augsberg and Karl-Heinz Ladeur, "Der Buchstaben Tödtet, Aber der Geist Machet Lebending?," *Rechtstheorie* 40 (2009): 431–71.

27. Derrida, "What Is a 'Relevant' Translation?," 195.

28. Richard H. Weisberg, "The Concept and Performance of 'The Code' in the *Merchant of Venice*," in *Shakespeare and the Law*, ed. Paul Raffield and Gary Watt (Oxford: Hart, 2008), 289–98.

29. Cf. Anselm Haverkamp, *Shakespearean Genealogies of Power: A Whispering of Nothing in Hamlet, Richard II, Julius Caesar, Macbeth, the Merchant of Venice, and the Winter's Tale* (London: Taylor & Francis, 2010), 10917.

30. Ino Augsberg, "Shylocks Anspruch," *Archiv für Rechts- und Sozialphilosophie, Beiheft*, no. 114 (2007): 257–67.

31. Rudolf von Jhering famously calls it a "lousy dodge" ("elender Winkelzug") (Rudolf von Jhering and Felix Ermacora, *Der Kampf um's Recht* [Berlin: Propyläen Verlag, 1992], 263–64). See Augsberg, "Shylocks Anspruch," 264n36.

32. See, for example, Lisa Lampert's interesting reading of the *Merchant* that analyzes the difference of gender and of Jewish and Christian identity by reference to their diverging hermeneutical practices in *Gender and Jewish Difference from Paul*

to Shakespeare (Philadelphia: University of Pennsylvania Press, 2004). Donaldson and others have pointed out how Portia's insistence that not an iota of blood is to be shed subverts the assumption of Jewish literalism. See Laura E. Donaldson, "Launcelot's Feast: Teaching Poststructuralism and the New Mestiza," in *Order and Partialities: Theory, Pedagogy, and the "Postcolonial,"* ed. Kostas Myrsiades and Jerry McGuire (Albany: State University of New York Press, 1995), 189. For a reading that conceives of the iota as a stand-in for the Jew itself, see again Lupton, *Citizen-Saints*, 92–94.

33. "Of course, as it is said, the letter killeth while the spirit giveth life. We can't help but agree . . . ; but we should also like to know how the spirit could live without the letter. Even so, the pretentions of the spirit would remain unassailable if the letter had not shown us that it produces all the effects of truth in man without involving the spirit at all. It is none other than Freud who had this revelation" (Jacques Lacan, "The Insistence of the Letter in the Unconscious," *Yale French Studies* 36–37 [1966]: 112–47). On the relevance of the pun in Shylock, see Haverkamp, *Shakespearean Genealogies of Power*, 109–17.

The Justice of Administration

8

A Postmodern *Hetoimasia*—Feigning Sovereignty during the State of Exception

Marinos Diamantides

THE STATE OF OUR CONSTITUTIONAL IMAGINATION:
COGNITIVE DISSONANCE, PERFORMATIVE CONTINUITY

> Today, there is no legitimate power left anywhere on earth. . . . The integral juridification and economization of the relations between humans and the confusion between what we can believe, hope, love, and that which we are required to do and not to do, to say and not to say, [condemns] all the powerful of the world themselves to illegitimacy.
>
> Giorgio Agamben, "L'Église et le Royaume"

Are the words those of a cynical old man, or do they aptly describe the state of crisis that modern constitutional imagination, in both its political and its legal versions, finds itself in? Since at least one leading constitutional legal theorist and one leading political theorist would not object,[1] I suggest the latter. Moreover, I am interested in how the crisis of legitimacy and sovereignty is experienced by many with a sense of certainty that the rule of law and democracy, currently "on the cross" as it were, will be resurrected. In this regard, my intuition is that the popularity of proliferating theories aimed at restoring legitimate order[2] is the irrational effect, rather than the rational cause, of people participating in such modern *rituals* as consensus-making procedures (even as they know that public opinion is manipulated), and voting, demonstrating with a raised fist, or applying for judicial review (even as they see that modern politics and law are like a dog that can't bite). This is to say that simply by doing such things—regardless of subjective belief in their value and efficacy—many of us performatively validate as a true social fact the postulate of sovereign self-constitution in the scissile form of constituent/constituted power. The latter is postulated in secular-modern constitutional theory under the name "constitutional paradox."[3] During the religious High Middle Ages, it was postulated by natural theologians as the "mystery" of God's split power: at once absolute and self-limited.

Hence the importance of theorists, including but—thankfully—not confined to Carl Schmitt,[4] who detect a lingering, unconscious, or affective, reliance on religion and corresponding political theology in the secular era. In particular, I largely agree with Giorgio Agamben's account of the continuing impact on Western legal and political imagination of Christian *economic-political* theology.[5] This imagination includes the postulate that society cannot exist otherwise than in relation to a sovereign power with a providential plan in the image of a throne, the acclamation of which is not diminished by its vacuity and impotence. Moreover, against advocates of modern "communicative reason," Agamben opines that acclamation is still at the center of the political apparatuses of contemporary secular liberal democracies, with premodern doxologies and liturgies replaced by communicative processes that generate public opinion and consensus shaped by modern media. The latter "not only . . . enable the control and government of public opinion, but also and above all . . . manage and dispense Glory, the acclamative and doxological aspect of power."[6] As I have argued with my coauthor,[7] attachment to the postulate of such *oikonomia* is indeed the key element explaining the continuing cunning of occidental public reason, which locks together, without fusing or separating, sovereign decision and implementation, principle and pragmatism, legal and political Right, and so on in a perpetual *renvoi* that needs perpetual adjustment; I like to picture this as "see-saw," the spectacle of which makes us presuppose sovereign will as the necessary "pivot." Insofar as there is indeed continuity between the premodern blind trust in theological postulates and our modern constitutional "counterfactual imagination," it is pertinent to evoke "political theology" in explaining how it is that we continue to experience the disorder that comes with the implosion of sovereignty with a false sense of continuity and order and how we continue to defer to pseudo-sovereign governments regardless of their impotence and the fact that they "abandon" us alternatively in the state of "human resources" and of "human waste."

Both elsewhere[8] and in what follows I support and nuance Agamben's claims. The support comes by way of endorsing the, counter-Enlightenment, claim that meaning, at its most fundamental level, is not conceptual but affective, and that, therefore, for the most part of human history, blind intersubjective trust was established by performatively validating religious postulates as true social facts. Indeed, for the anthropologist Roy A. Rappaport, linguistic animals alone suffer the fear of being lied to and the anxiety that comes with the ability to imagine contestable alternatives. In view of this, he argued, human communities created "Ultimate Sacred Postulates," namely, cosmological axioms that are unfalsifiable because of their "substantial vacuity"—bearing no relation to material *significata* (from Gods who chose one species or society over another, to "self-evident" secular "truths," for example, that working on a piece of matter or an idea turns it into one's property).[9] The common performative validation of such postulates provides an irrational basis for trusting *some* others with whom we experience the disorder of constant, contingent, change with a (fake) sense of identity, order, continuity, and certainty. For the greatest part of human history, it has been the universal feature of traditional religions to render such postulates "sacred," that is, unquestionable. Although expressed through traditional myths, scripture, or the like, and through dogmatically defended modern "secular" principles or policies, say neoliberalism or the eventual prevailing of the proletariat, these postulates are effective regardless of the participants' subjective dis/belief insofar as they are embedded in beloved icons (e.g., the Cross on which death is defeated), formulaic imaginations (e.g., the world as God's *oikos*, or his absolute but self-limited power), and rituals (say the signing of a constitution, or raising a revolutionary fist together with comrades). From such postulates flow lower-order postulates including, I propose, what Roscoe Pound called "*jural postulates.*"[10] Here is not the place to explain my position on the difference between Pound's view that said postulates are universal and Joseph Kohler's view that law is relative to the civilization of a time and place (Kohler was the inspiration for Pound's "jural postulates"). Suffice it to say that in a *Westernized world* any universal "golden rule" is likely to be subject to the aforementioned particular cunning of occidental public reason, namely, the constant *renvois* between sovereign decision and implementation, principle and pragmatism, and so on.

In what follows I turn my attention to the sovereignty crisis in Greece in order to show, first, how modern, secular acclamations of the rule of law and democracy are in synergy with more colorful ethno-religious images and rituals that most of us tend to dismiss as just innocuous "folklore." Second, and here is the bit where I sympathetically critique Agamben, I discuss a series of images from such rituals, which speak to a richer and more complicated account of the development of "Western" economic-political theology than Agamben's, one that is both occidental and Eastern, or "Byzantine." It would be very flawed to interpret these as a sign that Greece remains "Byzantine" underneath the "veneer" of her Westernized modern form. Rather, the open reference to Byzantium in Greek ethno-religious spectacles is here seen as an opportunity to study the *repressed* ("Eastern") side of Western political and legal imagination, in which the *renvois* between law and administration was openly seen as anomic or anarchic, often at the expense of the dignity of the imperial throne, leading to various coups that were not justified with reference to some legal right or revolts—rather than revolutions—which were not authorized with reference to political right. It developed in the first millennium of the Christianized Roman Empire and can be called the "prehistory" of the following millennium, the era of "law *and* revolution," in which the *anomic* side to government was repressed under a consciousness ever more preoccupied with the (see-saw like) oscillation between autonomy and heteronomy that in constitutional terms takes the form of the "paradoxical relation" between constituent and constituted power. It was via this repression that violence could be cloaked by *juris-dictio*: the violent positing of a legal or political right that is *at the same time* a right to posit it, as if its cause lies "outside" itself. This "mythologization" of violence, to paraphrase Walter Benjamin, had *not* been so successful in the preceding era (contrary to the now discredited view of Eastern *basileis* as omnipotent "emperors and priests"). The Byzantine "game of thrones" was a time when Christianity's incoherent attempt to bring about a fraternity of equals, just as the church was endorsed by a hierarchically organized polity employing coercion and favoring some over others, had not yet been absorbed into the cunning of public reason, but was embarrassingly visible. Today, the material ruins of this political theology exist only in Russia and southeast Europe, but its significance for the entire Western paradigm, deeply buried underneath the cunning of public reason, is only exposed when, in the era of Bush and Trump but also of capitalism without even the semblance of liberalism, it becomes difficult to hide *anomie*.

Last but not least, I turn my attention to speculations about the possibility to finally rid ourselves of our deeply seated attachment to said political-economic theology and to live together not under a presumed throne that "authorizes" anomie but as *inoperative* beings whose proximity is not a sovereign gift but a fact with ethical consequences. In circumstances of "governance without sovereignty" and "Empire of Management," it is not necessary that we, respectively, nostalgically, harken to visions of national self-determination / Class victory, or substitute the comfort of participating in empty rituals of democracy with those "bonding" rituals that multinationals oblige their employees to participate in. The situation, rather, *could* give rise to a different sort of constitutional reflexivity whereby we both admit our powerlessness to escape those anonymous forces of anarchic management of populations by way of sovereign will *and* assert an anarchic sense of ethical responsibility to be responsible *for one another*. Such an ethos would desecrate the sovereign throne and embrace contingency with a sense of infinite responsibility beyond all postulated certainties, forsaking the comfort of old and new religions. In this regard, however, my rather somber conclusion is inspired by other images from Greece, this time of stray dogs, namely, semidomesticated, nonlinguistic, inoperative, social animals who are truly without want of gods. The first was photographed napping on the Hellenic president's throne—an

Figure 1. Thessaloniki, Greece, 28/11/11. This stray dog climbed onto the Hellenic President's chair.

Figure 2. Athens, Greece: shot of "Loukanikos," the Greek riot-dog, in front of anti-austerity protesters. Unknown photographer.

Figure 3. Syntagma Square, Athens, Greece: stray dog lying in front of SYRIZA's electoral sign that reads "Hope is Coming," Unknown photographer.

accidentally perfect symbol of the potential to substitute inoperative life for sovereignty in the core of our political and legal imagination.

The second was eponymous and became world famous: Loukanikos, the riot dog, featured as the "2011 person of the year" by *Time* magazine.

Having accompanied anti-austerity demonstrators on various occasions, it ended up as pinup for those still seeking to storm the Bastille even as there is no center of power *to* storm. He is a perfect metaphor for Alexis Tsipras, the political underdog-turned-poodle. The third dog is as anonymous as the first, but its posture perhaps points to an ethos that may help us escape the fate of would-be fighting dogs that end up fully domesticated poodles: it is seen dozing off in Athens's Syntagma Square before the slogan that brought Tsipras to power: "Hope Is Coming."

GREECE'S OWN EMPTY THRONE: A POSTMODERN *HETOIMASIA*

The centre of the governmental machine is empty. The empty throne, the *hetoimasia tou thronou,* that appears on the arches and apses of the Paleochristian and Byzantine basilicas is perhaps, in this sense, the most significant symbol of power.

The empty throne is not . . . a symbol of regality but of glory. . . . Glory precedes the creation of the world and survives its end.

Giorgio Agamben, The Kingdom and the Glory

Late modernity at once constitutes itself as the constant management of interminable crises and states of exception *and* is imagined as an advanced, if precarious, stage in the rise and rise of "Juridical Humanity" and "Democracy." Ours is a world formally divided among sovereign states but, in effect, a global society in which myriad and diffuse, transnational, deterritorialized powers with particular agendas—from multinationals to global nongovernmental organizations, from the World Trade Organization to fundamentalist sleeper cells—operate in networks that, taken together, deprive states of their role as comprehensive order and welfare providers to their citizens and even sideline them in the effort to play the role of maestro among such transnational organizations as the WTO, the International Monetary Fund (IMF), and the European Central Bank (ECB).[11] Many a citizen realizes that the rule of law and democracy have given way to "administration without sovereignty,"[12] involving the constant management of two types of populations, competitive "human resources" and collateral "human waste": "illegal" migrants/refugees kept in detention if lucky enough to survive their trips over nineteenth-century borders; sweatshop laborers, often minors, in places where slums are next to mega-malls selling grand pianos; and many more, including the newly impoverished southern European millennial immigrants to the north working on zero-hour contracts for corporations that pay little or no tax; to those are added numerous others who, for various reasons, refuse or are unable to join in the spirit of relentless competition. Yet, while national governments are effectively reduced to the role of police—immigration control and tax collector—a role a handful of them play on a global scale on account of their military might, many citizens still atavistically validate them as the holders of that fantastic superpower to constitute and defend organized human communities that we call "sovereignty" and which lies at the center of the occidental legal and political imagination.

For a contemporary example of the state we are in, one can do worse than look at Greece—the birthplace of the question around democracy and the rule of law—which, has, since 2009, experienced a great incursion into its legal and political systems by the (neoliberal) dictates of its international creditors, verging on outright abandonment of respect for the country's liberal-democratic constitution. This has happened both openly/directly and secretly/indirectly through the actions of other governments in coordination with high-level international "expert" bureaucrats. Characteristically, as the *Financial Times* has revealed,[13] pressure by the then president of France and the German chancellor (in conspiracy with the president of the European Commission) led to the undermining of newly elected Greek prime minister George Papandreou when he dared to propose a referendum on the austerity-for-funding memorandum, his resignation, and the cancellation of said referendum. After two interim PMs served briefly, an ex-ECB employee and a judge, a coalition of the two traditional parties of power, left and right, grudgingly began to implement Troika-imposed austerity and liberalization measures in exchange for emergency financing (for they were all too conscious of their foreseeable losses in the next elections). As is well known, the austerity measures caused a great deal of suffering (Greece now tops the European suicide statistics charts, whereas it used to be at the bottom). As has been widely commented, much of this effectively meant the abandonment of the rule of law and democracy in relation to constitutionally guaranteed rights, directly of workers and pensioners and, indirectly, of most of the population.

During the dismantling of what had become, since the eighties, a generous welfare state (funded increasingly by European Union (EU) grants and loans and also marred by extensive patronage and corruption), the society-state bond was severely tested. During this time new anti-austerity political movements worked hard to draw energy toward organized protests and strikes and *away* from the increasing incidents of vilifications of the state (see my discussion of figures 14 and 15 later on) and from civil-society initiatives such as exchange markets and soup kitchens, accusing them, respectively, of nihilism and "putting a human face on neo-liberal capitalism." Finally, under the slogan "Hope Is Coming" and with the grand promise of "tearing apart" the memoranda by the passing of just "one law with just one clause," SYRIZA, the anti-austerity coalition of some of these "radical left" movements of protest, eventually won a weak majority in the 2015 elections and formed a coalition with ANEL, a small party of ethno-religious nationalists. As is widely known, not only was their manifesto not implemented but, surreally, substituted by the most intense austerity program ever, minus, this time, the protests, since their erstwhile agitators were now comfortably seated in parliament and hastily rubber-stamping every single demand of the Troika (e.g., under SYRIZA Greece had its most extensive privatization ever—including all national airports and the railways). Indeed, the Troika has since publicly praised the SYRIZA-ANEL government as the most compliant yet.

In this regard, I submit, the combined effect of mediatized legal *and* political reactions to the implosion of Greek sovereignty was, effectively, to help generate false consensus that the handling of the sovereign-debt crisis was still a matter of sovereign decision. Starting with *legal* developments, the Greek Council of State, in its first case reviewing the constitutionality of the measures demanded by the Troika, accepted as true the state attorney's proposition that the so-called Economy Protection Acts—in which whole segments of the first, of eventually three, "Memoranda of Understanding," which had been agreed to after Papandreou's forced resignation, between the technocratic Greek government and the Troika in exchange for emergency funding of the Greek state, were included *verbatim*—were *expressions of Greek sovereignty*, the Greek people's Will constitutionally generated in Parliament.[14] The laws in question had been passed with a slim majority and were retroactively ratifying a wide range of measures already implemented using decree-laws ("acts of legislative content") as foreseen in the Constitution's Article 44.1 in cases of "extraordinary circumstances of an urgent and unforeseeable need." The case focused on the relevance of Article 28, paragraphs 2 and 3, of the Constitution, which requires a supermajority of three fifths of the total number of members of Parliament whenever a bill proposes to "limit the exercise of national sovereignty in favor of agencies of international organizations when this serves an important national interest and promotes cooperation with other States."[15] It is pertinent to note that Article 28 had been originally included in the 1975 Constitution as a way to signal Greece's determination and readiness for joining the EU (Greece eventually acceded to the then EEC in 1981). By majority the Council of State disagreed with the Athens Bar's submission that the laws fell within this article's ambit on the basis that the austerity and economy restructuring measures, introduced by decrees and validated by the Acts, were an exercise of sovereignty, even as they had been devised "in collaboration with" Greece's international partners; therefore, the constitutional requirement that laws surrendering sovereignty be voted by a supermajority of the full house was not relevant. In typical positivist spirit the court agreed that whether there had been a de facto limitation of national sovereignty constituted a political, not legal, issue, and, therefore, the courts had no jurisdiction; whether an additional majority was politically preferable in view of the significance of the measures concerned internal, nonjusticiable, parliamentary process.[16] What is lost to the rhetorical "glorification" of (absent) sovereign decision in the case of the Council of State's decision is the court's own realist insight: the *memoranda* are *not justiciable* because they are *neither* international agreements *nor* national laws; expressions of neither political nor of legal power, they are, rather, "informal technical frameworks" drawn up by experts who, presumably, act as the long hand of the increasingly unpredictable markets. A second, depressingly sincere, remark of the court came in relation to the question of whether the constitutional duty of the Greek state to preserve the dignity of its citizens had been breached. In sum, the pay cuts and so on did not by themselves endanger the *sustenance* of the affected citizens; by equating human dignity with bare survival, the court presented us with a proxy description of what Agamben calls *bare life*.

Given that Greece avails of a system of diffuse and incidental control of constitutionality of laws, it is also pertinent to note subsequent lawsuits, some of which led to decisions that found the austerity measures to be *unconstitutional*. For example, the Athens Court of Peace agreed with the complaint of workers in the Athens Underground that their pay cuts were unconstitutional on the basis that, under Article 28, a parliamentary supermajority is needed to surrender sovereignty under specific circumstances of urgent national imperatives.[17] Disagreeing with the view of the Council of State, this court bravely announced that the "Economy Protection Acts" *did* amount to a decision to surrender the management of the national economy to foreign experts and so ought, in principle, to have been voted according to Article 28. Moreover, the court declared, to much approval by anti-austerity media, that "giving the international markets the reassurance that Greece is becoming more competitive," as the state attorney had submitted was a major objective, did *not* amount to a "national imperative" for the purposes of Article 28. Finally, the Economy Protection Acts had disproportionately infringed on basic human rights, including social and economic ones, in accordance with the Greek Constitution and several international treaties to which Greece is signatory. The pay cuts were not proportionately scaled according to the level of income and, thus, fell foul of doubly entrenched human and social rights (both directly in the Greek Constitution and indirectly by various international treaties to which Greece is a signatory via the Greek Constitution's Article 28 (para. 1) that proclaims such treaties to be inviolable by Greek law). What is lost to the rhetorical "glorification" of democracy and human rights by the anti-austerity decisions of this lower court—celebrated as David versus Goliath—is recoverable in the irony of its stating at once that (1) "sending signals of competitive reform" to the international markets (in order to be recognized as once again creditworthy) could not be used as "urgent grounds" to issue law decrees that infringed on workers' rights under international law; (2) the latter is superior to Greek law by virtue of Article 28, which, as we saw, had been originally introduced in the constitutional text law *in order to signal*, back in 1975, that the Greek state was "serious" in its intention to join the then EEC—namely, a postpolitical transnational enterprise. Beyond the irony, however, the court lost the opportunity to confront the main problem: Who decides the existence of an emergency that justifies decree laws, the Greek "sovereign" or the various networks of bureaucrats? A similar decision from an even lower court[18] declared unconstitutional the compulsory redundancy of janitors in the Ministry of Finance inter alia on the basis that "solvency by itself does not constitute a superior public interest" (talk about sovereignty *by fiat*!).

Turning from legal to political shows of "David versus Goliath," the eventual betrayal of the 2015 anti-austerity referendum result by Prime Minister Alexis Tsipras—a still relatively popular figure who was, before, an advocate of "radical" uses of constituent power leading demonstrations, strikes, and the like with a raised fist and was endorsed as such by such prominent Euro-Atlantic left public intellectuals as Slavoj Žižek (who thought he had found his "socialist Thatcher"[19])—is interesting as a case of staging impotence as if temporary, tactical, retreat that does not lessen the glory of its intentions. As such, it masks the anomie of Greece's crisis management no less than the courts' legalism. A month after his January 2015 electoral victory a (sincerely benevolent) Tsipras, with over 80 percent of popular support behind him, was televised standing before Parliament *crying* and committing to a much lighter version of his manifesto pledges. In his televised state address in the aftermath of the July 2015 referendum, after "fifteen continuous hours" of unsuccessful pleas to creditors to accept the anti-austerity will of his people, as the newly reopened state TV informed us, Tsipras appeared tired, with a highly visible canker on his lips, announcing a second election. This time he was promising to manage the austerity with as much concern for the weaker sections of society as possible. He won the election after just one month in the midst of great confusion, as all banks had closed. If we needed a contemporary example of Christ-like "glory" of the impotent and humiliated yet gloriously promising sovereign, this is it. Such theater, during an advanced stage of the "state of exception," masks the fact that when Greece's liberal-constitutional democracy retreated, the constituent potential of the likes of the *indignados* of *Syntagma* (Constitution) Square in Athens prevailed only superficially. At closer inspection what prevailed was, rather, the *syntagma* of the *force-of-law*, namely, the unreal "relation" between power and law that becomes apparent in the confusion between acts of the executive power and acts of the legislative power in such instances as Roman dictatorship, the French Constituent Assembly of July 8, 1791, the Nazis' formulaic claim "the words of the Führer have the force of law,"[20] and, in the case at hand, the dictates of Greece's debt-colonial masters. That said, as Agamben argues, today's situation is analogous not to dictatorship but to the Roman institution of *iustitium*—a "standstill" or "suspension of the law."[21] In Greece, at a time when the established Conservative, Liberal, and Social Democratic Parties could no longer serve as a legitimating reference for those anonymous forces that dictate the policies of nation-states, technocrats and jurists but also charismatic leaders who start as stray underdogs and end as docile poodles were better suited to implement neoliberal policies while acting out the (Christ-like) role of the tortured-yet-triumphant defender of, respectively, the Greek state and people. Such spectacle distracts from the degree of anomie by focusing public attention to the role of sovereign who is thus agentifying what in reality are fragmented, anonymous, and anarchic processes of management of populations.

GIORGIO AGAMBEN

Agamben has offered us tools to understand both the above-discussed predicament of *iustitium* and its mystification. He teaches that the human animal is not defined by power—be it in the sense of Platonic idealism, as *dynamis* or potential power, or of Aristotelian realism, as *energeia* or actual power—but by *powerlessness*. We are primarily "inoperative" and contemplative beings or, in the Hebraic lexicon, *sabbatical*.[22] His related thesis is that the countless changes in the way that populations in the West (and, through imposition, everywhere) are governed fall within a singular (secularized Christian) biopolitical paradigm—the "Western juridico-political machinery of government"—in which said inoperability is efficiently "captured" for the benefit of established power through the *fiction* of sovereignty, which hides that in effect lives are managed as things.[23] He argues that this situation is, first, courtesy of the dominant strands in Greek philosophy[24] in which the human was conceived in the form of a strictly binary articulation—"*zoe/bios*"—in such a way that ill-fitting forms-of-life (understood as inseparable from their form and its context, i.e., lives lived through multiple selves in various contexts) are "abandoned" as expendable "bare lives."[25] Since then, to be "inoperable"—to oscillate between actuality and potentiality—is, at best, seen as an apolitical vice (e.g., hedonistic laziness or disgruntled cynicism) and, at worst, is the forced status of designated bare lives that become the object of anomic violence (the long-term unemployed, the zero-hour contract workers, or, worse, the *sans papier*, the immigrants in detention centers).[26] Further, in *State of Exception*, Agamben teaches us that "sovereign" power is nothing more than the attempt to annex the anomie to which such "bare life" is subject through the legal fiction of "exception," namely, by establishing an artificial relation between anomic violence and law where no such relation truly exists.[27]

Finally, in *The Kingdom and the Glory*, Agamben explains the historical success of this model, where abandonment occurs via inclusion, with reference to the Christian "*political-economic*" theology that developed under ecumenical synods (which were called, chaired, and had their decisions enforced by the state). The focus is mostly on the Nicene Creed and Trinitarianism: when a divide was conceived within the One God (incidentally, some twenty years ago, the same Creed was at the heart of Harold Berman's distinct arguments).[28] This splitting of God's being from His praxis occurred in order to postulate, against Gnostics and others, that the Glory of Divine Providence is unaffected by the existence of evil. As such, the Triune God is the original model of "absolute yet divided" power that is quite unlike both Aristotle's *prime mover* and the, entirely otherworldly, Jewish God, who is a static single transcendent monarchy closed in on *Godself*. No sooner was this split conceived than theologians proposed to manage the "relations" between God's three holy persons in a way that also "accounts" for contingency: with reference to the classical discourse on *oikonomia* (administration of the house, the art of managing the *oikos* that for the Greeks lived outside politics; domestics managed it on behalf of a largely absentee landlord). An article of faith among the followers of the most important churches for millennia, Trinitarianism suggests that evil occurs as part of such mysterious and anarchic Divine *oikonomia* that comprises creationism *and* freedom. It advances a notion that God in freedom (not out of necessity) relates Godself to what is not God, that is, to the world. This *anarchic* freedom to be differentially Godself in a unique and mysterious *oikonomia* of the divine life is what makes creation possible—or, such was the Nicene "ultimate sacred postulate," as the anthropologist of religion would call it.[29] Earthly sovereignty was reconceived by analogy and in the *image* of such a Triune God—a God postulated as a cybernetically closed "set of relations" of his three hypostases. Indeed, almost two millennia later it is as "relational" that the modern legal theorist conceives sovereignty.[30] Imagined thus, sovereign power is believed to master contingency and to "contain" every possible difference, everything that was, is, and will be. Inside this total circle[31] the God-like sovereigns are "locked" together, without ever fusing or separating, a series of binaries: the particular and the universal, which the ancient philosophers had sought to distinguish (Platonic idealism) or collapse (Aristotelian realism); the transcendental and the immanent—originally correlating respectively to the inflexible and commanding rule of the Old Testament's God and the flexible and dispensatory rule of the Son of Man; and, equally, in the last millennium, the notion of God's *potentia absoluta* and *potentia limitata*, from which was derived the modern secular idea of constituent/constituted power (which in late modernity, after the killing of the God of ontology, ceased to be a mystery and was renamed a "paradox"[32]).

More efficient than the Roman practice of hiring *claquers* to applaud the emperor, the Nicene theology made possible a new image of government in which the earthly sovereign comes to be seen as mirroring God's eternal Glory regardless of how much misery he presides over. That God-like kings "reign but do not govern" means that they at once authorize and remain unaffected by the shortcomings, or even impotence, of government decisions and administrative measures. Government is, thus, "always already" legitimate in a circular way, as anarchically and as gloriously as the creator God. Again, this image contrasts both with Aristotle's idea of God (*qua* transcendent principle in any movement who leads the world as a strategist leads his army) *and* the biblical God (who commands and invites into a covenant): both were overcome by the new imagination of a monarch who "hidden in the room of his palace, moves the world as the puppeteer leads his puppets on strings."[33] The "hidden" or mysterious element is paramount, for sovereignty cannot be incessantly glorified if associated with the person of any particular mortal monarch.[34] Agamben, further, explains this

Figure 4. The *Hetoimasia* (Greek ἑτοιμασία, "preparation"), Preparation of God's "empty throne," Arian Baptistery, Ravenna, Italy, early sixth century.

ineluctable glorification of the sovereign office by reference to the postulate of God's *throne*, which, in the Abrahamic tradition, was created by God *before* the world (therefore, existing independently of it). He points to the paleo-Christian images titled *Hetoimasia tou Thronou* ("preparation of God's empty throne").

The fact that the throne is not *actually* empty—this one (Figure 4) bears a cushion, *crux gemmata*, and cloth and is flanked by Saints Peter and Paul—can be interpreted to mean that, as this chapter suggests, our political and legal imagination is never a tabula rasa. Conceptual innovation and critical thinking in modern times still go side by side with an affectively effective sense of certainty and continuity that is embedded in familiar images, emblems, architectural styles, metaphors, and so on. From bowing to the constitutional text to raising a revolutionary clenched fist, we performatively validate as a true social fact a power of self-constitution that is not there. The image—involving an "empty" divine throne surrounded by angels—is emblematic of the domestication of the political and legal imagination of the Christian subject (and, arguably, the modern secular one, too) into a new paradigm in which politics becomes unthinkable without a providential sovereign overseeing the prudential management of beings and/as things. The *Hetoimasia*, then, should not be taken literally to mean the act of "preparing" the throne for the elected to use but, on the contrary, of postulating and glorifying it as if it had always been ready and as if it were a substantive quality of the created world. The world, therefore, is a quality *of* government and not the other way around! Hence our inability to think "anarchy" otherwise than as chaos, and our deference to, and abandonment by, pseudo-sovereign governments, regardless of their disastrous action or inaction.[35] It could also be said that the *Hetoimasia* is a visual record of what Derrida called the "counter signature" of God that, regardless of secularization, still lies behind modern declarations of independence,[36] which preps us to accept government even when we realize that nobody really is in charge, that not only is the "king" naked but dead and buried: because we cannot imagine a world without *a* "throne." The modern death of the God of ontology, as well as the frequently exposed vacuity of our governments, is of no consequence to their respective metaphysical glorification *as if* indispensable. This assessment has sobering implications for democratic theory, just as much if not more than Michel Foucault's view that we did not really slay the monarch, which Agamben echoes.

In summing up the significance of this imagination for European political and legal culture ever since, Agamben points to how two antinomical paradigms have been *functionally* related. One is "political theology," which founds the transcendence of sovereign power on the single God; the other is "economic theology" (strictly speaking not a theology but the displacement of the denotation of Greek *oikonomia* onto the theological field of Trinitarianism, as discussed above), which effectively replaces transcendence with the idea of an *oikonomia* conceived as the *constant activity of immanent ordering*—domestic and not political in a classical sense—of both divine and human life. The coupling between these two paradigms, he argues, takes the form *not of concepts or even beliefs* but of ritualized *acclamative performances* that glorify sovereign providential power come what may. As stated earlier, against advocates of modern "communicative reason," Agamben opines that, today, public opinion and consensus shaped via the media perform a function analogous to premodern doxologies and liturgical acclamations.

In the preceding section I looked at how Greece's courts and politicians respectively validated as a true social fact the sovereignty of the Greek state and people in times of *iustium*. There is, however, synergy with the country's more colorful—explicitly ritualistic—public events. Modern Greece's national rituals include two national parades. While March 25 commemorates the war of independence from the Ottoman Empire, October 28, known as *Ohi* (No) Day, commemorates the rejection by the Greek dictator Metaxas of the ultimatum made by the Italian dictator Benito Mussolini on October 28, 1940, the Hellenic counterattack against the invading Italian forces during the Greco-Italian War, and the Greek Resistance during the Axis occupation. On October 28, 2011, at the height of the first phase of the Greek sovereign-debt crisis, the Hellenic president—a purely ceremonial post—hastily left the stage from which he was presiding over the parade in Thessaloniki, following vociferous booing by the attending crowds, who were angry at the austerity measures passed by the country's elected government at the dictate of the country's lenders. Once the president had paid the price for the people's dissatisfaction by leaving, the parade—a doxological event par excellence—continued before the empty presidential throne, and order was restored.

After the Hellenic president's abrupt departure, the national parade he was meant to watch continued before his empty chair flanked by his admin-

Figure 5. Thessaloniki, Greece, 28/11/11. With thanks to photographer Mr. I. Vassilakakis for his kind permission.

istrative and security staff, military officers, and clerics. This seems to suggest that the latter chorus matter more than the sovereign himself. The incident confirms that the empty throne is not a symbol of regality but of perpetual glory. The legalistic interpretation of this is effectively that of Ernst Kantorowicz[37]: in polities shaped as the corporate body of Christ, thanks to the conceptual labor of the medieval scholastics who combined Roman law with Christian theology, there can be no interregnum. Moreover, from Thomas Hobbes to Hans Kelsen the idea is that no unified "people" can exist but for their submission to a sovereign office that is unbound by law. The other side to this is the unquestionable "primacy of the political." From Hannah Arendt to Claude Lefort the disappearance of the sovereign leader as a political body—the putting to death of the king, as Kantorowicz called it—has been optimistically interpreted as a founding moment of modern secular democracy precisely because it made the seat of power, "hitherto" occupied by an eternal substance transcending the mere physical existence of monarchs, into an empty space where groups with shared interests and opinions can succeed each other; democracy, therefore, is celebrated on account of its vagueness, its incompleteness, against which totalitarianism is said to establish itself: no divine right, no transcendental *arche*. Government power in this optimistic view can no longer be tied to any specific program, goal, or proposal: it is nothing but a collection of instruments put temporarily at the disposal of those who win a majority. Likewise, the view proposed by "radical" Greek political forces embracing "agonistic" politics and asserting the primacy of "the political" over law (as Schmitt did in his famous debate with Kelsen) was that the juridification/constitutionalization of political matters is bad in the best of times and certainly not an antidote to the managerialization/privatization of Greek public life. They were the ones who encouraged the crowds to boo, after all. From their perspective the significance of the aforementioned Thessaloniki incident ends with the hasty departure of the Hellenic president: strip the liberal façade of legality! Shout out justice and raise your fists! Rebel! Storm the Bastille! Neither the fact that there is presently no Bastille (no one center of power) to storm nor the fact that the people appreciated the orderly spectacle of the parade before an empty presidential chair flanked by military and clerical dignitaries seems to matter much in their strategic calculations. Their view of the empty throne would be effectively that of Lefort: the killing of the premodern monarch revealed that the throne is always essentially empty, *its emptiness making agonistic politics possible*. If managers have usurped the throne, nevertheless, a revived

Politics, with a capital *P*, can still reoccupy it. Just as the submission to the absolutist "divine right" required a religion that was not only, and not primarily, conceptually but ritually—affectively—effective, the "civil religion" that, as Jean-Jacques Rousseau argued more explicitly, must be added to the persuasiveness of the social contractarian hypothesis mostly associated with Hobbes and John Locke, must, to be effective, be enhanced through (non-rational) acclamatory/doxological performances that give rise to a consensus that sovereignty must be presupposed as phoenix-like or rather Jesus-like. In crisis-hit Greece this task was perfectly performed by the media, politicians, lawyers, and some public intellectuals who encouraged the enraged public to continue to rely on law and/or politics.

WESTERN POLITICAL-ECONOMIC THEOLOGY IS NOT JUST OCCIDENTAL

Returning to the aforementioned incident in Thessaloniki, I note that the Hellenic president's chair bore the two-headed eagle symbolizing the Byzantine Empire as well as the modern Greek Orthodox Church, both important components in modern Greek national fantasies.

This prompts me to discuss some little-known particularities of religion and power in Byzantium. My findings suggest that the field of political theology is much too complex for such universalist assertions as Jean Bodin's, Hobbes's or Schmitt's (in brief, that "all societies" require a sovereign decider who presides over a law he is not bound by), but also, of Agamben's rather incomplete view of a "Christian-Western" model of governance that centers

Figure 6. Thessaloniki, Greece, 28/11/11: the Hellenic president's chair with a "double-headed eagle."

on a mutual "see-saw" between ever-glorious if impotent sovereignty and efficient if mundane and anarchic administration. Indeed, a closer look at the political theology of the Eastern Empire and Church reveals that Agamben is wrong to suggest that sovereignty and administration were in a fined-tuned synergy already since the development of Trinitarianism.

As I have argued elsewhere, based on the assessment of Gilbert Dagron's brilliant scholarship,[38] the Christianization of the Empire was a negative development for the authority of the imperial office, which henceforth was mired in a "legitimacy deficit" at the very foundation of the political presence of the Byzantine *basileus*, producing the *consciousness of the inherent vacuity and precariousness of the political*.[39] The stories of the many Eastern emperors who were neither anointed nor "born in the blue," and who ended up toppled and publicly humiliated, banished, or grotesquely tortured, bear evidence. According to the rather incoherent political theology of the peculiar, populist, "Republic,"[40] and first-ever "welfare state,"[41] that was the Christianized Eastern Roman Empire, the sovereign was always suspect and potentially illegitimate—a false Melchizedek (Hebrew "righteous king")—and only tolerated insofar as his administration was *actually* conducive to "*salus populi*" (by "people" I mean not everyone equitably but the *filoi*[42] [friends] among Christians and certainly not "obstinate Jews," "pagans," and "heretics" even if these were all Roman citizens). While Agamben in *The Kingdom and the Glory* usefully points out how it was in Byzantium that law acquired a dispensatory character, he misses out on the fact that the Byzantine state was a state of open patronage; dispensation from the rigors of the law and welfare "benefits" openly came hand in hand with clientalism, as they were not benefiting everyone but the emperor's supporters and friends—the *filoi*.

In sum, contrary to what most of us learned at school—if anything—the Byzantine *basileus* was not a super-autonomous sovereign unbound by law and combining imperial and sacerdotal power. In fact the Eastern *basileus* was only an "as if" *pontifex maximus* and only an "as if" Christian priest. In addition, there was no tradition of dynastic succession by primogeniture or anointment. Without such knowledge one can make too much of Justinian's *Digest* stating that the emperor was the source of all law (sec. 1.4.1) and, therefore, not bound by them (sec. 1.3.31), even if he abided by them voluntarily (*Institutes*, sec. 2.17.8). Justinian's restating of Ulpian's *princeps legibus solutus est* must be taken with a big pinch of (Eastern) Christian salt.

In reality, Justinian found out, the emerging Christian *ecumene*—not yet the universal space over which the Catholic Church would eventually claim authority—was not so governable by lawgiving. Justinian did issue an impressive six hundred laws over thirty-nine years, but that is already less than the earlier record. Imperial legislative production aimed for codification slowed down exponentially after the fifth century, when the second and longest phase in Byzantine legal history begins. It is during these long nonrevolutionary years of established and triumphant Byzantine cultural, military, and economic supremacy that, as Agamben notices, Byzantine lawgiving, in the form of *Novels*, took on its characteristic *dispensatory* nature, while Byzantine politics, as Agamben fails to note, acquired a characteristic obsession with the "social question" that increased patronage politics. In sum, a closer look at Byzantine legal and political history than Agamben allowed himself reveals that the merging of the Christian notion of God's anarchic praxis with, respectively, the Greek and Roman legal concepts of *epieikia* and *aequitas* occurred less in the name of universal salvation as (Catholic) Agamben implies than that of an insecure emperor presiding over networks of influential individuals or classes of individuals (laypeople, officials, clerics) whose interests occasioned from time to time the issuing of a dispensatory law *in exchange for* acclaiming the—usually usurper—*basileus*.

Figure 7. The humility of Byzantine sovereigns. Emperor Leo the Wise (r. 886–912 CE).

Figure 8. The mortality of Byzantine sovereigns. Emperor Alexander (r. 912–913) Mosaic detail, *Hagia Sophia*, Constantinople/Istanbul.

That post-Justinian ruling via law became decreasingly tenable also brought about a transformation in spectacles of power. Characteristically, postcoronation performances in the Hippodrome often explicitly represented the violent or conspiratorial events that brought each emperor to power. In response, a new attribute of imperial virtue was born: calculated humility and shows of imperial mortality. Thus Leo the Wise (r. 886–912), whom Agamben picks as exemplary for the turn toward *oikonomia*, is depicted on his knees before Christ (Hagia Sophia, Constantinople/Istanbul) (Figure 7).

In Figure 8 we see Emperor Alexander (r. 912–913) in the Hagia Sophia: in his left hand he holds a *Globus cruciger* and in his right hand the *akakia* (ἀκακία, lit. "guilelessness") a cylindrical purple silk roll containing dust symbolizing the mortal nature of all men and held by Byzantine emperors during ceremonies (it had developed from the *mappa*, the cloth used by the Roman consuls to start the races at the Hippodrome). That said, shows of humility had to be matched with bread for the masses or at least a large-enough power base. A Byzantine emperor, unlike say Prime Minister Tsipras today, could cry all he wanted and show off his cankers, but if the people went hungry along with his client power-base he could expect not reacclamation—in order to manage the situation as best he could—but a gruesome end. The difference between Byzantium and the second millennium is that sovereigns in the former could neither afford to forget the social question nor successfully hide their investment in economies of partial compassion and anarchic management of suffering behind some principle of legal or political justice. The ethos of the Byzantine sovereign never quite extended to the self-righteousness we find in, say, Shakespeare's Richard the Third.[43] Thus, while Agamben in *The Kingdom and Glory* is right to point out that in Christian political economic theology the sovereign is imagined by analogy to the Triune God qua sum total of the relations between his constituent "persons," he is wrong to, anachronistically, suggest that the figure of the impotent and tortured yet still-acclaimed Roi-Méhaigné[44] was a direct outcome of this imagination. In fact this figure, straight out of the Arthurian legends that Byzantines had no idea about, was absent from public imagination in places like Russia or Greece before they were influenced by their occidental neighbors.

The ways Byzantine political theology produced a "legitimacy deficit" and a compensatory obsession with the social question in what was a strongly centralized state should be studied and contrasted to the subsequent millennium's (occidental) self-confident political theology that gave rise to a public reason that generates "legitimacy surpluses" by centering on an "abstract," always already legitimate, fulcrum of political power that can be stored in institutions and, paradoxically, augmented by division[45] in the context of a weak Holy Roman Empire "presiding" over numerous kingdoms. This confident public reason has its roots in late medieval occidental "natural theology" that replaced Byzantium's "legitimacy deficit" with a "deficient immanence," a sense of absolute secular power without telos, which translated into cognitive or normative certainties. In its eastern version Christianism, as an official state religion, had openly been embarrassing: at once claiming to be a fraternity of equals that is better than a hierarchically organized society and in bed with a polity employing coercion and allowing favoritism of some citizens over others.[46] What, if anything, bound together Byzantines in a whole? Roman citizenship? Membership in the church? Networks of friends supporting each other in what was a fallen and irredeemable word before the Second Coming? Eastern political theology offers no answer. By contrast, the Catholic Church in pre-Reformation Europe developed tools that "explained away" such embarrassments through such means as the principle of "Two Powers" (the investiture contests further introduced the principle of "dualism in authority" that has migrated from pope-emperor to pope-prince, through to king-people); "just war theories"; and such "principles" as "unity in diversity" and "omnipresence with centralization." These new tools meant that what was once an embarrassing Christian imbroglio—a fraternity of "equals" housed in a stratified and anarchically managed imperial household—became a righteous dualist battle over who has the "right" to head the household in the name of God: the pope or the king? Likewise, since then, our image of the state economically retains two different modes of association deriving from Roman law: the idea of the state as *societas* and as *universitas*.[47] Since then, public law "can be understood realistically only once we have grasped that the modern state in general . . . rests on an unresolved tension between . . . two irreconcilable modes of government," namely, *societas/universitas* and a *corporation/communitas*.[48] Moreover, the sacrament of the Eucharist—the symbolic communion that joins members to the mystical body of Christ—changed. Thus, after the mid-twelfth century, the term *corpus mysticum* was transferred to the church, which was now also called *Corpus Christi* or *Corpus Naturale*; thus, "the mystical force and passion surrounding the old notion was brought to sustain the whole society of Christians and its power structure. In the papal bull of *Unam Sanctum* the church was already described as *unum corpus mysticum cuius caput Chris-*

tus, one mystical body whose head is Christ."⁴⁹ Post-Reformation Protestant thinkers transferred this image to the nation-state headed by a prince. If in the church-society the force fusing the members into a whole was the sacrament of symbolic communion that joins members to the mystical body of Christ, in temporal societies this force was nationalism.

If we turn to theology proper, we find that the interpretation of Trinitarianism that (Catholic) Agamben generalizes as "Christian," in which the glory of the anointed/elected sovereign is generally acclaimed regardless of impotence and human misery, is in fact merely *occidental* and was developed only in the second millennium of Christian political-economic theology. The difference *within* Western theology (Greek-Eastern and Latin-occidental) refers to the famous theological schism over the "correct" version of the Christian Creed and the related *Filioque* controversy in the eleventh century. Does the Holy Spirit "proceed" only from the "Father," as the Greeks had it, or, additionally, from the Son? The difference between Christo-centric Occident and *pneumato*-centric East (spirit-centered) East is more easily gauged in Doménikos Theotokópoulos's *The Dormition of the Virgin* painted before

Figure 9. *The Dormition of the Virgin* by Domenikos Theotocopoulos ("El Greco"), painted before the artist migrated to the Occident.

this artist migrated to the Occident (sixteenth century; Cathedral of Syros, Greece): there, it is the Holy Spirit, not Jesus, that takes center stage, ready to transport Mary to heaven.

Agamben does not take into account the fact that only in occidental Christianity was the third participant of the Trinity, the "Holy Spirit," *confiscated* on behalf of Jesus and his "vicars" on earth—such as popes who could thence anoint German kings as "Holy Roman emperors," kings with "divine right," and, eventually, the Protestant-cum-secular self-divinized bourgeois individuals qua contracting people—giving rise to something missing altogether in the first one thousand years of Christian Empire: the *postulate of legally right or politically just sovereignty*. Law and politics became each other's "dangerous supplement": neither could be free from the other. It is not enough to credit Catholicism for making possible royal absolute right, which opened the way to subjective rights. In parallel, through their self-appointment as vicars of Christ, the popes also offered a *model for a new type of subjectivity*: the *justifiably rebelling* individual who would, henceforth, increasingly often, assert a "spiritualized," extralegal and extrapolitical, "right" to reject tradition and law *not because they do not serve human happiness but as a "perversion introduced by the princes of the world,"* to use the formulation of Anselm of Lucca. And also to point out and declare war on the Antichrist, including, later, the pope himself, an accusation that in modern times is often leveled in a secularized form, at particular "enemies of the people." Moreover, this new "rightful" aspiration to power and liberty of medieval individuals and their corporations was, from the start, guaranteed by the Catholic Church, "establishing itself a[s] feudal court for the world at large" and lending "spiritual justification to . . . social change," with the pope acting as "trustee of all Christendom against imperialism."[50] For "the Pope [Gregory VII], who for a thousand years had anxiously avoided calling himself universal . . . because he feared that the expression would be derogatory to the other churches, was now settled, as Paul's vicar, on the universal apostolic throne of the world. . . . Gregory is the man who discovered the fusion of omnipresence and centralisation, the anti-classical and anti-pagan concept of the Middle Ages."[51] This is still relevant insofar as the modern secular state replaced the church; indeed, by granting the free right to appeal to every Christian soul, the popes did no less than invent the modern idea of omnipresent but centralized government.[52]

What in Agamben passes as the canonical version of the Trinitarian Credo is thus, partly, a particularly occidental version, the result of a theological variation/innovation of Nicean Trinitarianism, which is still anathema to the self-proclaimed "orthodox." The variation was formalized when the *Filioque* clause was inserted into the Roman rite in 1014 C.E. at the request of a German King (Henry II) eager to cause a rift with Constantinople, by a pope (Benedict VIII) who was grateful for the king's help in restoring him to the papal throne. Opposing this, the Eastern Patriarch Photius, in arguments he presented to the Latin pope, complained that with the insertion of the *Filioque* to the Creed, "The monarchy of the Father" was destroyed and "the reality of the personal, or hypostatic existence, in the Trinity was relativised."[53] In Eastern theology the *anarchos* Father remains the sole cause (*aitia*) and the principle (*arche*) of the divine nature of the Son and the Spirit.[54] Contingency, therefore, is not understandable in Eastern theology in terms of rational relation but of explicitly anarchic divine will. In other (theological) words, contrary to the concept that prevailed in the Augustinian Occident and Latin scholasticism, thanks to which a natural theology emerged that eventually prepared the ground for the Reformation and the Enlightenment, Eastern Christian theology still derives divine providence—from the hypostasis of the Father alone—not from his "common essence," qua "relationality," with His Son via the Spirit. The opposite is true in Catholicism and Protestantism to which modernity's autonomous individuals and their corporations, with their "natural" rights or/and self-standing "universal" aspirations, *owe their genesis*. Here, contingency is imagined as amounting to the incessant play between *two* rational forces, for example, in jurisprudence of natural and positive law, in constitutional theory of constituent and constituted power, in philosophy between universal and particular, in economics between protectionism and free trade, and so on. Although such binary metaphysics are traced to ancient Greek thinkers, the point is that only in the last millennium were these properly "economized," namely, thought of as pairs not capable of fusion/synthesis or separation, with the state recognized as their indispensable pivot. While Hegelianism de-economizes past versions of said binaries, it does so at the cost of allowing new ones to act as the "motor of history" in perpetual "progress."

These two versions of Trinitarian economic political theologies, I submit, correspond to two *overlapping* versions of Western *political-economic theology*: Eastern and occidental. Starting with the latter, it refers to the Trinitarian scheme that Agamben zeroes in on in *The Kingdom and the Glory*. It is the one we are all more familiar with, for it relates to the second millennium from which modernity sprang, that is, the period of occidental might now drawing to a close, a.k.a. the era of "Law *and* Revolution" that reached its peak with the French, American, and Russian revolutions and the constitutional-statist settlements that followed them. It emerged gradually in the context of animosity against the Eastern Roman Empire by the self-styled "Holy Roman Empire" and, in reverse, of the animosity of the Eastern Church against the older Roman Church whose primacy it coveted. It found a theological expression in the theological schism over the occidental church's alteration/simplification of the Trinitarian credo, which represented the equalization, in glory, of God and the Son of Man. It enabled the emergence of a nonapophatic "natural" theology that at once made God dependent on human reason and deified the latter until, eventually, God became unnecessary, and natural theology became natural philosophy; occidental theologians of the High Middle Ages used such theology to solve the problem of God's power in relation to evil *not* by evoking an utterly mysterious *oikonomia* (this is the hallmark of Byzantine theology—Agamben confuses this when he retroactively attributes to Byzantium the occidental invention of a sovereign glory that distracts from anarchic administration) but by *splitting His power into two rather than three: potentia absoluta* and *potentia limitata*. In parallel, and in the context of rivalry between church and empire, contemporary "political theorists" problematized similarly the old Roman idea of "power with authority," by turning into a "theory" the distinction between the so-called Two Powers that Pope Gelasius had introduced several centuries earlier, in an entirely different context, that is, between two principles governing the world: the "sacred authority of bishops" (*auctoritas sacrata pontificum*) and the "royal power" (*regalis potestas*). It is on this basis that, since the eleventh century's Gregorian reforms and the so-called Papal Revolution and throughout the era of Law and Revolution, political and legal innovation is tied, in the occidental imagination, not to dissatisfaction and will to power but to a (false) claim to "restore" what is deemed—now as legally, now as politically—right. Revolution, in other words, became synonymous with the decision of competent authority to promote universal emancipation—obscuring *oikonomia*.

Underneath the layers of this dualist, occidental, political-economic theology lie the ruins of the earlier, more obviously anarchic and embarrassing, "Byzantine," variety—one that is less studied and only exposed whenever the circumstances are so dire that the anarchy of administration without sovereignty becomes apparent, just as in the Greek crisis. For of course, even in places like modern Greece, whose theology is "Eastern," the prevailing *political* theology is occidental. Studying the repressed Byzantine non-occidental side to Western economic-political theology is a scholarly endeavor worth pursuing inter alia, for it stops us reifying only *some* peoples/countries as failing to meet the standards of modernity's "civil religions," say, "constitutional patriotism" or "internationalist class solidarity." Studying the visual/ritual references to Byzantium in Greece's national "folklore" is an opportunity to *speak directly to the repressed side of Western political and legal imagination,* namely, the one that developed in the first millennium of Christianized Roman Empire. The repression occurred in the second millennium, the age of "law and revolution," when this first formative stage in the accommodation of the cult of Jesus in Roman juridico-statist ideology and institutions came to be seen as a "perversion" of what a Christian polity must be, the result of an error in the "flawed" political theology of an "improperly Christianized," "caesaropapist Byzantium." This repression also took the form of the self-serving fantasy that said "error" was heroically "corrected" by adopting the dualist political theology-cum-political theory of Two Powers, and of *potentia absoluta–potentia limitata* that, eventually, gave rise to the secular constitutional paradox of *constituent/constituted* sovereignty. What this "paradox" conceals is the ignominious *oikonomia* that in Byzantium was for all to see. By today, this repression and this fantasy are shared by each and every man-in-the-Occident. Greeks are not spared even if, by reaction, the counter (modern) fantasy of an "orthodox" or "genuine" dogma rose among those living in what was once a great power but which had been in decline even before the sacking of Constantinople by crusaders, was then conquered by Latin and then Ottoman powers, and, in the modern era, succumbed to Russian and then Western European patronage. If we set aside the identity implications of the so-called East-West schism, we can, more fruitfully, consider "Western" political theology to be both occidental and eastern. If so, then this "Western" political theology can be thought of as one that openly assumes a political/legal right to govern in the name of universal salvation, the hallmark of the age of law and revolution, but *discreetly* counsels "getting into" bed with any patron/patronized in the interest of only some over others, the hallmark of the Byzantine age. Thus conceived, Western political theology is to be seen as *schizophrenic*; it is one that openly commits to the hard but glorious labor of striking a "delicate balance" between principle/rule and exception but discreetly relies on the inglorious and iniquitous management of affairs in a permanent, all-encompassing, state of exception. Said Western political theology may have been abandoned conceptually, but it still holds supreme at the level of affect among Westerners (religious or secular), duping them to imagine themselves as forever heroically balancing principle and pragmatism. This attitude, however, appears as *hypocrisy* to Westernized non-Westerners who endorse conceptually the globalized political and legal values that sprang from Europe as rational/universal but do not share the Western subjects' affective, irrational, confidence in their righteousness. This, at least, is my impression whenever I find myself face-to-face with refugees who are not welcome to the continent from which the Good News of the Universal Rights of Man sprang.

Returning to modern Greece, Figures 10–13 show how widely doxological power is still exercised through kitsch, neo-Byzantine, rituals in this country the Constitution of which, after all, begins with the words "In the name of the Holy and Consubstantial and Indivisible Trinity." In Figure 10 we see the Hellenic president and professor of constitutional law, Prokopis Pavlopoulos, on his knees in a scene of devotion during a formal attendance at mass in a Greek Orthodox Church. Note the Byzantine double-headed eagle on his chair on the right. His formal presence in this site and the double-headed eagle on his chair and also, though not visible in this image, on the carpet are not exceptional or coincidental. In fact, neo-Byzantine imagery and rituals are rife in public life; the Constitution provides for freedom of religion but also declares the Eastern Greek-Orthodox Church to be "predominant."

Figure 10. June 2016: Hellenic President and Professor of constitutional law Prokopis Pavlopoulos. With thanks to photographer Mr. George Ferdis.

A Postmodern Hetoimasia   219

Having replaced his ostensibly religious predecessors, the self-declared atheist Tsipras quickly learned to participate in such ethno-religious rituals as being sprinkled with holy water in Parliament, which correlates with the medieval *Byzantine* practice of the church blessing, but not anointing, the sovereign. Here, following elections in which his party for the first time climbed to the second position and could finally eye power, Tsipras accepted for the first time to be sprinkled with holy water by the Greek Orthodox archbishop during the Parliament's inauguration. The Communist Party leader on the left looks on rather disapprovingly.

The point here, however, is not to judge this politician for his populist flirting with religion. While Tsipras's ideology is the product of secular modernity, where state power must be exercised with the authority of the people delegating authority in substitution of the medieval Catholic Church, the medieval Byzantine ritual church blessing, but not anointing,

Figure 11. 2012: The Parliament, Athens, Greece.

Figure 12. January 2015: Piraeus, Greece.

of the sovereign in which Greek prime ministers participate, speaks to a premodern theology that rejects the notion that *any* power can be authoritative before the "Second Coming." There is, hence, a dissonance between the spirit and affect of such modern Greek ethno-religious spectacles. Or consider the rite of releasing a dove on Epiphany. Weeks before his electoral victory Tsipras releases a dove symbolizing the Holy Spirit, handed to him by Greek-Orthodox priests, during Epiphany.

As is the case with similar rituals (see Figure 11), the significance he probably attributed to this publicity stunt ("hope is in our hands," "vote for change") contrasts with this Byzantine ritual's embedded theological message: the Holy Spirit is only fleetingly in the hands of the mortal sovereign who is bound to disappoint until the Lord himself saves us in the Second Coming. On a visit to Mount Athos the young prime minister asked to be left alone with a miraculous icon of the Virgin cradling Jesus. The byzantine sovereign must constantly seek the mediation of the Virgin, since he, as someone loving power and life, has no access to God. He also declared that the church would continue to be untaxed, and his government abolished neither militaristic national parades nor such rituals as receiving holy relics or the Easter "Holy Light" with head-of-state honors, as SYRIZA had vowed to do. Every year since the late 1980s the so-called Holy Light that "miraculously self-ignites" during Easter in the Greek-Orthodox portion of the Holy Sepulchre Church in Jerusalem, Israel/Palestine, is flown to Greece and received with head-of-state honors by the Greek government.

Now, the Greeks' exposure to such images and rituals in which lie em-

Figure 13. The so-called Holy Light.

bedded those postulates of a Christian political theology the Occident loves to hate is not without consequences. If the IMF/EU/ECB treated Greece in fact as a debt colony while, in principle, dealt with it as a sovereign nation, and if the international Left rallied to support SYRIZA's rise but has since fallen silent, this is likely to reify the key message of Eastern (Byzantine) political theology: in the end, inglorious *oikonomia* is all there is, and, since this world cannot be one of equality until the Messiah comes, preferential treatment in order to survive—ignominiously—is the best we can aim for. In this regard, the fact that Greece-in-crisis was treated by both neoliberals and their opponents as a petri dish is likely to enhance the sorry fantasy that it is the Greeks' destiny to occupy the position not of citizens but of clients, both domestically and internationally. After all, the Byzantine sovereign exercised *oikonomia*—that is, dispensation from the austerity of the law because he could—as *Dominus Mundi* to placate the *filoi*, not to save humanity. At the same time, the fact that Eastern theology does not know of a sovereign whose religious or legal or political legitimation may survive his failure to actually provide welfare makes Greeks more likely to suspect that, especially today, when governance is postsovereign, would-be populist saviors are morons or, potentially, useful idiots. In this regard, it is worth recalling that, apart from protesting with a raised fist, voting in elections and referendums and filing complaints in courts, some Greeks had a different reaction. In Figure 14, an angry crowd stands before the Greek Parliament that it had no intention of "storming," with many participants holding up not a raised fist but their open palms: this is an ancient gesture of disdain, which in Byzantine times was used also against disgraced emperors held to be "false messiahs." Similarly, in Figure 15 a student is seen parading before the Republic's representatives *almost to script* except that he allows himself a small but expressive deviation from the ritual: he turns his face away from the stage to which he directs his open palm. It would be as much a mistake to dismiss Greeks extending their open palm to their representatives as uncivil or to see here only a sign of impending revolution, as it was racist in the not-so-distant past to look out for noble savages. They were neither cuing revolution nor acclaiming: *they were ridiculing the very order that they performatively served*. Though little, this is not nothing. It shows that postsovereign "civilization" need not be accompanied by reverence for fake sovereignty. But it also shows that we have learned to tie our survival to marching to the drum of a missing sovereign.

Figure 14. Not quite storming the Bastille.

Figure 15. A Greek student parading before the Republic.

CONCLUDING THOUGHTS: TOWARD A CONSTITUTIONAL ETHICS

Returning, for a final time, to the Thessaloniki 2011 parade incident, I note an incident that happened toward the parade's end: the president's evacuated "throne" was impromptu made use of by a passing stray dog, which climbed on it and took a nap in the autumn sun (Figure 2). This image would, surely, be an irrelevant if amusing aside for both liberal constitutional legalists and advocates of agonistic politics. At best they may see in this image a tragicomic depiction of sovereignty "going to the dogs," since administration has been "allowed" to escape control by democratic legislatures as a result of the surge of cosmopolitan *lex mercatoria* and of deterritorialized regimes of "governance without government." As for Agamben, he might have seen in the dog's ephemeral place on the throne the perfectly ironic depiction of his two major theses: first, the dog-on-the-throne graphically depicts the centrality of *bare life* in a regime where the flourishing of a community is necessarily predicated on the existence of those abandoned within it. Second, he might have commented on how the accidental presence dog-on-the-throne did not desecrate the throne in the long run, since the spectators' enjoyment of the empty throne's glory was such that they continued to stand orderly. Empty or not, even with a dog on it, the "throne" remains the central symbol of sovereignty's inexhaustible glory in the Christian/post-Christian constitutional imagination. Third, judging by his version of the so-called turn to "new materialism" and the emphasis on the supposed agency of bodies as such,[55] the stray-dog-on-the-throne might be interpreted as pointing to the *potentially* effective profanation of the "throne" and, consequently, of the anarchic administration of lives as things that the throne falsely "authorizes," by such "forms of life" as are only included-as-abandoned, expendable lives in the zone of in-distinction between animality and humanity. Is Agamben arguing here for some sort of rightful revolution even if by desecration? Would that not be terribly Catholic and so "last millennium" of him? If so, is he not again forgetting that *desecration with compliance* is already part of the Western economic-political imagination if only in a repressed manner, as exemplified by Figures 14 and 15?

An alternative reading of the Thessaloniki parade continuing before an empty throne that was soon occupied by a dog is possible. The dog's accidental ascendance cannot act as a sign of possible desecration of the throne by us humans inasmuch as we remain in love of gods, unlike dogs. Minus the sovereignty-worshipping, the image of the dog-on-the-throne can be read as retroactively turning Greece's annual independence parade into not (necessarily) more than a festive congregation of *people on their day off*, where "people" signifies neither an aggregate of "individuals"—as in social contract theory—nor a substantive "we" with distinctive unifying elements, be that a "nation" or a "class." Rather, faced with a stray dog napping on their throne, "people" *could* mean the anarchic being together of "inoperative forms of life" (as Agamben calls it, i.e., not dependent on the metaphysical animal/human or *zoe* and *bios*) *and*, perhaps, also as Levinas called it: radically passive ethical subjectivities singularized by a desire to be for-each-other as a unique other (i.e., not dependent on the metaphysical distinction friend/enemy) who come to imagine ways to justify their unjustifiably selective proximity.

Thus interpreted, the parade loses its ritualistic efficacy. Each spectator would begin to realize that she or he stands not before a throne but before each other in a situation of inescapable "proximity" in Levinas's use of the term, namely, an ethical face-to-face.[56] Proximity in this sense does not exhaust itself in physical contiguity or common identity but, instead, issues from the *unraveling* of the latter and leads to the *questioning* of the very "rightfulness" or raison d'être of the former. The corresponding ethics of responsibility differs from both liberal and Marxist moralities. Starting from the former, say Rawls's "justice as fairness,"[57] the Levinasian view of responsibility differs on at least two crucial points. While the "veil of ignorance," on which Rawls's principle depends, is a hypothetical thought experiment of the self, Levinas's ethical responsibility is a real feeling of persecution and shame. Rather than imagining an original position of abstract individuality where social place is hidden as the basis for deciding how resources should be shared, in Levinasian "ethics as first philosophy" subjectivity is individuated by exposure to its others' suffering/abandonment in humanity's *oikos* and embarrassed by the fact that it is unable to justify occupying a particular "place under the sun" instead of someone else. Insofar as the contingency of its privileges and identity are fully exposed, the ethical subject, per Levinas, succumbs to an anarchic, gratuitous, and infinite sense of responsibility for the very accident of its birth in this or that position of privilege vis-à-vis others. Turning to Marxist morality, Levinasian ethics shares its preference for materialism over abstraction, but, unlike Marxism, it does not presume that secular modern humans have altogether given up the comfort of their gods[58] even if we should. In this sense Levinas's ethics is a form of shameful *religare* that is yet to supplant traditional religions. Central to the former is the "idea of infinity which comes to mind" that, like the postulates of traditional religions, has no signified but, unlike them, is not validated as a true social fact via rituals; on the contrary, it is experienced when the rituals' emptiness is felt. This idea of infinity as sign of godless transcendence is central to Levinas's ethics of proximity based on obsessively dedicating one's self to the misfit other. Thus sociality is the result of an infinite ethical command: open up to the stranger, *religare*! It is important to stress that Levinas refers to "infinity" as the only idea that is not produced by the subject but signifies a meaningless yet irreducible exteriority, in contrast to the philosophical "absolute" that lends itself to great minds who, heroically, hover above their prejudices, able to conceive of the veritably "new." Levinas's "infinity" is like the Eastern Christian Holy Spirit: untamed, it comes fleetingly to mind and prompts us to look away from our group navel. The philosopher's absolute is like the confiscated Holy Spirit of the occidental theological imagination. Alas, it is also a bit like the dove that the would-be redeemers of this world seek to capture: it shits on us a range of unintended consequences and collateral damage.

A marriage of (what Agamben calls) human *inoperativity* with (Levinasian) *anarchic ethical responsibility* points toward a different kind of constitutional imagination that, instead of attempting to answer the questions of *idem* and *ipse* collective identity (respectively, "what are we?" and "who are we?"),[59] *questions our very right to be* part of each and every separate, privileged, or privilege-seeking group *and* exposes our will to "justified" power as existentially inauthentic. The postulate of "autonomy" should be questioned as much as that of the heteronomy it replaced. The constitutional "paradox" of constituent-constituted power should be shamefully exposed as a game of "see-saw" that detracts from the arbitrariness of *oikonomia*. With this in mind the image of the stray dog on the Hellenic president's throne in the aforementioned Thessaloniki incident not only illustrates what neither courts nor politicians were prepared to admit—that, in fact, sovereign power has "gone to the dogs"—but, more important, that the words "we the people" can refer to inoperative sociality without the auspices of a national sovereign *and* without universal justification vis-à-vis any *third* who is excluded or, rather, as in the Western, secularized-Christian biopolitical model, included in a disadvantaged position. This ought to give rise to an infinite sense of uneconomizable responsibility that unsettles the *oikos* of humanity. While those spectators in Thessaloniki who ended up seeing a stray dog sitting on the symbol of their presumed sovereignty—the throne—managed to enjoy each other's presence on their day off together, many third others surely *did not*. The term *third* on this occasion could mean anyone: from those many non-Greeks who were once living in Thessaloniki before wars, "population exchanges," and the Holocaust led to "homogeneity" through to all those undocumented refugees currently residing in Greece, unwanted here or elsewhere in Europe, to all future generations that will inherit our fiscal and moral debts, and, further, to all those millions of peoples in much poorer countries that have never been paid much attention to by the IMF as the relatively still-prosperous Greece. In Greece as elsewhere, the crisis has yet to lead to such constitutional reflexivity whereby we both *acknowledge our powerlessness to escape* those anonymous forces of anarchic management of populations inside the global human "household" through traditional liberal and political ideals *and* assert an anarchic, infinite sense of responsibility (contrary to what the impending future order of illiberal capitalism may hold).

NOTES

1. The former is Martin Loughlin: "We live today in an age simultaneously marked by the widespread adoption of the idea of constitutionalism, of ambiguity over its meaning and about its continuing authority. Far from being an expression of limited government, constitutionalism is now to be viewed as an extremely powerful mode of legitimating extensive government. Where this form of constitutionalism positions itself on the ideology-utopia axis . . . has rarely been more indeterminate . . . notwithstanding the liberal gains . . . the significance of the idea of the constitutional imagination has never exhibited a great degree of uncertainty" ("The Constitutional Imagination," *Modern Law Review* 78, no. 1 (2015): 25. The latter is Wendy Brown: "Continued belief in political democracy as the realization of human freedom depends upon literally averting our glance from powers immune to democratization, powers that also give the lie to the autonomy and primacy of the political upon which so much of the history and present of democratic theory has depended" ("We Are All Democrats Now . . . ," in *Democracy in What State?*, ed. Amy Alen [New York: Columbia University Press, 2011], 54).

2. H. Vorländer, for one, identifies the following new versions of constitutionalism: societal constitutionalism, creeping constitutionalism, compensatory constitutionalism, pluralistic constitutionalism, multilevel constitutionalism (containing the notion of a constitutional compromise or settlement), cosmopolitan constitutionalism, and global constitutionalism (with variations in the form of transnational constitutionalism, where mention is made of a constitution of humankind, and global civil constitutions) (quoted in F. Venter, *Constitutionalism and Religion* [Cheltenham, U.K.: Edward Elgar, 2015], 57). Brown, in turn, counts the many *desiderata* of democratic theory: "democracy-to-come, democracy of the uncounted, democratizing sovereignty, democracy workshops, pluralizing democracy and more" ("We Are All Democrats Now," 45).

3. See Martin Loughlin and Neil Walker, eds., *The Paradox of Constitutionalism* (Oxford: Oxford University Press, 2007).

4. E.g.: "All significant concepts of the state are secularised theological concepts" (Carl Schmitt, *Political Theology: Four Chapters on the Concept of Sovereignty* [Chicago: University of Chicago Press, 1996], 36); and more generally, "The metaphysical image that a definite epoch forges of the world has the same structure as a form of its political organization" (ibid., 46). "Can we not admit that, despite all the changes that have occurred, the religious survives in the guise of new beliefs and new repre-

sentations, and that it can return to the surface, in either traditional or novel forms, when conflicts become so acute as to produce in the edifice of the state?" (Claude Lefort, "The Permanence of the Theological-Political?," in *Democracy and Political Theory*, trans. David Macey [Cambridge: Cambridge University Press, 1988], 215). "While weakening nation-state sovereigns yoke their fate and legitimacy to God, Capital . . . becomes God-like: almighty, limitless, and uncontrollable. In what should be the final and complete triumph of secularism, there is only theology" (Wendy Brown, *Walled States—Waning Sovereignty* [Zone Books, 2010], 66).

5. Giorgio Agamben, *The Kingdom and the Glory: For a Theological Genealogy of Economy and Government* (Stanford, Calif.: Stanford University Press, 2011).

6. Ibid., xii.

7. Marinos Diamantides and Anton Schutz, *Political Theology: Demystifying the Universal* (Edinburgh: Edinburgh University Press, 2017).

8. Ibid., esp. chap. 5, "Political Theology beyond Schmitt."

9. Roy A. Rappaport, *Ritual and Religion in the Making of Humanity* (Cambridge: Cambridge University Press, 1999).

10. He argued that in order to evaluate conflicting interests in order of priority, every society takes for granted certain basic assumptions, usually implicitly formulated, upon which its ordering rests. These he called *jural postulates* of the legal system of a particular society. Cf. R. Pound, *Introduction to the Philosophy of Law* (New Haven, Conn.: Yale University Press, 1922).

11. See, e.g., Martin Loughlin, "The Rise of the New Ephorate," in *Foundations of Public Law* (Oxford: Oxford University Press, 2010), 448: "Decisions taken by independent central banks, the energy sector regulators, the various inspectorates (schools, health and safety, pollution pension, police, and prisons), and a variety of miscellaneous bodies (such as, in the United Kingdom, the National Institute for Health and Clinical Excellence . . . or the information Commissioner) often have greater impact on public policy formation than decisions of ministers and other elected politicians." For discussion of other transnational examples of the "new ephorate," see, among others, Gunther Teubner, *Constitutional Fragments: Societal Constitutionalism and Globalisation*, trans. Gareth Norbury (Oxford: Oxford University Press, 2014); and Marcelo Neves, *Transconstitutionalism*, trans. Kevin Mundy (Oxford: Oxford University Press, 2013).

12. See, e.g., Alexander Somek, "Administration without Sovereignty," in Petra Dobner and Martin Loughlin, *The Twilight of Constitutionalism?* (Oxford: Oxford University Press, 2010), 267–68.

13. Peter Spiegel, "How the Euro Was Saved," *Financial Times*, May 11, 2014.

14. Case 668/2012 concerning the constitutionality of Laws 3833/2010 and 3845/2010.

15. Per paragraph 2: "Authorities provided by the Constitution may by treaty or

agreement be vested in agencies of international organizations, when this serves an important national interest and promotes cooperation with other States. A majority of three-fifths of the total number of Members of Parliament shall be necessary to vote the law ratifying the treaty or agreement." Paragraph 3 proclaims: "Greece shall freely proceed by law passed by an absolute majority of the total number of Members of Parliament to limit the exercise of national sovereignty, in so far as this is dictated by an important national interest, does not infringe upon the rights of man and the foundations of democratic government and is effected on the basis of the principles of equality and under the condition of reciprocity" (www.hri.org/docs/syntagma/).

16. The minority dissented on the basis that the agreed measures had been agreed by subjects of international law, were very detailed, and concerned the strictly timed implementation of structural reforms of the wider public sector including public administration, local authorities, salaries, pensions, and the economic policy that affects the interaction of public and private sectors and taxation; their implementation is closely monitored by representatives of the lenders and constitute a vital condition for the continuing financing of the Greek state. Moreover, the relevant laws were not based on reasoned arguments and detailed data proving that the austerity and restructuring measures were proportionately dictated by an important national interest in the sense that they were the only solution and complying with the principles of equality and proportionality.

17. Case 599/2012.

18. *Protodikeio* Athinon Number 1584/2014.

19. See https://www.newstatesman.com/politics/politics/2013/04/simple-courage-decision-leftist-tribute-thatcher (accessed April 17, 2013).

20. Giorgio Agamben, *State of Exception*, trans. Kevin Atell (Chicago: University of Chicago Press, 2005), 38.

21. Ibid., 41.

22. "Man is the Sabbatical animal par excellence . . . He has dedicated himself to production and labour, because in his essence he is completely devoid of work [opera]" (Agamben, *Kingdom and the Glory*, 246). Aristotle skirts this issue, Agamben notes, while, for example, the Jewish tradition of a creator God who rested on the seventh day, through the associated rituals of the Sabbath, put man's inoperativity at the heart of its metaphysical understanding of the world.

23. "Inoperativity is the political substance of the Occident, the glorious nutrient of all power" and the "internal-motor" of the machinery of government (ibid., 245).

24. On the losing side of history, other Greek philosophies such as Skepticism, Cynicism, and Epicureanism (which had placed the form and movement of matter in the chance movements of primitive atoms) were vilified by Roman statesmen—

perhaps due to their uselessness in capturing inoperative life for the state. In this connection I find it apposite to add that while the first loud roaring of this "machinery" that runs on human inoperability occurred in the Rome of Stoic Seneca and institutionalized *homo sacer*, its conceptual possibility dates back to the third century B.C.E., when stoicism brought together platonic idealism and Aristotelian materialism's by virtue of a new additive—the postulate of the logos, carried forth by the pneuma that "structures" or economizes the tension between the two competing ontologies of power that Plato and Aristotle had respectively prioritized (*dynamis/energeia*). In sum, if ancient Greek idealism and realism were at odds in their respective ontologies of constitutional power, the appearance in the scene of the Stoic *logos* and *pneuma,* first, and the Triune God-like sovereign, second, made possible their cybernetic synergy.

25. The term is not to be confused with the biological, "natural" or animal, side of human life, which the Greeks call *zoe* and opposed to *bios*; "bare life" signifies neither a thing nor a being but an indistinct in-between that can be treated indifferently: it stands for the rejection/abandonment of plural, contingent, contextual, forms-of-life in the statist-juridical tradition that took hold in republican Rome in which particular forms-of-life come to signify only an indistinction between *zoe/bios*, nature/logos, body/soul, animality/humanity, etc.

26. Agamben has used the term to describe a most horrific exemplification of this status in modernity in the concentration camp's *Muselmann*: Giorgio Agamben, *Remnants of Auschwitz: The Witness and the Archive,* trans. Daniel Heller-Roazen (Cambridge, Mass.: Zone Books, 1999). There is an abundance of literature now using the term *bare life* to describe the continuum of various "expendable" lives: from "Third World" immigrants or child workers to the Western precarious workers who would be better off signing up for benefits than working, and even the well-fed but suicidally stressed business manager (or even the academic who must "publish or perish").

27. Agamben, *State of Exception*, 59.

28. Harold Berman, "Law and Logos," *DePaul Law Review* 44, no. (1994): 4.

29. Rappaport, *Ritual and Religion*.

30. "In the relationship between ruler and ruled sovereignty belongs to neither but the relationship itself" (Benedetto Croce, *Politics and Morals,* trans. Salvatore J. Castiglone [New York: Philosophical Library, 1925], 14). See also Martin Loughlin, *The Idea of Public Law* (Oxford: Oxford University Press, 2004), 83–86.

31. "God's being as a unified difference of persons *already contains every possible difference,* including the difference of a created, 'exterior' world. . . . The only content of the transcendent order is the immanent order, but the meaning of the immanent order is nothing other than the relation to the transcendent end. *'Ordo ad finem'* and *'ordo ad invicem'* refer back to one another and found themselves on

one another. The Christian God is this circle in which two orders continuously penetrate each other" (Agamben, *Kingdom and the Glory*, 87).

32. Loughlin and Walker, *Paradox of Constitutionalism*.

33. Agamben, *State of Exception*, 9.

34. Cf. Rappaport, *Ritual and Religion*. In view of the uncertainty created by contestable lies and alternatives, Rappaport argues, it is the universal feature of religion to render certain postulates sacred, that is, unquestionable. As such, religion allows humans to live orderly with the permanent risk of experiencing disorder, namely, with the risk that inheres in our ability to lie or to oppose lies and to conceive of alternative worlds or discredit them. What Rappaport terms "Ultimate Sacred Postulates" take the form of cosmological axioms embedded in and expressed through myth, scripture, or the like, but also of "secular" principles or policies that correspond to *ultimate or basic values*, at the top of hierarchies of values. The "unquestionable," or "sacred," status of USPs derives from their "substantial vacuity" (427), namely, that their *significata*—e.g., Gods, ancestors, natural law, the scientific management of the earth's resources and the like—are unreal and beyond falsification.

35. Viewing the history and theories of the modern sovereign state in this light, one wonders whether, despite the various changes, politics is always thought not as the product of the differentiation between *oikos* and public domain but as the mystically totalized space in which this distinction can be made in the first place. Hence the openness to stasis, factionalism, civil strife, and anarchy that characterized the Athenian and Roman constitutions is in modernity abhorred/repressed as intensely as a serious family crisis, and "treason" as much as incest or infidelity; conversely, the ordered unity—guaranteed by the uninterrupted rule of a sovereign with a monopoly on violence—is, perversely, acclaimed as a precondition of the political. The Christian sovereign, that is, becomes the acclaimed paterfamilias of the *respublica christiana*—which, in all its various configurations, is always at once a *respublica* and a household—be it in the context of medieval political thought whose sovereign was the monarch issuing commands, or in the context of modern democratic theory where the sovereign guarantees the right conditions for the expression of the general will or for the organization of consensus. The problem with acclaiming the sanctified sovereign in monistic monarchical regimes based on divine right and modern pluralist democracies is that in *both* cases it gives rise to a "religion" of metapolitics in which the measure of every form of internal differentiation—namely, the pluralism that the former repress and the latter celebrate—is also a reinstatement of the aforementioned theo-political structure that, as totalizing context, evades scrutiny as such.

36. Jacques Derrida, "Declarations of Independence," *New Political Science* 7, no. 1 (1986): 7–15.

37. Ernst Kantorowicz, *The King's Two Bodies: A Study in Medieval Political Theology* (Princeton, N.J.: Princeton University Press, 1997).

38. Especially Gilbert Dagron, *Emperor and Priest: The Imperial Office in Byzantium*, trans. Jean Birrell (Cambridge: Cambridge University Press, 2003).

39. See chapter 5, "From Jerusalem to Rome via Constantinople," in Diamantides and Schutz, *Political Theology*. Cf. Marinos Diamantides, "Constitutional Theory and Its Limits: Reflections on Comparative Political Theologies," *Law, Culture and the Humanities* 11, no. 1 (2015): 109–46; and Diamantides, "God's Political Power in Western and Eastern Christianity in Comparative Perspective," *Divus Thomas: Commentarium de philosophia et theologia*, November 2012, 333–81.

40. Anthony Kaldellis, *The Byzantine Republic: People and Power in New Rome* (Cambridge, Mass.: Harvard University Press, 2015).

41. Alexander P. Kazhdan and Silvia Ronchey, *L'aristocrazia bizantina dal principio dell' XI alla fine del XII secolo* (Palermo, Italy: Sellerio Editore Palermo, 1997).

42. See Peter Brown, *Power and Persuasion in Late Antiquity: Towards a Christian Empire* (Madison: University of Wisconsin Press, 1992).

43. Consider this extract from the resignation speech of Justin II (r. 565–574): "You behold the ensigns of supreme power. You are about to receive them, not from my hand, but from the hand of God. Honour them, and from them you will derive honour. Respect the empress your mother: you are now her son; before, you were her servant. Delight not in blood; abstain from revenge; avoid those actions by which I have incurred the public hatred; and consult the experience, rather than the example, of your predecessor. As a man, I have sinned; as a sinner, even in this life, I have been severely punished: but these servants, (and he pointed to his ministers), who have abused my confidence, and inflamed my passions, will appear with me before the tribunal of Christ. I have been dazzled by the splendour of the diadem: be thou wise and modest; remember what you have been, remember what you are. You see around us your slaves, and your children: with the authority, assume the tenderness, of a parent. Love your people like yourself; cultivate the affections, maintain the discipline, of the army; protect the fortunes of the rich, relieve the necessities of the poor" (Theophylact Simocatta, quoted in Edward Gibbon, *The Decline and Fall of the Roman Empire* [New York: Modern Library, 2003], 790).

44. Agamben, *Kingdom and the Glory*, 106.

45. Cf. Chris Thornhill, *A Sociology of Constitutions: Constitutions, and State Legitimacy in Historical-Sociological Perspective* (Cambridge: Cambridge University Press, 2011). In his chapter on the "migration of legal forms from church to state" (37) from the High Middle Ages (from the second half of the twelfth century to the end of the thirteenth century), through early modernity (fourteenth–sixteenth centuries) to the Renaissance (sixteenth–seventeenth centuries), he points out especially the Catholic idea of centralized but omnipresent government needing

justification through law, and argues that not only did Roman law act as the conceptual framework by which the popes asserted the power to institute new laws (ostensibly analogous to that of Roman emperors) but in reality augmented it. The popes qua *lex animata* were perceived as if containing "higher law" than positive law, and this led to the notion of a "fulcrum of power" (27), that is, power that is at once absolute and legitimate. Likewise: "Modern societies are defined . . . by the fact that they require and produce, not autonomous political institutions, but rather autonomous reserves of political power" and that the autonomy of the state increases when more political power is first abstracted and then deposited into its hierarchical institutions (17). The church-cum-state thus established itself as the central institution in society and acquired systematically ordered powers of jurisdiction and legal regulation that distinguished it from local, personalized structures of feudal order. Moreover, once such a fulcrum was conceived, the necessity rose for an internal distinction between *potentia absoluta* / *potentia ordinata* of the God-like sovereign that we inherited as constituted power / constitutive power. Only after the distinction was theorized could law and politics begin to acquire autonomy from each other and from the personal arrangements of the feudal order.

46. This gave rise to the "somewhat confusing image of an imperial power organisation which professed also to be a community." See Sheldon S. Wilson, *Politics and Vision: Continuity and Innovation in Western Political Thought* (Princeton, N.J.: Princeton University Press, 2016), 119.

47. *Societas* suggests a partnership of humans who are tied to one another only by loyalty, not by the pursuit of a common substantive purpose or interest. This abstract loyalty can then evolve into a respect for legal rules where the law is obeyed not because it is a means to an end but because it is an expression of their kinship. The ruler of a state understood as *societas* is the guardian of the conditions that constitute the relationship, and obedience to the ruler/law is an "end in itself," not a means to an end. In turn, *universitas* is a "corporate association" where persons unite only, or primarily, to attain a common purpose/interest. Here the ruler is the owner or trustee of common property, and the manager of the group activities and policy is seen as far more important than law. See Michael J. Oakeshott, *On Human Conduct* (Oxford: Clarendon Paperbacks, 1991).

48. Martin Loughlin, *The Idea of Public Law* (Oxford: Oxford University Press, 2003), 20.

49. Wilson, *Politics and Vision*.

50. Eugene Rosenstock-Huessy, *Out of Revolution: Autobiography of Western Man* (Providence/Oxford: Berg, 1993), 529. Cf. Marinos Diamantides, "On and out of Revolution: Between Public Law and Religion," *Law, Culture and the Humanities* 10, no. 3 (2014): 336-366.

51. Rosenstock-Huessy, *Out of Revolution*, 36.

52. Ibid., 518.

53. John Meyendorff, *Byzantine Theology: Historical Trends and Doctrinal Themes* (New York: Fordham University Press, 1979), 92: "The *Filioque* dispute was not a discussion on words—for there was a sense in which both sides would agree to say that the Spirit proceeds 'from the Son'—but on the issue of *whether the hypostatic existence of the Persons of the Trinity could be reduced to their internal relations*, as the post-Augustinian West would admit, or whether the primary Christian experience was that of a trinity of Persons, whose personal existence was irreducible to their common essence. The question was whether tripersonality or consubstantiality was the first and the basic content of Christian religious experience" (94; emphasis added).

54. Ibid., 183.

55. Giorgio Agamben, *The Use of Bodies*, trans. Adam Kotsko (Stanford, Calif.: Stanford University Press, 2016).

56. The literature on this, by Levinas and others, is too large to cite. For a very preliminary understanding, see Marinos Diamantides, "'Face' and 'Other,'" in *Encyclopedia of Political Theory*, ed. Mark Bevir (London: Sage, 2009).

57. John Rawls, *A Theory of Justice* (Cambridge, Mass.: Belknap Press of Harvard University Press, 1971).

58. Cf. "Men . . . hide their actions under a strange veneer of ideology. . . . Marxism unveils our ideologies; it strips off the moral pretexts that cover our naked interests. But it cannot change human nature . . . Man is not naked and never will be" (Rosenstock-Huessy, *Out of Revolution*, 108–9).

59. Terms used by Paul Ricoeur, *Oneself as Another*, trans. Kathleen Blamley (Chicago: University of Chicago Press, 1992), 1–3. In connection to constitutional theory, see Hans Lindahl, "Constituent Power and Reflexive Identity: Towards an Ontology of Collective Selfhood," in Loughlin and Walker, *Paradox of Constitutionalism*, 9–24, esp. 14–17.

9

Contra Iurem
Giorgio Agamben's Two Ontologies

Laurent de Sutter

THE LIFE AND DEATH OF COMMAND

A Star Is Born

It was a summer day in 1963. The sun was hitting the rocks of the desolate plains of Basilicata, in southern Italy, depriving them of all the shadows from which could have benefited the ones who wanted to protect themselves from the burning rays. In a cellar away from the heat, a man suddenly stood and spoke to a small group of others; he told them that, one day, one of them would betray him—a prophecy to which a young man replied, like some of his comrades: "Will it be me, Master?" On the set of *The Gospel According to Matthew*, Pier Paolo Pasolini's gaze lingered on the thick black hair, both messy and shiny, that adorned the head of the young man who uttered this line. Like the rest of the actors chosen by the director, he was a complete stranger—or, rather, he was a stranger to the world of cinema and theater, the world of what Guy Debord would call, some years later, "spectacle." The young man was a law student, whom Pasolini had met during discussions in some literary and intellectual circles in Rome, and whom Elsa Morante, then the central star of these circles, had decided to take under her wing. At the time of the filming of *The Gospel*, the young student was twenty-two years old and had not yet published anything; his first text, soberly titled "Decadenza," appeared after the end of filming, in the sixth issue of the science fiction magazine *Futuro*, which would cease publication a few months later.[1] Yet he had impressed Pasolini enough to be included among the other artists and intellectuals whom, by contrast with the rest of the amateur cast that he had assembled, the director wanted to see in his film. Among these, one could recognize the writer Natalia Ginzburg, whose son, Carlo Ginzburg, was about the age of the young man—but also the poet and journalist Alfonso Gatto, whose collection *Poesie d'amore* had just been published, or the critic Enzo Siciliano, the then future president of RAI television. Pasolini had guessed that under the appearance of the reserved young law student to whom he had given the role of the Apostle Philip was hiding a talent that would one day rival that of his elders. The young man's name, as it appeared in the movie credits, already resonated with a strange authority, yet mixed with doubt—an authority similar to the one that blessed his gaze. His name was Giorgio Agamben.

Ending with Doubt

Agamben has never discussed the relationship he had maintained, at the time, with Pasolini—nor has he dedicated one single text to the work of the one who had been at the origin of his first appearance in the world of creation, and also one of his most important inspirations. Maybe, in his eyes, this appearance was some sort of a dress rehearsal, a clearing of the throat before the beginning of a speech: like the science fiction story that he gave to *Futuro*, his acting experience would know no tomorrow. Yet it was not insignificant that Pasolini gave him the role of the Apostle Philip, just as it was not insignificant that he would decide to finish the litany of concerns voiced by the servile followers of Christ by a shot on the young man. Incarnating Philip, Agamben was closing the series of the doubt—before that, a while later, Judas would take the floor to express it in turn, and Jesus answered, with the tone, demanding no reply, of the one who knows with an indubitable knowledge, "Yes, it's you." With the role given to him by Pasolini, he who was still only a law student, waiting to make the decisive encounter with Martin Heidegger, at René Char's house, in Thor, in the south of France, was completing its metamorphosis into something else.

Although he has often proposed definitions of philosophy, and could even give the impression that philosophy had always been at the heart of his business, it was (and still is) difficult to say whether this something else was a philosopher per se or a philologist, a theologian, a writer, or a mere erudite. The end of something was enacted, which opened before him a wide field of possibilities, of which the only element to be taken for granted was that Agamben would not become a lawyer—or, if it was the case, that he would become a lawyer in an oblique, crooked, biased, forever impossible to accept for other lawyers way. Indeed, since the publication of his first book, *The Man without Content*, in 1970, when he was twenty-eight, he has never stopped beating around law while, by turning around it, making it rotate, with him, on itself.[2] Law has remained the place that was, and still is, playing, for Agamben, the issue of the end of doubt, as well as one of the possibilities that this end inaugurates: law is the place of the certainty of uncertainty. Law is what must be doubted to the point where it may eventually open itself to the potentialities that only uncertainty allows for—against the obscure and short-sighted certainty of lawyers.

Esti *and* Estô

Fifty years after *The Gospel According to Matthew* was screened for the first time in a movie theater, the strange arrangement linking doubt, law, and faith in Agamben ended up taking a new form. In the closing chapter of the fifth volume of the second part of the huge work in progress that was then *Homo Sacer*, a volume published in 2011 under the title Opus Dei: *Archaeology of the Office*, he indeed offered a curious distinction.[3] We were wrong, he wrote: the philosophical history of the West is not the history of the figure of being, the history of an ontology that we would not manage to get rid of—any more than to satisfy ourselves with. This history, rather, is that of *two* ontologies, of which the ontology of being (the ontology of *esti*) is only one branch, the other being what Agamben called "the ontology of *estô*," meaning, the ontology of ought-to-being, the ontology of command.[4] Command or duty is not a mere deontic variation on the register of being but an ontological reality in itself, which is opposed in every way to the one of being, and defines an area of the world that the latter does not govern in any sense. In the history of the West, Agamben argued, it was possible to witness a sort of duel in which neither form of ontology ever managed to come out as the winner, but whose adventures sometimes led to a fragile moment of supremacy of one over the other.

Since Immanuel Kant, and with him, he added, the supremacy of one of the two ontologies has reached an unprecedented level in the history of the duel between the two: we now live, with hardly any remainder, in the world of the ontology of *estô*—we have become the exclusive subjects of command. In the eyes of Agamben, this was a nightmarish turn of events: the supremacy of *estô* over *esti* marked what he called the "catastrophic return of law and religion at the heart of philosophy."[5] When the ontology of command triumphs, what remains of being and of its potential in the field of philosophy eventually falls back in front of the demands of the thought of imperative and of duty, never to leave behind anything but the sheer power of violence. The oblivion of being of which Heidegger spoke thus took a singular face—a face where, suddenly, law manifested itself with the evil traits of metaphysics.

The Magic of the Imperative

A few months after the publication of *Opus Dei*, during a conference in Munich to which he had been invited by the von Siemens Foundation, Agamben resumed in a stylized manner the distinction suggested in the last chapter of his book.[6] He stressed in particular the importance of the imperative mode in the definition of the ontology of command: whereas being belongs to the order of description, command belongs to the order of limitation—command *intimates*.[7] Again, the imperative should not be seen as the simple expression of the deontic mode, transforming a state of affairs that would only be given, into a state of affairs to be respected, whether in the form of license, or that of prohibition. Rather, it should be understood as the tearing apart of being, and as the passing of his power through every state of affairs, leading to its reconfiguration according to concerns belonging to its own, without any consideration for what this being asked for or made possible. There was a strong link, in the language of Agamben, between power and command—just as, albeit in a nostalgic form, being was to be sided with what Baruch Spinoza called "*potestas*," but Agamben, true to Aristotle, preferred to call "possible."[8] Command was power in its opposition to the possible; it was the becoming impossible of the possible, its summation in the direction imposed by the imperative that each speech act using it was the carrier, the agent or the soldier. This command, and the ontology that it governed, repeated Agamben, was the proper of law and religion—but it also was, he added, the one of magic, as magic constitutes the introduction of necessity in the world of contingency.[9] There is a magic of the imperative that the logic of being cannot understand, or support, or justify, and yet, that supports and justifies law as well as religion. It was the magic of the imperative that Agamben saw dominating Western thought since Kant, ushering in the total reign of necessity, and the increasingly rapid disappearance of what could have avoided it—what Pasolini, in a letter to Franco Farolfi, dated February 1, 1941, had baptized with the fragile name of "firefly."[10]

Law as Evil

By making the history of command the essence of an alternative history of being, Agamben replayed, though he never admitted it, a distinction as old as the history of thought—or, at least, the history of this eccentric form of thought that bears the name of philosophy. The invention of philosophy, and its formalization in the restricted set of axioms and theorems that continues to define its mode of existence, has, since its origins, been conceived as opposing to law, religion, and magic (say, to the force of necessity) a higher order of reasons. *Law is evil*: this is the belief from which originated the story of being, as being forms the conceptual axis around which all categories of philosophy have articulated. Law is evil, since being is a concept of which it has no use whatsoever; it is evil to the extent that it does not care about being, and the consequences that its existence would be likely to produce. Rather, it is on the side of nonbeing, and of the sophisticated exercises in virtuoso manipulation of which Gorgias had extracted the lost treaty bearing this title ("Peri tou mê ontos ê peri physeôs," "Treaty on Nonbeing, or On Nature"), that one should consider as the kingdom of law, and of the ontology on which it relies. But in reality, things were more complex: the category of law simply did not exist in Greek thought—which only knew more or less arbitrary, more or less local, more or less singular decisions. The passage of the vocabulary of *thesmos* to the vocabulary of *nomos* did not happen before the time of Cleisthenes, at the moment of the birth of philosophy itself, as evidenced by a famous fragment of Heraclitus, reported by Stobaeus, and which one takes it offers the most schematic formulation of the conception shared by the Greeks:

> Those who speak thoughtfully must necessarily rely on what is common to all, as a city relies on its law (νομω), and does it more firmly. For all human laws (ανθρωπειοι νομοι) are fed by a single divine law. It dominates as it wishes; it provides for all, and rules over all. (Fr. 119)[11]

LAW AGAINST PHILOSOPHY

The Nomos *as Short Circuit*

The invention of the strange foil that *nomos* is, is the invention of philosophy itself: it is philosophy that has promoted the category of *nomos*, as well as the idea of order accompanying it, as defining a part of the world whose principles it was to set. There is a native pharmacological dimension of philosophy, which is the dimension of the establishment of the category of *nomos* as the foil of philosophy, its inverse, or its shadow, by philosophy itself. For Heraclitus, it was necessary to distinguish between the human and the divine *nomos*, the first ordering itself, in its hierarchy and structure, on the second—of which it only offered an imperfect and mundane version, just like, in Plato, the sensible would oppose the intelligible.[12] The key in this distinction was there: in the ordering of the world and its systematic redeployment according to a logic that, in fact, already belonged to what Agamben, more than two millennia later, would eventually call "command." One could even say that the invention of *nomos* constitutes some sort of a short circuit—the short circuit by which being was, from the moment of its very inception through philosophy, innervated by an ought-to-being of which it nevertheless formed the principle, unless it incarnated its material. *Nomos* is the ought-to-being of the world: it is the face that takes being once crossed by the command that is the requirement to reproduce the order governing the divine world—that is, the one of religion and magic as much as the one of the Idea. So there was a terrible paradox, in Agamben, to institute command as the locus of a second form of ontology, since it was philosophy, as the science of being, which introduced its concept—or, at least, possibility of its concept. Yet had Agamben not set the game of these two ontologies as a kind of dance that would be conducted sometimes by one, sometimes by the other, without specifying which one was at its origin, except that it would have to do with the very history of language? The philosophical *nomos* only becomes legal in its effectuation in the imperative; outside this effectuation, why wouldn't it be the mere description of a state of the world—an ordered state, certainly, but whose ordering would only be the product of a random given?

The Cicero Program

In fact, the divine order, of which the human *nomos* was the imperfect substitute, gave itself as such, without any justification coming to redeem the pure stochastic of its being—the fact that it was such, that it was ordered only because it was given. As long as the question of command remained internal to the field of philosophy, the catastrophic dance whose consequences Agamben observed in the contemporary world could not be launched: it lacked the radicality of an outside. *Nomoi* succeeding to *thesmoi* were not yet law, even though, without a doubt, he still belonged to religion, and to the magic that was attached to it; it was not yet *the practice of the imperative*, translating into the realm of actions the existence of an ontology of command. Beyond the condemnation of the sophists made by philosophers, one had to wait for the condemnation of lawyers, litigants, jurisconsults, by Cicero, to see the front line described by Agamben starting to produce its effects. For many, including Agamben himself, Cicero's legal thinking was to be found in his *De Officiis*, his treatise on the policy of public functions, and on the role that one had to expect for the law to play in the government of people and things.[13] Yet it is in the *De Legibus* that Cicero displayed all his hatred for lawyers; it was in this dialogue, of which we only have but a few fragments, that one could meet the traces of the desire to do away with law *in the name of philosophy*.[14] Cicero was not hiding how much the proposed reform of the fundamental laws of the city corresponded to a program: the practical realization of the ideals defended by Platonism, as reformulated by State stoicism to which he had attached his name. It was about to jettison the rhetorical sophistry, technical distinctions, and autistic ratiocinations of lawyers, in order to get back to the purity of principles, as they alone could redeem the inaccuracy and corruption of which the former were guilty.[15] But, as many historians have shown, Cicero's call remained unanswered—a way to say that law, in Rome, had acquired such an autonomy that no principle, no philosophy, could alter, if not the orientation, at least the nature anymore.[16] Law had forgotten all about being, and felt perfectly well about it.

Brief Description of a War

This cursive travel through the history of law could be much furthered, and show that the dividing line suggested by Agamben was a dividing line opposing, with the ontologies they defended, the two antagonistic practices that were those of law and of philosophy. In this *war*, the two most important moments were the Renaissance and the Age of the Conflict of Faculties—the first based on the opposition between lawyers and humanists, and the second between the faculties of law and of philosophy, fighting for supremacy in the field of thought. As Patrick Gilli described it, this was a war in the truest sense: with the determination of the superiority of one practice over another, it was up to the possibility of getting the ear of the Prince, and therefore the power to de facto govern, that was involved.[17] When Petrarch, in Letter XX, 4, of the *Familiar*, restated the criticism made by Cicero, he established the basic repertoire of what would be the humanist critique of law for subsequent centuries—namely, the distance of law toward nature, and then toward God.[18] The order established by God, for Petrarch as for the Greeks (and Cicero), was an order whose establishment testified to its given character, and therefore how it was doomed to eternity and the immutability of being: nature was the nature of things, the essence of things, the being of things. Law, however, only had access to the changing human scum of things; it only was concerned with the trivial quarrels by which humans tore themselves apart about goods whose being was determined once and for all by God. The ought-to-being, as manifested in the trials or acts of which jurists were the actors, was parasitic to being—or, rather, it was its perversion into casuistry, singularity, transition, or locality, that is, into anything that was the contrary of the Idea. From Lorenzo Valla to Erasmus, or from the Pogge to Cosma Raimondi, the variations on this main argument were used by humanists (with some exceptions, including Leon Battista Alberti) in their defense of the principles of philosophy against the casuistry of lawyers.[19] The entire modern history of thought will be the more or less voluntary and more or less belligerent, more or less violent, heir of these.

Philosophy Falling

Of this heritage Agamben was right to consider Kant the most important, although the more tortuous, beneficiary—it is thanks to him that the ontology of command catastrophically entered into the ontology of being and that, in philosophy, the imperative supplanted the indicative. Kant's maneuver could be explained according to various reasons, but the most important remained the strategic one: it was necessary to remove the power attached to the ontology of command from the hands of those who made use of it, and add it to the powers of the ontology of being. It was necessary to take the opportunity of the conflict of faculties so that philosophy could annex the power of law and lead the latter to finally lose any possible claim to supremacy in academic matters, while the philosophy faculty would receive the first place it turned.[20] For Agamben, this move implied a real degradation of philosophy, a parasitism thereof, by what, since the Greeks, had represented its evil obverse—a particularly dramatic parasitism insofar as it resembled a sort of suicide of philosophy itself. In attempting to establish the deontological as the last word of thought, Kant had sealed the fate of the ontological, doomed to be nothing if not *guided* by the vectors of order that the legislative imperatives of reason (be they political or moral) addressed to finite humans. The price to pay to ensure the supremacy of philosophy amounted to its overthrow; philosophy triumphed in the conflict of faculties only to turn into its own worst enemy; the thought of being was not wearing more than the name anymore, all philosophy having become, by definition, juridical. However, it was necessary to understand the scope of the disaster: it was less that philosophy felt as a discipline than that what the thought of being opened (the possible) was destroyed by the police management of the ought-to-being (the necessary). The philosophy of Kant, his whole theory of being (or what was left of it) was a thought of the necessary; while his philosophy was a thought of "one must"—and even, in very many respects, of "one has to," the renunciation to anything that might escape the inevitable, the finite, or the determined.

The Logic of Oath

In *The Sacrament of Language*, another volume of *Homo Sacer*, published three years before *Opus Dei*, a volume devoted to the "archeology of the oath," Agamben tried to define the functioning of the necessary, as the object of the imperative mode.[21] The institution he had chosen as instituting that mode, and as constituting its paradigmatic incarnation, infiltrating with its paradoxes every imperative speech, was that of the promise or sworn faith—in short, the oath. With the oath, the relationship between law, religion, and magic was exposed in its most purified form: each of these practices was only a way of seeing, a perspective on this institution that summarized them all. For what is an oath but a way to guarantee that it could be possible to ensure that a given word would lead to the consequences to which it committed the subject who uttered it? What is the oath but the establishing of a necessary link between the articulation of a proposition and the realization of what it promised or claimed to establish—depending on it being a promissive or assertive oath? For Agamben, the oath defined the imperative condition of language in that it bound it to the possibility of a name whose model could only be God—that is, a name that was the epitome of command.[22] Swearing is to provide evidence of the belief in the power of a name and transform this power into a weapon involving every name, every nomination, as each and every one of them is an act of command, since God is only God because it is a name that nominates. The imperative is the grammatical mode of the religion of name, and of the magic that supports this religion—the magic that, for all the civilizations that have known the oath, could be named "law": *law is the magic of name*. That is, it is the practice of the necessity involved in believing in the name, and of the attestation of this belief by the performance of an oath defined as the fulfillment of the necessary consequences of what was stated therein. Such was the curse of the imperative, whose philosophy, according to Agamben, had never stopped trying to guard itself—until Kant opened the doors.

INTRODUCTION TO THE THEORY OF MAYBE

What's Left

Philosophy is the preservation of the possibility of perjury where sworn faith is required; it is the ability of the desecration of the name where the name requires adherence, obedience, and repetition; it is the possibility of friendship in the age of generalized law. If one prefers: it is what, in the logos, remains preserved from any guarantee or any need—what, in it, continues to err between truth and error, and whose erring is being itself, as being is always experience. In the work of Agamben, this experience could take many faces, including, as a matter of fact, the one of childhood, desecration, friendship, nudity, or story—that is, the faces of the "form of life" as they are opposed to the "rule" of the necessary.[23] Always and everywhere, for him, "fireflies" continue to reappear as as much a residue or memory left behind, once destroyed by the incessant extension of the realm of command, at the heart of what should be its opposite. It took all the bad faith of Georges Didi-Huberman to refuse and consider these ghosts, as well as the experience of possibility that, in Agamben, always accompanied them—and to blame him for the pessimism he shared with Pasolini.[24] The big fat fireflies of which Didi-Huberman had undertaken to describe the "survival" in the little booklet that he dedicated to them were actually the fireflies of resistance: with them he preferred to fold the possibility of being into the need a simple alternative ought-to-being. For there to be an opportunity, it is in fact that there must be no actuality—but, as had been established by Gilles Deleuze when he distinguished the "virtual" from the "actual" to better emphasize their common reality, this does not preclude that this possibility could be part of being in itself.[25] The pathos of the destruction of experience that Didi-Huberman criticized in Agamben was not blindness toward what would remain of experience, as supposedly "indestructible": it is not what remains. The entire work of Agamben has only been the gigantic encyclopedia of these remains and of the possibility of experience left intact once their experience had been destroyed by the enslavement of being by command.

A Moment of Hesitation

However, why finish with law; why finish with command, rule, religion, magic, necessity—and the strange logical device by which the language of law loops on itself, and that has been called "state of exception"?[26] Agamben has never really delivered on this, as if he were hesitating to abandon what had been the first moment of his student, intellectual, and research life—that is, as if law were still part of his person. From this perspective, his hesitation might recall that of Deleuze, who in his video interviews with Claire Parnet, declared that if he had not studied philosophy, he probably would have studied law and become a judge—even though, in the book he coauthored with Parnet at the same moment, he eventually went on to write a sentence like this: "Rather being sweeper than judge."[27] The complex history of *logos* and its interaction with *nomos* did not stop with the triumph of command in Kantian thought; the dancing had resumed in the twentieth century in new configurations, of which it was not sure that they would entirely correspond with the ones that Agamben had in mind. Rather than conceive it under the form of a frontal opposition, perhaps one was to remember the invention of the Greek *nomos*, rather than its reinvention, in the age of Roman law, by Cicero, and then recall that it was not a dance for two partners—but three. True, there was *logos* and *nomos*, and *nomos* as the possible face of *logos*; but there was also *ius* and *lex*, and *lex* as what, in *nomos*, was a reminder of *logos*—while *ius*, however, was what subtracted radically from it. The necessity of which the linguistic form of the oath was the guarantor was not the only form of necessity; it was equally possible to imagine a kind of necessity that belonged not to warranty or language—a necessity that was also pure possibility. It was this second form of necessity that Agamben had never quite dared to refuse to see, and that made it so that, against all odds, his past as law student still continued to live in him, like one of those precious remains of which he wished to preserve the possibility of experience.

The Other Necessity

In *After Finitude*, Quentin Meillassoux had proposed a formula for this possibility: that of the "necessity of contingency"—that is, the necessity that nothing would have any necessity, and that any attempt to establish its necessity was doomed to failure.[28] Meillassoux's endeavour, since it was meant to challenge what he called "correlationism," aimed at the destruction of the link established, since Kant, between what we are capable of knowing and our finitude as human beings.[29] The principle of "One has to," which supported Kant's philosophy, and with it, the deontological-legal framework by which philosophy had abdicated any chance of still being able to measure itself decisively to the question of being, was a vain principle. The contingency of everything could hold only insofar as it was necessarily asserted—but this necessity, just as the Cartesian *cogito*, then allowed and rebuilt the entire world that the terrorism of contingency had destroyed. It was therefore no coincidence that the great work of Meillassoux, beside *After Finitude*, was an attempt to confront an issue long abandoned by philosophy: that of the establishment, in the realm of being, of what he called "God's non-existence." Just like Agamben, Meillassoux wanted to restore the existing ontological difference between the world of philosophy (and its ontology of being and contingency) and the world of religion (and its ontology of ought-to-being and necessity). But, unlike Agamben, Meillassoux wanted to achieve this recovery by the nondeontological, and even antideontological, reclaiming of necessity: by the instauration of a kind of sheer necessity—as pure as was the possibility for Agamben. For the one who observed the deployment of their respective work (which was a deployment apparently in a complete mutual ignorance) there, there also were lineaments of a curious as much as unexpected conjunction, in which possibility and necessity came to share their mutual characteristics. Necessity suddenly became the possibility of the assumption of the contingency of everything, and possibility became a special case of necessity—a case without law, without rule, without constraints, and without command: a pure *caso*, a pure chance, a pure *arbitrary*.

An Ontology of Maybeing

To the two ontologies distinguished by Agamben, was it then appropriate to add a third—the ontology of what evades being as well as command, and only gives itself as purely inconsistent, haphazard, and arbitrary occurrence? The ontology of being and *maybeing*, in which necessity and contingency would start dancing in turn, albeit on a quite different mode than that, hostile, which characterized the dance of *esti* and *estô*. This ontology would be concerned not by the indicative of description, or the imperative of prescription, but by the conditional of fiction; it would be an ontology of the potentialities specific to any illusion, provided there is someone to believe it or to act as if he or she believed. Of this ontology, law, magic, and religion would offer excellent examples, since the consistency of all that animates them only is the product of an effective fiction—a fiction whose effectiveness lies in the solidity of what is produced therefrom. Thus, in the case of law, this huge machine of fictions, it is less the methods of *juris dictio* that shape the ecology of cursed necessity, denounced by Agamben, than the legal act following any *juris dictio*, its immediate consequence, the next legal relationship. When a legal act is passed (say: an oath), it is not the act itself, as such, that is important: it is the *other* legal acts that this act allows, and which, retrospectively, *fabricate* the necessity of what he had it only possessed the virtuality.[30] But this virtuality, to quote Deleuze again, should be regarded as real, whatever its fictional, illusory, or even false character—since it is not being, or its ought-to-being, which is its transcendental. Any legal act belongs to the realm of *maybeing* surrounding the always singular and chancy case that provokes it, and of which only the chain of consequences, they also singular and chancy, will allow for the venturing of a fragile and provisional conclusion regarding being. Such is the nature of the possible: to open a virtuality in the absolute necessity of its contingency, as well as in the absolute contingency of the frail necessity that it attempts, by the fictional magic of its meager resources, to make consist.

Against the Law

On the set of *The Gospel According to Matthew*, was Agamben thinking that the doubt tapping his character, if it marked, for Pasolini, the end of a cycle (the insulation of the apostles from Judas the traitor), opened in a new one too? This new cycle of doubt, Agamben has never stopped trying to ward it off, by tracing, between philosophy and law, a kind of boundary relegating the former in the realm of error—instead of trying to conceive error as the locus of another regime of truth. It must be said that the history of law, as an instrument in the hands of each power claiming to be entitled to use it (from the church to alleged contemporary democracies), offered an inexhaustible reservoir of examples of violence carried out in its name, and in the name of what it was supposed to defend. Law has always been used as a bludgeon at the service of order, of command, of ought-to-being—even if the fact that it had been so did not mean that it *had* to be so, or that it was inevitable that it might continue for all eternity. On the contrary, the logic of the imperative is a logic of use: it is only one of the possible modes of the use of *maybeing*, orienting it toward the policing of the limitation of consequences, rather than toward their unlimited invention. Perhaps it was possible, then, to try to save Agamben from what might seem like a strange myopia concerning the mode of operation of law—a missing that Yan Thomas, who had been his friend, had named "operations."[31] What Agamben aimed at, and was right to aim at, was in fact *the* Law, the *lex*, as innervating *logos* with *nomos*, the device through which law could be domesticated, which philosophers kept dreaming about, and authorities of all kinds kept using with dramatic results—the device that was the obverse of law, rendering vain or empty the performance of its operations. The Law was the embodiment of the ontology of command, whereas law was the incarnation of the ontology of fiction, and of the preservation, in the virtualities of its *maybeing*, of all the real possibilities that its legislative functioning just kept crashing. Law was the best ally of Agamben, in his fight against the Law; it was just that he had to accept coming to terms with it so that it could dissipate the agonizing melancholy that darkened his face while, at twenty-two years old, he uttered his line: "Me too, Master?"

NOTES

1. Giorgio Agamben, "Decadenza," *Futuro*, no. 6, May 27–June 1964, 28–32.
2. Giorgio Agamben, *L'homme sans contenu* (1970), trans. Charles Walter (Belval: Circé, 1996).
3. Giorgio Agamben, Opus Dei: *Archéologie de l'office*, pt. 2, vol. 5 of *Homo Sacer* (2011), trans. Martin Rueff (Paris: Le Seuil, 2012).
4. Ibid., 115.
5. Ibid., 154.
6. Giorgio Agamben, *Qu'est-ce que le commandement?* (2013), trans. Joel Gayraud (Paris: Rivages, 2013).
7. Ibid., 32.
8. Giorgio Agamben, "La puissance de la pensée" (1987), trans. Joel Gayraud, *La puissance de la pensée: Essais et conférences* (Paris: Rivages, 2006), 233.
9. Agamben, *Qu'est-ce que le commandement?*, 42. For commentary, see Laurent de Sutter, *Magic: Une métaphysique du lien* (Paris: PUF, 2015).
10. Pier Paolo Pasolini, *Correspondance générale, 1940–1975*, trans. René de Ceccatty (Paris: Gallimard, 1991), 37–38.

11. Héraclite, *Fragments*, ed. Jean-François Pradeau, 2nd ed. (Paris: Flammarion, 2004), 175, 300. See the comments of Jacqueline de Romilly in *La loi dans la pensée grecque, des origines à Aristote* (Paris: Les Belles Lettres, 1971), 16.

12. Romilly, *La loi dans la pensée grecque*, 16.

13. Pierre Grimal, *Cicéron* (Paris: Fayard, 1986), 392.

14. Cicero, *Traité des lois*, ed. Georges de Plinval (Paris: Les Belles Lettres, 1959).

15. Ibid., I, IV, 14. *De Legibus* continues and develops the criticisms already formulated in *Pro Murena* (23–30) and *De Oratore* (1:236). See Georges de Plinval, introduction to *Traité des lois*, XII. See also Grimal, *Cicéron*, 272.

16. Aldo Schiavone, *Ius: L'invention du droit en Occident* (2005), trans. Geneviève and Jean Bouffartigue (Paris: Belin, 2008), 202.

17. Patrick Gilli, *La noblesse du droit: Débats et controverses sur la culture juridique et le rôle des juristes dans l'Italie médiévale (XIIe–XVe siècles)* (Paris: Honoré Champion, 2003).

18. Ibid., 163.

19. Ibid., 231.

20. Immanuel Kant, *Le conflit des facultés en trois sections* (1798), trans. Jules Gibelin (Paris: Vrin, 1935).

21. Giorgio Agamben, *Le sacrement du langage: Archéologie du serment*, pt. 2, vol. 3 of *Homo Sacer* (2008), trans. Joel Gayraud (Paris: Vrin, 2009).

22. Ibid., 78.

23. Cf. Giorgio Agamben, *Enfance et histoire: Destruction de l'expérience et origine de l'histoire* (1978), trans. Yves Hersant (Paris: Payot, 1989); Agamben, *Profanations* (2005), trans. Martin Rueff (Paris: Rivages, 2006); Agamben, *L'amitié* (2007), trans. Martin Rueff (Paris: Rivages, 2007); Agamben, *Nudités* (2009), trans. Martin Rueff (Paris: Rivages, 2009); Agamben, *De la très haute pauvreté: Règles et forme de vie*, pt. 4, vol. 1 of *Homo Sacer* (2011), trans. Joel Gayraud (Paris: Rivages, 2011); Agamben, *Le feu et le récit* (2014), trans. Martin Rueff (Paris: Rivages, 2015); Agamben, *L'usage des corps*, pt. 4, vol. 2 of *Homo Sacer* (2014), trans. Joel Gayraud (Paris: Le Seuil, 2015).

24. Georges Didi-Huberman, *Survivance des lucioles* (Paris: Minuit, 2009), 57.

25. Gilles Deleuze, *Différence et répétition* (Paris: PUF, 1968), 269.

26. Giorgio Agamben, *Etat d'exception*, pt. 2, vol. 1 of *Homo Sacer* (2003), trans. Joel Gayraud (Paris: Le Seuil, 2003). The doctrine of "civil war," recently formalized by Agamben, seems to constitute a direct consequence from his theory of the "state of exception." See Agamben, *La guerre civile: Pour une théorie politique de la "stasis,"* trans. Joel Gayraud (Paris: Le Seuil, 2015).

27. Gilles Deleuze and Claire Parnet, *Dialogues*, 2nd ed. (Paris: Flammarion, 1996), 15. For a comment, see Laurent de Sutter, *Deleuze: La pratique du droit* (Paris: Michalon, 2009).

28. Quentin Meillassoux, *Après la finitude: Essai sur la nécessité de la contingence*, 2nd ed. (Paris: Le Seuil, 2012).

29. Ibid., 18. For commentary, see Graham Harman, *Quentin Meillassoux: Philosophy in the Making* (Edinburgh: Edinburgh University Press, 2011).

30. Bruno Latour, *La fabrique du droit: Une ethnographie du Conseil d'Etat* (Paris: La Découverte, 2002). For more detailed commentaries on this point, see Laurent de Sutter, *Après la loi* (Paris: PUF, forthcoming).

31. Yan Thomas, *Les opérations du droit*, ed. Marie-Angèle Hermitte and Paolo Napoli (Paris: EHESS–Le Seuil–Gallimard, 2011).

CounterPlaces, CounterTimes

IV

10

Cities of Refuge, Rebel Cities, and the City to Come

Giovanna Borradori

The intensification of the processes of globalization transforms the city into a node of accumulation of financial and symbolic capital. If it is true that the city has never been more vulnerable to the systemic imperatives of the market, it is surprising that it continues to be the place where the deepest social and political transformations come to the surface. From Tahrir Square to Taksim Square, from Ferguson, Missouri, to Saint Paul, Minnesota, from sit-ins to die-ins, the crucial question is thus the following: What preserves the city as a space of dissent? The claim of this essay is that a critical reflection on the political agency of Northern and Southern cities, dispersed all over the surface of the globe, has to start from asking what it means, today, to occupy the pavement of their streets. The argument explored here is that, in this age of neoliberal policies of austerity, it is a certain experience of dispossession, rather than the quest for identification and recognition, that makes the city the core of a shared experience of refuge and resistance, and sometimes turns it into a site of rebellion.

In a 1974 short story by Ursula Le Guin, "The Ones Who Walk Away from Omelas," a town is celebrating the Festival of Summer. The sun is out: boats rig in the harbor and parades stream down the streets while music, dances, and wreaths of flowers entertain young families and elderly couples alike. All that happiness and well-being, however, depend on what Le Guin calls the "terrible justice of reality": an abandoned and abused child, permanently locked up in a windowless broom closet.

Le Guin locates the closet beneath one of the city's feature buildings: whether it is a public establishment or an elegant private home she doesn't say. What matters is that the filthy little closet is in a basement, out of view but acutely present to the consciousness of all discerning citizens.

The closet is a narrow and moldy space, barely three paces long and two wide. The door is locked at all times. The malnourished and naked child who is held captive in it looks no more than six years old, although he is probably ten. The ironclad rule is that whoever comes to see him may not talk to him. He is a specimen to be looked at in consternation and silence. Given the child's despicable destitution, even looking at him proves to be an almost impossible demand. "Its buttocks and thighs are a mass of festered sores, as it sits in its own excrement continually."[1] Instead of cleaning him, his caregivers yell at him and kick him when they want him to move. Most sadly, everyone knows that there was a time when even this child hoped to be released. He used to cry and promise that he would be good. Now he moans at the very most.

> They all know it is there, all the people of Omelas. Some of them have come to see it, others are content merely to know it is there. They all know that it has to be there. Some of them understand why, and some do not, but they all understand that their happiness, the beauty of their city, the tenderness of their friendships, the health of their children, the wisdom of their scholars, the skill of their makers, even the abundance of their harvest and the kindly weathers of their skies, depend wholly on this child's abominable misery.[2]

The people who get to see him are devastated. Most leave in tears, some in a tearless rage. They empathize with the horror: how can any decent human being accept the monstrous suffering of a child? Yet, in the face of their own powerlessness, people try to rationalize: is it worth sacrificing "the happiness of thousands for the chance of the happiness of one?" And acceptance slowly sinks in.

Then there are those who simply cannot accept it, and once in a while an adolescent who went to see the child does not go back home.

> They go west or north, towards the mountains . . . they walk ahead into the darkness, and they do not come back. The place they go towards is a place even less imaginable to most of us than the city of happiness. I cannot describe it at all. It is possible that it does not exist. But they seem to know where they are going, the ones who walk away from Omelas.[3]

Deflecting the suggestion that her story might be a footnote to *The Brothers Karamazov*, because of its strong reliance on the figure of the scapegoat, Le Guin said that Omelas is simply the palindrome for Salem, O(regon), a street sign that she read backward in the rearview mirror of her car while driving up the West Coast one bright summer morning. It may not be a quotation from Dostoyevsky, but Salem is not just the name of any West Coast sleepy town. For it was in the small village of Salem, Massachusetts, geographically nestled symmetrically from Salem, Oregon, on the East Coast of the United States, that the American Inquisition incarcerated, prosecuted, and executed scores of people accused of witchcraft.

The biblical horizon haunting Le Guin's narrative functions as a methodological premise of this essay. In the opening section, I succinctly describe one of the crucial mechanisms of neoliberalism as the millennial, and fundamentally Abrahamic, rhetoric of sacrificial attachment. It is the logic of sacrifice that, in today's political economy, authorizes the seemingly natural translation of social solidarity and political conflict into the polarized positions of debtor and creditor. This convergence of the religious and the economic is the background against which nations, as well as cities, are being refashioned as corporations, and the termination of social programs is presented as collateral damage.

In the wake of Le Guin's merciless gaze, I then embark on a critical reflection of what constitutes safety, safe spaces, and political subjectivity today. My point of departure is the biblical trope of the city of refuge, which is at the origin of the legislation regulating the right to asylum for refugees.

According to the Old Testament, God ordered Moses to found six exceptional cities designated to provide sanctuary to the manslaughterer, defined as the one who kills their neighbor unintentionally. The city of refuge was the topic of one of Emmanuel Levinas's Talmudic Lectures, and, through Levinas, it became an important figure of Jacques Derrida's reflection on cosmopolitanism, global governance, and the crisis of the nation-state.

For both Derrida and Levinas, the city of refuge is a trope marred in moral ambiguity: Like all legislation on human rights, including the right of asylum, the city of refuge too is suspended between idealism and hypocrisy. Within this general position, however, Levinas and Derrida interpret the city of refuge in distinct ways. For Levinas, the city of refuge is the emblem of the structural contradictions of the liberal city, a community in which we all as members unwittingly commit unspeakable crimes by participating in democracies founded on structures of injustice and oppression, both nationally and geopolitically. From Levinas's perspective, Omelas in its entirety could thus emerge as the quintessential city of refuge.

By contrast for Derrida, who embraces moral ambiguity as a space of hesitation and productive interruption of the neoliberal logic of debt and credit, the city of refuge illustrates an "elsewhere" to the *polis*, a city beyond the city, or perhaps the possibility of a city-to-come. This elsewhere, I suggest, is where the adolescents aim to go when they head out of town, unable to carry the unintended moral burden of the abandoned child who languishes in a broom closet.

Of this elsewhere Le Guin says that it is "even less imaginable to most of us than the city of happiness." It is a place that, she admits, she cannot describe but that the young people seem to sense in their bodies as they head out of town. From the island in the middle of the Atlantic theorized by Thomas More to the *derives* of the Situationists, this elsewhere has been imagined as a rural, bucolic, or insurrectionally playful "other" space. I offer to locate it in the deconstruction of the *oikos*, the core of the hierarchical metaphysics of the *polis*.

What I call the practice of *deconstruction by occupation* has been the trademark of recent movements of protest in the Middle East, Europe, Latin America, and the United States. Responding to calls uttered through social media such as Twitter and Facebook, crowds have been taking to the squares and the streets of cities around the world, and affirmed new political subjectivities. I want to ask: In the age of Twitter and Facebook, what exactly does it mean to appear on the pavement of those squares and those streets, and expose one's body to harm? And how does the new political subjectivity of those crowds relate to their exposed corporeality?

Ever since the iconic uprising that tore down the gates of the Bastille in 1789, demonstrations have been perhaps the most universal expression of political struggle in the history of modernity. I want to argue that there is something distinctive about today's popular uprisings. Unlike classic demonstrations, whose objective was to affirm the existence of an oppositional force and apply pressure, occupations of today's public space are aimed at physically and mediatically exposing human bodies in their vulnerability and precarity. From Tahrir Square, in Cairo, to Taksim Square, in Istanbul, from Ferguson, Missouri, to Saint Paul, Minnesota, crowds have formed and appeared in sit-ins and die-ins, using the body, individually and collectively, as the ultimate tool of political struggle.

Heading out of the neoliberal city and pursuing the city-to-come is for these crowds a gesture of dispossession, and not identification or narcissistic search for recognition, as it is commonly taken for granted. In my reading, today's demonstrating crowds are not moved by the utopian impulse of creating a new *polis*; rather, they work at disfiguring it, in the sense of dispossessing it of all signs of familiar belonging. From Zuccotti Park, in the heart of Wall Street, to the Pearl Roundabout, a crossroad at the outskirts of the business district in Manama, Bahrein, what I describe as *deconstruction by occupation* has been waged in the name of the body of the other: the marginal, the unseen, and the unaccounted subject.

In this perspective, the naked presence of the crowds that have recently occupied the pavement of many rebel cities lays claim to public space by exposing both their own fundamental injurability and that of those who exist outside the boundaries of the visible, the representable, and the immediately recognizable. This new *alliance*, as Derrida and Judith Butler call it, includes foreigners, immigrants, the undocumented, the squatters, the homeless, the unemployed, the only precariously employed, the handicapped, the uninsured, the refugees, the displaced, and the deported, among many others yet.

NEOLIBERALISM AS POLITICAL RATIONALITY

The focus on neoliberalism as a specific form of political rationality clarifies a deep historical transformation in the relation between markets, states, and civil society. Since the capillary deregulation of the financial markets implemented by Ronald Reagan and Margaret Thatcher in the 1980s, neoliberals have argued for the privatization of state assets, the territorial dispersion of production through subcontracting, and a shift in tax policy that favors the upper echelon of wealth accumulation. Central to this line of neoliberal thinking is the social Darwinist idea that the market naturally pays people what they are worth.[4] Intervening in the market thus distorts fair distribution.

While late twentieth-century politics has seen corporate wealth either buying, or becoming, the political elite, a mark of the new millennium is what Wendy Brown has called the *merging of corporate and state power*. Not only are state functions outsourced, from prisons to the military, and corporate CEOs appointed as cabinet secretaries, but state power is, as Brown states, "unapologetically harnessed to the project of capital accumulation via tax, environmental, energy, labor, social, fiscal, and monetary policy as well as an endless stream of direct supports and bailouts for all sectors of capital."[5]

In this perspective, neoliberalism is the form of political rationality that "renders every human being and institution, including the constitutional state, on the model of the firm and hence supplants democratic principles with entrepreneurial ones in the political sphere."[6] Echoing the raison d'état of the old realists, this kind of market democracy makes the contemporary state into an actor and a facilitator of global financial health. "The people are reduced to passive stockholders in governmentalized states operating as firms within and as weak managers of a global order of capital without: an order that has partly taken over the mantle of sovereignty from states. Nothing made this more glaringly apparent than state responses to the financial capital meltdown in the fall of 2008."[7] In a late modern twist on commodity fetishism, democracy is thus reduced to a brand and the bond of solidarity into a strong credit rating.

While the political core of the *demos* is quantified in terms of the human capital, citizenship is encouraged as a radically vulnerable subjectivity, haunted by the perspective of unemployment and saddled with debt. Salvation, in this light, is redefined as the lifelong project of self-investment.

In a marked departure from the classical empiricist definition of the human subject as the agent of needs, the neoliberal subject is an agent of financial responsibilities. The agony of the Fordist model of labor and the neoliberal reliance on disposable forms of employment have enabled the rise of a flexible workforce that can be hired and fired at will. This shifting in the conception of what constitutes a subject, objecting to injustice and fighting for rights, becomes the internalization of failure and self-blame. The well-being of the economy designates the horizon of the common good, the metrics against which actions and decisions about oneself are made in the interest of all. As entire populations are subject to the prospect of appreciation and depreciation, they are also groomed to face the possibility that none of their basic needs will be met. In this perspective, solidarity and conflict, the distinctive experiences of homo politicus, are translated into the objective conditions of homo economicus: credit and debit. Today's responsible citizen does not rely on Kantian dignity but on the macroeconomic imperative of growth and a good credit rating.

As typical neoliberal subjects, the inhabitants of Omelas are held hostage by the incantations of summer festivities. For them and for us, membership in the city is structured as a *spectatorial relationship*, in which the spectacle of what is desirable and enjoyable depends on the spectacle of what Jacques Rancière has called "the intolerable image."[8] In Le Guin's story, this is the image of the battered child, the sacrificial lamb to which everyone is silently indebted. On the global stage of today's political and media apparatus, the intolerable image is the thousands of nameless, and mostly faceless, victims that shake the conscience of the global North: from the so-called tribal violence that rips apart the promise of political cohesion in places like Afghanistan to the suicide bombings that punctuate ordinary life on the streets of Baghdad; from the atrocities against the civilian population committed by drug cartels in Mexico and Colombia to the trickle drowning of thousands of migrants imported as cheap labor from impoverished regions of the world.

Le Guin's story denounces thus two distinct "regimes of visibility": the visibility of what lies within the audience's threshold of moral tolerance and the visibility of what lies beyond it, the intolerable image. This is the collateral moral damage that Le Guin's short story, "Those Who Walk Away from Omelas," stages in its stark, iconic terms.

CITIES OF REFUGE

The notion of collateral damage lays well-disguised roots in the economy of sacrifice, which renders the utilitarian calculus of profit maximization a less secular operation than it seems. As Le Guin's narrative makes clear, the designation of certain subjects, or populations, as expendable relies on their previous dehumanization, which is a kind of "consecration," to use Agamben's language,[9] aimed at enhancing the threshold of collective tolerance for the suffering and abandonment of given others.

While classical Greek tragedy focuses on the heroism of those who elect to be sacrificed to maximize the common good, the Abrahamic tradition devotes considerable attention to the moral status of the agent of manslaughter. The position of the individual who kills unintentionally shares the moral ambiguity of the community that lies at the receiving end of sacrifice, for those who benefit from a sacrificial offering commit murder without intending to so.

In the Old Testament, Moses founds six cities of refuge to provide the man who kills his neighbor unintentionally with a safe haven. Each of the six Levitical towns, named Golan, Ramoth, Bosor, Kedesh, Shechem, and Hebron, is set up to work as a geographic, social, and political shield against the avenger of blood, who would otherwise take a life for a life. The morally undecidable status of the manslaughter is mirrored in the fact that residence in the city of refuge is a cursed blessing: while it offers fugitives safe haven, it also holds them in exile from their home.

In a late text titled "Cities of Refuge,"[10] Levinas sees the connection between the ethical ambiguity pertaining to individual crimes of manslaughter and the political ambiguity pertaining to the sacrifice, or consecration, of certain lives as expendable in order to enhance the greater good, which is what happens in Le Guin's Omelas. In his commentary on the passage about the cities of refuge in Makkot 10a, Levinas reads the biblical city of refuge in terms of the *liberal city*, an expression that defines the moral agency of those living in the affluent societies of the global North. "In Western society—free and civilized, but without social equality and a rigorous social justice—it is absurd to wonder whether the advantages available to the rich in relation to the poor—and everyone is rich in relation to someone in the West—whether these advantages, one thing leading to another, are not the cause, somewhere, of someone's agony?"[11]

Similarly to the six Levitical cities of refuge, the purpose of the liberal city is to guarantee the safety and prosperity of its citizens against the anger of the avengers of blood, whether these avengers are in faraway countries or at the social, cultural, religious, or economic margins of the liberal city itself. Levinas underlines that the apparently primitive figure of the avenger of blood is in fact the voice of social injustice that the city of refuge is designed to contain. "Does not the avenger or the redeemer of blood 'with heated heart' lurk around us, in the form of people's anger, of the spirit of revolt or even of delinquency in our suburbs, the result of the social imbalance in which we are placed?"[12]

Yet the moral ambiguity of the city of refuge cannot be reduced to the shielding of the isolated incident of manslaughter. Rather, it raises the question of a political space in which innocence is measured on a purely subjective scale, guilt is objectified and institutionally forgiven, and reparation is exorcised. As Levinas writes, the issue of refuge has a geopolitical, and even civilizational, scale. "The city of refuge is the city of a civilization or of a humanity which protects subjective innocence and forgives objective guilt. . . . A civilization of the law, admittedly, but a political civilization whose justice is hypocritical and where, with an undeniable right, the avenger of blood prowls."[13]

In Levinas's analysis, the concept of refuge is the crux of the hypocrisy of the liberal city, in which capitalist accumulation is sheltered from its moral responsibilities, whether those responsibilities play out in terms of a positional geopolitical privilege or in terms of the gross inequality of opportunities besieging distinct populations within it. If the structure of the liberal city is indeed that of the city of refuge, liberal citizenship as such would be marred by the ambiguous status of the manslaughterer: those who are half guilty as a consequence of having harmed or even killed, but also half innocent because they did not intend to do so.

Liberal citizenship, from Levinas's angle, comes with an implicit participation in a system of oppression and structural violence. By replacing the normative foundation of Kantian dignity with the macroeconomic imperative of growth and a good credit rating, which holds each and every subject solely responsible for his or her performance, our neoliberal city renders this ambiguity even less legible.

Judaism is the religion of a fugitive population, seeking refuge against oppression and enslavement. In the Talmudic passage Levinas takes up in "Cities of Refuge," a rabbi asks why cities of refuge are needed, given that the Torah is the ultimate refuge. The answer offered by another rabbi catches Levinas's attention: one might be interrupted while reading. It is precisely the moment of interruption that breeds the danger of making careless mistakes that may lead to incidents and even murder.

The figures of interruption and inattention play a key role in Levinas's interpretation of the cities of refuge. Reading in general, which includes the Torah, should be interpreted not as an abstract undertaking but as a practice. As such, reading depends on material conditions that are not only beyond our control but are unique to a place and a time, a given set of circumstances, and the rhythms of individual human subjects. The interruptions and potential inattention that haunt the practice of reading also haunt the city's political space, where allowances and adjustments are made in response to the singular material underpinnings of human life.[14] While the cities of refuge in Makkot 10a give voice to the dilemma of how to live together given a specific and irreducible constellation of events, in Levinas's text they appear juxtaposed to the figure of the heavenly Jerusalem: conceived as the ultimate refuge in which perfect wakefulness reigns, this is a polity in which no careless errors are made, no one is a manslaughterer, and no one is a fugitive seeking refuge.

The true meaning of Zion, for Levinas, "is not one more nationalism or particularism; nor is it a simple search for a place of refuge. It is a hope for a science of society, and of a society, which are wholly human."[15] The new vision of humanity that Levinas calls "the humanity of the Torah" is "a completely different mode or potential of spirituality a new attention to the human, and placed, as it were, above humanism, which will enlighten us in the Jerusalem of the Torah, which is perhaps defined as a consciousness more conscious than consciousness."[16]

Derrida both admires and fears what he perceives as Levinas's fascination with the heavenly Jerusalem, the city that does not produce refugees: a political space so mindful of itself that the allowances and adjustments that are the essence of the urban condition are not needed, and no sacrifice is made to enhance the common good.

In "A Word of Welcome,"[17] Derrida grapples with two competing readings of Levinas's treatment of the juxtaposition of the liberal city and the heavenly Jerusalem: on the one hand, Derrida does not exclude that Levinas's interpretive scheme may point to a problematic teleological end of politics. On the other, he is convinced that Levinas's legacy may lie in a *hyperbolic conception of politics*, a politics beyond politics, a yet-unseen approach to living together that Derrida takes upon himself to develop further than Levinas himself. Derrida's crucial claim in substantiating this second line of interpretation is that, in order to push Levinas's vision of a hyperbolic politics forward, there is no need to turn to ethics, as Levinas seems consistently to do.

According to Derrida, what lies beyond the city's walls is not limited to the face-to-face relation that Levinas sees as ordering and ordaining human agency, and that depends on the human subject's inability to remain indifferent to the suffering of the other, because the other's vulnerability would naturally cause a rupture in the self. For Derrida, the *outside* of politics has to be produced from within it, by a patient, rigorous, and interminable work of deconstruction. This process has to target the political frame of action in its entirety, encompassing the conceptual scaffolding of political theory as well as the institutions that shape the way politics deploys itself, always in a singular manner, in a given context, and at a given point in time.

I wish to suggest that Derrida's interest in imagining new political institutions has to be understood in the perspective of such a hyperbolic politics, whose responsibility is to address the needs of those amassed beyond the walls of what Levinas calls the liberal city: those avengers of blood who do not find a place in the city of refuge. One of these institutions is the International Parliament of Writers, which in 1996 sponsored the creation of the International Cities of Refuge Network.[18]

The parliament is a transnational institution devoted to the protection of the right of free speech exercised by writers, journalists, and intellectuals, against the many political entities willing to employ physical force in the pursuit of censorship. The parliament was constituted after the brutal murder of the Algerian writer Tahar Djaout, in 1993, and sponsored the signing of a petition to form the European Charter of the Cities of Asylum. The Indian writer Salman Rushdie gave the inaugural speech of the Parliament, thus making Ayatollah Khomeini's 1989 fatwa against his *Satanic Verses* a key reference to its scope. When, in 1996, Derrida was asked to address the parliament and to detail his own vision of the cities of refuge, a number of cities had already been engaged to act as safe havens for persecuted and endangered writers.

The parliament's project of an International Cities of Refuge Network represents, for Derrida, a symptom of the crisis of the international political order that has developed in the wake of the Enlightenment hypocritical ideals. The parliament has, therefore, the conditions to be a literal embodiment of cosmopolitan solidarity, but only if it remains sharply vigilant in its attempt to reimagine a global political constellation that does not replicate the Enlightenment's exclusionary mode of operation. The network will fulfill that potential only if it extends its welcome beyond the already established writers and journalists featured in Rushdie's inaugural speech, and exemplified in his persona.

In his address to the parliament, Derrida calls for a new Charter of Hospitality, whose normative principle should be the protection "of the foreigner in general, the immigrant, the exiled, the deported, the stateless, or the displaced person."[19] If Levinas's approach to the ethical significance of the biblical trope of the cities of refuge is to reconstruct its deepest moral lesson, Derrida proceeds to deconstruct it, by issuing a call for anonymity. The cities of refuge should exist, for him, in the name of the anonymous, the nonaligned and nonidentified or identifiable within recognizable labels and groups. As Sean Kelly aptly suggests, "Identifying the one who is without a culture, without a name, and without a mode of being-home associates the Derridean city with foreigners in their foreignness as opposed to foreigners as actual, or even potential, compatriots."[20]

In Derrida's perspective, anonymity also provides a useful critical angle from which to approach the crucial questions of refuge in relation to humanitarian aid: Who is in the position of offering refuge and to whom? Is refuge truly available in a situation of structural disparity of opportunities?

On November 13, 2015, after a series of coordinated mass shootings against civilians in several locations of Paris, including the Bataclan Theatre, the Stâde de France, and several cafés and restaurants, a national state of emergency, or more precisely state of urgency (*état d'urgence*), was declared by President François Hollande and has not yet been rescinded at the time of this writing. This response to the attacks bears juridical similarities to the Patriot Act, implemented by the Bush administration in the United States in the immediate aftermath of the bombings against the World Trade Center and the Pentagon on September 11, 2001. Unlike the Patriot Act, however, the French *état d'urgence* lays its foundations in French colonial history and, more specifically, in the first eruption of the Algerian conflict, in the mid-1950s. At that time, the French government created the *état d'urgence* in order to manage the Algerian crisis without having to resort to the state of siege (*état de siege*), which would have meant to formally acknowledge being at war. Under the *état d'urgence*, as of July 23, 2016, 3,600 houses have been raided, 5 of which led to a terrorism-linked judicial investigation.

Since the first Algerian uprising in 1955 and before to the November 13, 2015, attacks, the *état d'urgence* had been declared five times in France: in 1955 and 1958, in response to events in Algeria; in 1961 because of a military coup; in 1984, in connection with independence claims in the overseas department of New Caledonia; and in 2005 to help manage civil unrest in several French metropolitan areas. The year of Derrida's address to the Parliament, 1996, was a particularly dark moment in terms of France's reputation as a country granting refuge and asylum. That year a certain self-congratulatory image of France as *terre d'asile* and *terre d'acceuil* mutated into the much less friendly image of France as the core of Fortress Europe, a continent whose internal free circulation is maintained at the expense of the closing of the external borders. This is due to promulgation of the so-called Debret Laws, a hostile new legislation affecting immigrants and the undocumented, or the *sans pa-*

piers, which was protested by robust demonstrations in the streets of French cities large and small.

Derrida's address to the Parliament engages this historical and political background by shifting the horizon of the discourse of refuge from the defense of freedom of speech, which had been Rushdie's focus, to the theme of hospitality to the foreigner. The overarching argument of Derrida's address to the Parliament is that to offer refuge is to offer hospitality, but a hospitality worthy of its name cannot but be offered to foreigners in their utter foreignness. This is the spirit of Derrida's own "audacious call" to the Parliament to imagine "a genuine innovation in the history of the right to asylum or the duty to hospitality."[21] The cities proclaimed and instituted as cities of refuge are independent from one another, and their bond of solidarity will, in and of itself, be a challenge to the state. As Derrida clearly states, "Whether it be the foreigner in general, the immigrant, the exiled, the deported, the stateless or the displaced person (the task being as much to distinguish prudently between these categories as is possible), we would ask these new cities of refuge to reorient the politics of the state."[22]

If refuge ought to offer hospitality, the city of refuge cannot be understood as a simple enclosure, a safe space in which those who escape violence and persecution find physical protection. This kind of enclosure would quickly transform the city into what Michel Agier has called the "city-camp." A city swallowed in the logic of containment of the humanitarian camp.[23] While there is no doubt that the biblical trope of the city of refuge is at the origin of the right to asylum, humanitarian law, and the industrial and military apparatus that accompanies it, for Derrida the city of refuge still harbors an untapped potential to disturb the fundamentals of all these domains.

Hospitality and protection, however, are not easily disentangled. All modes of hospitality are constrained by the host's own *construction* of what the foreigner needs and wants: by how the host imagines the foreigner as an agent worthy of protection and care. Security thus draws the perimeter of what Derrida calls "conditional hospitality." As Derrida notices in his address to the Parliament,

> The Constitution of 1946 granted the right to asylum only to those characterized as persons persecuted because of their "action in the name of liberty." Even though it subscribed to the Geneva convention in 1951, it was only in 1954 that France was forced to broaden its definition of a political refugee to encompass all persons forced into exile because "their

lives or their liberties are found to be under threat by reason of their race, religion, or political opinions."[24]

Even the Geneva Convention, therefore, in its definition of the conditions of the right to asylum, lags far behind the right to universal hospitality, the Third Article of Kant's classic 1795 treatise, *Toward Perpetual Peace*.

> Here, as in the preceding articles, it is not a question of philanthropy but of right. Hospitality means the right of a stranger not to be treated as an enemy when he arrives in the land of another. One may refuse to receive him when this can be done without causing his destruction; but, so long as he peacefully occupies his place, one may not treat him with hostility.[25]

Based on what Kant identifies as the human species' "common possession of the surface of the earth," this right to universal hospitality is subject to Derrida's critique: although Kant frames it as unconditional, this is not a right of residence but of temporary sojourn, and limited to conditions of peaceful cohabitation. The right of states to deny residence is a limitation that points to the exclusionary scope of cosmopolitanism since its very inception. If the cosmopolitan right to universal hospitality has been so poorly translated in the modern juridical framework, it is because Kant himself had placed it under the sovereignty of individual states. This is why Derrida believes that the city has a yet-untapped role to play in matters of the politics of asylum and refuge.

In this spirit, Derrida exhorts the Parliament to make sure that any future elaboration of the Charter of the Cities of Refuge contains provisions that strictly limit the "new police powers," which he sees operating at both the national and the international scales. Derrida could not be more in tune with the issue of police brutality against migrants and marginalized populations that haunt our own political scene. Recently at the forefront of the political agenda of movements such as Black Lives Matter in the United States and PRI (Parti des Indigènes de la République) in France, the reduction of police harassment and brutality was for Derrida a fundamental component to reimagining refuge. Hospitality means "to restrict the legal powers and scope of the police by giving them a purely administrative role under the strict control and regulation of certain political authorities, who will see to it that human rights and a more broadly defined right to asylum are respected."[26] Both Walter Benjamin and Hannah Arendt, who experienced being refugees firsthand, had already noticed the increased powers of the police in handling refugees. For both of them the police emerge as an anonymous, faceless, formless and ultimately spectral force, whose legitimate powers of enforcement, under the banner of security and protection, easily convert into the sprawling of illegitimate and discriminatory practices.

REBEL CITIES AND THE CITY-TO-COME

In 1996 Derrida's address to the International Parliament was dedicated to the refashioning of the bond of solidarity within the Network of the Cities of Refuge. The insurrectional tone coloring the original title of Derrida's address, "Cosmopolites de tous les pays: Encore un effort!" was lost in the generic English translation, "On Cosmopolitanism." My reading of this text hopes to give it back its original mobilizing spirit.

Delivered in the midst of a tense political climate, which pitted the French government's tough stance on immigration against grassroots movements defending the rights of immigrants and the undocumented, the tone of Derrida's address speaks of a new political subjectivity that I dare call the city-to-come and that, I claim, seems to have come to fruition two decades later.

Since 2009, a wave of demonstrations and prolonged occupations of public spaces around the world has demanded a more reasonable distribution of wealth, more democratic forms of government, racial justice, and the end of police brutality. In line with Derrida's injunction, I suggest that the occupations, die-ins, and sit-ins organized by these movements maintain the city as the core of a shared experience of refuge and resistance, and sometimes turn it into a site of rebellion. Similarly to those few adolescents from Omelas who, upon seeing the locked-up child, do not go back home and voluntarily abandon their homes, the crowds that have flooded the urban pavements of large and small cities give voice to a certain experience of dispossession, rather than the quest for identification and recognition. By occupying a square or a park, they divest the square or the park of its ordinary function, and in so doing expose the core of dispossession and expropriation of these designated public functions.

Although these demonstrations and occupations have taken place for very different political purposes, the startling effect of the crowds of bodies that put themselves at risk of violence by the police, the military, and sectarian strife has been their very own exposure as vulnerable bodies. In Tunis and New York, London and Manama, crowds of people have come together to affirm what Elaine Scarry has called the most "incontestable reality":[27] this is the body exposed in its vulnerability to pain and injury, the body as the original site of reality. "What is remembered in the body is well remembered,"[28] Scarry writes, pointing to the fact of pain's inexpressibility and the impossibility of destroying a sufferer's language.

Exposing one's body's to the possibility of being mutilated and maimed, or even annihilated, by external force is to affirm it as the most incontestable reality. This is one fundamental implication of appearing on the pavement of a street or a square, which is perhaps intensified given today's prevalence of digital social life. But appearing on the street is also a matter of exposing the body's given characteristics and social intelligibility, its shape, gender markers, and melanin gradient, to being abused and violated. As bodies are exposed in their nakedness and injurability, the social realities of neglect and abandonment, physical assault, verbal aggression or symbolic diminution are all exposed as ways in which specific bodies are apprehended differentially from others.

When crowds become exposed bodies, an individual body becomes distinct from the body of single individual: it becomes a body that appears among others, in its corporeality and materiality, interdependence and injurability. The city-to-come names this specific phenomenology of bodies, which appear together and in between one another. In their very appearing together and in between one another, these bodies expose both their new *legibility*, in terms of pure corporeality, and their persistent *illegibility*, within the economic terms of the politics of austerity. By exposing their bodies in their utter destitution, these crowds deconstruct the neoliberal construction of the radically disembodied subject: a subject always already saddled with debt, delivered over to sacrifice, which feeds into the image of a disintegrated *demos*, whose only salvation is in the lifelong project of self-investment.

The amassing of bodies in the streets of our neoliberal cities has certainly made a claim in the public space. But we would miss something crucial were we to take the publicity of that space for granted. For it is the very public character of the space that, by and through these acts of protest, has been made, once again, the object of dispute. As Butler noticed,

> Though these movements have depended on the prior existence of pavement, street, and square, and have often enough gathered in squares, like

Tahrir, whose political history is potent, it is equally true that the collective actions collect the space itself, gather the pavement, and animate and organize the architecture.[29]

The bodies of those occupying public space, in their nakedness and injurability, performatively disfigure it and reconfigure it. Mobilized by social media, these crowds have moved from the squares and iconic monuments and locales to the back alleys, turning anonymous intersections where violence is so prevalent that it goes unnoticed into a spectacle of their own. These crowds have taken over different names and changed their aims as the global audience kept watching. It happened, for example, to the movement of Occupy Wall Street, which, after being evicted from Zuccotti Park, in downtown Manhattan, relocated to the shores of Staten Island. There, in the aftermath of the devastation of Hurricane Sandy, it went on to occupy the discursive practices of relief agencies and became Occupy Sandy.

> So when we think about what it means to assemble in a crowd, a growing crowd, and what it means to move through public space in a way that contests the distinction between public and private, we see some way that bodies in their plurality lay claim to the public, find and produce the public through seizing and reconfiguring the matter of material environments.[30]

Ever since Plato analyzed the constitution of the polis for the Western imagination, the city has been identified in terms of the distinction between private and public spaces. By occupying the pavement of its streets and squares, back alleys and intersections, crowds of people with political projects that are structurally open to further adaptations divest and dispossess the abstraction of the distinction between private and public. By producing the public as the material environment that supports human existence as fragile and interdependent, bodies are exposed in their capacity of acting together.

> No one body establishes the space of appearance, but this action, this performative exercise happens only "between" bodies, in a space that constitutes the gap between my own body and another's. In this way, my body does not act alone, when it acts politically. Indeed, the action emerges from the "between."[31]

The space of appearance created by the amassing of bodies on the city pavement requires the mobilization of a specific kind of collectivity, which

Butler calls an *alliance* and Derrida referred to in his attempt to imagine a new bond of solidarity within the Network of the cities of refuge. Reading Derrida through Butler, we may picture an *alliance of cities* along the model of the *alliance of bodies* that physically expose themselves to harm and, in so doing, performatively produce a new configuration of public space: the city-to-come.

The city-to-come is thus the name of a new collective agency that owns up to the experience of dispossession that being a body implies. In this sense, the city-to-come emerges not only when a mass of bodies occupies the pavement of streets and squares, back alleys and intersections, but discursively too, when bodies and not people are referred to as political agents: bodies in their actual and potential exposure to abandonment and harm, anonymous and faceless bodies, bodies that, because of their different melanin gradients, appear on distinct scales of fragility and interdependence. Speaking in the name of their own injurability, more than to themselves these bodies have called attention to the unseen and the unaccounted for: those who exist outside the boundaries of the visible, the representable, and the immediately recognizable, all those foreigners, paperless, homeless, deported, incarcerated humans who are not allowed to mourn in public.

NOTES

1. Ursula Le Guin, "The Ones Who Walked Away from Omelas," in *Masterpieces: The Best Science Fiction of the Twentieth Century*, ed. Orson Scott Card (Ace Trade, 2004), 216.
2. Ibid.
3. Ibid., 217.
4. Elisabeth A. Povinelli, *Economies of Abandonment: Social Belonging and Endurance in Late Liberalism* (Durham, N.C.: Duke University Press, 2011), 17.
5. Wendy Brown, "We Are All Democrats Now," *Kettering Review* 29, no. 1 (2011): 46.
6. Ibid.
7. Ibid.
8. Jacques Rancière, "The Intolerable Image," in *The Emancipated Spectator* (New York: Verso, 2009), 83–106.
9. See Giorgio Agamben, *Profanations* (Zone Books, 2007).
10. Emmanuel Levinas, "Cities of Refuge," in *Beyond the Verse: Talmudic Readings and Lectures* (New York: Bloomsbury, 2007), 34–52.
11. Ibid., 40.
12. Ibid.

13. Ibid., 51.

14. See Oona Eisenstadt, "The Problem of the Promise: Derrida on Levinas on the Cities of Refuge," *Crosscurrents* 52, no. 4 (2003): 474–82.

15. Levinas, "Cities of Refuge," 52.

16. Ibid., 38.

17. Jacques Derrida, "A Word of Welcome," in *Adieu to Emmanuel Levinas*, trans. Pascale-Anne Brault and Michael Nass (Stanford, Calif.: Stanford University Press, 1999), 15–123, 135–52.

18. See International Cities of Refuge Network, http://www.icorn.org/.

19. Jacques Derrida, "On Cosmopolitanism," in *On Cosmopolitanism and Forgiveness* (New York: Routledge, 2001), 4.

20. Sean K. Kelly, "Derrida's Cities of Refuge: Toward a Non-Utopian Utopia," *Contemporary Justice Review* 7 (2004): 427.

21. Derrida, "On Cosmopolitanism," 4.

22. Ibid.

23. The camp-city is the result of the massive use of the "camp formula" in the most dispossessed regions of the world. "The camps are both the emblem of the social condition created by the coupling of war with humanitarian action, the site where it is constructed in the most elaborate manner, as a life kept at a distance from the ordinary social and political world, and the experimentation of the large-scale segregations that are being established on a planetary scale" (Michel Agier, "Between War and City: Toward an Urban Anthropology of Refugee Camps," *Ethnography* 3, no. 3 [2002]: 320). With the movement of displaced and refugee populations from the global South to the global North, the sociospatial form of the camp that has become a city, the camp-city, finds its mirror image: the city-camp, the city that has become a camp.

24. Derrida, "On Cosmopolitanism," 10–11.

25. Immanuel Kant, "Toward Perpetual Peace," *in Practical Philosophy* (Cambridge: Cambridge University Press, 1999), 328–29.

26. Derrida, "On Cosmopolitanism," 15.

27. Elaine Scarry, *The Body in Pain: The Making and Unmaking of the World* (Oxford: Oxford University Press, 1987), 27.

28. Ibid., 152.

29. Judith Butler, "Bodies in Alliance and the Politics of the Street," European Institute for Progressive Cultural Politics, http://eipcp.net/transversal/1011/butler/en.

30. Ibid.

31. Ibid.

11

A Ghost Story
Electoral Reform and Hong Kong Popular Theater

Marco Wan

Marcus Woo's *Find Ghost Do the CE* was staged in Hong Kong during Occupy Central, the 2014 protests sparked by local discontent with the mainland Chinese government's proposed legal framework for the selection of the city's leader. The play's title, a transliteration from the Cantonese dialect and perhaps more elegantly translated as "Let us ask a ghost to become the Chief Executive," alludes to the unpopularity of the city's current leader: the Cantonese expression "to find a ghost to do something" suggests that the thing to be done is so undesirable that no human being would be willing to do it. The play is the eleventh part of an ongoing series of satirical performances titled *East Wing, West Wing* that engages with topical political, legal, and cultural issues of contemporary Hong Kong. In addition to Occupy Central, the play addresses other controversies around the time of its performance, such as the rise of "localist" Hong Kong culture, the delay of major construction projects, and skyrocketing property prices, to name but a few. That this particular installment in the series was performed in the midst of one of the most momentous protest movements in postcolonial Hong Kong makes it of particular relevance for the investigation of Hong Kong identity, and in particular the ways in which legal debates such as those sparked by the electoral reform package shape identity and cultural production.

Cultural identity is a complex and at times contentious notion, and for Hong Kongers, this complexity is heightened by the uneasy mix of "Britishness" and "Chineseness"—themselves cultural and racial categories that need to be placed in quotation marks—arising from the city's peculiar politico-historical circumstances. Hong Kong was returned to China on July 1, 1997. As a former British colony, the way of life and values in contemporary Hong Kong are arguably shaped by a continuing colonial culture. On the other hand, the city's transformation into a special administrative region (SAR) of China has meant that Hong Kongers are developing a greater sense of affinity with the motherland. During the 1980s, when China was making tentative moves to open itself up to the world, Hong Kong functioned as a bridge between the mainland and the rest of the world such that at the time, the "British" and "Chinese" dimensions of Hong Kong identity were imagined to be more harmoniously balanced: Hong Kongers were "Westernized" enough to understand the developed world, yet Asian enough to navigate the dark continent of the Middle Kingdom. In the time of postcoloniality, however, this balance between "East" and "West," which had served as the foundation for Hong Kongers' self-perception for so long, has come under increasing pressure. Hong Kongers often find themselves torn between pride in China's growing economic power and grave concerns about its political repression. They also find themselves torn between nostalgia for the economically prosperous times of colonial governance associated with the 1980s and early 1990s, and doubts about the relevance of colonial values and structures for the future. Identity in postcolonial Hong Kong is arguably marked by a longing for a colonial past (whether real, imagined, or romanticized) and an affective investment in the Chinese present that are both opposing and intertwined, such that "the issue of becoming Chinese again" after the handover "cannot be discussed without reference to its Britishness."[1] The tensions between the past, the present, and the culturally uncertain future have led one critic to argue that Hong Kong identity has become "schizophrenic," torn between two sets of values that are hard to reconcile.[2]

Some commentators have interpreted Occupy Central as the direct result of the clash between an expected allegiance to China as the new sovereign and the lingering influence of colonial rule. They have called for the purging of such colonial influences from Hong Kong society, and for the need to reestablish a sense of pride in the city's Chinese heritage. As Qi Pengfei argues, "To promote universal suffrage in Hong Kong... the authorities should first complete the historic task of 'decolonizing' the SAR society and help its residents develop a sense of belonging."[3] To use another vocabulary to describe the current political and cultural tensions, the postcolonial situation can be said to be a time in which the Chinese sovereignty that has been reestablished to great fanfare is haunted by the ghost of the city's coloniality, and the expected allegiance to the motherland is troubled by nostalgia. The calls for an end to the colonial influence are in effect calls to exorcise the ghosts of the past.

In this essay, I draw on Jacques Derrida's discussion of hauntology in *Specters of Marx* to analyze the question of Hong Kong identity as refracted in one instance of popular theater: Woo's *Find Ghost Do the CE*. I also consider the relationship between spectrality and justice. The reference to ghosts in the title of a play in which ghosts never actually appear—in which, in fact, the search for ghosts never even takes place—raises questions about the nature of a ghost, about its place in contemporary Hong Kong, and about the ways in which it would communicate with the audience. Specters, Derrida tells us, can never be simply relegated to the past. Indeed, they are not simple presences that can be traced to a single temporal origin or external invasions that can be purged from the polity. As *revenants*, they are always already there, constitutive of the very notion of identity and problematizing linear temporal conceptions such as the figural divide between "pre-" and "post-"1997. When read together, the notion of spectrality and Woo's play suggest that exorcism of colonial ghosts is not an option. As we will see, justice requires that we learn to speak to ghosts.

In the first section, I discuss different reactions to Occupy Central to establish the political and legal context of Woo's play. I also demonstrate the ways in which Derrida's discussion of hauntology can provide a useful point of entry into questions of coloniality, Chinese sovereignty, and Hong Kong identity. In the second section, I address the place of ghosts in Woo's play, and in the third section I provide a close reading of its key moments. In the conclusion, I show that it is only by giving ghosts their due that one can do *justice* to Hong Kong identity.

OCCUPY CENTRAL AND THE SPECTER OF COLONIALITY

Occupy Central is usually regarded as a reaction to the slow pace of electoral reform in Hong Kong. Spearheaded by two professors and a Baptist minister, it dovetailed with local student movements and became a mass demonstration during which protestors blocked the city's main traffic thoroughfares for over two months. The organizers argued that the existing electoral system, under which a pro-Beijing committee pre-screened the candidates for Hong Kong's top post, did not constitute genuine democracy. They demanded elections, which would give effect to substantive voting rights, and which would ensure "equal weight for each vote" and "no unreasonable restrictions on the right to stand for election."[4] The movement was galvanized by the decision of the National People's Congress Standing Committee issued in the summer of 2014, which imposed further restrictions on the selection of candidates.[5]

While the public discourse on Occupy Central has revolved around the question of selecting the chief executive, some commentators have observed that the movement is also indicative of a continuing colonial influence in post-1997 Hong Kong. For these commentators, the movement both reflects and enacts a fundamental tension between a longing for the values of the old order and the reality of the new regime. Writing in the *Asia Times*, Crystal Lin discerns that "what arguably underlies the protests is not so much the design of the 2017 elections, but rather a mistrust over the implications of Beijing's invisible influence over Hong Kong's governance."[6] She further notes that "a fundamental legacy of British rule was to instill a rule of law environment and ethos" which guaranteed equal access to justice, a system of checks and balances, transparent government, and judicial independence. She acknowledges that there was no democracy during the colonial period, but notes that "there was something greater: public trust in governance." She argues that Hong Kongers who witnessed the political repression across the border came to appreciate the freedoms that they enjoyed under the British. Lin's analysis can be said to reflect a strong sense of colonial nostalgia: the colonial past is associated with liberty, social order, and public confidence, all of which are being eroded under Chinese sovereignty. Hers is by no means a singular view: as another commentator remarks: "Democracy as it exists in Hong Kong is a legacy of British colonial rule. Few Hong Kongers would claim otherwise."[7]

Pro-China commentators, however, question the narrative of colonial benevolence by people such as Lin. Writing in the *China Daily*, Lau Nai-keung accuses Lin of "deception" and of painting an unjustifiably "rosy" picture of the past.[8] He argues that her description of colonial rule "resonates well with the young people of the city" only "because they did not experience the colonial era first hand." He highlights the 1967 riots, which were led by leftists rebelling against the colonial regime, as an episode of brutality against the Hong Kong people by the British police force that undermined Lin's rosy depiction. He also notes that the existence of a "special branch" of the royal Hong Kong police largely operating in the shadows before 1997 undercuts her narrative of accountability and transparency. For Lau, colonial nostalgia is only maintained because "dissidents and their leaders conveniently forget many things." Yet even though Lau argues against colonial nostalgia in Hong Kong, his comments can be read as further confirmation of its persistence: not only does he acknowledge that Lin's narrative appeals to many young Hong Kongers, but the fact that he felt the need to respond to it at all arguably testifies to its importance.

The voices of commentators such as Lin and Lau suggest that even though the time of postcoloniality is also the time of Chinese sovereignty, it is also a time in which this sovereignty consistently finds itself haunted by the ghost of the colonial past. The rhetoric of Chineseness is undermined by a sense of longing for an era, real or imagined, in which Hong Kongers' sense of self and of their relationship to China was less problematic. Postcolonial time, then, is a time out of joint: the Chinese present is also the time of an invisible but palpable coloniality, a past that not only makes an isolated appearance but is always already imbricated in the here and now. How, one might ask, should we think about the nature of this ghost, its relationship to cultural identity, and its place today?

The disruption of time constitutive of contemporary Hong Kong identity, as well as the ghostly echoes of coloniality in the city's political, legal, and cultural discourse, may stand to be illuminated by Derrida's discussion of hauntology in *Specters of Marx*.[9] Derrida posits that thinking about specters requires a fundamentally different mode of analysis, for "the spectral . . . is *never present as such*" and is "neither substance, nor essence, nor existence."[10] To approach ghosts, then, is first and foremost to rid oneself of the impulse to seek a concrete presence. A specter is neither unambiguously present nor unequivocally absent. More important for my purposes, specters lead us to rethink what we know of temporality: a spectral moment is "a moment that no longer belongs to time," in the sense of a linear relationship between past, present, and future.[11] As Fredric Jameson explains, spectrality can be thought of as "what makes the present waver," revealing it as not quite what it seems to be.[12]

Spectrality is part of a broader conception of what Derrida calls a hauntology. A portmanteau word combining *haunting* and *ontology*, a hauntological approach to a text problematizes distinctions such as presence and absence, real and unreal, and being and nonbeing. It also reconfigures temporal distinctions such as before and after. Derrida's argument is meant to be an interrogation of ontology: as Warren Montag observes, "to speak of specters, the lexicon of ontology is insufficient. Ontology speaks only of what is present or what is absent; it cannot conceive of what is neither."[13] Hauntology's interrogation of our foundational ideas about existence or reality can also shed light on the complex, heterogeneous, and ephemeral aspects of identity in modern-day Hong Kong, for it can provide one way to understand the city's relationship with its own coloniality. The colonial past is neither completely over nor unequivocally contemporaneous, neither dead nor alive, neither absent nor present. To conceive of coloniality as a specter or a ghost is to understand that the seemingly confident Chinese present in Hong Kong, which began with the temporal dividing line of July 1, 1997, is a "living present" that is "scarcely as self-sufficient as it claims to be," and that "we would do well not to count on its density and solidity, which might under exceptional circumstances betray us."[14] In other words, coloniality is not simply a past that continues to operate in the present but a moment that exposes the "*non-contemporaneity with itself of the living present.*"[15] The colonial dimension of identity, which is neither tangibly there nor unambiguously gone, does not allow any easy opposition between Hong Kong's (British) past and its (Chinese) actuality, and the ceaseless negotiation of this complex cultural dynamic is part of what makes Hong Kongers who they are. Hong Kong is no longer a "borrowed place" living on "borrowed time," as one Australian journalist famously called it, but a city in which cultural identity defies time as we know it.[16]

In this light, the calls for the purging of colonial ghosts, tantamount to calls for chasing away the past, are misunderstanding the very nature of Hong Kong as a postcolonial space. Coloniality, at least as part of contemporary Hong Kong identity, is not an invasion from the outside, nor can it be excised from the cultural fabric of the city. It is a revenant, a specter that one finds is always already there, and as such, "one cannot control its comings and goings because it *begins by coming back.*"[17] It is a disruption of the Chinese present, but is already integral to it. Calls for exorcism, chasing away, and moving beyond the past return us to the ontological condition that a hauntological reading of Hong Kong culture problematizes. Understanding the ghosts of coloniality requires a different analytic frame. In the following section, I argue that *Find Ghost Do the CE* enacts precisely such a hauntological reading of Hong Kong culture and identity.

A PLAY WITHOUT A GHOST

Find Ghost Do the CE comprises a number of skits satirizing different dimensions of Hong Kong politics, law, and culture. As a play performed during Occupy Central, much of its satirical force was directed at the electoral reform package, as well as the unpopular leader of the city. One of the most curious aspects of the play is that it does not actually contain a ghost, or even a search for one for the position of chief executive, as suggested by the title. The prologue notes that the content has changed because, according to Chinese folklore, it is bad luck to put on a play about ghosts. Woo also jokes that since "ghost" in the Cantonese dialect is slang for a foreigner, the script was changed in case the government accused the theater troupe of "introducing foreign forces" into the city, a reference to the conspiracy theory that Occupy Central was an anticommunist movement funded by foreign entities such as the CIA. Yet the prologue's brief justification about the title's purported irrelevance does not exhaust the question about the intriguing absence of ghosts in the play.

This is especially so because ghosts featured prominently in the play's advertising material throughout the entire duration of the show's run. Several ghostly figures can be seen on the poster. The image is framed by two ghoulish figures, dressed in white and with squiggly tails for legs. In the center, a stern-looking man with an ashen face stares implacably at the viewer, and next to him is another figure with a white squiggly tail. All these figures are set against the backdrop of a night sky and a moon mostly hidden by clouds that is reminiscent of a horror film. Moreover, the press release underscores the play's ghostly theme: it explains that ghosts are an organizing thread of the play because "the word *kwei* (ghost) is of multiple layers of meanings."[18] As the description notes, the semiotics of *kwei* in Cantonese is rich and varied, and its meaning changes according to the context. The expression "ghosts fighting ghosts" refers to people who are on the same side bickering with each other; "wasting ghost" refers to excessive spending; and "the drawing of ghosts' feet" means avoiding responsibility.[19] The press release suggests that the multiple significations of *kwei* in Cantonese is key to the play's meaning, and that heterogeneity, plurality, and the disruption of any purportedly monolithic understanding of Hong Kong's language or identity constitutes one way to understand the ghost in the play, despite its seeming absence.

I would suggest that even if the prologue or perhaps the playwright does not believe in *kwei*, a ghost does haunt the play, and it is the ghost of coloniality. Neither present nor absent, it is invisible to the audience, yet its importance is everywhere felt. Contra the prologue, the play's strange title is in fact an important indicator of how to interpret it, and the seeming clumsiness of its English transliteration is significant to the play's thematics. The phrase "Find Ghost Do the CE" is linguistically neither Cantonese nor English but also both at the same time: it is a string of English words put together in a Chinese syntactic frame, but does not make sense in either language. The play's title, like the Hong Kong identity with which it engages, is neither Chinese nor British, yet it is constituted by elements of both. The title's strangeness can be interpreted as an indication of the spectrality at work in the play, a spectrality that operates through the interrogation of oppositions such as colonial history and Chinese actuality, foreignness and domesticity, betrayal and allegiance.

Far from being detached from the play's content, as the prologue suggests, the title is a key to understanding the play's deconstruction of the cultural, affective, and political divisions that have become increasingly prominent in Hong Kong. It has become commonplace locally to say that Hong Kong has become a more divided society because of Occupy Central. Those who supported the movement became known as "Yellow Ribbons" and those who opposed it became known as "Blue Ribbons" because of the color of the garments that they wore. There were frequent clashes between the two camps on the streets and in the subway system.[20] In the private domain, the divisions have at times strained family relations.[21] The play's hauntological reading of Hong Kong identity problematizing cultural divisions between "the colonial" and "the Chinese," as well as temporal divisions such as "past," "present," and "future," can be regarded as one step toward subverting those broader divides that have hardened because of the protests.

SEARCHING FOR SPECTERS

It is perhaps unsurprising that *Find Ghost Do the CE* would become the site for the interrogation of fundamental oppositions in Hong Kong culture, or that it would produce some of the most formidable challenges to the official rhetoric of Chinese sovereignty, for Woo himself is acutely aware of the continuities between art and reality, and in particular between theater and society. At the end of one of the performances, Woo makes a few remarks about the nature of his play to the audience. He begins by noting that one usually believes what is happening "outside" to be real, while what happens "here" in the theater to be nothing but make-believe. Yet he goes on to posit that what happens "outside" on the streets of Hong Kong during the time of the Occupy movement—the student demands for democracy, the clashes between the protestors and the police, the conflict between the "Yellow Ribbons" and the "Blue Ribbons"—is also a form of performance. Everyone is playing a role, however provisional and unintended, and the movement is a form of experimental theater in which the distinction between actor and audience constantly evolves. He calls Occupy Central a "collective and creative enterprise," which, like *Find Ghost Do the CE,* is a cultural product reflecting the conditions of contemporary Hong Kong. He concludes by collapsing the distinction between theater and society, saying that the "play outside will continue for a long time" even if the one inside the theater has to come to an end. Woo's comments make clear that the division between art and reality is blurred at best, in that both are cultural texts which open themselves up to interpretation. As such, the play is invaluable for the study of Hong Kong culture and identity and the way they are shaped by legal debates. However, I would further suggest that the play's cultural significance goes beyond Woo's own explication of its *raison d'être*, and that it is only by interpreting the play's interpretation of Hong Kong's cultural condition, rather than taking Woo's comments at face value, that one could approach the ghosts of contemporary Hong Kong.

Ghostly Echoes

Find Ghost Do the CE opens with a section reflecting on one of the most popular television shows in Hong Kong's entertainment history, *Enjoy Yourself Tonight*. Known affectionately as *EYT*, it was a variety show that first aired in 1967 and continued until a few years before the handover, in late 1994. It ran at 9:30 and 11:00 P.M. every weeknight, and launched the careers of some of the most iconic local television personalities and movie stars, including Lydia Shum Din-ha, Carol Cheng Yu-Ling, and Ivan Ho Sau-shun. The show consisted of singing, dancing, and TV drama. Up to this day, the lyrics of the show's opening theme song, as well as the words of the closing, "Good Night Song" by Hong Kong–born composer Joseph Koo Kar-fai, are still known to many Hong Kongers.

It is perhaps unexpected for a satirical drama critiquing the issues surrounding Occupy Central and electoral reform to begin by returning to a variety show that had ended long before those issues were on the horizon. One way to approach the place of *EYT* in the play is to examine the issues or events it is placed in dialogue with. *EYT* is introduced against the backdrop of the narrator's litany of legal and political problems in post-1997 Hong Kong, including not only electoral reform but also the 2003 demonstration against the introduction of national security legislation; the protest against the introduction of national education, which many people regarded as a tactic to "brainwash" the next generation of Hong Kongers; and the use of tear gas against peaceful protestors during Occupy Central. In contrast to the grim reality of the present, *EYT* is presented as "a happy collective memory" for Hong Kong. The terms *simple* and *happy* are used repeatedly throughout the play when referring to *EYT*.

The significance of *EYT* becomes clearer when one places the program in historical context. It began in November 1967, toward the end of the 1967 riots, and was taken off the air only a few years before the end of colonial rule. The show is therefore associated with a more politically stable and economically prosperous period of colonial governance. The memory of the popular variety show therefore arguably evokes not only elements of the entertainment program itself but the positive sentiments associated with the three decades during which it was aired. The return of *EYT* can therefore be understood as a symptom of colonial nostalgia, a proxy for a better time when everything was (mis-)remembered as "simple" and "happy." The narrator yearns for the play to be given the same name as the TV show, and this yearning reflects a longing for the past in the present, for Hong Kong to be able to approach its current dilemma as if we were still in the time of *Enjoy Yourself Tonight*. The nostalgia surrounding the play's reference to the program, and which raises the possibility of blurring the distinction between 2014, 1974, 1984, and 1994, can be interpreted as a ghostly manifestation that exposes the temporal contradictions of Hong Kong identity.

Music, especially in the form of tunes instantly recognizable to members of a group or community, can create a sense of cohesion and is often an important aspect of cultural identity. The narrator uses *EYT* as a springboard into the popular music of the period, and the play's engagement with the so-called Cantopop from the 1960s to the 1990s is also telling. He notes that the music to "Teddy Boy in the Gutter" (1967), one of the most popular Cantonese songs in the 1960s, was actually written by Jule Steyn for the film

Three Coins in the Fountain (1954). One of the most famous songs of Hong Kong popular culture is therefore actually not Chinese at all. Yet it is not entirely foreign, for few Hong Kongers would know that the music actually has a non-Chinese origin. The same goes for many of the most popular, and most recognizable, tunes that have become the bedrock of Hong Kong popular culture: the narrator notes that the music for Leslie Cheung's 1984 hit "Monica" is in fact by a Japanese composer, as is the music for Alan Tam's equally catchy "Love Trap" (1985). Moreover, the queen of Cantopop, Anita Mui, has reinterpreted music from Germany, Japan, and Scotland, and the iconic George Lam often found inspiration for his songs in the work of German, Russian, and Israeli artists. The detour into the origins of Hong Kong's pop music from the 1960s to the 1990s depicts Hong Kong culture of the late colonial period as much more cosmopolitan than Hong Kong culture around the time of Occupy Central, which some argue has become obsessed with being faithful to its Chinese heritage. Woo's play implies that the international cultural connections permitted by the previous regime enabled local culture to flourish from cross-fertilization, while the turn toward the motherland had the effect of snuffing out creativity. By returning to the international influences that were already part of Hong Kong's popular music, ghostly echoes of which were always heard if not necessarily registered, Woo's play challenges the view that Hong Kong culture is necessarily "Chinese" at the core, or that its acquaintance with "Western" art forms is only skin deep. *Find Ghost Do the CE* suggests that Hong Kong culture, and Hong Kong identity, has always been haunted by the voices beyond the walls of political sovereignty.

Laughing at Superstition

The section of the play that refers to the mystical or the supernatural most explicitly is a parody of a popular TV show about feng shui, or the ancient Chinese art (or superstition, depending on one's viewpoint) of living in harmony with nature. The term *feng shui* literally means "wind" and "water," and those who follow its precepts believe that we sometimes unknowingly place ourselves against the rhythm of the natural order, perhaps by living in a building that disrupts the natural energy flow of an area, or by placing important objects of furniture in a space with bad energy. A feng shui master's advice usually takes the form of guidance on where one should live or how someone should organize his or her living space. The language of feng shui is often highly metaphorical, in that it is usually premised on double meanings of cultural texts, such as buildings or interior design, which escape the eye of the uninitiated. These meanings often contradict the official rhetoric associated with these texts. In other words, feng shui can be regarded as a discourse attuned to how cultural texts can be haunted by multiple significations, incompatible meanings, and subversive undertones.

One of the main objects of parody in this part of Woo's play is the Western Kowloon Cultural District, a site that the Hong Kong government has earmarked for the development of the arts, including the visual arts, music, and theater. The policy objective was to transform Hong Kong into the arts hub for East Asia. However, the development of the site has been repeatedly delayed. When the legislature approved the funding for the project in 2008, the government aimed to open the first part of the development in 2015. However, the project was severely delayed because of overspending and other unforeseen circumstances. The lack of progress stunned many people working in the performing arts, and some of them have noted that the delays could stifle artistic production, as it would be difficult for them to secure funding from investors if it is uncertain that there would be a viable venue for the performances.[22]

The official website of the cultural district confidently announces that it will "establish a new vibrant cultural quarter located on a dramatic harbourfront site in the heart of Hong Kong."[23] It further notes that it would become "one of the world's largest cultural quarters, blending art, education and public space." The skit playfully questions the development's self-conception by drawing on the figurative language of feng shui. The character of the feng shui master begins by reminding the audience that the project was supposed to be complete by the time of the play, but that there was no official opening on the horizon. The West Kowloon Cultural District is both "something"—websites, a designated area, a promenade by the harbor, promises of future development—and "nothing." It hovers between absence and presence; it is always eagerly anticipated, and projects have been planned around it, yet the space never quite materializes.

She goes on to note that the residential buildings nearby, which are supposed to be luxury apartments, are in fact shaped like an altar with incense to the trained eyes of a feng shui master. She posits that a building shaped like an altar so close to the cultural district projects an image of deathliness on it; it is as if the altar and the incense were there to mark the passing of a project that was already dead. She also critiques the plan for the cornerstone of the project, a museum of visual culture known as M+ that is scheduled for completion in 2018. The design of the museum itself has been presented as an architectural gem, but she points out that the building in fact looks like a tombstone. She speculates that the resemblance of M+ to another symbol of death could explain the multiple delays with the cultural district. Finally, she points out that another building on the site is shaped like a paper lantern that is normally used during Chinese funerals. The entire project, then, has an aura of mortality to it.

The play's turn to the discourse of feng shui as a way to critique the government's project can be read as a hauntological reading of its grand narrative of Hong Kong's place in East Asia in the era of Chinese sovereignty. Despite the government's grandiose pronouncements about the cultural district's ability to turn Hong Kong into an art hub, the repeated delays mean that many people in the art community have lost confidence in the project, and in their minds it is already dead. The reliance on the contradictory, plural, and at times surprising significations of the various buildings to which the figurative language of feng shui gives rise enables the play to express discontent with the project's development through a linguistic register familiar to the Cantonese-speaking audience, most of whom would have been exposed to the basic vocabulary and concepts of feng shui regardless of their attitudes toward it. The comparisons of the site to the altar, the incense, the tomb, and the paper lantern expose the official rhetoric as rigmarole; the dual meanings of feng shui discourse reveal a signification that undercuts whatever might be printed on the website of the cultural district. The haunting comes not from the outside but from the very shape and design of the project. It is constitutive of it. In the play, the supposed beacon of cultural development is always already inhabited by death.

Of course, Woo's play does not at all suggest that the logic of double meanings and mystical analogies of feng shui should be taken seriously. Indeed, the skit's humor can be said to stem from how it holds the assumptions and conventions of the discourse up to ridicule: with enough imagination, anyone can assign meanings to random objects, be it a museum, an apartment building, or a chair. However, it is precisely the free association enabled by the discursive space of feng shui that allows the play to find a style and a language to critique the delays in the project. The challenge that the ghostly meanings pose to the Western Kowloon Cultural District at every turn interrogates its monolithic, positive, and confident self-presentation. The parodic reliance on feng shui thus provides an alternative discourse, however fictive, silly, or downright superstitious, to address the community's concerns about the site, and about the empty governmental rhetoric of turning postcolonial Hong Kong into an arts hub. Moreover, this aura of deathliness surrounding the attempts at cultural development by the post-1997 government forms an implicit contrast with the flourishing of popular music in Hong Kong during the colonial period that precedes the skit on feng shui. In other words, the play is structured in such a way that the efforts at developing local culture and identity through the arts in the era of Chinese sovereignty is implicitly found to be wanting when compared with the natural cultural cross-fertilization that took place in the 1970s, 1980s, and 1990s discussed above, thereby further undermining the official rhetoric. The colonial past, though intangible, constantly disrupts the postcolonial present, making it waver.

Believing in Ghosts

The play's final section presents a series of proposals for improving governance in Hong Kong. It is by far the most didactic part of the performance, and its tone changes from humorous to solemn, from entertaining to probing. I am concerned here less with the concrete proposals, such as decentralization of power or development of research institutions, than with the specter of coloniality that the play unwittingly evokes. *Find Ghost Do the CE* does indeed find a ghost, in that it conjures up the specter of coloniality without knowing it. One of the key questions in the final section is "How can Occupy Central be like *Enjoy Yourself Tonight*?" Another is "How can we change the problem of electoral reform into a song that makes us happy?" Both questions refer to the markers of colonial time, including *EYT*, the popular music of the period, and the presumed happiness of Hong Kongers in the 1980s and 1990s. At the end of the play, the colonial past returns to haunt it, in that these questions seek to conflate the Chinese present with the British past, to solve the current political and legal problems of electoral reform with the comedic and musical formulas from the time of colonial rule, to find in the tensions of Occupy Central the "happy" and "simple" mood of pre-1997 Hong Kong.

One character describes the colonial period as a time in which "everyone is happy," including entrepreneurs, the arts community, and the local population as a whole. As he speaks, the colonial flag is projected onto the screen. The symbol of the past appears in the present. On one level, such references to the past can be dismissed as a simple, and misguided, romanticizing of the time of imperialism that naively neglects its darker side. Yet such dismissal would be problematic in that it would assume that the colonial past could be straightforwardly excised from the collective memory of the postcolonial present. In light of Derrida's discussion in *Specters of Marx*, it would perhaps be more productive to think of such evocations as the "non-contemporaneity with itself of the living present" that Derrida identifies as characteristic of spectrality, and that I take to be constitutive of the temporal disjunctures of identity in contemporary Hong Kong. The play keeps referring to the past, sometimes consciously, sometimes unwittingly. At times, it romanticizes this past. Such evocations, such ghostly visitations not only in the final section but in the entirety of the play, bear witness not simply to an inability to let go, but more interestingly to a certain way of approaching the here and now in which the past, the present, and the future blend into one another, so that coloniality and Chinese sovereignty, history and contemporaneity, *Enjoy Yourself Tonight* and Occupy Central, are all part of the same postcolonial moment in which Hong Kong currently finds itself. Spectrality in post-1997 Hong Kong does not simply mean holding on to or learning from the past but thinking of identity and culture in such a way that markers of linear time no longer make sense. To conceive of oneself, and of one's relation to reality, in terms of this temporal disjuncture is part of what makes Hong Kong identity unique. Hong Kong is no longer a "borrowed city" living on "borrowed time." It is a city that exists in a "spectral moment."[24]

CONCLUSION: SPECTRALITY, JUSTICE, AND HONG KONG IDENTITY

At the beginning of *Specters of Marx*, Derrida says that he will speak about ghosts "in the name of justice."[25] Justice, he tells us, "will never be . . . reducible to laws or rights"; it is both more important and more elusive. How might we understand his remarks about justice, and about the relationship between specters and justice? One clue comes toward the end of the book: "Present existence or essence has never been the condition, object, or the *thing* [*chose*] of justice."[26] In other words, to do justice is to recognize that one must move out of the certainty of the ontological analytic frame, to move from "linking an *affirmation* (in particular a political one), *if there is any*," to "a radical experience of the *perhaps*."[27] In other words, to do justice is to move toward the recognition of plurality and undecidability, to deconstruction, to hauntology. It is in this sense that justice, for Derrida, is "not yet there" and "no longer present": to conceive of justice in the vocabulary of presence or of an unequivocal, monolithic there-ness would be to return to ontology.[28]

In this light, doing justice to cultural identity in postcolonial Hong Kong would consist of two intellectual adjustments. First, it would involve moving beyond the conception of "coloniality" and "Chineseness" as two sides of a binary opposition, or to assume that "British" values or ideas are somehow an identifiable presence that could be resurrected intact or simply excised from the city's cultural matrix. To return to the beginning of this essay, calls to purge coloniality from the fabric of Hong Kong society are problematic because there is no insidious colonial mentality or value system *there* to be excised.

Second, it would involve giving the complexity, irreducibility, and temporal multiplicity of Hong Kong identity their due. It would mean understanding that specters, hauntings, and the inhabitation of a time out of joint are precisely what make Hong Kong unique. Contradictory, wavering, and intangible conditions are part of what constitutes Hong Kong identity, and if we insist on exorcising ghosts, we may end up one day losing the fascinating pluralities that make "Hong Kong" as we know it. In other words, rather than attempt to exorcise the specter of coloniality, we should learn to speak to it. Only by doing so can we move toward being *just* to Hong Kong identity. In the current political climate, such a move away from an ontological conception of Hong Kong identity as something made up of building blocks, one Chinese, one colonial, may be impossible. Yet as Derrida reminds us, "one must remember that the impossible . . . is, alas, always possible."[29] Woo's *Find Ghost Do the CE* constitutes a first step toward this act of justice.

NOTES

I would like to thank Daniel Matthews and Andrew Counter for their comments on this essay.

1. Howard Y. F. Choy, "Schizophrenic Hong Kong: Postcolonial Identity Crisis in the *Infernal Affairs* Trilogy," *Transtext(e)s Transcultures: Journal of Global Cultural Studies* 3 (2007): 55.

2. Ibid.

3. Qi Pengfei, "'Colonial Mentality' Still Haunts Hong Kong," *China Daily*, June 26, 2015.

4. *Occupy Central with Love and Peace: Manifesto*, http://oclp.hk/index.php?route=occupy/eng_detail&eng_id=9 (accessed July 16, 2014).

5. *Decision of the Standing Committee of the National People's Congress in Issues*

Relating to the Selection of the Chief Executive of the Hong Kong Special Administrative Region by Universal Suffrage and on the Method for Forming the Legislative Council of the Hong Kong Special Administrative Region in the Year 2016 (adopted at the Tenth Session of the Standing Committee of the Twelfth National People's Congress, August 31, 2014).

6. Crystal Lin, "Ideological Dilemma Grips Hong Kong," *Asia Times*, October 24, 2014.

7. Brian Hioe, "The Impossibility of Democracy in Hong Kong?," *New Bloom*, September 2, 2014, http://newbloommag.net/2014/09/02/the-impossibility-of-democracy-in-hong-kong/.

8. Lau Nai-keung, "Young People Ignorant about Colonial Hong Kong," *China Daily*, November 5, 2014.

9. For a helpful discussion of the major theoretical approaches to cultural hauntings, and in particular of the differences between psychoanalytic and deconstructive approaches, see Colin Davis, "*État présent*: Hauntology, Spectres, and Phantoms," *French Studies* 59, no. 3 (2005): 373–79.

10. Jacques Derrida, *Specters of Marx: The State of the Debt, the Work of Mourning, and the New International*, trans. Peggy Kamuf (New York: Routledge, 1994), xvii.

11. Ibid., xix.

12. Fredric Jameson, "Marx's Purloined Letter," in *Ghostly Demarcations: A Symposium on Jacques Derrida's "Specters of Marx"* (London: Verso, 1999), 38.

13. Warren Montag, "Spirits Armed and Unarmed: Derrida's *Specters of Marx*," in *Ghostly Demarcations*, 71.

14. Jameson, "Marx's Purloined Letter," 39.

15. Derrida, *Specters of Marx*, xviii.

16. Richard Hughes, *Borrowed Place, Borrowed Time: Hong Kong and Its Many Faces*, 2nd ed. (London: Deutsch, 1976).

17. Derrida, *Specters of Marx*, 11.

18. "*East Wing West Wing 11*—Find Ghost Do the CE," press release, June 2014.

19. Ibid.

20. Liam Fitzpatrick, "Hong Kong Is Bracing Itself for More Anti-Occupy Violence," *Time*, October 4, 2014, http://time.com/3462996/occupy-hong-kong-central-democracy-blue-ribbon-anti-protest/.

21. Chris Lau and Shirley Zhao, "Hong Kong Families Split over Support for Occupy Central Protest," *South China Morning Post*, November 17, 2014.

22. Vivienne Chow, "West Kowloon Arts Hub Delays Threaten to Choke Hong Kong Drama and Music," *South China Morning Post*, June 8, 2014.

23. West Kowloon Cultural District, http://www.westkowloon.hk/en/the-district (accessed July 21, 2015).

24. Derrida, *Specters of Marx*, xix.

25. Ibid., xviii.
26. Ibid., 220.
27. Ibid., 42.
28. Ibid., xviii.
29. Ibid., 220.

12

Appearing under Erasure
Of War, Disappearance, and the Contretemps

Allen Feldman

> As for the Thing, it is true that it "commands," but it makes no demand. It is in this way that it differs so greatly from the Voice. It does not address itself to you, it does not have an addressee at all. You are its intimate interlocutor. It expects no recognition because it is not your addressee. It does not speak an unknown or untranslatable language. It simply does not speak. Let us say that it dwells in your home but as if it were outside. In truth, since it is already there and you know nothing of it, do not even hear it, even as the voice of a stranger, cannot measure its time with you or know that its moment of "already been" has not yet arrived, it is therefore you who is instead made homeless and historically dislocated by it.
>
> —JEAN-FRANÇOIS LYOTARD, "Anamnesis of the Visible"

BREACH OF PROCEDURE

We are living the time of wartime as a largely unwitnessable time out of time, as a fall out of conventional time that fractures any idea of progress and political achievement. Jacques Derrida names such temporal dislocation the *contretemps*, which is poorly translated by the English *accident*, and better glossed as "countertime."[1] The contretemps carries the formative sense of a mishap as a blow to the body. The phrase *à contretemps*, originally a seventeenth-century category of fencing and combat, diversely signifies an inopportune movement of a weapon, a false time, a motion out of time, an unexpected and untoward event, a reversal, a random but intervening occurrence, being in countertime and the unaccented portion of a rhythmic pattern. It is related to the anachronic in being *up against* directional time. *Allumage à contretemps*, cross-fire, encompasses the self-cancellation of a force caught by and between its own violence, that turns against its violence with violence, and is no less destructive for this self-effacing retroaction. I contend in this essay that the recursion of *allumage à contretemps* is the condition of possibility for indemnifying war crimes such as collateral damage and enforced disappearance.

As inessential, rigorous necessity and catastrophic disruption, the possibility and actuality of the contretemps conditions all proper and programmed temporality such as war, law, securitization, and democracy as their inadmissible contingency. The contretemps is the rupturing of a directional and linear temporality of which *jus ad bellum* was once the highest expression. The contretemps of collateral damage becomes the alibi—the elsewhere—of an unreliable enemy who has failed to appear at the proper geopolitical coordinate and has remaindered inappropriate civilian targets in its place. The encyclopedia of collateral damage that is "regime changed" Iraq with its discountable casualties, leaked torture photography, infrastructure failure, imploding democracy and proliferating sectarianism, became the contretemps that provisioned an alibi for Obama's return to the "good war" in Afghanistan. A contretemps recently befell democracy closer to home in the coming to power of a counterfactual American presidency. It is but a brief slide from the contretemps of confected Iraqi WMDS and 9/11 culpability, whose fabulation justified invasion, to the current contretemps of executive rule by "alternative facts." This nondescript slippage is the passage that Derrida terms *à pas de loup* that is essayed by a beastly and predatory sovereign. This is the mode of motion of the contretemps that seemingly unfolds intangibly from nothing and nowhere:

> To move à pas de loup is to walk without making a noise, to arrive without warning, to proceed discreetly, silently, invisibly, almost inaudibly and imperceptibly, as though to surprise a prey, to take it by surprising what is in sight but does not see coming the one that is already seeing it, already getting ready to take it by surprise, to grasp it by surprise.[2]

For Derrida, a contretemps interrupts any cultural predication of synthetic time by accelerating "the separation of monads, infinite distance, the disconnection of experiences, the multiplicity of worlds, everything that renders possible a contretemps."³ The historical experience of the contretemps desynchronizes internal-time consciousness and the institutionalized metrics that compress the differentia of social time and space into the measure and meaning of the contemporaneous. The contretemps forecloses accessible pathways to a center, to a subject, to a privileged reference, but is also a surplus effect and externalized cost of production of closed systems and bounded networks:

> Dates, timetables, property registers, place names, all the codes that we cast like nets over time and space—in order to reduce or master differences, to arrest them, determine them—these are also contretemps traps, intended to avoid contretemps, to be in harmony with our rhythms by bending them to object measurement, they produce misunderstanding, they accumulate the opportunities for false steps, or wrong moves, revealing and simultaneously increasing this anachrony of desires in the same time.⁴

The contretemps, by disfiguring a sequence of closure, negatively outlines a failed autopraxis (*Eigenpraxis*), a syntactical continuum of embedded and deployable objects and operations that cease to cohere into a grammatical and operative series.⁵ The anachronous accident assaults molar institutions through its seemingly acausal infiltration. With the advent of the contretemps, the portentous breaks into our universe in the form of a parallel creation, "a breach of procedure" that disrupts extant moral order and social syntax.⁶ The contretemps does not achieve the status of a codified norm and is denied the stature of a legible action. In its anomic illegibility, the contretemps is the action of a nonaction, a "cipher in algorism," that is a figure of occluded and exscribed insignificance in a computational enclosure that proves determinant in the last instance. The causality of the contretemps has to be retrofitted *ad seriatum* from an abruptly inceptual and derivative punctum—the emergency zone triggered by the collision of system and event that now rules as a commanding anachrony. This is the shock of exception profiled against eventless continuity.⁷ In its radiating afterlife and afterimage, the wound of the consequential contretemps cannot be sutured. It unfolds as the cause of the cause that is prognosticated ex post facto, and thwarts the capacity of a sovereign subject or apparatus to catch *its causality* in the act.

The contretemps remediates the aesthesis of witnessing and historicity in interrupting the presumed contemporaneity and synchrony of the present.

It disrupts the aphoristic presentness of the present as the atemporal form assumed by rationality, plenitude, and the self-evident. "Conversely, no contretemps, no aphorism without the promise of a now in common. For there is no contretemps, without the pledge, the vow of synchrony, the desired sharing of a living present."[8] The contretemps disperses repetition as *a future present*, as the transmission of the *same* through time that is expected to secure life, habitation, and orientation. For Derrida, such axiomata are foregrounded against a negativity from which the contretemps unfolds as "the background of a shadowy zone against which it stands out, this—the self-evidence of self-evidence . . ."[9] The contretemps bifurcates the scenic affirmation of the self-evident and riddles its fixed schema with puncturing anomaly—chronotopic black holes. It appears as off-center envelopment by the incalculable "that allows the motif of calculability to be thought as what it is."[10] Giorgio Agamben identifies analogous negativity in the aleatory conjuncture of the singular, the nondescript, and the contingent that coincides with the apparitional infrastructure of the contretemps: "Nondescript is the figure of pure singularity. Nondescript singularity has no identity, is not determined in relation to a concept . . . the nondescript is a singularity plus an empty space."[11] Michel Foucault similarly points to the abyss of contingency that is exposed by the contretemps upon which the self-evident resides: "The politically intelligible appears against the background of emptiness and denies its necessity."[12] Foucault's necessary "emptiness" speaks to the aleatory contretemps *against which* systematicity and repeatability are forearmed and by which they can be disarmed in the refutation embodied by the catastrophic. Foucault here coincides with Althusser's possible-impossible aleatory, the empty site of the nonanteriority of meaning that is occupiable by a constitutive political practice lacking any transcendental ground. In its contravention of the calculable, the contretemps disinters the buried anachronous origins of historicity—the narratological apparatus of causation, seriality, and sequence stationed as guard against the contretemps. If the condition of historicity is *presence* continuously temporalized as the past, the now, and the future, then the shattering of such scenic affirmations by the contretemps opens "intemporality," what Derrida names the "ahistoricity of history."[13] Against this anchoring ahistoricity of presence, the contretemps unfolds as radical temporalization and anachronic acceleration. Caught in the net of the contretemps, the political shows itself as indeterminate underneath its schematized categories. Reiner Schurmann observes of the epochal contretemps of the self-evident: "To say that ultimate referents have lost their credibility is no longer a philosophical topic but has become a popular commonplace. The fissure in the constructs of a legitimating First has turned into a rent open for public inspection. . . . each construct of normative validity appears retrospectively as having depended on one thetical referent construed as fully present to itself. In a first approximation, transgression is the effect of a power of dissolution counteracting the formative, law-bestowing force at its core."[14]

THE ACCIDENTALIZATION OF THE ACCIDENT

This essay contends that the contretemps has now reemerged as a mediology of counterinsurgent rule under which *jus ad bellum* no longer fulfills the normative tasks that have been historically assigned to it. A polemological sovereignty multiplies, virtualizes, partitions, and thereby indemnifies its destructiveness through the contretemps. Under the regime of the contretemps, a no longer ipsocratic, executive power is amplified through its self-division into the presenting fact and the extrafactual surplus of its prosecutory force. The immunizing doctrine of collateral damage elevates the contretemps to a normalized rationality of *jus ad bellum*. This doctrine, which poses the accident as an anticipated, external and disposable intrusion, effectively reconstitutes executive power in situ as a contrivance and entrapment of the accidental. Collateral damage inflicted on noncombatants by drones is excused as "scenario fulfillment" (errant threat perception) by their human operators, or as anonymizing "crowd killings" in which "unintended" deaths are treated as algorithmic cacophony with little utilitarian or moral consequence. Related aleatory temporalities permeate the containerization of war. The latter is the deconsolidating dispersal of the productive sites of power and the concussions of its violence. Containerized warfare is the offshoring and geopolitical camouflaging of site-specific performances of power and privation. Containerization addresses how an organ of violence, like the border, domestic policing, outsourced mercenaries, the drone kill chain, the detention center, "enhanced interrogation," the "kill list," and proxy wars, amputates itself from an authorizing or underlying body politic and command structure and becomes self-organizing as the autopoetic trajectory of ever-shifting centers and points of force. Containerized war now unfolds as a series of countertimes, as "rhythmed anachronies" and as "moving errors whose errance is both finite and infinite, aleatory and programmed."[15] As in transnational capitalist-corporate containerization, such polemological self-division and dispersion magnifies predation, occludes accountability, and preempts dejustifying witnessing. Through containerization war itself has been subjected to an extraordinary rendition to the "black sites" of disavowal and deniability.

The contretemps as a denegation of war unfolds (*explicatio*) a sovereign will to unwill violence. Here the executive power does not choose to be nonviolent but makes *of its* violence *a nonviolence* (or a *sub rosa* and *sub voce* violence) in being underwritten by the accidental. The programmed contretemps is a political denegation that consists of polemological power "presenting [its] being in the mode of not being it."[16] Denegation is a nomination that simultaneously unnames itself, an enunciation that renounces itself. Under a regime of denegation the enunciation of law opens nonlaw and the unstable vibration between law and nonlaw as di-visualizations of sovereignty. For denegated warfare, as force retracted in enactment, becomes a constitutive power that seizes, secures, and perverts the very epistemological and moral ground that measures its violence, including that very ground-seizing act. Derrida describes such an *allumage à contretemps* that overflows normative justification and inflates power through self-division and generative discordance:

> The One divides and opposes itself, opposes itself by posing itself, represses and violates the difference it carries within itself, wages war, wages war on itself, itself becoming war [*se fait le guerre*], frightens itself, itself becoming fear [*se fait peur*], and does violence to itself, itself becoming violence [*se fait violence*], transforming itself into frightened violence in guarding itself from the other [*il se garde de l'autre*], for it guards itself from, and in, the other, always, Him, the One, the One "different from itself."[17]

Consider how François Hollande cut off the random killing of Parisians on November 13, 2015, from the damage of his bombing campaign in Syria. Under the ceremonial facade of retribution and resecuritization, Hollande effectively escalated France's grayed-out anti-ISIS bombing. The killing, mutilation, and displacement of not only ISIS but contiguous, expendable, and uncountable Syrian noncombatants drove the future anterior of the tit for tat 2015 Paris attacks as the catastrophe *that will have been*. Hollande and his advisers calculated the civic sacrifice of random domestic deaths at a temporal distance as corollary to vertical killing at a geographic distance in Syria. Bombing Syria was to become the temporal prepossibility of the Bataclan and other massacres and ultimately of the contrived accidentalization of the collateralized Parisian victims cordoned off by Hollande as casually external to his already in-place warmaking. The contretemps at Paris already happened before it happened as the final node of the kill-chain preassembled by the French assault on Syria.

Benjamin Netanyahu also pursued a strategy of autoimmunization by contretemps when mournfully speaking to CNN of the Gazan civilians killed by Israeli missile strikes in 2014: "All civilian casualties are unintended by us but actually intended by Hamas. They want to pile up as many civilian dead as they can, because somebody said they use, I mean it's gruesome, they use telegenically dead Palestinians for their cause. They want the dead, the more the better."[18] In Netanyahu's phantasmagoria, each "carefully" launched Israeli missile is subject to a mishap in its refunctioning by a Hamas imputedly committed to the mechanical mass production of televisual Palestinian dead. The Israeli first-person shooter, morally inoculated by the Holocaust with an a priori *and* racialized incapacity for atrocity, discharges a ballistics of innocence. The Israeli missile assault was described by one Israeli government spokesperson as restricted by "hesitancy and care," and as ultimately in search of a "sustainable quiet."[19] Under this polemological regime of "care and quietude," civilian causalities in Gaza are imputedly emplotted by Hamas. Israel's launched ordinance becomes the inadvertent prosthetic of the Palestinian will to telegenic death. The "true violence" of Gaza is cast in lead by Netanyahu as the self-enclosure of the agent and patient of force exclusively within the Palestinian body politic.

Derrida distinguishes the accidental contretemps—the singular accidentality of the accident—from the essential contretemps; the latter is the "non-accidental" accident.[20] The essential contretemps as the time of war times manifests as the programmed accidentalization of the accident. This accidentalization of war refers not to war as inconvenienced by mishaps but to political mobilization of the *accidentalized as war by other means*. The suffix shifts the root term from the intransitive to the transitive, in the sense of to make, to conform to the thing expressed by the derivation. The doubling of the stem word in the theorem "the accidentalization of the accident" implies a deliberate normative action on the accident as concept and event. The neologism "accidentalized" refers to a historical mishap or contretemps that has befallen the essence of the inessential or nonexemplary accident. Accidentalized war is also a catastrophe that has befallen the prestige and finality of the political terminus now placed under erasure by the seemingly infinite plateau of the medium of the contretemps without ends or end. This process culminates in a war that has purloined its own purposiveness. The prescriptive promise of *jus ad bellum* and the very act of its disavowal as such undergo their own contretemps as a fall out of perceptible time.

As a structuring threshold or borderline event, the essential and needful accident overturns the philosophical dicta that the perfection of substance is far more perfect than the objective perfection of the accident—the latter is the project of the necessary contretemps as desired and designed anachrony. Derrida asserts that the infelicity of the accidental contretemps "remarks the essential contretemps which is as much to say it is not accidental."[21] Derrida's "remark" indicates a relation of repetition, simulation, tracing, and mimesis between the extrinsic and essential accident. However, the interface between model and copy is haunted by dislocating acts of surrogation where too faithful a copy infiltrates and suborns the original to the point of indistinction. Through parricidal assault on the original, the copy effaces the paternal position through a disruptive countertime arising from its similitude. The "re-mark" indicates that the threshold between the essential and nonessential accident is porous. The prognosticated accident is subject to, and can inadvertently trigger, an aleatoric cascade. Here the inessential contretemps becomes the concept of the concept of the essential accident that conveys what is unthinkable within the design of its necessity—there is no pure accident, be it essential or extrinsic. There can be a contamination of the calculated contaminant, a mishap can befall the concept, status, and experience of the needful accident that ruptures its prognostic architecture.

Accidentalization stands in relation to its etymon as rationalization stands in relation to Reason, as reification stands in relation to the concept of the thing, that is, as the historical unfolding of the effective denegation of the concept. Here the Heideggerian practice of *Durchkreuzung* is apt; a pivotal and anchoring term is typographically crossed out and over and thus placed *under* erasure (*sous rature*) to signal its historical and semantic inoperability. In being retained in the text beneath the mark of its defacement, the deferred concept signals a flashing accident zone—a contretemps has befallen the concept in its historical trajectory, which becomes an operative vacancy within a discursive practice. An apparatus that places entities under erasure while archiving their anachronistic gravitational pull gathers contraries into a single constellation that resembles the *allumage à contretemps*—crossfiring as denegation, dis-jointure, and discordance. This cross-firing or inter-de-face-ment is not solely an after-image of the now-concussed referential punctum; what has been placed under erasure is cast as bearing its own self-cancellation across time as the intrinsic catastrophic structure of its being.

An entire politics of securitization is predicated on the reverse time axis of the essential accident. Derrida implicitly aligns the essential contretemps with the apotropaic and the *pharmakon as* both curative prosthetic and dangerous toxic supplement:

> The purity of the within can henceforth only be restored by accusing exteriority of being a supplement, something inessential and yet detrimental to that essence, an excess that should not have been added to the unadulterated plenitude of the within. The restoration of inner purity must therefore reconstitute, recite—and this is myth itself, the mythology, for example, of a logos recounting its origin and returning to the eve of a pharmacographical assault.[22]

As simultaneously pathogenic and prophylactic, the pharmacographical contretemps both assaults and underwrites securitization, which proceeds by means of apotropaic mobilization—alarms, alerts, shibboleths (passwords and color codes) and insulating checkpoints. Pharmacographical assault, as irruptive event or computation, can serve as a retentional apparatus, an archival substrate-support, for an executive power that redefines and renews itself by re-calling and simulating asymmetrical counterconcepts, such as the faceless terrorist, the errant migrant, and the transnational parasitical virus.[23] The apotropaic alarm, signaling the misarrival of the catastrophic, points to, fabulates, and secures the contretemps as the needful *pharmakon*-toxin/remedy. As I have written elsewhere:

> The apotrope is both a figure of warning and of termination, it promises the circular finality of preemption, making what is supposedly before—the threat to be averted—an afterward—an epilogue and supplement to the rhetoric of the averting gesture. The apotrope cannot be brought into play without this compression and reversal of the time of threat and its redress. The promissory redress of the apotrope precedes and frames threat, pushing it back in chronology in forwarding it in consciousness. The homeopathic apotrope does not pledge to end the threat that is simulated and averted, however it pledges the end of the latter's anomic repetition beyond apotropaic containment.[24]

Werner Hamacher translates contretemps as *Unzeit*, as an anachronous pre-essence that refuses "every compossibility and every co-presence and therefore also every place within a time series, a place that could be put before or after another."²⁵ The denegated contretemps is the "pre-possibility of all temporal possibilities that does not precede these within a time series; rather it precedes the latter as the nonlinear—nongeometric and nonmetrical—play of various times and time-possibilities, and precisely therefore *lies within these as what is absolutely external to them*" (emphasis mine).²⁶ Such anachrony can be embedded in the planning, execution, and political neutralization of an act of force in media res or ex post facto. Hamacher's denegating description evokes the countertemporality that Avital Ronell refers to as "operations of destruction operating 'inoperably' from a time and space that destroys time and space."²⁷ Such operations often extract surplus value from the misarrival of the contretemps. As Jean-Luc Nancy observes of the Fukushima disaster, the essential accident, under the rule of Capital, must be conceptualized as "plus d'une catastrophe," as simultaneously more-than-a-catastrophe, in its calculability, risk assessment, and potential value convertibility, and no-more-a-catastrophe, as an utilitarian algorithm of Capital for extracting surplus value through disaster accumulation. For Nancy, considering the conflation of more-than and no-more-a-catastrophe, "It is this equivalence that is catastrophic."²⁸

APPEARING UNDER ERASURE

Invisibility in everything is the thing we aim at in modern war.

Solomon J. Solomon

The accidentalization of war crimes reaches aporetic intensity in the orchestrated vanishing of noncombatants and combatants in pogroms of enforced yet disavowed disappearance that are frequently dissimulated as anomalous mishaps by the abducting power.²⁹ Accidentalized disappearance is not limited to war, as the recent disappearance of the Saudi journalist-in-exile Jamal Ahmad Khashoggi in Turkey confirms. The Office of the United Nations High Commissioner for Human Rights defines disappearance as "the arrest, detention, abduction or any other form of deprivation of liberty by agents of the State or by persons or groups of persons acting with the authorization, support or acquiescence of the State, followed by a refusal to acknowledge the deprivation of liberty or by concealment of the fate or whereabouts of the disappeared person, which place such a person outside the protection of the law."³⁰ The use of the modifiers "enforced" and "involuntary" by human rights organizations as certifying nomenclature confirms the predominant orchestration of disappearance as accidentalized violence that extends from abduction to the postmortem disposition of bodies. Disappearance considered as accidentalized war runs counter to human rights and legal perspectives that treat political disappearance as an extrinsic mishap that befalls the otherwise normal proceduralism of the state and the law and which can be rectified by the rehabilitation of the latter. However, the emergence of enforced disappearance as a counterlaw and as the countertime to extant law is implied by the writ of habeas corpus—the having of the body as law has its history of exscription in the loss of the body to law, of its being beyond law and the necessity of its being written into law. To think through this aporia is to step back, in part, from the worthy tomes of empirical data on enforced political disappearance (that are merely the tip of an unquantifiable iceberg) collated by human rights organizations and to think through the making of the missing as sustaining a metaphysics of executive power.[31]

Practices and campaigns of enforced or involuntary disappearance are linked to the spatial and visual logic of genocide, though they differ in crucial ways. In pogroms of disappearance, as with genocide, one population claims a nomos of the earth for itself and denies another the right to cartographic legitimacy and security. Hannah Arendt supported the capital penalty for Adolph Eichmann based on the principle that he was complicit in an apparatus of deportation and extermination that had denied the right of Jews to share the earth. On this basis, Eichmann had forfeited his right to share the earth with others—imprisonment would not suffice.[32] Judith Butler, following Arendt (though not her advocacy of the capital penalty), declares genocide to be impermissible, for we have no choice with whom to cohabit on the earth. Butler asserts, as existential fact and ethical a priori, that diversity precedes birth and cohabitation.[33] Both genocide and enforced disappearance attack the right to appear on the earth and declassify persons and populations as proper to the terrestrial surface. A regime of vanishment defaces any evidence of the victim's present and prior terrestrial anchorage. The proprietary right of the nation-state is advanced through the serial voiding of a right to the earth for the vanished en masse or in series. The rhizomatic dispersion and cordoning off of the disappeared from molar space in turn enhances the circulating spectrality of an executive power that gives itself an immaterial anchorage through its attrition of somatic and biographical gravity—the missing become sheer effluvia—ephemeral historical dust that fuels power and fear.

The publicness and systematicity of certain genocidal operations is precipitated by its large-scale infrastructural mobilization, and justifying propaganda. In contrast, enforced disappearance is accidentalized, randomized, silenced, and rendered unmotivated and acausal by the disappearance of disappearance. Both the vanished and the act of vanishment are literally placed under erasure (sous rature), not completely voided, but subsumed under the quasi-opacity of a retraction and redaction of an act that is rescripted as a nondescript mishap inflicted on those who henceforth will become procedurally nondescript. Disappearance and its aftermaths are often designed to simulate the extrinsic and nonexemplary accident—the pure aleatory contretemps in order to inhibit the capacity of political and legal witness to catch its causality in the act. The missing are denied political exemplification in the midst of the orchestration of their vanishment.[34] The anonymization of the missing achieves the dephenomenalization and demanifestation of the event that persists as a public secret whose force lies in its political and epistemological remotion (its etymon, *remōtiō*, means the act of moving a thing back, withdrawal, removal, or elimination of a condition or factor, recession, and distance).

Accidentalized disappearance is structured around a political technology of ellipsis that informs the act, its aftermath, and cultural memory of the latter. If, as Bernard Stiegler proposes, grammatization/discretization are axial to a technical history of memory, under the dispositivizing apparatus of disappearance these operations inform a techno-political history of forgetting or programmed unrecalling that evoke *Unzeit*.[35] Disappearance that containerizes the absentee within the contretemps generates an inverse discretization; rather than assemble the encapsulated bodies of the vanished into discrete units and syntagmatic ensembles, their doubled subtraction as act and archive promotes systemic inattention—a politics of the unretainable. This grammatology of enforced disappearance produces repeatable nonmemory—the loss of loss. The disappearance machine, like any grammatology, is "cut as well as cutting with regard to the living present of life or of the living body: it is an effect of the cut as much as it is a cause of the cut."[36] Derrida speaks of bodies as *insectum*, which means cutting into and sectioning, to have the body divided into segments; to insect is to separate, to dissect, and to intersect, and to hunt and catch insects.[37] The disappeared in being rendered culpable (*coupable*) become cuttable and cut from society, family, their bodies, biographies, and deaths. Whether an occurrence authored by an executive power becomes event or nonevent is here a matter of aleatory depoliticization and dehistoricization, as a machinality that cuts into the flow of events that could have been enchained and historicized. This disappearance of disappearance, of the loss of loss, is the essential contretemps passed off as the elliptical action of a nonaction in which the disappeared become ciphers in algorism.

The regime of vanishment that disavows its disapparitions commits to the objective perfection of the accident by fabricating the nonexemplarity of the disappeared. The apparatus of disapparition provisions an alibi or elsewhere for the disappeared by removing any terrestrial imprint and trace of the internal deportee and denying any rationality to the latter's abrupt unbecoming. The illogic of the alibi is extended to claims that the disappeared abdicated their lives and their survivors for an elsewhere where they remain perpetually incommunicado—this is the u-topia of the disappeared, the nonplace of their mostly wall-less confinement, the countergeography of interminable displacement without end. This sequence of retraction, demanifestation, and disavowal is a double burial and banishment of the disappeared behind the dispositivizing alibi. The vanished have a diminished phenomenological relation to the earth, and this persistent condition of political flotation eventually washes over any imprint on the earth they left prior to being exiled.

The regime of vanishment stubbornly resists such qualifying supplements as "enforced" and "involuntary" by enforcing mischance and the accidental through the elaboration of intimidation and symbolic terror by explicit threat and whispered innuendo, which promise further "randomized" subtraction for those who speak and seek out. The regime simulates structural indifference that morbidly envelops the survivor-families as much as the subtracted. Either the initial detention/abduction is greeted with a frozen bureaucratic silence or an undocumented arrest and fictive release or escape is recited to exonerate custodial responsibility. The public media frequently say little or nothing about a disappearance as pattern or policy, preferring to treat each instance as episodic if reported at all. The officiating bureaus of the police, the public prosecutors, and the courts extend the stigma of culpability to the families, who are criminalized for re-calling those who have become politically and culturally uninheritable. The local community where disappearance occurs has little alternative but to respond with self-protective unknowingness, an enforced *agnosia* of those surviving its wake—they forgo vocal witnessing as inviting their own eventual vanishing. Only the most stubborn of kin resist this foreclosure, withstanding the years in which the missing remain under erasure, insisting on their living-on and survival until shown otherwise in the form of a corpse or its fragments and not even then, rejecting the part for not being the whole that was originally stolen. In the exhumations performed by the South African truth commission, the survivors of the disappeared grasped at any material fragment of usually incinerated remains as a fossil of the withdrawn persona, as if they required proof not only of their abduction and execution but of a prior life before the spirit was rendered bone.[38] These fragments, once ritually reburied, enabled the dead to be treated as ancestor figures for the survivor-families in subsequent mortuary rites. In the documentary film *Nostalgia for the Light*, a Chilean woman, whose brother was abducted by the Pinochet regime, searches for decades through the Atacama Desert where political prisoners were incarcerated and/or summarily executed. She eventually recognizes, authenticates, and eulogizes a detached, half–buried foot and sock, mummified by desert aridity, as belonging to her brother, yet this is ultimately unsatisfactory because it merely points to what will never be returned.[39]

A recent transitional justice report from Sri Lanka attests to disappearance as a political technology that crosscuts sharply divergent ideological postures of justified warfare. The sheer ideological indifference of the viral practice begs the question of an inadmissible, excluded third terrain of ideological projection, underwriting the act's internal logic and effacing the various political demands that supposedly animated the politically disparate agents and objects of vanishment. Enforced disappearance emerges as a purposiveness without purpose—as a contretemps that befell any recognizable political teleology. The report describes the following personae and scenes of enforced disappearance (my annotations in brackets):

> Village roundups by of Tamil and Muslim civilians [wartime and postwar] and Sinhalese civilians during the Southern [JVP] insurrections [by student/peasant Marxist rebels] by the police, army and intelligent services.
> White van abductions of Tamil, Muslim and Sinhalese civilians including human rights defenders, journalists, workers, students and others. [The ubiquitous and otherwise unmarked white van deployed by intelligence and police agencies was so firmly wedded to imaginary of disappearance that it may have been adopted by antistate organizations to cover their tracks when engaged in similar abductions.]

- Surrender and subsequent disappearance of Tamil combatants [LTTE–Tamil Liberation Tigers of Tamil Eelam] to the Sri Lankan armed forces and police particularly during the last stages of the war [2008–9].
- Disappearance of families of LTTE combatants, including very young children.
- Injured persons left behind in hospitals in LTTE controlled areas or driven away by police and army vehicles.
- LTTE and TMVP [Tamil Makkal Viduthalai Pulikal] abductions of child soldiers whose current location is unknown.
- Indian Peace Keeping Force abductions of Tamil and Muslim civilians.
- JVP [Marxist] abduction of Sinhalese civilians.
- Disappearance of Tamil and Muslim fisherman by the LTTE and Sri Lankan navy.
- Abduction of Tamil civilians by other Tamil militant groups.
- Disappearance during rehabilitation of LTTE ex or suspected combatants.
- Disappearance in IDP camps of Tamil, Muslim civilians and combatants.
- Disappearance of [state] combatants and police missing in action.
- Disappearances that took place across the island in the context of pervasive abductions.[40]

The final item registers both a certain causal circularity and perhaps the exasperation of the reporting organization, an NGO–sponsored task force of local lawyers, academics, social workers, mental health specialists, and civil society activists. It inadvertently records the empirical fact that a contretemps has befallen any criteria of political utility in Sri Lanka during its wars. The final item is effectively the meta-structure of which all the preceding deprivations of liberty and life partake, yet is included in the very series it totalizes. The list ends by asserting disappearances occurred "in the *context* of pervasive abductions." This is a conceptual palindrome consuming itself in a tautology wherein disappearance disappears within itself and causes itself. The terminus of the list is neither outside the series nor gives itself to repetition in the series; it halts the orchestrated sequence of abductions and returns the reader to the beginning of the list as if winding it up one more time for its procession toward its non-end. This is confirmed by the fact that disappearances continue to occur after the ostensive termination of all hostilities and the military triumph of the state in 2009. The terminal item is the undecidable element, an absent cause that renders all the preceding instantiations possible and which demands evocation while remaining unpresentifiable—excluding in its inclusion. The underlying apparatus of vanishment that is "the reason" of the chain is not determinable—it is opaque to historical presentation and rationality. "Context" is exposed here as inadequate to any commensuration of these events, targets, and patterns of vanishment. Context is precisely what is lacking here, not in terms of an event history or political motivations, but as what is expected to weave together the heterogeneity of ideologies and practices through the leveling uniformity of a mediating purposiveness and rationality. Rather, enforced disappearance is its own surplus value, generating itself from itself. The final item on the list confesses that there is no context for "context" here, and this cutting away of ground announces the contretemps as a mishap assaulting the identifiability and necessity of context. The list is left to symptomize a sphere of political unmaking by which various executive powers delimited their terrain of jurisdiction and dominion—not over the expected amassed corporeality of subjects or even over the bent bodies of the subjugated, but over the faded footprint, the whispering and barely limned trace of the vanished, of persons and bodies withdrawn and remanded to dust and wind.

The disappearance of disappearance captures errant temporalities and topologies that Orlando Patterson associates with slavery, in particular social death and natal alienation (in this case cloaking both the disappeared and their affected peers, families, and related survivors).[41] The disappeared and their affected families are afflicted with the contretemps of a denuded life-death that beyond any biological certainty is a socially and politically enforced interstitiality—a demission of life and death without their archivization. The missing, suspended within an attenuated life-/death-world of abduction, detention, and decertified death, are presumed to be alternatively detained or deleted by inhumation or incineration. Social death in Patterson is enchained to natal alienation where the enslaved are forcefully estranged from their natality in all of its biosymbolic nuances that have been explicated by Arendt.[42] Natal alienation removes the disappeared from the sites of their birth as kin, subjects, and citizens, from their ascendants and descendants, and from the general biopolitical condition of *natio* that constitutes the civil subject in the nation–state. The missing are a spectral trail of atomized revenants that nonetheless become the determination in negation of those who are contingently permitted to enjoy being-with and living-on in the now-tattered facade of civil society. For Arendt, natality is not just biological; it is the ability to bring something new into the world, to initiate the unprecedented and the unrepeated, and this potentiality too is denied the disappeared and their stranded survivors. The missing are not only abducted and vanished for what they have done and said or for who they are (and many times not even that), but for what they can politically become. In appearing under erasure the disappeared are exscribed as the extremity, the without, of what is normed as the political. They are jettisoned as the media by which the political moves outside itself to delimit itself. If, as Arendt and Butler claim, unwilled proximity and unchosen cohabitation are preconditions of our political existence, enforced and disavowed disappearance interdicts political natality and possibility through the banishment of potential political interlocutors from the earth.

Involuntary and disavowed disappearance is the engineering of history, the orchestration of historiographical surfaces through the incision of black holes that puncture and fray the social fabric with dark matter exerting immense gravitational pull on those who remain and furtively remember. The socius that is scarified by repeated acts of disappearance assumes the labor of relegating the missing to deeper and deeper levels of historical oblivion through their complicit and enabling silence. With the contretemps of enforced disappearance the future is abducted—disappearance devours historical time, it detours historicity, biographies, and life chances through executive fiat. For survivors and others who are affected, the nonlife of living with and after the disappeared replaces natality and the inception of the new. Time stops with an act of enforced disappearance. Each moment that goes by without searching for, and calling to, or demanding an accounting of the vanished, in other words, without activating them temporally, implants them deeper within an encrypted abyss. The society that transcribes its self on the silence of the missing, on their scattered selves and bodies, and the compulsory privatization of the memories of survivor families, resides on the immemorial as that which cannot be accessed or historicized as it persists outside finite time.

DEVOURMENT

Examining disappearance and its computational accidentalization needs to address the sensory content of a phantasm in which the vanished have disappeared outside their disappearance. A tropology of devourment haunts a regime of vanishment, an autonomic cannibalism, wherein the disappeared, the event of their disapparition, and the sociocultural memory of the event are mechanically and voraciously consumed by an executive power and its automation of fear. The anthropophagic disappearance of denizens, subjects, or citizens, and the autoconsumption of the regime's own acts through the signifier of the accidental is an ultimate assertion of an impunity that repels any historicizing and juridifying predication of the regime's own praxis. The regime of redaction is the gradated disappearance and autoconsumption of the executive power itself to the degree that it was ever defined by a duty of care, law, and citizenship and is meant to be responsive to habeas corpus.

In the two volumes of *The Beast and Sovereign*, Derrida discusses the voracity of the sovereign become beast, cannibalism, and the anthropophagic consumption of the posthumous. Derrida asserts that only an anthropos can be "anthropophagic" and disappearance as the auto-cannibalism of a political order confesses the anthropophagy that is recognizable in Thomas Hobbes's discussion of internal war as intestinal discord. Only the cannibal can be truly inhuman in devouring within its species.[43] Irrespective of its structural indifference, institutional mechanisms, and designed acausality, the regime of vanishment requires human cogs of inhumanity to advance its procedural voracity for names, bodies, and disposability. For Derrida, postmortem disposal is ultimately a passage through space and time linked to procedural technicity, sovereignty, and the *fort/da*—the play of the here and there, of the here and gone as the play of missing-missed presence.

> How and to what will they proceed in the time that follows the deceding? To decede, to proceed, to retrocede: it is indeed a matter of a procedure, a path, a movement along a path, a path of departure or return; it is indeed a matter of progress or regression or digression, of process and processing, proceeding and procedure, and so already of arrangements that are both technical and juridical, which have themselves left the order of what is called in the current and belated sense nature. We are already either in the opposition of nomos, tekhnē, thesis to physis in the late and derived sense, or else in that différance (with an a) of originary physis, which takes the forms of law, thesis, technique, right, etc.[44]

Extrajudicial enforced disappearance cannot take place in the absence of technicities of proceeding, deceding, and a retroceding of the act itself in the fabrication of its acausality. Nor can it take place without an element, time frame, and locus of haptic and optical interface—no matter how episodic and encrypted it leaves a trace structure. For the encounter that results in involuntary disappearance to take place, there must already have been a disapparition chain in the making that requires a having and haptics of the body—techniques of identifiability, a chronology, cartography, and optics of surveillance, standing against all spatial and temporal dispersion by promising a rendezvous predicated on the exclusion of the nonsynchronous in the very action of haptic interface—the teleocratic accident must have its procedural essentialisms. Despite its ultimate project of dispersal, enforced disappearance must cast its nets over time and space in order to arrest and master difference. This begs the question of under what historical conditions does difference becomes so ubiquitous, so generic, as to be implanted in the masses of the nondescript in excess of any datable political antagonists.

The cannibal is traditionally seen as antithetical to executive power. However, Michael Taussig envisions colonial and neocolonial phobias of the cannibal as the hallucinogenic re-creation of the sovereign colonizing self in a fantasized antiself. This transverse mimesis politically embodies the fear of constituted power of "being consumed by difference" as embodied by the phantasmic cannibal.[45] Can programs of enforced disappearance be construed as the preemptive consumption of difference that is seen as potentially engulfing? Would this explain the interdiction of natality as the foreclosure of future political interlocutors? There is no doubt that this regime also transcribes difference onto those it wipes off the earth in that very act. Returning to Taussig's mimetic anthropophagy, it can be suggested that a regime of vanishment turns to political cannibalism, not only to preemptively consume difference, but to procedurally make the difference to which it could be seen and imagined to ingest and dispatch.

Here "à pas de loup" returns as a contretemps that marks the secrecy and deniability that informs the architecture of accidentalized disapparition. Derrida stresses the intangibility of the passage of the sovereign, silent, and randomized predator: "insensible because one neither sees nor hears it coming, because it is invisible and inaudible, and therefore nonsensible, but also insensible because it is all the crueler for this, impassive, indifferent to the suffering of its virtual victims."[46] The clandestine organization of disappearance, its containment within the accidental and the aleatory, attests to the power and privation of a simulacrum that seeks to be ungraspable and intangible. This silent/silencing forceful disapparition magnifies fear through the expansion of its powers of self-virtualization. This apparatus of disframing and occlusion grips the living made missing and intensifies the radiating reach of its political dispositivity as the mode of motion of warfare. This is the vertigo of a deliberate disframing: "the radical off-centredness of a point of view that mutilates the body and expels it beyond the frame to focus instead on dead, empty zones . . . the use of the frame as a cutting-edge, the living pushed out to the periphery beyond the frame . . . the focusing on the bleak or dead sections of the scene."[47]

In *Beast and the Sovereign II*, Derrida relates the experiences of being devoured and of being incinerated or inhumed while alive to the corpus as property and legal personality. The proprietorial corpus partakes of a sovereignty under which the living possess the contractual right of deciding on the disposition of their living body and their posthumous remains. Derrida questions to what degree this right remains enforceable both within and beyond life and in relation to the writ and existentials of habeas corpus.

A writ of habeas corpus is a demand to produce the body that has fallen under question as to its status and disposition between life and death, to bring the body before a space of witnessing and certification as a proof of life or death. The writ and range of habeas corpus includes not only the physical body but any trace, imprint, or recording of the state's physical contact with or proximity to the body, however fractured, damaged, and classified these intersections might have been. Habeas corpus depends not on the ordinary jurisdiction of the court for its effectiveness but on the duty of care of an executive power in relation to the entirety of its subjects and denizens, both voluntary and involuntary, enfranchised or not. The writ gives habeas corpus terms of reference to restore the disappeared to a spatial location and can delimit a political cartography of absence parasiting the political community. According to the writ, the executive power cannot immunize orders or acts of detention from review by holding a detainee beyond the writ's territorial reach; the writ thus becomes an interrogatory remapping of the executive power that defines its deliberately darkened frontiers beyond its formal frontality or strategic dispersion. As a spatial predicate, habeas corpus implicitly recognizes a constituted right to civic and terrestrial habitus that would include the right to one's own body that is radically overturned by involuntary disappearance. The demand of habeas corpus is a belated appeal to the state and the nation to become accountable for the fate and location of citizens and noncitizens who have previously been denied the right to cohabitation by whatever agency, be it the state, parastate, and antistate apparatus. For Derrida, this right is haunted by the possibility of a cannibalism that collapses and compresses life, death, and disposal:

> But having my remains at their disposal can also take place before I am absolutely, clearly and distinctly dead, meaning that the other, the others, is what also might not wait for me to be dead to do it, to dispose of my remains: the other might bury me *alive, eat me or swallow me alive, burn me alive*, etc. He or she can put me to a living death, and exercise thus his or her sovereignty.[48]

Derrida phobically associates habeas corpus with the "living dead" and to living burial as anthropophagic. He relates sovereignty to a decision on the state of death or nondeath by a third party, which can also license and ensure a discreet locus and technique for the disposition of the corpse or corpus. Corpse disposal requires a social contract between the living and the dead, and among the living themselves that is mediated by a third as "a force of institutional coercion [that] . . . guarantees it and can oblige the inheritors to obey its instructions."[49] Derrida provisionally situates the posthumous within a legal order. However, a sovereign regime of vanishment places the disappeared as socially dead, natally estranged and biologically terminated, and uncertified as such, outside the accustomed laws and contracts of postmortem disposition. Here, the state-that-disappears abrogates its social contract with both the living and the dead concerning the postmortem—the latter is now consigned to the extrinsic accident that disperses and disorders the posthumous—the corpse, as concept and event, despite being beyond death, affect, and lived time, suffers a contretemps.

Denied disappearance is a political computation to not to decide on the state of death, to withhold death and posthumous disposition from the disappeared and a possible community of witness. Sovereignty here occupies a threshold that de-juridifies death by abandoning any civic purview over the disposal of the dead—the clandestine mass grave, without markers, speaks of a withheld civic jurisdiction over the postmortem. The frontier of life/death is here structured by a zone of indistinction in which there is no clear delineation between bios and zoe (enfranchised and disenfranchised life), to use Agamben's schema. Derrida writes:

> The dead person no longer has the corpse at his or her disposal, there is no longer any habeas corpus. Habeas corpus, at least, is not a habeas corpse, supposing there ever were such a thing. Habeas corpus concerns

the living body and not the corpse. Supposing, I repeat, that there ever were a habeas corpus for the living body. Because you can guess that I believe that this habeas corpus never existed and that its legal emergence, however important it may be, designates merely a way of taking into account or managing the effects of heteronomy and an irreducible non habeas corpus. And the non habeas corpse, at the moment of death, shows up the truth of this non habeas corpus during the lifetime of said corpus.[50]

Habeas corpus is a fiction in being vulnerable to the suctioning of juridical life from out of the still-breathing body or to the sliding of the body, living, dead, or neither, out from under the category of the subject. The "non habeas corpse" is a anthropophagic potentiality, a teleocratic power of a sovereign apparatus that predicates habeas corpus by skewing the body in the direction of a contretemps intrinsic to law and civic membership, the "non habeas corpus." The computational contretemps of the corpus is its becoming corpse before dying—death and demise are here severed. The contretemps of the corpse is to be alienated from death. The posthumous comes before expiration as the future anterior of the disappeared who are buried in reverse. Under disappearance, the corpse that precludes the condition of habeas, of self-possession, property, and sovereignty, already happens, in essence, before it happens, prior to biological deceding; it becomes an anachronistic pre-essence that refuses every place within a time series, a place that could be put before or after another, such as the sequence that governs life and death. Where no such distinction between bios and zoe, before and after, or life and death can operate, where the living body is virtualized and accidentalized as a denegated corpse in order to preclude the juridical personality of the corpus, there is only an unlife and an *Unzeit*, as that which cannot assume the historicity of its own death, its own finitude, as proper to its life. Derrida names this (dis)continuum that supplants the civic construct of life/death "sur-vivance," a concept that bears within itself all the errancy of an essential contretemps afflicting the law and societal ontology.[51]

Biopower enfranchises citizens to the same degree that it can expel them from civil securities embodied in Foucault's maxim, "make live and let die."[52] Derrida indirectly intervenes in this teleocratic thesis to assert that both the living and deceased body, the natal and postmortem body, reside under the same regime that at its core treats the quick and the dead with minimal or, at the most, a highly precarious differentiation between the biopolitical and the thanatopolitical. He terms this indifference of life and death *survivance*, which is not reducible to survival, which presupposes recovery and recuperation. Under survivance, each declension of bios and thanatos infiltrates the other with the bleed-through of mirror images. Derrida addresses this interstitially as an apparatus of power, a political technology and expropriated right that extends beyond life and death into a third artificed domain required by the executive, who administrates the dispensability of both by passing off one as the other—in which to-make-live is to also redistribute immanent death by assigning it to dispensable others as both promise and actuality. There is a politics of survivance, as a countertime that initiates political undecidability such as that which structures enforced disappearance. Survivance is suspended between the active and the passive, life and death, corpus and corpse, as indicated by the "ance" ending, which retraces the deferment conveyed by *différance*. Survivance renders death itself, once an object of central civic administration, disposable and abandoned—to defer death as an event just as much as enforced disappearance seeks the deferral of natality. Survivance removes the power of being able to die, to be capable of death as death, and the power to ethically and juridically decide on postmortem disposition as a sociocultural acknowledgment of death. Derridean political anthropology here is a political anthropophagy as an a priori dispossession informed by the structural immanence and slippage of the non habeas corpus and non habeas corpse under a sovereign apparatus. Derrida disrupts the anamorphosis of Agamben's biopower wherein the political sequence from zoé to bios is the becoming subject of substance, and the making of bare life, the disqualifying passage from bios to zoé, is the becoming substance of the subject.[53] In both survivance and enforced disappearance, both subject and substance, corpus and corpse and their biopolitical rites of passage become unavailable.

Derrida's non habeas corpus implicitly poses the question of not what life justifies its inconsequential expenditure but what forms of death no longer count as civically eligible as death, such as the drowned Syrian asylum seeker. The transnational abandonment of the latter to fragile boats and winter seas extends the acausal and aleatory fictions of an extended kill chain of enforced disappearance. The current political inhospitality afforded enforced exile proceeds *à pas de loup*, in being a remote and silent killing by the action of inaction that encrypts and falsifies the death of asylum seekers as aleatory catastrophe. In so doing, this protocol of inhospitality occludes the transnational kill chain of migrant death at sea as an essential, computational contretemps and disavowed complicity of the Asad regime and its Russian and Iranian allies and their adversaries, ISIS, the EU, the Saudis, and the Emirati powers.

> Survivance in a sense of survival that is neither life nor death pure and simple, a sense that is not thinkable on the basis of the opposition between life and death, . . . a survival that is not more alive, nor indeed less alive, than life, or more or less dead than death, a sur-vivance that lends itself to neither comparative nor superlative, a survivance . . . (that) . . . is without superiority, without height, altitude or highness, and thus without supremacy or sovereignty . . . the survivance I am speaking of is a groundless ground. . . . It [Ça] begins with survival. And that is where there is some other that has me at its disposal; that is where any self is defenseless. That is what the self is, that is what I am, what the I is, whether I am there or not.[54]

Derrida maps an interstitial terrain between Agamben's bios and zoe, a domain of their mutual inoperability and abandonment. This passage insists on survivance as an unplaceable locus "without superiority, without height, altitude or highness"—that is, without the sovereignty, ipseity, and autonomy of death or life, which infer anterior self possession—"And that is where there is some other that has me at its disposal."[55] Survivance as political technology is the essential accident that has befallen the relation between life and death, and thereby disrupts biopower.[56] Derrida insists on a differentiation between habeas corpus and habeas corpse but also recognizes a pervasive oscillation between these two unstable fictions that populate the interstitiality of survivance. The accidentalized indecision of disavowed disappearance is indexical of an emerging political locus where both habeas corpus and the corpse are concomitantly precipitated from what Derrida terms an "irreducible non habeas corpus." Within this reduction, a regime of vanishment reenacts a foundational asynchronous moment of state formation wherein citizens are legislated to appear under the ungrounded charter of a law founding violence—to let appear *and to make disappear*—no political appearance without political disappearance.[57] No biographical dispensation without the contretemps of biographical annulment.

What archival act remains if what survives is only the indifference and indistinction between the quick and the dead and the severe compression of the meshwork that binds them together and rapidly exchanges their positions as mutually unarchivable and thus as the expendable memory of both the corpus and the corpse. Only memory can decree such forgetting, only forgetting remembers to dispense with the memory of the opposition of life and death. Can we ask ourselves what such forgetting expends, in what political currency or general equivalent, and at what cost to the inequivalent and the singular? Forgetting the disappeared is a silent sovereignty and the sovereignty of a silence that exceeds death. The missing and the dead can be forgotten, but forgetting never dies—forgetting is the ultimate survivance, for it is the condition of possibility by which entire political orders live on in denial and denegation of their historicity.

INHERITING THE UNREADABLE

The phenomenology of disappearance coincides with the atopology of Derridean justice, which is organized around the "not there" and responsibility for what has no living manifestation other than survivance.

> If I am getting ready to speak at length about ghosts, inheritance, and generations, generations of ghosts, which is to say about certain others who are not present, nor presently living, either to us, in us, or outside us, it is in the name of justice. Of justice where it is not yet, not yet there, where it is no longer, let us understand where it is no longer present, and where it will never be, no more than the law, reducible to laws or rights . . . the principle of some responsibility, beyond all living present, within that which disjoins the living present, before the ghosts of those who are not yet born or who are already dead, be they victims of wars, political or other kinds of violence, nationalist, racist, colonialist, sexist, or other kinds of exterminations, victims of the oppressions of capitalist imperialism or any of the forms of totalitarianism. Without this non-contemporaneity with itself of the living present, without that which secretly unhinges it, without this responsibility and this respect for justice concerning those who are not there, of those who are no longer or who are not yet present and living, what sense would there be to ask the question "where?" "where tomorrow?" "whither?"[58]

Derrida's historical revenant induces an infectious and unhinged historicity, in which any condition of the presence of the present and of directional futurity as a future presence is unavailable to justice. He here turns the essential contretemps against itself by suggesting justice can occur only through a contingent conjuncture to come and not by calculation, which infers justice must arrive from a disjunctive not-yet and never-been as if it were a deframing and dismediating arch-contretemps that becomes all the more necessary in being incomputable.

Derrida's formulation of the intemporality and nonsynchronicity of the nonpresent challenges the synchronizing command of postwar prescriptive silence that seeks to arrest and synchronize polemological difference as a politically disruptive countertime. The eventual lowering of the political volume of the war damaged is, more often than not, advocated by the postwar culture of the state and upheld by many NGOs and human rights activists: the latter two agents frequently propose that those submitted to gross violations of human rights, once having been permitted to give pro forma witness, now need to turn the page of history and memory—to take up the labor of disappearing disappearance for the sake of a self—and national therapeusis, through which the polity can recover from "ambiguous loss." This was the prescription of many South African truth commissioners for any act of apartheid-era human rights violation.[59] In the film *Nostalgia for the Light*, the survivors of the disappeared, in search of their remains in the Atacama desert, portray themselves as being treated as a "leprosy" in today's Chile. In contemporary Sri Lanka, the state is preparing to commodify the process of neutralizing its disappearance-history through fiscal reparation. The legislated Office of Missing Persons has been given the undeclared mission to use silencing payoffs to massage the memory of collateral survivors of disappearance, most of whom are impoverished because of the loss of key wage earners. In the legislation pertaining to this bureau, the administration and funding of forensic investigation and the recuperation and reconstruction of bodily remains have an uncertain standing. Reparation and perhaps official memorialization here precede and take the place of a forensics of disappearance in the fullest sense of the term in which the Roman *forensis* referred to the deliberation and assemblies of the public forum. The cutting-off effect of "putting behind," the insecting of a disappearance historiography promises a future of presumptive certitude—"reconciliation" and peace dividends, fiscal or otherwise. However, it requires the disappeared to be encased in a petrified past sealed by formal memorialization and monetization. However, Derridean justice requires an unpredictable past and an anachronistic futurity, as countertimes that rupture the self-evidence of self evidence, the presence of the present. For the commemorative monument, designed as a symmetrical reversal of a history not-well-lived, betrays the disappeared in functioning as an adequation machine that renders their pain and suffering and that of their respective survivors commensurable, exchangeable, and politically digestible.

The immemorializing monument inverts the hidden mass grave in claiming to emplace a regime of vanishment upright into the artificial and arresting light of law and collective commemoration when perhaps one should be contemplating the shadowy recesses, the occlusion and the demission of time to which the missing and their families were consigned by an occluded executive act. The potential horror of commemorated disappearance for the survivors who live on is the profanation of the particularity and singularity of the once-visible and living missing and of the intense particulars of their abduction, possible execution, and bodily disposal. To homogenize the latter, to make the effective singularity of such acts commensurate through memorialization, is to reenact the leveling, collectivizing, and compressive logic of disappearance in its presumed condemnation and redress. The culminating effect of the passage from the disappearance of disappearance to memorialization as the arrest of disappearance is to alibi the latter by consigning it elsewhere in the petrified cold case file of the archival monument, under which the disappeared no longer belong to time but to the immemorial. Derrida, fully aware of the immemorial kernel haunting memorialization, stresses that justice cannot be limited to the living and the appearing that would align it to presence, simultaneity, to collective autoaffection and to national synchronicity. Through memorialization the disappeared and the institutions of vanishment would also become synchronized and eventually anachronistic to the very degree that their legacy is enframed as deformed time that has now been straightened through legal and sculptural orthotics. Anachronistic confinement is merely another form of cannibalism, an anthropophagy of time by time.

Memorialization reduces legacy and inheritance to pure readability. The legibility of the victims of vanishment promoted by im-memorialization insists on the convergence of the missing with productivity, information, and a mastery of difference that the vanished never attained, as confirmed by their submission to a program which insisted that they do not belong and should never have belonged to the space and time of the nation. Neither memorialization nor exhaustive forensic excavation can fully redress their suspended animation, their imposed survivance, which through disavowal and impunity has been parasitically interwoven into the present texture of the afflicted society as the silent trace on which it is founded. "If the readability of a legacy were given natural, transparent univocal, if it did not call for and at the same time defy interpretation, we would never have anything to inherit from it. . . . One always inherits from a secret."[60] Inheritance invariably entails a cut, most primordially between what is valorized as worthy of inheriting and what is deemed to be uninheritable, which is not an absence, a nothing, or a lack, but that of the past which is refused a proper name, "because the proper of the proper name is always to come."[61]

THE NAME OF THE NAME

> There would not be any contretemps, nor any anachrony, if the separation between monads disjoined only interiorities. Contretemps is produced at the intersection between interior experience (the "phenomenology of internal time-consciousness," or space-consciousness) and its chronological or topographical marks, those which are said to be "objective," "in the world." There would not be any series otherwise, without the possibility of this marked spacing, with its social conventions and the history of its codes, with its fictions and its simulacra, with its dates. With so-called proper names.
>
> Jacques Derrida, "Aphorism Countertime"

The Sri Lankan report on enforced disappearance previously discussed returns a list of transgressions that, in their flattened enumeration, mutes the political horror that lies behind its dry rehearsal of typified agents or targets. Here gross and collectivizing appellations of typified victims and organizational acronyms struggle to provision motivation, rationality, and victim eligibility that these same signifiers effectively frustrate in their excision of specificity and singularity. In many ways, these enlisted appellations with their sharply demarcated ideological programs and historical justifications function, not as context or as historical causation but as aphorisms—self-referential condensations, concentrates, and insected units of political normativity and motivation (*aphorismos* means "delimitation," its etymon, *aphorizein*, "to define," and *horizein*, "to separate"). In conjunction with the act of disappearance, they inflict a nominalist catastrophe on the missing—were they abducted because of their objective guilt, or did they acquire a name and political value through vanishing? Were they a political force prior to being disappeared, or did they authorize a politics in their disapparition. Typifying appellations, through which political antagonists interface, converge, and transpose political positions, become a terrain of power/knowledge that remains without name and ideological designation in belonging to the order of the contretemps.

The disappeared and the collaterally damaged carry the death of the proper enemy as a structuring essential contretemps, without witnessing that death; they are wedded to the death of the absent enemy, the proper and capitalized target, through an elongated and immaterial kill chain. There is often no actual relation between the disappeared and the structuring enemy, for what is set up as the proper enemy is more often than not phantasmic—a malleable void that the disappeared, once rendered nondescript, are conscripted to fill through anonymization, biographical attrition, and cannibalization. Their disembodiment embodies the nominalism of aphoristic interruption and foreclosure as a medium of connecting without connection. Thus the kill chain, which seems to underwrite and unwrite these figures, is spun out into invisibility and elliptical disconnection enabling the chain's prolongation into the bad infinity of endless dislocation. The collaterally damaged and the disappeared vanish under the aphorism of the enemy that affects their very being, yet they are merely *the name of that name* which is not a name. They are rendered ineffable under aphoristic sentencing that befalls them as a hammering accident. The victims-targets, and even their survivors, have no part in the enemy but are of him by virtue of the accident of names, given and taken; they are a spun fragment of a name that restages what is not there—the reason and measure of war. They are the nonname of the "enemy" that their confinement, wounds, and death incarnate and nominate. The disavowed vanished and collaterally damaged become unspeakable and unthinkable because of the essentializing accident of the imprisoning and insecting name. All names of such targets assigned by war function as needful accidents, as mishaps, and as anachronous inadequations that befall the damaged before, during, and after their death. This suggests that aphoristic naming is the protological contretemps and essential accident that occurs at and as the inception of war, as the medium of an always unhinged commensuration by which accidentalization is triggered as a sustaining terror and insecting fate. The most sovereignly and lethal of aphorisms, which inaugurates both war and the inevitability of the contretemps, is the invocation: "In the beginning . . ."[62] War begins, lives on, and terminates in aphoristic certitude. The terrorizing aphorism sentences, abbreviates, dissociates, encapsulates, enframes, and enables an automatism of the name beyond life and death; it cuts off time and insects space, for it is "an economy or strategy of mastery that knows very well how to potentialize meaning . . . it says the truth in the form of the last judgment, and this truth carries [*porte*] death."[63] Derrida associates aphoristic power with a sovereign power that gives and suspends death, that is with survivance: "Because it traces, aphorism lives on [*survit*], it lives much longer than its present and it lives longer than life. Death sentence [*arrêt de mort*]. It gives and carries death, but in order to make a decision thus on a sentence [*arrêt*] of death, it suspends death, it stops it once more [*il l'arrête encore*]."[64] This suggests that interstitial survivance is the (post)materialist support and substrate of an aphoristic politics: "A given series of aphorisms crosses over into another one, the same *under* different names, *under the name of the name.*"[65] This crossing over and under and tracing through is imbued with a compulsive and repetitive automatism and a mediology. "This machinality virtually entrusts the trace to the survival in which the opposition of the living and the dead loses and must lose all pertinence, all its edge."[66] Aphoristic power is erected on the plateau, the *res extensa*, the compressed nonverticality of the *Unzeit* and nonlife of survivance. As accidentalized, insecting, and crushing nominalism, war is the power of aphorism weaponized that sentences the vanished and collaterally damaged to the unwitnessable death of their death that, despite this privation of mortality, is incapable of returning life.

NOTES

1. Jacques Derrida, "Aphorism Countertime," trans. Nicholas Royle, in *Psyche: Inventions of the Other*, vol. 2, ed. Peggy Kamuf and Elizabeth G. Rottenberg (Stanford, Calif.: Stanford University Press, 2008), 227–42.

2. Jacques Derrida, *The Beast and the Sovereign, Volume I: The Seminars of Jacques Derrida* (Chicago: University of Chicago Press, 2011), 2.

3. Derrida, "Aphorism Countertime," 130.

4. Ibid., 129–30.

5. Cornelia Vismann, "Cultural Techniques and Sovereignty," *Theory, Culture & Society* 30, no. 6 (2013): 83–93.

6. Roberto Farneti, "Of Humans and Other Portentous Beings: On Primo Levi's *Storie naturali*," *Critical Inquiry* 32, no. 4 (2006): 726.

7. However, in Carl Schmitt's state of exception, as the politicized time of an anticipated threat, the contretemps does not appear as politically generative. This is due to its undoing of the ipsocratic sovereign subject. Incalculable violence overturns the Schmittian sovereign's imperative to preemptively identify the structuring public threat that inaugurates the state of emergency. This is why the essential, designed and needful contretemps is constitutive of sovereignty and the state of

exception, though it suggest the structuring enemy is a fiction. (See my discussion of the contretemps as pharmakon below.)

8. Derrida, "Aphorism Countertime," 131.

9. Jacques Derrida, *Heidegger: The Question of Being and History*, ed. Thomas Dutoit, with the assistance of Marguerite Derrida, trans. Geoffrey Bennington (Chicago: University of Chicago Press, 2016), 141.

10. Ibid., 133.

11. Giorgio Agamben, *La communauté: qui vient*, trans. Reiner Schürmann (Paris: Roche, 1990), 68–69.

12. Michel Foucault, "Friendship as a Way of Life," in *Foucault Live: Interviews, 1961–1983*, ed. Sylvère Lotringer (New York: Semiotext(e), 1996), 312.

13. Derrida, *Heidegger*, 141.

14. Reiner Schurmann, "Legislation-Transgression: Strategies and Counter-Strategies in the Transcendental Justification of Norms," *Man and World* 17 (1984): 363.

15. Derrida, "Why Does Peter Eisenman Write Such Good Books," in *Psyche*, 114.

16. Jacques Lacan, *Écrits: The First Complete Edition in English*, trans. Bruce Young (New York: W. W. Norton, 2002), 748.

17. Jacques Derrida, *The Politics of Friendship*, trans. George Collins (New York: Verso, 1997), 109n13.

18. "Netanyahu: Israel Seeks 'Sustainable Quiet' with Gaza," CNN staff, July 21, 2014, http://www.cnn.com/2014/07/20/world/meast/mideast-crisis-blitzer-netanyahu-interview.

19. Q&A: Paul Hirschon, Israeli Foreign Ministry Spokesman, www.livestation.com (accessed July 10, 2016).

20. Derrida, "Aphorism Countertime," 131. See also Werner Hamacher, "N'essance," *Oxford Literary Review* 36, no. 2 (2014): 212.

21. Derrida, "Aphorism Countertime," 131.

22. Jacques Derrida, *Dissemination*, trans. Barbara Johnson (Chicago: University of Chicago Press, 1981), 128.

23. See Dagobert Frey, "Zum Problem der Symmetrie in der bildenden Kunst," in *4./5. Heft 1949: Studium generale; Zeitschrift für die Einheit der Wissenschaften im Zusammenhang ihrer Begriffsbildungen und Forschungsmethoden* (Berlin: Springer Verlag, 1949), 268–78. Frey opposes symmetry, associated with law to the accident in aesthetics. Reinhart Koselleck, in his historical analysis of Schmitt's friend/foe binary, proposed that all political concepts have their counterconcept, the most extreme being asymmetrical or incongruent concepts that exclude mutual recognition between the interfacing alterities. The generative accident is locatable under Koselleck's schema of temporalized and asymmetrical counterconcepts that precipitate deterritorialization and dislocation. See Reinhart Koselleck, "The Historical-Political Semantics of

Asymmetric Counterconcepts," in *Futures Past: On the Semantics of Historical Time*, trans. Keith Tribe (New York: Columbia University Press, 1985), 155–91.

24. Allen Feldman, *Archives of the Insensible: of War, Photopolitics, and Dead Memory* (Chicago: University of Chicago Press, 2015), 89.

25. Hamacher, *N'essance*, 214.

26. Ibid.

27. Avital Ronell, *Loser Sons: Politics and Authority* (Urbana: University of Illinois Press), 87–88.

28. Jean-Luc Nancy, *After Fukushima: The Equivalence of Catastrophes*, trans. Charlotte Mandell (New York: Fordham University Press, 2014), 6.

29. Solomon J. Solomon, the painter, was one of the inventors of camouflage in World War I.

30. See http://cambodia.ohchr.org/sites/default/files/InfoNotes/003_InfoNote E.pdf (accessed January 12, 2017).

31. The following phenomenology of enforced disappearance draws on my witnessing of testimonies given by the affected families of the disappeared and in conversations with the latter in Cape Town, when attending hearings of the Truth and Reconciliation Commission from 1997–2000. A discussion of the disturbing dialogical soundscape and bodyscapes enacted by these women at the TRC is discussed in my *Archives of the Insensible*, 295–310.

32. Hannah Arendt, *Eichmann in Jerusalem: A Report on the Banality of Evil* (New York: Penguin Random House, 1963), 266, 268, 277, 279. Arendt in this formulation ignored the Israeli state's own investment in withholding terrestrial right and facticity from the Palestinians who were disappeared as an earth-bound people in all but name.

33. Judith Butler, *Parting Ways: Jewishness and the Critique of Zionism* (New York: Columbia University Press, 2013), 23–24, 125–26.

34. Feldman, *Archives of the Insensible*, 338.

35. Bernard Steigler, *For a New Critique of Political Economy*, trans. Daniel Ross (Cambridge, U.K.: Polity, 2013), 31–32.

36. Jacques Derrida, *Without Alibi*, ed. Peggy Kamuf (Stanford, Calif.: Stanford University Press, 2002, 133.

37. Jacques Derrida, *The Beast and the Sovereign, Volume II: The Seminars of Jacques Derrida*, ed. Michel Lisse, Marie-Louise Mallet, and Ginette Michaud, trans. Geoffrey Bennington (Chicago: University of Chicago Press, 2011), 135.

38. Feldman, *Archives of the Insensible*, 308–9.

39. *Nostalgia for the Light*, dir. Patricio Guzman (Icarus Films, 2011), DVD.

40. Final Report on the Consultation Task Force on Reconciliation Mechanisms, no. 17, November 2016, 1:180.

41. See Orlando Patterson, *Slavery and Social Death: A Comparative Study* (Cambridge, Mass.: Harvard University Press, 1982).

42. See Hannah Arendt, *The Origins of Totalitarianism* (New York: Harcourt, Brace, 1973), 473; Arendt, *The Human Condition* (Chicago: University of Chicago Press, 1958), 177; and Arendt, *Love and Saint Augustine* (Chicago: University of Chicago Press, 1996), 51.

43. Derrida, *Beast and the Sovereign*, 142–43.

44. Ibid., 126.

45. Michael Taussig, *Shamanism, Colonialism, and the Wildman* (Chicago: University of Chicago Press, 1988), 104–26.

46. Derrida, *Beast and the Sovereign*, 1:6.

47. Pascal Bonitzer, "Deframings," in *Cahiers du Cinéma vol. 4: 1973–1978: History, Ideology, Cultural Struggle*, ed. David Wilson (New York: Routledge, 2000), 198–99, 200.

48. Derrida, *Beast and the Sovereign*, 1:127; emphasis mine.

49. Ibid., 1:143.

50. Ibid., 1:144.

51. Ibid: 130.

52. Michel Foucault, *Society Must Be Defended: Lectures at the Collège de France, 1975–76*, ed. Mauro Bertani and Alessandro Fontana (New York: Picador, 2003), 241.

53. Giorgio Agamben, *Homo Sacer: Sovereign Power and Bare Life*, trans. Daniel Heller-Roazen (Minneapolis: University of Minnesota Press, 1998).

54. Derrida, *Beast and the Sovereign*, 1:130.

55. Ibid.

56. See my discussion of biopower as thanatopolitics in Feldman, *Archives of the Insensible*, 365–68.

57. Enforced disappearance advances the non–habeas corpus of survivance yet overturns Derrida's postmortem opposition between inhumation as immobilization and incineration as dispersion. The vanished, whether secretly living, buried, or burnt, are both immobilized and dispersed in being denied any artifactual containment that could serve as a prompt for witnessing.

58. Jacques Derrida, *Specters of Marx: The State of the Debt, the Work of Mourning and the New International*, trans. Peggy Kamuf (London: Routledge, 1994), xviii.

59. Allen Feldman, "Memory Theaters, Virtual Witnessing, and the Trauma-Aesthetic," *Biography* 27, no. 1 (2004): 168.

60. Derrida, *Specters of Marx*, 11:130.

61. Ibid., 19.

62. Jacques Derrida, "Faith and Knowledge," in *Acts of Religion*, ed. Gil Anidjar (New York: Routledge, 2002), 76.

63. Derrida, "Aphorism, Countertime," 128–29.

64. Ibid., 131.

65. Ibid., 132.

66. Derrida, *Beast and the Sovereign*, 2:14.

Contributors

Giovanna Borradori is professor of philosophy and chair of philosophy at Vassar College. She specializes in European philosophy of the nineteenth and twentieth centuries. In recent years, her research has focused on the aesthetics of architecture and the philosophy of terrorism. She is the editor of *Recoding Metaphysics: The New Italian Philosophy* (Northwestern University Press, 1988) and the author of two books: *The American Philosopher* (University of Chicago Press, 1993) and *Philosophy in a Time of Terror: Dialogues with Jürgen Habermas and Jacques Derrida* (University of Chicago Press, 2003), a "philosophy best-seller" translated in ten languages.

Marinos Diamantides is a professor of constitutional law and political science, and director of the LL.M. in constitutional law, theory and politics at the School of Law, Birkbeck College, University of London. His research includes award-winning work on the significance for jurisprudence of the ethical philosophy of Emmanuel Levinas, as well as investigations into political theology and public law. His books include *Political Theology: Demystifying the Universal* (Edinburgh University Press, 2017, with Anton Schutz); *Law, Islam, and Identity* (Routledge, 2011, with Adam Gearey); *Law, Levinas, Politics* (Routledge, 2009, 2nd ed.); and *The Ethics of Suffering: Modern Law, Philosophy, and Medicine* (Ashgate, 2000). He is currently working on a book on political theology and constitutionalism. He has held visiting appointments at University of Kyoto, Japan; University of California School of Law, Berkeley; Cardozo School of Law, New York; and Hebrew University, Israel.

Allen Feldman, professor of mediology at New York University, a pioneer in the ethnography of violence, the body, and the senses, is the author of *Archives of the Insensible: Of War, Photopolitics, and Dead Memory* (University of Chicago Press, 2015) and *Formations of Violence: The Narrative of the Body and Political Terror in Northern Ireland* (University of Chicago Press, 1991). He has conducted ethnographic research on the politicization of the gaze, the body, and the senses in Northern Ireland, South Africa, and the post-9/11 global war on terror. His research and teaching interests include visual culture, political aesthetics, political animality, and the political theology of media.

Stanley Fish, in addition to being one of the country's leading public intellectuals, is a prolific author whose works include over two hundred scholarly publications and books. He has written for many of the country's leading law journals, including *Stanford Law Review*, *Duke Law Journal*, *Yale Law Journal*, *University of Chicago Law Review*, *Columbia Law Review*, and *Texas Law Review*. His most recent, and best-selling, works are *How to Write a Sentence: And How to Read One* (2014), and *Think Again: Contrarian Reflections on Life, Culture, Politics, Religion, Law, and Education* (2015). His newest book, *The First: How to Think about Hate Speech, Campus Speech, Religious Speech, Fake News, Post-Truth, and Donald Trump*, is forthcoming in April 2019. He is also a contributor to *The Opinionator* blog for the *New York Times*.

Peter Goodrich is professor of law and director of the Program in Law and Humanities at Cardozo School of Law, visiting professor of law at NYU Abu Dhabi, and Distinguished Visiting Professor of Law at Hong Kong University School of Law. His most recent books are *Schreber's Law: Jurisprudence and Judgment in Transition* (Edinburgh University Press, 2018); *Legal Emblems and the Art of Law* (Cambridge University Press, 2014); and with Valérie Hayaert, *Genealogies of Legal Vision* (Routledge, 2015). He is also the co-author and creative director of two documentary films, *Auf Weidersehen—'Til We Meet Again* (Diskin Films, 2012); and *Of Many* (Spicy Icy Productions, 2014).

Pierre Legrand teaches law at the Sorbonne, where he directed the postgraduate program on globalization and legal pluralism for over fifteen years. He publishes in English and French, and his work has been translated in seven languages, including Chinese (Mandarin), Portuguese, Russian, and Spanish. He teaches and writes about salient theoretical issues arising from comparative interventions in a globalizing world, and seeks to revisit the conventional models governing comparative study by defending an oppositional stance vis-à-vis the core traditional epistemological assumptions held by orthodox comparativists. His publications include numerous articles and books. In recent years, he has written extensively on the relevance of Jacques Derrida's work for comparative legal studies and for law in general, including "Siting Foreign Law: How Derrida Can Help," *Duke Journal of Comparative and International Law* (2011); a contribution to *Derrida and Legal Philosophy*, ed. Peter Goodrich et al. (Palgrave Macmillan, 2008); and a chapter on Derrida and law for the *Blackwell Companion to Derrida*, ed. Zeynep Direk and Leonard Lawlor (Wiley-Blackwell, 2014). He is preparing *Negative Comparative Law* for Routledge, a critical conspectus on the theory of comparative research in law.

Bernadette Meyler is Carl and Sheila Spaeth Professor of Law and professor (by courtesy) of English at Stanford Law School. She has published extensively on constitutional law and law and the humanities, including *Theaters of Pardoning* (Cornell University Press, forthcoming), *The Oxford Handbook of Law and Humanities* (Oxford University Press, forthcoming), *Common Law Originalism* (Yale University Press, under contract), and *New Directions in Law and Literature* (Oxford University Press, 2017).

Michel Rosenfeld is University Professor of Law and Comparative Democracy, Justice Sydney L. Robins Professor of Human Rights, and director of the Program on Global and Comparative Constitutional Theory at the Benjamin N. Cardozo School of Law, Yeshiva University. He is the author of several books, including *Affirmative Action and Justice: A Philosophical and Constitutional Inquiry* (Yale University Press, 1991), which in 1992 was named outstanding book on the subject of human rights in the United States by the Gustave Meyers Center; *Just Interpretations: Law between Ethics and Politics* (University of California Press, 1998); *The Identity of the Constitutional Subject: Selfhood, Citizenship, Culture, and Community* (Routledge, 2010); and *Law, Justice, Democracy, and the Clash of Cultures: A Pluralist Account* (Cambridge University Press, 2011). He is the coeditor of several volumes, including *Hegel and Legal Theory* (CRC Press, 1991); *Deconstruction and the Possibility of Justice* (Routledge, 1992); *Habermas on Law and Democracy: Critical Exchanges* (University of California Press, 1998); *The Oxford Handbook of Comparative Constitutional Law* (Oxford University Press, 2012); *Constitutional Secularism in an Age of Religious Revival* (Oxford University

Press, 2014); and *The Conscience Wars: Rethinking the Balance between Religion, Identity, and Equality* (Cambridge University Press, 2018).

Bernhard Schlink, a recurring visitor to Cardozo School of Law since 1993, is a professor emeritus of public law and legal philosophy at the Humboldt University of Berlin, and previously taught at the University of Bonn and the Johann Wolfgang Goethe University in Frankfurt. From 1987 to 2006, he was a justice on the constitutional court for the state of Nordrhein-Westfalen, Münster. He has written several books on constitutional law, fundamental rights, the separation of powers, and police law; he edited, with Arthur Jacobson, *Weimar: A Jurisprudence of Crisis* (University of California Press, 2000).His many novels include the international best seller *The Reader,* which was translated into fifty-five languages and made into an Oscar-winning film.

Jeanne L. Schroeder is a professor at the Benjamin N. Cardozo School of Law, New York City. She practiced in corporate finance for twelve years as an associate at Cravath, Swaine & Moore and a partner at Milgrim Thomajan & Lee. Her scholarly interests range from finance law doctrine to feminist jurisprudential theory. Her current work is on the law and theory of payments and the law of blockchains. She has developed a feminist theory of law and economics incorporating the political philosophy of G. W. F. Hegel and the psychoanalytic theories of Jacques Lacan. Her books on this subject are *The Vestal and the Fasces: Hegel, Lacan, Property, and the Feminine* (University of California Press, 1998), *The Triumph of Venus: The Erotics of the Market* (University of California Press, 2004), and *The Four Lacanian Discourses: Or Turning Law Inside Out* (2012).

Laurent de Sutter is professor of legal theory at Vrije Universiteit Brussel (Brussels, Belgium). He is the author of several books dedicated to the relationship between law and transgression, translated into various languages, the most recent being *Métaphysique de la putain* (Léo Scheer, 2014), *La voie du droit* (Dalloz, 2014), *Striptease, l'art de l'agacement* (Le Murmure, 2015), and *Magic: Une métaphysique du lien* (PUF, 2015). He is also the managing editor of the Perspectives Critiques series at Presses Universitaires de France, and of the Theory Redux series at Polity Press. He serves as an editor of *Law & Literature,* as a member of the Editorial Board of *Décalages, An Althusser Studies Journal,* and as a member of the Scientific Committee of the Collège International de Philosophie.

Katrin Trüstedt is assistant professor in the Department of Germanic Languages and Literatures at Yale University. Her research is situated at the intersection of literature, law, and philosophy, and engages with early modern, modern, and contemporary German and English literature. She is the author of *Die Komödie der Tragödie* (Konstanz University Press, 2011) and coeditor of *Happy Days: Lebenswissen nach Cavell* (Fink, 2009). She is currently finishing her second book on figures of "Stellvertretung" (advocacy, agency, representation, substitution) in rhetoric, law, and literature.

Marco Wan is associate professor of law at the University of Hong Kong, where he directs the program in law and literary studies. He is also managing editor of *Law and Literature*. His first book, *Masculinity and the Trials of Modern Fiction* (Routledge, 2017), was awarded the biannual Penny Pether Prize from the Law, Literature and Humanities Association of Australasia. He is currently working on a monograph on law and Hong Kong cinema, and is coediting (with Peter Goodrich and Christian Delage) a collection of essays on law and new media.

Index

à pas de loup, 291, 308
abduction, 41–43, 45–47
accidentalization, 294, 296–297, 299–300; of disappearance, 299–301
acclamation, 59, 79, 80–81, 83–84, 90, 93, 190, 204–205
administration, 5–6, 55–57, 59, 66, 79–82, 92, 93, 195, 199, 201; bureaucratic, 65–67, 82, 93, 199
aequitas, 209
Agamben, Giorgio, 5–8, 55–58, 66–68, 69–70, 77–85, 91–93, 149, 157, 190–195, 198, 200–206, 207–208, 211–215, 223, 240–244, 293; as actor, 234, 247
Agier, Michel, 265
aleatory (cascade), 296–297, 301, 308, 312
Althusser, Louis, 293
anachronic, 291, 293–294, 296, 298
Andrewes, Lancelot, 29–31, 44, 50
angelology, 8, 204
anomie, 193, 199, 201–203, 213–215, 245–247, 292
anonymity, 263–265
Anselm of Lucca, 214
Antigone, 12
Antonio, 172–175
apophasis, 216
aporia, 163, 300
apotropaic, 298
apparatus, 6–8
Arendt, Hannah, 206, 266–267, 300, 305–306
Aristotle, 54–55, 200, 201, 202, 237
arms, 24–27

ars iuris, 5
Atell, Kevin, 164
Aufhebung, 168–169
Augustine, Saint, 30, 215
author, 24, 27, 38
authority, 129–130, 216
autopoiesis, 70
autopraxis, 291

Babel, Tower of, 109
Badiou, Alain, 48, 166–167
Balke, Friedrich, 162
Balkin, Jack, 161
bare life, 198, 201, 223
Bassanio, 178–180
Beardsworth, Richard, 162–163
Benjamin, Walter, 170–171, 184, 192, 266–267
Bennington, Geoffrey, 163
Berman, Harold, 201
Bernstein, Richard, 132
Bible, 11–12, 20, 22, 29
biopolitics, 200–201, 312
Blackstone, William, 26
Bob Jones University v United States, 176
bodies, 268–270
Breyer, Stephen, 27
Brown, Wendy, 226, 258
bureaucracy. *See* administration
Butler, Judith, 257, 268–269, 300, 306
Byzantium, 207–209, 211–214

Calcagno, Antonio, 167
Campillo, Antonio, 160–161

Camus, Albert, 56, 152
Cantopop, 281–282
Cardozo Law School, 58, 112, 140
ceremony, 295. *See also* ritual
Chea, Pheng, 160, 163
child, 254–255, 256, 259
China, 273–275, 287
Christ, 30, 80, 82, 90, 191, 200, 206, 213, 235
Christianity, 56–58, 78–83, 171–173, 177, 180–183, 190–192, 206, 207; Catholicism, 84, 87, 89, 209, 212, 215; Orthodox, 190, 192, 207–215, 219
Cicero, 240–241, 244
citizenship, 158, 258–259
city, 253, 256, 259; camp, 271; liberal, 260, 263; neoliberal, 257; of refuge, 255–257, 259–261, 263; to-come, 267, 268, 270
collateral damage, 291, 294
coloniality, 277, 285, 287
command, 236–239, 242–243
consensus, 16–18, 32, 47, 59, 63, 64–65, 76
constitution, 155, 189, 193, 196–198, 222, 258; Greek, 198–199
constitutionalism, living, 27, 32
counterfactual reconstruction, 58, 60
contretemps (*à pas de loup*), 290–291, 294, 296–298, 308, 317
Cover, Robert, 175, 180, 183
critical legal studies, 4, 58, 60–61, 73, 147, 161
Croce, Benedetto, 229
Cronos, 150, 151
Cross. *See* Christ
crumbling, 28, 31, 44, 50
Cunningham, Timothy, 26

Dagron, Gilbert, 208
dance, 239, 240, 244, 245–246
death (penalty), 107, 151–154
Debord, Guy, 234–235
decision, 153–154, 158
declarations of independence, 154, 155, 204, 231
deconstruction, 3, 7, 57, 60–61, 72–75, 78, 83, 84, 86, 93, 112, 115, 121–123, 126, 127, 129–131, 152, 153, 161, 256, 262, 279
Deleuze, Gilles, 243–244
democracy 75, 83–85, 152, 155–157, 166, 195, 258; to come, 75, 76, 151, 156–157, 166
deontology, 242, 245
Derrida, Jacques, 3–4, 7–8, 54–56, 58, 64, 65, 67–68, 72–77, 82–83, 86, 89–90, 105, 113–133, 148–162, 167–173, 255–256, 262–264, 274–277, 286–287, 290; and language, 106–112, 120–121, 150
Descartes, René, 149
destinerrance, 129
Deuteronomy, 174–175
dialogue, 64–67
dictionaries, 25–29
Didi-Huberman, Georges, 243–244
différance, 128, 156, 312
différend, 111–112
diligence, 29
disappearance, 299–301, 304–305, 306–307
disframing, 309
dispensation, 190, 209
dispositor. *See* apparatus
District of Columbia v Heller, 24–29, 32–34, 41
dogmatics, 113–123, 191
dogs, 190, 193, 222, 223
Dostoyevsky, Fydor, 255
Doyle, Arthur Conan, 44
Durst, David, 162
Dworkin, Ronald, 67–69, 98

Eagleton, Terry, 132
Easterbrook, Frank, 27
Eichmann, Adolph, 300
ellipsis, 151–152
Enlightenment, the, 67, 68, 84, 150, 263; counter, 191
Enjoy Yourself Tonight (EYT), 281–282, 285
epistemes, 148–149
esti, (and *estô*), 236–237, 246
état d'urgence, 264
ethics, 57–58, 74–76, 122; of difference, 76–77, 122
event, 157–158, 159, 166–167, 301–302
evil, 34, 50
exception (state of), 55, 59, 78, 264
existentialism, 76, 130
exscripting, 300, 306

face of the other, 122, 127
falsification, 2–3, 15, 18, 31–32, 38, 45–49
father, (name of), 3, 78, 80, 82, 83, 90, 200
Faust, 12
feng shui, 282–283
Feyerabend, Paul, 46
Filioque, 213, 215, 233
Fink, Bruce, 39, 40–42
Fish, Stanley, 38–40, 44, 46, 50
form of life (*forma vitae*), 201, 223, 243
foreigners, 263–265, 270, 278–279

Foucault, Michel, 147–148, 152, 157, 158, 159, 160, 204, 293, 311
Franklin, Ben, 154
Freie Rechsschule, 15–16
French (language), 106–109, 119–121
friends (*filoi*), 75, 78, 165, 208–210, 213, 220
Freud, Sigmund, 39, 50, 55
Fuller, Lon, 32–34

Geneva Convention, 265, 266
genocide, 300–301
ghosts, 272–273, 276–278, 286–288, 306, 314
Gilli, Patrick, 241
glory, 59, 80–81, 83, 90, 190–192, 199, 202, 204–205
God, 154, 191, 193, 201–204, 224, 242–243; death, 204; non-existence, 245
Goodrich, Peter, 161
governance, 5–7, 78,80, 81–83, 92
grammatology, 4
Gratiano, 180–181
Greenstein, Michael, 183
Guerlac, Suzanne, 160, 163
Grundnorm, 62

habeas corpus (writ), 300, 309–311
Habermas, Jurgen, 59, 64–65, 76, 84, 97
Häglund, Martin, 152, 154, 164, 165
Hamacher, Werner, 298–299
Hamas, 296
Hamlet, 12, 23
Hart, H. L. A., 32–34, 48, 50, 62
hatter, 154–155
hauntology, 274, 276–277, 310, 314
Heidegger, Martin, 74, 109–110, 121, 149, 150, 152, 162–163, 236, 297
Hegel, Georg, 115, 168–169, 183
Heraclitus, 238–239
Hercules, 68
hermeneutics 1–2, 5, 8, 46, 175; biblical, 2–3, 11–12, 20, 23; exegetical, 175, 177; legal, 11–12, 16–20, 23; literary, 12, 20, 22; of suspicion, 4, 7
historicity, 293–295
Hobbes, Thomas, 206, 207
Hollande, François, 264, 295
Holmes, Oliver Wendell Jr, 45
Hong Kong, 272–273, 275–277, 278–285, 287
hospitality, 158, 159, 163, 263, 265
Hume, David, 45, 54
Husserl, Edmund, 159

hyperlaw, 114, 116
hypotheses, 14, 42, 43, 45–46, 49

image, 259
imaginary, 40, 49, 192–198
indeterminacy, 60, 116, 147, 161, 164, 165, 166
indignados, 200
induction, 44–46
injustice, 258
inoperativy, 193, 201, 225, 228, 298, 313
interpatrari, 1
interpretation, 2, 6–8, 12–15, 20, 114–120, 128–130, 132–133, 158, 171, 174, 176; analogical, 178; arrested, 180; correct, 38–39, 43, 141; and desire, 32, 42, 130–133, 174–176; disingenuous, 33–34, 44–45, 50; failed, 34–35, 48; hauntology, 114–117, 121, 129, 130–131, 133; and justice, 12, 15, 90–94, 174–178; play, 105, 116, 130; and psychoanalysis, 39–42, 117; work of, 181. *See also* hermeneutics
invagination, 114
iustitium, 200, 205

Jameson, Frederic, 276
Jefferson, Thomas, 154–155
Jerusalem, 262
Johnson, Samuel, 26
Jonas, Eric, 162
judges, 15, 19, 43, 49
jural postulates, 191
jurisgenesis, 175, 177
jurisprudence, 57–58, 62–63
jus ad bellum, 291, 294, 296
justice, 54–56, 63–65, 67–68, 74, 83, 93, 121–123, 154, 170–172, 224, 274, 286–287, 314–315; ghosts, 286–287, 314; racial, 266, 267; of reality, 253; to come, 314; transitional, 303
Justinian, 208–210
jurisdiction, 192; contract, 63, 155, 310; impossibility of, 65, 89–90, 93–94, 122, 127; mercy, 168–169, 171, 178; spectre of, 157; as supplement, 123–125; unconditional, 159–160; and wit, 180–182

Kant, Immanuel, 38, 42, 44, 63, 64–65, 74, 89, 159, 164, 241–243, 245, 259, 266
Kantorowicz, Ernst, 206
Kashoggi, Ahmad, 299
Kekulé, August, 15
Kelly, Sean, 263

Index

Kelsen, Hans, 6, 55, 62, 118–121, 130, 139, 141, 206
Kennedy, Duncan, 4
kingship, 56
Kohler, Joseph, 192
Kowloon, 28

Lacan, Jacques, 39, 42, 181, 185
Lakatos, Imre, 46
Lampert, Lisa, 184–185
law, 3, 7–8, 12–15, 54, 64–66, 92–94, 105–106, 110–114, 116–118, 127, 130–132, 175–180, 197, 212–215, 236, 244–245, 295; autopoietic, 70–72, 79, 81; code, 119; contract, 179–180, 223, 310; counter, 300; criminal, 179–180; curriculum, 4–5, 113, 119–120, 141–142; Debret, 264–265; determinacy, 122–126; as difference, 130–134; and economics, 68–70; as evil, 238; and force, 123; internal, 55, 119–120, 131, 169–170; Jewish, 169, 174, 184; letter of, 170, 175, 180–182; natural, 67, 115, 122, 123, 142; Nazi, 33–34, 200; nonlaw, 295; political, 177, 196–200, 213–215; posited, 114, 118, 120–122, 126–128, 198, 242; post-metaphysical, 64; practice, 19–20, 22–23, 113; private (civil), 179–180; pure theory, 6, 118–120, 121, 124; revolution in, 192; rule of, 80, 81, 82, 84, 196; student, 234, 244; theory, 57, 58–59, 92–95, 240–246; of usury, 174
lawyers, 240, 241
Lefort, Claude, 206–207
legal realism, 15
legitimacy, 59, 63, 78, 81–83, 90–91
legislature, 17–18, 23, 33, 68–70
Legendre, Pierre, 174, 182–183, 193
Legrand, Pierre, 96
Le Guin, Ursula, 254–255, 259
Leitch, Vincent, 153
Leo the Wise, 211
Levinas, Emmanuel, 122, 162–163, 224, 255–256, 260–261
liberalism, 200–201, 255; neo, 191, 200, 255, 256, 257–259
lifeworld, 66–67
Lin, Crystal, 275, 276
Locke, John, 207
Loughlin, Martin, 226, 227
Loukanikos, 194
love, 29, 30
Luhmann, Niklas, 70–71, 79, 81
Lupton, Julia, 174

Luther, Martin, 15
Lyotard, Jean-François

M+, 283–284
management, 193, 206–207
Magdalen, Mary, 30
magic, 238, 239
Marx, Karl, 224
Mauss, Katherine Eisaman, 169–170
McCormick, John, 150
media, 190
mediology, 294
Meillassoux, Quentin, 245
Mendeleyev, Dmitry, 15
Merchant of Venice, 168–169, 171–179
mercy, 168–172, 178
Metaxas, 205
Meyler, Bernadette, 166
Miller, J. Hillis, 118
monolingualism, 108–110
Montag, Warren, 277
Morante, Elsa, 235
More, Sir Thomas, 256
Moses, 255, 260
Mussolini, Benito, 205

Nai-keung, Lau, 275–276
Nancy, Jean-Luc, 128, 299
Netanyahu, Benjamin, 296
Neuman, Meredith, 29
Nicene creed, 203
Nietzsche, Friedrich, 74–75
nihilism, 4, 116
Nomos and Narrative, 180
norms (*nómoi*), 12–14, 17, 23, 55, 71–72, 179–180, 238–239, 244
nostalgia, 281
Nostalgia for the Light, 303, 315

oath, 242–243
Occupy, 257, 269–271, 281, 284–285; Central, 272, 278
oikonomia, 2, 5, 7, 56, 59, 66, 68–71, 79, 81, 82, 90, 190, 201–203, 211–215, 220–222, 256
Omelas, 254–255, 256, 259, 267
ontology (dual), 236–237, 238–241, 245, 286; anontology, 245–246

papacy, 214, 216
Papandreou, George, 196
Parliament of Writers, 263, 265, 267
Parnet, Claire, 244

Pascal, Blaise, 124
Pasolini, Pier Paolo, 234–235, 238
Patterson, Orlando, 305
Paul, Saint, 170, 175, 181; throne (empty), 81, 90, 92, 203
Pavlopoulos, Prokopis, 218–219
Peirce, Charles Sanders, 41, 44
Pengfei, Qi, 274
Petrarch, Francesco, 241
pharmakon, 298
philosophy (war of), 240–242, 245
Plato, 178, 200, 239, 240, 269
pluralism, 78, 85, 86, 89–93; comprehensive, 86–87, 93
Political theology. *See* theology
Popper, Karl, 45–46, 50
populism, 191, 208, 219, 221
Portia, 170, 171, 178–180
positivism, 55, 63, 95, 106, 113, 116–123, 127, 130, 198; post-positivism, 106
Posner, Richard, 69
Pound, Roscoe, 191
principle, 67–68
providence, 59, 68, 80, 82, 190, 204
psychoanalysis, 39–44
proportionality, 19
punishment, 147–148, 151

Rancière, Jacques, 259
Rappaport, Roy, 191
ratio scripta, 127
Rawls, John, 63–64, 67, 76, 84, 224
relever, 168
resistance, 243, 256–258
revolution, 192, 216, 217
Rheichman, Ronen, 184
rhetoric, 178
Ricoeur, Paul, 125
ritual, 57, 190, 192–196, 204–205, 223
Ronnel, Avital, 298
Rosenfeld, Michel, 140
Roudinesco, Élizabeth, 148, 159
Rousseau, Jean-Jacques, 63, 64, 65, 207
Rushdie, Salman, 263, 265

sacrifice, 254, 259–260
salus populi, 208
sans papier, 201, 265
Sartre, Jean-Paul, 76
Scalia, Antonin, 24–26, 31–34, 35, 41–42, 44–45
Scarry, Elaine, 268

Schlink, Bernhard, 2, 22–24, 31, 38–40, 42–44, 46, 48–50
Schmitt, Carl, 55–57, 58, 62, 78, 150, 165, 190, 226, 319
Schurmann, Reiner, 293–294
seasoning, 178–179
Second Amendment, 24–26, 41
secularization, 56, 59, 62
sentences, 29–30
Shakespeare, William, 169, 211
Sherlock Holmes, 42–44, 49–50
Shylock, 169, 171, 172–173, 175–180
Simons, Jon, 162
Sisyphus, 56
Smith, Adam, 81
social welfarism, 65–66
societas, 232
Solomon, Solomon J., 299
Sophocles, 12
sovereign, 55–56, 78, 80–82, 90–92, 150, 151–153, 155, 162, 165, 189–193, 195–198, 200–203, 211–215, 221, 229, 310; apparatus, 300, 301, 302, 305, 311; Chinese, 272–273, 284; exception, 157–158, 195, 244, 319; polemological, 294; silent, 313; subject, 292, 306
spectacle, 7, 57, 59, 191, 211, 218–220, 259, 269
spectrality, 114–115, 117, 157, 276–278, 286
Spinoza, Baruch, 237
Spivak, Gyatri, 106
Sri Lanka, 303–304, 315
stare decisis, 19
Steigler, Bernard, 301
Stevens, John Paul, 24, 35
sublation, 169
suicide, 196
Supreme Court, 176
survivance, 312–313
symbolic, 39–43
syntax, 25–26, 28, 29
SYRIZA, 194, 196, 197, 220–221

Taussig, Michael, 308
teleology, 158–159, 167
temporality, 148–150, 152, 157, 163–164, 272–274, 285–287, 290–293
terrorism, 77, 90, 158, 264, 298
textuality, 24–28, 31, 32, 44, 114–117, 129, 172, 175–177, 181
theology, 78–80, 198–201, 206, 207–210, 215–218, 224; economic, 200–204,

theology (*continued*)
  207–209, 211–212; political, 56, 62, 78–79, 150, 190, 193, 204, 208–212
Theotokópoulos, Doménikos, 213–214
Thomas, Yan, 247
Thornhill, Chris, 231–232
throne (empty), 81, 90, 92, 194–196, 202–206, 207–210, 222
trace, 118, 128–130, 132, 308
translation, 105–106, 109, 168, 170–174, 180
trifles, 42–43, 48
Trinity, 201–203, 208–211, 213, 215
Troika, 196–197
truth, 48, 50, 147; commissions, 303
Tsipras, Alexis, 194, 199, 219–220

unconditional, 157–159
Unger, Roberto, 119
United Housing v Forman, 48
universal, 57, 65, 68, 72, 74–79, 82–86, 89; pluralist, 89–90

veil of ignorance, 224
Vico, Giambattista, 1–3
Ville, Jacques de, 155, 163
violence, 77, 90, 124–128, 144, 162, 176, 201, 269, 275, 294–298; arche, 124; as vigilance, 127
visibility, 259, 268, 290, 295; invisibility, 299

war, 291, 294, 318–319; accidentalizes, 296; containerized, 294–295, 301; crimes, 291; Sri Lanka, 304
wit, 180–181
Woo, Marcus, 272, 274, 278, 279–280, 282–283, 287
World Trade Organization, 195

Zeus, 150, 151
Zion, 262
Zoé, 310, 311, 312
Žižek, Slavoj, 39, 199
Zuccotti Park, 257, 269

just ideas

Roger Berkowitz, *The Gift of Science: Leibniz and the Modern Legal Tradition*

Jean-Luc Nancy, translated by Pascale-Anne Brault and Michael Naas, *The Truth of Democracy*

Drucilla Cornell and Kenneth Michael Panfilio, *Symbolic Forms for a New Humanity: Cultural and Racial Reconfigurations of Critical Theory*

Karl Shoemaker, *Sanctuary and Crime in the Middle Ages, 400–1500*

Michael J. Monahan, *The Creolizing Subject: Race, Reason, and the Politics of Purity*

Drucilla Cornell and Nyoko Muvangua (eds.), *uBuntu and the Law: African Ideals and Postapartheid Jurisprudence*

Drucilla Cornell, Stu Woolman, Sam Fuller, Jason Brickhill, Michael Bishop, and Diana Dunbar (eds.), *The Dignity Jurisprudence of the Constitutional Court of South Africa: Cases and Materials, Volumes I & II*

Nicholas Tampio, *Kantian Courage: Advancing the Enlightenment in Contemporary Political Theory*

Carrol Clarkson, *Drawing the Line: Toward an Aesthetics of Transitional Justice*

Jane Anna Gordon, *Creolizing Political Theory: Reading Rousseau through Fanon*

Jimmy Casas Klausen, *Fugitive Rousseau: Slavery, Primitivism, and Political Freedom*

Drucilla Cornell, *Law and Revolution in South Africa: uBuntu, Dignity, and the Struggle for Constitutional Transformation*

Abraham Acosta, *Thresholds of Illiteracy: Theory, Latin America, and the Crisis of Resistance*

Andrew Dilts, *Punishment and Inclusion: Race, Membership, and the Limits of American Liberalism*

Lewis R. Gordon, *What Fanon Said: A Philosophical Introduction to His Life and Thought.* Foreword by Sonia Dayan-Herzbrun, Afterword by Drucilla Cornell

Gaymon Bennett, *Technicians of Human Dignity: On the Politics of Intrinsic Worth*

Drucilla Cornell and Nick Friedman, *The Mandate of Dignity: Ronald Dworkin, Revolutionary Constitutionalism, and the Claims of Justice*

Richard A. Lynch, *Foucault's Critical Ethics*

Peter Banki, *The Forgiveness to Come: The Holocaust and the Hyper-Ethical*

Peter Goodrich and Michel Rosenfeld (eds.), *Administering Interpretation: Derrida, Agamben, and the Political Theology of Law*

www.ingramcontent.com/pod-product-compliance
Lightning Source LLC
Chambersburg PA
CBHW030432300426
44112CB00009B/962